A435 *Francis J. Scanlon*

SCIENCE AND CULTURE SERIES
JOSEPH HUSSLEIN, S.J., Ph.D., GENERAL EDITOR

THE EMANCIPATION OF A
FREETHINKER

THE
EMANCIPATION
OF A
FREETHINKER

BY

HERBERT
ELLSWORTH
CORY

THE BRUCE PUBLISHING COMPANY
MILWAUKEE

Nihil obstat: MATTHAEUS BRITT, O.S.B., Censor librorum
Imprimatur: ✠ GERALDUS SHAUGHNESSY, S.M., S.T.D., Episcopus Seattlensis
14 Novembris, 1940

(Third Printing — 1943)

CISTERCIAN ABBEY
OUR LADY OF THE GENESEE

To

FATHER WILLIAM J. O'BRIEN,
*whose genial piety inspired me to search systematically
for that which is evidently so real to him;*

FATHER JAMES B. McGOLDRICK, S.J.,
*whose erudition and holiness and patient dialectic
exorcised my last arrogant negations;*

FATHER FRANCIS A. POPE, O.P.,
*with deepest gratitude for years of continued counsel,
so detached and so purehearted*

PREFACE BY THE GENERAL EDITOR

PERPHAPS the best description we can give of this book is to call it the intellectual Odyssey of an agnostic. The quest undertaken is a search for evidence of God, His revelation, His Church. It is not a planned voyage, but dependent upon wind and wave and circumstance. It leads through important sections of literature, through modern sciences, and the discordant philosophies defended in the great secular universities of our day. It ends, after more than two decades of years, within the safe harbor of St. Augustine's City of God.

In writing the foreword to this uniquely constructed book the best service I can render the reader is to give the plan and method of the volume, without anticipating the author's thoughts and discussion. The life story narrated is typical, in many ways, of the lives of millions of men and women in our de-Christianized civilization. The longing for God experienced by him is at the heart of thousands whose days are void without Him. They are part with the author in his adventure.

His environment is that of the modern secular university. It is there his Odyssey begins. It is there it ends. And in his observations on others, be it said at once, there is no intended bitterness regarding anyone; Protestant, agnostic, or atheist. Through all these stages he himself passed. Least of all is there any reflection on comrades and faculty members with whom he associated. His sole purpose is to be of benefit to all.

Emotion is strictly excluded from his quest. It is a search purely rational, intellectual, and concerned only with factual evidence.

With the author's acquaintance made, we quickly find ourselves at home with him, first at Brown University, then at Harvard, where he receives his doctorate. In both institutions our interest is mainly literary, while always catching the significance of the religious note in the literature under observation. The same is true as we enter with him the University of California. Here he remains for nine years as a member of the teaching staff. Unique in his method it is that we follow, as it were, through the courses with him, studying closely in the present instance the character, no less than the literary production and religious convictions of men like Alfred the Great, Spenser, Dryden.

California, however, presented other attractions than those purely academic. Visits to the less opulent quarters of the city and contact with radical thinkers of the Marxian type had a twofold effect. Together with a worthy zeal for the disinherited there developed in our hero a cast of Marxian intellectualism that found expression not merely in proletarian oratory, but in a published volume. His own serious reaction to this served for a cure of the red rash, and yet embedded in his work were seeds of better things. Reference to this book naturally leads on to extensive discussion of the important *Rerum Novarum* and *Quadragesimo Anno*, exemplifying the Vatican attitude on the labor question.

From the University of California we pass on to Johns Hopkins; from literature and sociology to the physical sciences. Four years devoted to postdoctorate courses in biology now follow, with ample opportunities for psychological and psychiatric studies, including a three-semester course in psychoanalysis. Nor is the original quest forgotten during these years of mature scientific investigation.

Here, in particular, mention may be made of the various philosophies, materialistic or vitalistic, that constitute the atmosphere of secular universities. No little attention especially is given by the author to emergent evolution. Yet he believes that physics, so fruitful of new philosophies, is unconsciously verging toward scholasticism. This opens up, on the writer's part, an exposition of the Thomistic theory of prime matter and substantial form, offering an excellent introduction to this Greco-scholastic philosophy, as best adapted for lucid application to modern discoveries in physical science.

His entire chapter on "Orientation," with its constructive scientific application of Aristotelian Thomism, its thrilling account of earth formation, earth rhythms; the struggles of land, air, water, and the resultant harmony — is perhaps unsurpassed in its kind. It will not be found wanting under scientific scrutiny, and bespeaks the necessity of an infinite Master Mind. In the words of St. Paul: "The invisible things of him from the creation of the world are clearly seen, being understood by the things that are made: his eternal power also and divinity" (Rom. 1:20).

Fitfully, and as occasion served, the author's quest has thus been carried onward, not without prayers at times, nor yet without lapse, on the other hand, into a period of contented atheism. From this state of a quietistic spiritual nihilism he is snatched, however, and with the reassertion of reason soon arrives within sight of his goal. He has finally reached the harbor. Before him rises the City of God, and over its bastions and battlements, like a celestial light, rests the divine promise that the gates of hell shall not prevail against it — a promise made good now through twenty centuries: through Roman persecution, through Aryan heresy, through Eastern Schism, and the Great Western Schism, through Saracen invasion, through "Reformation" and "Enlightenment," through Renan and Napoleon.

There is just one way of leading men back to God, and that is by giving them the intellectual evidence for the existence of God and of a divine revelation to man. But it was easier for St. Paul, when speaking to the men of Athens, to begin with the Unknown God whom actually they worshiped, than for us to start with the Forgotten God. Paganism, however perverted and licentious in belief and practice, still held to at least the essential truth of the existence of Deity and its relation to men. Even at the very heart of pagan polytheism there remained a survival of the true doctrine of one single God, but metamorphosed by it into a supreme ruler over gods and men.

With the finding of God, of revelation, of the Church, by way of purely human reason, our author's Odyssey had ended, but at the same time a new world had opened up before him, seen with a newness of vision and a child's freshness of heart, all of which still needed to be pictured. New beauty lay revealed and a largeness of liberty enjoyed only by the children of God. Nor did reason suffer because of the faith embraced, which itself was most conformable to reason. In the words of the Vatican Council, "faith frees and guards reason from errors, and furnishes it with manifold knowledge," and as Pope Leo XIII adds, "what is opposed to faith is equally opposed to reason."

Faith is above, but never contrary to reason or true science, nor does faith ever force us to discard anything that science can prove to demonstration. "We cheerfully and gladly declare," writes the same Pontiff, "that whatever has been wisely said, whatever has been profitably discovered and ascertained by anyone whomsoever, should be accepted" (Encyclical, *Aeterni Patris*). What larger charter can there be of intellectual freedom!

As the reader must already have surmised, not more than about one tenth of the entire volume is autobiography. The other nine tenths are concerned with evidence and exposition. Yet like a cord of many colors the author's narrative runs through it all, binding into unity all its parts.

With the creed of a Godless world discredited, with civilization crumbling into chaos, there is need of just such a volume. "Not by bread alone doth man live," may be amplified today by adding, "nor yet by science and machine alone." It is God and the word of God that men need most. Reason will find Him for us; faith will give Him to us. And no one labors in vain who humbly and honestly seeks for Him.

Most consoling of all truths taught by the Catholic Church is her doctrine that from the beginning of time to its end, none shall ever have been lost eternally who did what lay in him, who followed out, as best he knew and could, the will of God. "How good, indeed, to those who seek Thee, but oh, to those who find, how inexpressible!"

Clearly, then, the watchword of our age and of the generation that is to follow, must be: "Back to God." In this mission the book of Dr. Cory should always hold its distinctive place.

JOSEPH HUSSLEIN, S.J., PH.D.,
General Editor, Science and Culture Series

St. Louis University,
April 23, 1941.

AUTHOR'S PREFACE

In September, 1933, at the age of forty-nine years and eleven months, I was received into the Roman Catholic Church. A gentle nebulous Congregationalist Christianity had sustained me for something like the first eighteen years of my life. If it had been one of the more vinegar-visaged kinds of Protestantism, it would have failed me much earlier. Its liberality saved it. But under the first onslaughts of the great unbelievers of the nineteenth century, poetic and scientific, it foundered.

For years, as an agnostic humanist, I dallied with the protean forms of liberalism, until I had found them all too lacking in real liberality. I then became a radical, about 90 per cent Marxian communist. That was about 1917. By 1920, while still unable to find any arguments which conclusively disproved the existence of God, I thought it worth while to try out atheism as an hypothesis. This, instead of leading me away from belief in a Deity, brought me closer to it because of certain grave difficulties, notably the problem of good and the problem of the origin and objective validity of the rational process, which forced me gradually to the conclusion that some sort of theistic hypothesis was much more reasonable than its antithesis. But what influenced me most at this time was a study of the biological sciences. This I continued for four years, in the laboratories of Johns Hopkins University, whither I had turned from the teaching of English Literature during nine previous years at the University of California, a task for which I had been prepared by a doctorate at Harvard.

Meanwhile, however, the social question remained profoundly in my thoughts and I began to suspect that Marxian communism was far too bourgeois and conservative to solve the vexing problem. Since I was determined to become a radical of the most uncompromising sort, it was only a question of time when I would slough off the shallow skepticism or solipsism from Descartes to Hume and Kant, and from Hume and Kant to Bergson, Russell, and Dewey. Bound to discover the validity of common sense, that is to say of critical common sense, I was destined to discover the *philosophia perennis,* scholasticism. Here at last, I could only capitulate to the conservative and yet ultrarevolutionary truths of the pure Tradition of Christianity.

The arguments — biological, psychological, sociological, historical philosophical, and theological — which lead to Catholicism form a colossal web of uncounted strands converging from every side to a common center. I have sketched in this book a number of these arguments, though, of necessity, only roughly. I am forced to content myself with a general perspective rather than an array of detail which would require a library. I have quoted freely from a great number of wise men. Indeed, I hope that if the reader goes over my pages skimmingly he will always choose my quotations in preference to my own reflections.

As I look backward over the years I am often amazed and annoyed at the obstinacy with which, in the face of innumerable and unusual opportunities, I resisted the truth. I realize now that my brooding fear lest some one of my wishes might dictate some one of my thoughts bordered at times on the psychopathological. At all events, I can fairly say that my long pilgrimage to Rome has been one of growingly relentless reasoning coercing an increasingly stubborn and more or less emotional resistance. Yet all my efforts would have availed me naught without the grace of God.

Even before I accepted the whole great truth, I was tormented persistently with a desire to share my ever more densely thronging and spacious discoveries with others in writing. Of course, I spurned the temptation. In fact, I continued even after my conversion to reject all such impulses for more than a year. Finally, about six years ago, I began, in a quiet and very leisurely manner, to write this book. Since then it has claimed many of my best and happiest moments. But I have never been in the least haste because every year, every day, every hour of meditation has increased my appreciation of the terrible depth of St. Augustine's aspiration: "Lord, let me know myself and let me know Thee. Let me know myself that I may hate myself; let me know Thee that I may love Thee."

No sooner was I converted, than all my incipient complacency or pride was subjected to a most wholesome castigation by friends and foes. Within twenty-four hours I had received a postal card, anonymous, bemoaning my "surrender to superstition." The katharsis still continues with increasing vigor and sweep. One and all, superficial and searching, these animadversions are very nourishing. The simplest was a remark, current among some of my acquaintances, that I was conquered by my

wife's convictions along with her beauty. Far be it from me to deny that
Mary was what the metaphysicians call an "efficient instrumental cause."
But this book, mere sketch though it be of the myriad converging strands
of reasoning which drew me Romewards, ought to convince my more
romantic (and cynical) friends that the process — for better or worse —
was considerably more complicated than they at first surmised. As for
Mary, she never expressed her hopes for my conversion by a single
syllable except, as I later learned, in her prayers. But what a poet like
Coventry Patmore would call her "great and gracious" example was —
and is — a powerful inspiration.

Among my less informal critics, and among the experiments and books
which mold their lives, I searched and still search for a single example of
a single incongruity between even one scientific formulation, adequately
verified, and a single religious dogma, traditionally venerable. Add to this,
that after some twenty-five years of wide exploration in modern philosophy, from Descartes to Dewey, I still await the appearance of a single
understanding refutation of even one of those five *a posteriori* rational
proofs of the existence of God which St. Thomas Aquinas favored, and
which he made the crown of a philosophy independent of all authority
and based on no assumptions whatever, except — if you want to call it so
— the assumption that if men seek arduously and sustainedly there is a
considerable likelihood that they will find out some of the truth about
things. I have learned that, as a fact, everything proves the existence of
God and leads to inferences concerning His nature. Though naturally
limited, since we are finite and He is infinite, such inferences quite suffice
to prepare the way for a scientifically historical demonstration that on a
certain occasion He assumed human flesh, lived and died humanly, and
rose again from the dead divinely in Palestine where He founded a
Church — one Church, concerning which He promised that the gates of
hell shall never prevail against it. So triumphantly has this promise been
verified throughout two thousand years of history that it evoked, even
from the grudging Whig, Macaulay, the famous acknowledgment that
the Papacy still remains, "not in decay, not a mere antique, but full of
life and youthful vigor," sending forth her missionaries as of old, and
with the number of her children greater than in any former age. "And she
may still exist in undiminished vigor when some traveler from New Zealand shall, in the midst of a vast solitude, take his stand on a broken arch
of London Bridge to sketch the ruins of St. Paul's."

Like all converts I have often heard, at second or third relay, that I shall regret my rash move. "Poor man," one observer was quoted as saying, "I *think* that he is sincere. I suppose that he has as yet no inkling of the way in which Catholics treat their converts once they have them in the fold." This remark is not wholly devoid of truth. For I can testify that, during these past eight years, many Catholics have been much more kind to me than I deserve. Not that they regard my entrance into the Church as epoch-making — old Catholics are well acquainted with prodigal sons. And for this very reason I cannot help being surprised that, in their indefatigable hospitality, they waste so many good fatted calves.

As to my possible regrets, I may — after referring the reader to the latter part of this book — content myself at this point with one brief paragraph, not too swaggering, I hope.

It was not until the day of my first Holy Communion that I found I had attained, for the first time, to what in the strictest sense of the word may be termed happiness in contrast with mere pleasure. I was tempted almost to believe that I had already achieved the greatest possible happiness. I have found out that I was wrong. For each year, notwithstanding the onset of trying vicissitudes, perhaps somewhat more than the average number which anyone expects, this happiness has intensified undreamably, even to the point of incorporating into itself a good deal of the pain that I have experienced. And daily I realize ever more and more that even this increased happiness is as nothing when contrasted with that which awaits all of us when we face our greatest opportunity — death — if by perseverance we come to that magnificent adventure in a state of grace.

What I am now about to write may seem priggish. But I am really obliged to do it. To compare one's self with a saint borders on the sacrilegious for, though Catholics never worship saints, they know, from centuries of amply verified experience, that God will often honor those whom His Church has officially declared to be in His Communion in heaven, by answering their intercessory prayers for us. Yet when one's life — at such a far distance! — parallels sufficiently that of a certain saint to induce one to lean heavily upon him at every step of the way, what then can the poor weakling do but make his confession of allegiance as an autobiographer and enlist the services of his illustrious champion in defense of the faith which they share?

Among all the many saints to whom I owe unpayable debts, Augustine, more than any of his fellows, has throughout my whole life fanned incandescent in me the flame of a rationally grounded hope. It is for this reason that I have looted his philosophy for preludial quotations for each of my chapters, and I have taken refuge under his ægis at many a climax in the text.

He lived in an age startlingly similar to this. For apostates like Hitler and Stalin in our day he had, in his own boyhood, an equally powerful and no less futile Julian the Apostate. There will always be such, heedless of the fates of their predecessors, as long as Satan is allowed to remain at large to blind men who freely will to emulate his pride with their pride, rather than to make that loving surrender to God which is the only unequivocal freedom. So great and so many were the cataclysms which St. Augustine's contemporaries survived, thanks in no small measure to him, that we may hope to see mankind today survive similar debacles, and we may hope — or regret — that the Day of Judgment is probably not, after all, hard at hand.

In contrast with the showy schemes of Hegel, Marx, Spengler, and the rest, St. Augustine's *City of God* is the only philosophy of history which in all ages and in all places has never failed to fit the facts. Unperturbed by the Vandals who were raging around the temporal city (partly of God, partly of Satan) wherein he died, he departed on the supreme adventure full of the rapture of his own immortal sentence: *Fecisti nos ad Te et inquietum est cor nostrum donec requiescat in Te*. "Thou has made us for Thyself, and our hearts are restless until they find rest in Thee." And to him today, more than to any other mortal, I owe the guidance which lead me *ex umbris et imaginibus in veritatem,* "out of the shadows and the phantasies into the Truth."

The Doctor of Grace remains today the supreme searcher of souls. Contrasted with his child psychology for instance, the experiments of John B. Watson — although indubitably of very high value — are like the discoveries of a small boy blowing his first soap bubbles. And with this very soul-searching turned outward, St. Augustine penetrated farther than any philosopher who ever wrote into the mysteries of the "human caravan" in its tortured and often triumphant quest of the true God.

An unbaptized son of a pagan and long himself a pagan, St. Augustine received the grace of faith, partly, we may be sure, because of the prayers with which his Christian mother, St. Monica, stormed heaven for his conversion. Yet even as a pagan, Augustine was, like all agnostics and atheists in all times, at least negatively aware of the great sentence which we have already quoted from him. "I was utterly empty," he cried in his *Confessions* — and how often over long years my own heart has throbbed with the rhythm of his lamentations — "I was utterly empty . . . my soul was sick and sore, and threw itself into the external world." Observe that, contrary to the Freudian pseudo-scientific myth with which the Viennese psychologist warps his many important contributions, Augustine did not take to religion because he was starved sexually. No, Mr. Edward I. Watkin in his book *The Bow in the Clouds,* is right in this matter about the saints. W. D. Lawrence, the "naturalistic" novelist, became hyper-sexual simply because he was starved religiously in his early life, as the pathetic, abortive, quasi-mysticism of his later years reveals. Thus also James Joyce — whose *Ulysses* is perhaps the most appallingly lonely book ever written. But Augustine, a perfect antithesis to these men, clearly discerned, without becoming in the least a jaded roué, that even in his worldly adventures he was really seeking God.

Arthur Symons once wrote that the four greatest autobiographies are those of Augustine, Cellini, Casanova, and Rousseau. But, whatever their greatness, of the last three, how paltry they stand confessed in contrast with the first, how feverishly unfinished! And in contrast, how majestically humble is the climax of the *Confessions* of the mighty Christian: *O veritas, veritas, quam intime etiam tum medullae animi mei suspirabat tibi!* — "O Truth, Truth, how did the inmost marrow of my soul sigh for Thee even then!"

So Augustine stands out pre-eminently as the apostle whose longest apostolic wanderings were within the labyrinthine mazes of his own soul. Consequently, he was always purifying the various sciences of their prejudiced assumptions. Would that our brilliant and profound mathematicians and physicists like Eddington and Schrödinger, Jeans and Einstein, did so today with one half of Augustine's cunning. He, like Descartes, but over a thousand years before the great French geometrician, and more clearly than he, dared even to doubt that he doubted. But unlike Descartes, he did not become so enmeshed in skepticism as to take such desperately sophistical measures to escape it.

St. Augustine moved forward much more cautiously and, in spite of, nay perhaps because of his thirst for God, rather fearfully. His Manichæan period has a very modern appearance and reminds me today of that current philosophy of a finite God who is good but "in trouble," which enlisted for a few years my rather suspicious allegiance. It was at the time when I yielded to the genial and racy eloquence of William James. With such a background, how warmly could I share Augustine's inward-looking suspicion of ecclesiastical authority, so defiant, so prolonged! But how completely, too, have I in consequence been able to understand the wisdom of his final acceptance of it! With the eagerness of a hunter I dogged his footsteps. Closely I observed how — after he had reacted from his worldliness to the attenuated spiritualism of Neo-Platonism; after he had learned from an intensive study of Holy Scripture that one can abuse the spirit as well as the flesh; after he had come, through the aid of St. Paul, to a complete understanding of Charity and found the only true freedom under the authority of a Church which showed him the way to love his neighbor as himself because of his love of God — how then, at last he was able to burst forth with the rapturously reasonable: "Love and do what thou wilt; whether thou hold thy peace, of love hold thy peace; whether thou cry out, of love cry out; whether thou correct, of love correct; whether thou spare, through love do thou spare; let the root of love be within, of this root can nothing spring but what is good."

Then, too, uprose that understanding which kept his faith impregnable, nay full of high victory even as he saw the enormous Roman Empire groan and crash around him just as Western European Civilization groans and crashes around us today. For he knew that the Church, whose authority he had accepted would somehow, even if need be in some catacombs, survive every whirlwind-reaping until the end of time. Jubilantly might she cry: "Christ is my beginning, Christ is my root, Christ is my head!"

HERBERT ELLSWORTH CORY

ACKNOWLEDGMENTS

Thanks are due the following publishers for permission to quote from their works:

The Paulist Press, for the quotation from *The Question Box,* by Father Bertram Conway; P. J. Kenedy and Sons, for the quotation from Leen's *The True Vine and Its Branches;* Dodd, Mead and Company, for quotations from G. K. Chesterton's *What's Wrong With the World;* W. W. Norton and Co., Inc., for quotations from *The Biological Basis of Human Nature,* by H. S. Jennings; Charles Scribner's Sons, for quotations from *The Sources of Religious Insight,* by Josiah Royce, and the *Degrees of Knowledge,* by Jacques Maritain; Longmans, Green and Co., Inc., for quotations from G. H. Joyce's *The Principles of Natural Theology,* Fulton J. Sheen's *God and Intelligence,* Fouard's *The Last Years of St. Paul, Electromagnetics,* by Alfred O'Rahilly, and *Salve Mater,* by Frederick Kinsman; D. Appleton-Century Co., for the quotation from Fulton J. Sheen's *Moods and Truths;* Ginn and Company for quotations from *Select Translations from Old English Prose,* edited by Albert S. Cook and Chauncey B. Tinker; the Macmillan Co., for quotations from *The Spirit of Catholicism,* by Karl Adam, *The New Testament of Our Lord and Saviour Jesus Christ,* by F. A. Spencer, O.P.; and Sheed and Ward for quotations from Huby's *The Church and the Gospels,* Christopher Dawson's *The Making of Europe* and *Progress and Religion,* Michael Müller's *St. Francis de Sales,* Maritain's *An Introduction to Philosophy,* Arnold Lunn's *A Saint in the Slave Trade,* Leen's *The Holy Ghost* and *In the Likeness of Christ,* Davis' *Moral and Pastoral Theology,* Grandmaison's *Jesus Christ,* Arendzen's *The Holy Trinity,* Brodrick's *St. Peter Canisius,* Gregory's *The Unfinished Universe,* Hughes's *A History of the Church,* and Karrer's *Religions of Mankind.*

CONTENTS

THE EMANCIPATION OF A FREETHINKER

CHAPTER I

THE OLD FAMILIAR FACES

"Thou hast made us for Thyself, O God, and our hearts are restless until they find rest in Thee."

MY EARLIEST memory of the holy Catholic Church I cannot localize in time. I must have been a rather small boy when my mother, a restless Congregationalist, took me to the Providence Cathedral to what, from my dim memory, I now fancy, was probably a Requiem High Mass for some departed soul. The first appeal which the one complete faith made to me was through my nostrils, invaded by the fragrance of incense.

Nobody but a materialist or a spiritualist need be amused or shocked by this. A materialistic psychologist might reason that my present inferences and consolations are proved worthless by this apparently trivial beginning. For he is often a victim of the fallacy of origins, the notion that a lofty belief might not have been remotely stimulated by some vulgar impulse. A man's nose may inflame his soul. And his soul, perchance, may be at that very time listening, however unwittingly, to some message from the Holy Ghost. But of course the materialist does not believe in a soul. On the other hand, the spiritualist is shocked at the thought that the faintest religious glimmer should owe its existence in any way to matter which he would like to explain out of existence. He has forgotten that Jesus called His material body a temple. The spiritualist has turned his back on the cornerstone sentence of the Christian faith wherein St. John, writing of the incarnation of Jesus Christ said, "And the Word became flesh."

My mother was a sort of ecclesiastical gypsy. Born of Anglo-American Puritan parents and reared a Congregationalist, she nonetheless loved to steal into every available sort of church, from Jewish synagogue to Christian Science temple. Finally, after having entered the Anglican Church she died, in the baptism of desire, just as she was planning to take instructions to unite herself to Rome.

My father was, as Chaucer would say, "a verray parfit gentil knight." But unfortunately, like Don Quixote, he was born after the days of

3

chivalry were gone. He was honest. He was tender. And for a while his virtues brought him, even in the business world, great success. But he was too little of this world. He turned out to be a failure, a failure who will inspire me to the end of my days.

Father, humble as he was, never lost a sweet dignity in the midst of defeat, but moved, slightly bewildered, through the mart, much like Spenser's Sir Guyon or Temperance through the dim, gold-gloomed cave of Mammon, with a steady courage and a sober cheer. He knew naught of Spenser or any other poet. He was in fact all but illiterate. Nor did he care for such churches as he knew. Of Anglo-American parentage, like my mother, there was yet no Puritan rigor in him and the Congregational church brought him some peace for a while. But he soon left it for his own simple meditations. He had a deep wistful piety shadowed by many a naïve doubt. Often, after I went to college, and seemed to him to be a youth of towering erudition, he would approach me shyly with his difficulties. I, who by this time had become myself a most unwilling unbeliever, answered him, as hopefully as I could, out of my wish to believe, but with a sinking recognition of the fact that I was a blind man trying to lead the blind. More and more my fear that my wish to believe would hypnotize me fused with that most subtle form of pride miscalled "intellectual honesty" to paralyze my reasoning.

I. BOYHOOD AND ADOLESCENCE

But to retrace my steps. I was perhaps about twelve when my mother suggested that I might become a member of our church. I was at that time as much of a sinner as a normal boy could be at that age. I was a chronic liar, at times a pilferer, a member of a gang of vandals who made life miserable for our neighbors, and proudly profuse in that unseemly language by virtue of which so many boys strive to attain what they presume to be manhood. Yet I was capable of occasional fits of remorse — particularly after I was punished. Lacking access to the Catholic confessional, the Sacrament of Penance, which today strengthens me in my crises, I fear that my repinings were more of the nature of attrition (based on the fear of God, the pains of hell, and my mother's violent wrath) than of contrition (rooted in the love of God). I read and enjoyed the Bible. But I rioted over Homer and Dumas, Virgil and Scott, Ariosto, Sir Thomas Mallory, and garishly covered dime novels about the Wild West. All stories of adventure, distinguished or trashy, were my meat and drink; but I would have been as bored as the un-converted St. Ignatius Loyola with the lives of the saints. Still, I could pray, at times, with real fervor. And since I loved my mother as well as feared her, it occurred to me that it would be a nice thing to gratify her desire.

As a consequence, I appeared before a company of deacons, business-men who knew little more about religion than I did. No classes, no catechism, no reading, no instructions. One solemnly bearded gentleman asked me if I prayed. I replied very sincerely that I did, and that I certainly derived help therefrom. With no more ado I was accepted and allowed on "communion" days to eat a little dry cube of homemade, leavened bread which vaguely *symbolized* the body of Jesus, and to take a sip of grape juice which even more pallidly symbolized the blood of our Lord. But I would not belittle the gentle moods of exaltation that often came to me then though they sometimes seem a bit funny, in retrospect. For they had the tang of reality.

One day, a few years later, when I had well passed the portals of adolescence and had acquired a substantial knowledge of the much graver sins which beset that period, I was in church, dreaming my way through a sermon, very serious and very long, when I suddenly descried a fair-haired boy some four or five years younger than myself. I, weighed down by my vices, was abruptly stung into writing under that inspiration my first poem, which began as follows:

> Sweet Innocence, thy charming face
> Bears not a sign of this sad place
> To which thou'rt born.

I quote these silly but very sincere lines as an instance of the ponderous piety of which I was capable now and then.

In the main, my impressions of orthodox Congregationalism past and present are very delightful and respectful. I shall never, for instance, forget the benign lady who taught my Sunday school class. For six days a week she toiled and moiled in a dingy office. On the Sabbath she endured with a smiling resignation our impudent quips and yawns. Despite our rudeness we esteemed her. And although she was not learned, she was strong in her faith and taught us more with the homely example of her simple holiness than many more skillful and well-informed teachers could perhaps have done. We had sincere ministers who were particularly helpful in their pastoral calls. But the easygoing liberalism of the creed of my childhood, like all versions of Protestantism, is headed sadly but surely toward unbelief. Today some of the most brilliant Congregationalist pastors, like those of some other Protestant creeds, are making a brave rally in defense of a God, but a very unorthodox one. As long ago Calvin, obsessed with the omnipotence of God, forgot all about His mercies, today many descendants of Calvin, inspired now by John Stuart Mill and William James, have decided that God is benevolent but not all powerful. Else how could He allow evil to exist? I shall have more to say about this thesis later. For in after years I adopted it myself for a time. But I now see that it foreshadows the death of all reasonable faith.

I am glad to be able to confess that, while I dallied with the mythological God "in trouble" of William James, and with H. G. Wells's sentimental vision of an imperfect Deity like a "radiant youth," I did at least see through the rather conceited sophistries of those who, like George Eliot and Hugo Munsterberg and George Santayana, have recommended as a substitute for the belief in personal immortality a most unrealistic pseudo-physical and pseudo-biological faith in an "immortality of influence," in being a "precursor of a noble race," surviving in "those who follow." Quite appositely Fathers Bakewell Morrison and Stephen J. Rueve, in their compact and wise little book, *Think and Live,* see in this particular bromide a piece of self-assurance, entertained "with naïve disregard of the possibility that one's descendants may be veritable bluebeards."

But I was yet a long way from knowing that: (1) God's Existence, Omnipotence, Mercy, Justice, and Love can be proved by the unaided reason, in spite of the "refutations" of mere travesties of the arguments of St. Thomas Aquinas by men like Kant, Mill, the Cairds, McTaggart, and Ward; that (2) scholasticism at the meeting point of philosophy and psychology can prove the spirituality and simplicity (incorruptibility) of the rational human soul; that (3) such a God would never deny the natural desire of such a soul for pure and perfect eternal happiness; that (4) the historical existence of Jesus Christ can be proved just as surely by the unaided reason as the existence of Alexander or Napoleon or Woodrow Wilson; that (5) in spite of the mutually homicidal vagaries of the so-called higher critics, the same reason without appeal to authority can prove that Jesus Christ declared Himself to be true God as well as true Man and that He told the truth; that (6) since He promised us immortality, we can base our belief on Divine Revelation the existence of which, as we have just seen, can be proved by the combined arguments drawn from philosophy, psychology, and history without any reliance on any ecclesiastical authority whatsoever.

II. EARLY FRIENDSHIPS

Meanwhile, my heroic mother became a proficient linguist and was thus enabled to help my father by teaching French and German in the Providence Evening High School. She had an excellent speaking technique, but no wide acquaintance with the literature of these languages. So, as I entered the Providence Classical High School, she became a freshman in Brown University. And when I finished my freshman year at our Alma Mater she left it with a master's degree and an added equipment of Spanish and Italian. Her insatiate passion for languages, which led her to accost every alien ragman and garbage carrier who tarried at our door and to converse in strange tongues with every friend who shared her interests, brought us both the priceless friendship of another exuberant linguist, Ellen L. Virgin. Miss Virgin is a richly learned Catholic, and my meeting with her marks one of the most radiant milestones on my road to Rome.

It was Ellen who introduced us to the Storers in Newport, Rhode Island. I had previously spent many a summer in that quaint old town. As a boy I had left my scalawag pals in Providence, to play here for a brief season with two lads, the Allens, who were sons of a gentle, devoted Methodist minister. I all but lived at his home. I loved the white-haired mother. I discovered *The Last of the Mohicans* with the two sisters. I was regular at church and prayer meeting. It was a sort of retreat, a purgation. Methodism has divided into a score of jangling sects. Its attitude toward holy Mother Church is often ignorant and hostile. But through these memorable Allens I owe to the church of the illustrious John Wesley a considerable debt.

There is a part of Newport little known to any but her natives. The tourist traverses Bellevue Avenue, the Cliff Walk, and the Ocean Drive where the marble mansions of the Vanderbilts and the rest of that sort, on the verge of the tumultous ocean surf, set him agape. Old Newport ends where Touro Street becomes Bellevue Avenue. But turn your back on Bellevue Avenue and all its sound and fury, signifying nothing. Retrace your steps along Touro street, named after the fine old Jew, past the Park which is his memorial, with its "Old Stone Mill" which dreamers like to believe to be a trace of the early Norse explorers of Vinland, past the Jewish synagogue wherein I spent an unforgettable evening, past the little cemetery of Touro's kith and kin which the now most unjustly despised Longfellow celebrated in song.

How strange it seems! These Hebrews in their graves,
   Close by the street of this fair seaport town,
Silent beside the never-silent waves,
   At rest in all this moving up and down!

The trees are white with dust, that o'er their sleep
   Wave their broad curtains in the south wind's breath,
While underneath these leafy tents they keep
   The lone, mysterious Exodus of Death.

And these sepulchral stones, so old and brown,
   That pave with level flags their burial place,
Seem like the tablets of the Law thrown down
   And broken by Moses at the mountain's base.

Now saunter on ever westward through the old city square with its statue of Admiral Perry, across the main business thoroughfare, Thames Street, which a good broad jumper could take at one leap. Angle your way through meandering crooked lanes, under temples of maple trees which mellow with their shade the dinginess of thronging proletarian cottages. At length you come, let us hope at sunset, to a heavily shaded, ambrosial aisle called Washington Street, on the verge of murmurous Newport harbor. Here a fine old house shelters the Storers.

Dr. Storer, a Boston Unitarian convert to the Catholic faith, had been forced to relinquish his surgery because of a septicemia which resulted from one of his operations. He bore his infirmity with a fine combination of Christian realism and good cheer. He had no doubts of the reality of evil, spiritual and physical, and he had no doubts of the reality of the all-pervasive, abounding love that God has bestowed upon all of us. His son, Bellamy, then ambassador to Italy, I never met. It was his daughter, Agnes, close friend of Ellen Virgin's, with whom we spent most of our hours.

On a little incline looking out over the quiet-colored waters of the harbor, with its distant portals leading to the sea, its light-bejeweled islands and its goodly company of far-traveled ships, stands a charming stone house which had been given by Agnes to the nuns of the Cenacle when the Masonic French government of the early 1900's expelled them from their native home. Here mother and Ellen went into retreat, and here, too, I first came to know some of the Sisters of our faith fairly well and learned how comical is the pity which many non-Catholics lavish on supposedly brokenhearted nuns. Here I saw women immensely happier than any human beings I had seen before.

III. FIRST CONTACTS WITH CATHOLICISM

But I, alas, was also a good deal of a neopagan in those days. It was Ellen Virgin who ushered me into the study of Father Dowling, then rector of the Providence Cathedral, destined to die an archbishop in St. Paul. My callow undergraduate days were then drunk with the music of Swinburne's poetry. My lips burned with his naughty phrases about

> The creeds that spit on Christ

And about

> The lilies and langours of virtue,
> The roses and raptures of vice.

and

> Thou hast conquered, O pale Galilean,
> The world has grown grey with thy breath.

Unsmilingly, but most heartily, Father Dowling echoed antiphonally my pæans about my beloved poet, but with discerning judgment. Not a word about Catholicism or any religion. No, the Church could wait.

Just here I can imagine some Mr. Worldly Wiseman remarking: "At last I understand why this man praises the Catholic Church. He was and is a violent and whimsical emotionalist. How easy for him to pass from the rhapsodies of Swinburne to the superstitions of Rome!" Yes, I was excessively emotional. And often my fervors veered from paganism to Catholicism. In the Antwerp Cathedral I all but knelt before the impetuous colossal picture of "The Descent from the Cross," by Rubens. In Boston I felt a vague but genuine religious exaltation when the symphony orchestra played the "Symphony in D-Minor" of César Franck. I admired St. Francis of Assisi as the most Christian of Christians because he expanded the love of all men to a loving sermon to the birds and to an effectionate greeting of his gray brother, the wolf. When, at Brown, I studied seventeenth-century poetry, I shared the ardors with which Richard Crashaw, that learned Catholic son of a Puritan divine, extolled St. Teresa.

So again, in Cologne I lay awake many a night and contemplated the ghostly grandeur of the cathedral spire. In the cathedral at Rouen I witnessed a georgeous processional proclaiming that the spirit of St. Joan of Arc, the victim, not of holy priests, but of scheming politicians, was still alive. In Notre Dame I sensed the triumph of spirit over matter as my eyes swept up along the soaring vaulting which has for centuries so audaciously defied the mechanical Law of Gravitation.

But I feared my own emotions. The salt of honest doubt withheld me. And now I realize that I was right. The Roman Catholic Church has no camp-meeting lust for emotionally intemperate turncoats, for those of us who are outside and who have not as little children been born and nursed within her cool shadows before the glow of stained-glass windows or before the sumptuous splendor of the high altar. She expects that her own children will learn to reason, as best they may with lisping lips. Her catechism helps them, if they will, to think for themselves, to bow before her, not with blind fear, but with love and reason. For love without reason is not love; and reason without love is not reason. Many of her children are content to forget her first lessons and to surrender to super-stition, lukewarmness, or apostasy. But if they have learned to love her deeply enough, they will continue to reason and so return to her sooner or later. And for those of us who were not brought up, from some cause or other, in her love, if we will but listen to our deepest impulses and reason unflinchingly long enough, we will learn to love. And she will not ask of us more than our opportunities allow. If we do not spurn our own modicum of piety and good will she in turn will not spurn us whatever we may happen to be, or wherever we may happen to find ourselves. For African Bushman and Roman Catholic, Russian Communist and New England Victorian; for Brahminist, Mohammedan, Shintoist, Confucian-ist; for Agnostic and Atheist there is always the voice to be heard which the pagan convert, St. Augustine, heard when he wrote: "Thou hast made us for Thyself, O God, and our hearts are restless until they find rest in Thee."

CHAPTER II
ALMA MATER

---

*"For God is more truly thought than expressed;
and He exists more truly than He is thought."*

I BELIEVE that Freud is right when he says all of our spontaneous day-dreams are egoistic. I remember once luxuriating in the fantasy that my chum and I had devoted ourselves to several days of tortured meditation which culminated in the complete solution for all men for all time of the riddle of the universe. Our brows were furrowed and distorted by the awful vigil. But our very disfigurement only deepened the love that mankind must have for us who had saved them forever from the distress of thinking any more about ultimate questions. I suspect that many of us in our mature years, in a sort of rationalistic arrogance, retain some vestige of the grotesque daydream which I have just described. Excessive rationalism, though not so common, is quite as possible as excessive emotionalism. There are many of us who refuse to believe in God until we know as much as God does. This was a vain hope which I was in due time to entertain, more or less unconsciously, for many years. I find that it lingers in the minds of many of those of my friends who are older as well as those who are younger than I.

I. COURSES AT BROWN

I found time, at Brown, to take two courses in philosophy, a study which I was unable to resume until I was well launched in my teaching at the University of California in Berkeley. My second course at Brown was in the history of philosophy. It seemed to me then, and for some years thereafter, the most broadening study that I had ever attempted. Indeed, in a certain sense, it was, but to a degree of tenuity that was almost nihilistic. I became, by turns, a Platonist, Cartesian, Kantian, Hegelian, Pragmatist, Neo-Realist, until, like Omar, at the end of the course, I "came out by the same door where in I went."

At Brown I also carried on for two more years my classical studies.

11

I was charmed with Horace, Catullus, Tibullus, Propertius. Always deeply and wistfully concerned with immortality, I was uplifted by the hope which Socrates is made to express in Plato's *Apologia*. I was so delighted with the Greek melic poets that I made a versified translation of one of them in the margins of a book only to remember, to my horror, that the volume had been loaned to me by my professor. The rereading of all of the *Prometheus Bound* of Aeschylus, on the eve of an examination, was a glorious experience. How I reveled in the Firebringer's rebellion against Jove! Grandest of all was my experience of "the surge and thunder of the Odyssey." In my enthusiasm I often translated neither wisely nor too well. Once, while I was rendering a bold paraphrase of a passage from one of Lucian's satires, I was vaguely and bewilderingly aware that my professor was squirming in his seat as though he was attired in a hair shirt. I was soon to learn the cause. "Mr. Cory," said he, when I had sat down complacently, "your translation reminds me of an elegant torso. The trunk is beautiful; the arms, the legs, and the head are all missing."

I was aflush with the Renaissance and the Reformation. These seemed to me to be the high watermark in the ebb and flow of human souls. I actually believed that the so-called free spirits of this period really had revived, after the long, dark night of the Middle Ages, the knowledge of Greek. And why shouldn't I? For the histories which I was taught, ancient, medieval, renaissance, and modern, were all written by men steeped, as I now know, in a one-sided even if forgotten Protestantism. And worse than that, these men honestly believed that their works were nonsectarian. How well I realize today the truth of the saying of Hilaire Belloc's, in his *Survivals and New Arrivals* that so-called nonsectarian education is pretty generally, though more or less unconsciously, anti-Catholic!

My work in the social and natural sciences and in mathematics was superficial. I did relish a year in the botanical laboratory and some accompanying field work. But this was merely because I learned the names and appearances of many flowers which I could star-scatter through my callow poetry. I feared the sciences most sentimentally and morbidly because, with Edgar Allen Poe, I believed that the men of scalpels and acids had driven the nymphs from the streams, the mountains, the forests, and the oceans, and had silenced the pipes of Pan.

Little did I realize that a fuller acquaintance with the sciences at Johns Hopkins, some twelve years after, was to do much to restore my ability to reason to God's existence. Meanwhile, they seemed to make it clear that miracles were unbelievable and that consequently one of the arguments for the divinity of our Lord was absurd. Jesus now became for me a glamorous human figure, perhaps historical, perhaps legendary. I am sorry to say that my portrait of Him was almost as saccharine and as materialistic as Mrs. Eddy's. I remembered His kindness to publicans and to the woman taken in adultery. But I forgot that He called some of the Pharisees "whited sepulchers" and drove the money-changers from the temple with a scourge.

The kind of Jesus that I now believed in was somewhat like the Jesus who haunted the neurotic imagination of Nietzsche when he stigmatized Christianity as a slave-morality, a conspiracy of the unfit against the fit. Poor Nietzsche! How little he understood the same Darwin from whom he caught a catchword or two! By fitness to survive, Darwin meant any attribute, however degenerative from our point of view. Thus the hermaphroditic tapeworm is the fittest of the fit in its own particular environment.

II. MILTONIC REFLECTIONS

For some years I had wavered between music or literature for my vocation. At Brown I specialized in English. The question arose — journalism or literature? My mother used often to tell me a story about her father, George Washington Cook, which may have had its influence. My maternal grandfather, an expert mathematician in navigation and mechanics, was self-taught. He ran away from Tiverton, Rhode Island, to go down to the sea in ships with the New Bedford whalers. But he was a sober lad. And his life as a whaler and as a pilot in the Civil War did not deter him from study. Now when I was an infant, father and mother and he stood by my bedside solemnly forecasting my career. After derisively rejecting all other possibilities, my grandfather manifested great enthusiasm at the mention of a college professorship. And so it came to pass. At Brown I read omnivorously in the modern literatures from the Renaissance to the present day. The Elizabethan period was my favorite and I loved to emulate the Dionysiac prose of that time. So heady was the wine that some ten or twelve years afterward, when I submitted to Professor George Lyman Kittredge the manuscript of my *Edmund Spenser, a Critical Study,* he returned it with some friendly comments but with the emphatic admonition to "de-Swinburneize" it.

On the whole, however, my greatest inspiration came from Milton, and not the youthful Milton, if you please, but the majestic singer of *Paradise Lost, Paradise Regained,* and, above all, the rarified *Samson Agonistes.* I pondered long over the much discussed question of the theme of *Paradise Lost.* I was delighted with Paul Elmer More's charmingly argued thesis that the theme is the Garden of Eden. But I came to believe that More was wrong. I decided to take Milton at his word when he said that his epic was written to "justify the ways of God to man." The mature Milton was a good antidote for my apoplectic Elizabethanism.

Now, since I had concluded that Milton meant what he said, it was easy to discern that the hero of *Paradise Lost* is Adam, and its theme, original sin. This view readily disposes of the romantic theory that Satan, because of the grandeur with which he is portrayed in the early books, is really the unacknowledged hero. The whole point is that Satan retrogresses from his primal Luciferean splendor to become a thing unspeakably grotesque and groveling. Adam appears at first quite unlike the typical hero of an epic. And he sins. But at the end, when Eve and he are taking their repentant departure from the Garden of Eden, he becomes grand, humble, and heroic in his resignation, in his contrition.

I never felt that Milton was completely successful in justifying the ways of God toward man. And, as a Catholic today, I do not expect anybody this side eternity to fathom completely the mystery of original sin. According to both reason and revelation, God gave Adam and the rest of us a responsible free will. If He had withheld free will and forced us to be good, man would have been a lower creature. But it is strange that in these ruthless days so many men whine against God because He did not make mollycoddles out of us — and then go on believing that He does not exist. He sent His Son to redeem us in an agony of which only a Man-God could be capable.

It is clear, as I came gradually to see, that if there is a God, and if, because He loved us in His thoughts from eternity, and so created us in fact — created us to love Him and to become like Him — He would of necessity endow us with free will. For coerced love, like a square circle, is intrinsically contradictory. And even almighty God, as St. Thomas Aquinas frequently reminds us, cannot violate the Law of Contradiction, cannot create the intrinsically contradictory. He cannot make x be both x and non-x at the same time and in the same respect. He can raise a Lazarus from the dead. But He cannot make a Lazarus both dead and not-dead in the same instant. Now, love is in its essence a free surrender.

The lover always says to his beloved "Thy will be done," and so makes the freest of all acts. Love unfree is as intrinsically contradictory as a square circle. So God created us free to love Him. Mankind sinned in using the freedom which God gave to turn away from Him. God, who is the absolute opposite of all tyrants, respected that freedom and left mankind to find its way back to Him. But He also imprisoned Himself in the womb of a Jewish girl, from which He emerged clothed in humanity, in order to show men by example how to endure sufferings even the most extreme, and how, victorious even over death, to enter into His celestial presence, there to remain forever.

Now, however, difficult though the doctrine of original sin may be, it is vastly superior to all others that men may wish to substitute for it: Buddhistic pessimism, Mohammedan and Calvinistic fatalism, or the spiritualistic efforts to explain evil away as error. Verily a rose by any other name would smell as sweet, and so evil with any name is just as nauseous and noxious. How bleak, too, is Martin Luther's opposite view that man is hopelessly evil, a creature to be saved not by his good deeds but merely by faith, a view which John Dewey still confuses with Christianity. Catholicism, always true to the golden mean between two extremes, believes that man needs both faith and good works for his salvation. Rousseau's theory of the natural goodness of man is the silliest of all. He thought that if man could shake off the incubus of the preacher, of the teacher, and of the king, he would assert his native ability for purity. But preachers, teachers, and kings are men. Why, then, are they bad? According to Luther, man is hopelessly evil. According to Rousseau, man is ridiculously good. According to the unnatural "naturalists," who espouse some highly speculative theory of evolution, or some soulless "psychology" or the "mores" sociology of a William Graham Sumner, man is neither good nor bad, but morally neutral. They would substitute for rational ethical standards the view that ethical codes are mere formulations of experiences which are all quite justifiable in their given environments as devices for "adaptation." They will blandly refuse to condemn any of these "mores" anywhere — until somebody does something repellent to *them*, whereupon they suddenly flame up with moral indignation. According to Catholicism, always sane and temperate, man is both bad and good with an excellent fighting chance, if he cooperates with God's grace, of walking more and more in the ways of righteousness. He has the threefold concupiscence of the flesh, the eyes and the pride of life — but he also has a conscience, that is to say, a warning voice bidding him to do the right thing, coupled with more or less ability to reason it out. Conscience is not a myth or a mystery; it is a practical judgment perfectly familiar to every man, not infallible, but not unreasonable.

Milton, as we know, became an independent, the extreme left wing of Puritanism. As such he is claimed as an ancestor by both conservative Baptists and liberal Unitarians. I felt that he was the latter, and I tried Unitarianism under a most eloquent and scholarly preacher. But I soon gave it up with a feeling of emptiness. Its communities are sweetly and pensively anarchic. For a while I was proud of my Puritan forbears. What champions of freedom! Beginning as low churchmen, then becoming dissenters, and finally independents. I was full of the superstition that this was freedom. Low churchmen, dissenters and then nonconformists, independents, and then what? Such "freedom" reaches its inverted and inevitable apotheosis in agnosticism or atheism. That is precisely what it did for me. Such "freedom" is but the inheritance of original sin, a pride, in its ultimate development, like that with which Lucifer hurled himself out of heaven into hell.

My favorite poem of Milton's was his last, the magnificently bleak drama, *Samson Agonistes*. *Paradise Regained* is transitional. For all its austerity it reveals a wistful reminiscence of the sensuous Spenser, and of Spenser's even more sensuous — and violently Puritan — early followers. One of these, Giles Fletcher, in his *Christ's Triumph and Victory*, had dealt with the theme of our Saviour's temptation, often with quaint, stiff beauty, occasionally with religious fire that burns clear white even today. Fletcher's Satan, disguised as an aged hermit, is no more than Spenser's magician, Archimago, who masqueraded in similar fashion to deceive the Red Cross Knight or Holiness. Like the Red Cross Knight, Jesus is brought to the "Cave of Despair" in a passage in which Fletcher follows his master almost verbatim. Satan then tempts Christ with the true luxurious abandon of the Renaissance. Our Lord's possible worldly ambition is tested by Presumption in her airy pavilion,

> Over the Temple, the bright stars among.

He is then brought to the "Bowre of Vaine Delight." At this point Fletcher imitates jauntily and prettily, Spenser's account of the Bower of Bliss wherein the voluptuous enchantress, Acrasia, seeks to seduce Sir Guyon (Temperance). According to Giles Fletcher's eroticism:

The garden like a Ladie faire was cut,
That lay as if shee slumbered in delight.

On "a hillie banke" her head is laid, white and red roses for her face,
and for her hair, marigolds, that "broadly shee displaid," but at night
"with green fillets in their prettie calls them bound."

This is exactly what we should expect from a pleasure-loving worldly
son of the Renaissance. These furtively voluptuous Puritans were fain
to decorate the spare lines of the Scriptural stories with delight upon delight until they forgot the *motif* of their poems in their naïve joy in the
World and the Flesh.

Milton seems to have planned a conscious revolt against the Bower
of Bliss device. "Set women in his eye and in his walk," said dissolute
Belial to Satan meditating an assault on Jesus. But Satan rejects the
advice with superb scorn. Here the poet speaks *in propria persona*. Practice, however, fell somewhat short of what Milton intended in theory.
As Spenser tempted Sir Guyon with Philoteme (Worldly Ambition) and
the lascivious Acrasia; as Giles Fletcher followed by choosing Ambition
and Wantonness; so Milton, following at a somewhat greater distance,
did nothing more than discard the allegory and subject our Lord most
inappropriately to somewhat similar epicurean allurements.

But in my favorite of his poems, *Samson Agonistes*, Milton, in music
most rarified, spoke of his own griefs and closed with a hymn of victory
so austere that to the weak majority of men it sounds like despair. When
I was a sophomore this drama left me cold. But it helped me when a
senior to recover, for fleeting moments, the faith which was now submerged in agnosticism.

It is difficult for us to realize with sufficient dramatic intensity the
awful depth of the spiritual tragedy that reached its catastrophe for
Milton with the restoration of the Stuart monarchy. *Samson Agonistes,*
if we understand it with dramatic sympathy, should appeal to us more
than any of Milton's other poems. For while this grand poem groans
and burns with his sorrow over his blindness, his bitterness toward
women, the defeat of his political cause; while it breathes his large
hatreds and his petty hatreds, yet from the depths Samson emerges. The
poem trumpets forth Milton's love and fear of God, a God as terrible
as the Hebraic Jehovah, but a God who has His appeal to all good
fighting men. Well was it, as Gilbert Keith Chesterton observes in *The
Everlasting Man,* that the God of the Jews was a jealous God. For this

chosen people was surrounded by alien tribes with a myriad of alien and often degraded gods. Chesterton notes (following, I suppose, recent anthropologists like Father Wilhelm Schmidt) that polytheism, far from preceding the worship of one God, is always a sign of degeneracy. How much easier it is to agree with your neighbors in a flabby way, to promise to worship their gods if they will worship yours! How often the Jews approached the brink of this abyss of liberalism only to be drawn back by a Moses or by the later Prophets to that unalienable loyalty, to that majestic monotheism which establishes their supreme religious genius! And Milton reawakened this great theme in a sublime fanfare. He drew proudly aloof from his age and rose above it — not selfishly, but to show to his distracted fellow men the only tolerable goal for a triumphant life. Like Samson he rose above his own gloom to forge out the proud faith that is uttered in the noble stoical lines of Manoa:

> Come, come; no time for lamentation now,
> Nor much more cause. Samson hath quit himself
> Like Samson, and heroically hath finished
> A life heroic.

It is so easy nowadays to jeer at high heaven that the last words of Milton's last chorus will appear to many a superficial reader to bear the taint of a facile optimism. But when I ponder them in the perspective of the poet's bitterest of life struggles I seem to find the awe of divine things in their burnished calm. And some forty years of further meditation on the possible ways of a possible Providence have at last, by the grace of God, turned the faint, evanescent hopes of those days into a firm, supra-rational faith.

> All is best, though we oft doubt
> What the unsearchable dispose
> Of Highest Wisdom bring about,
> And ever best found in the close.
> Oft He seems to hide His face,
> But unexpectedly returns,
> And to His faithful Champion hath in place
> Bore witness gloriously; when Gaza mourns,
> And all that band them to resist
> His uncontrollable intent.
> His servants He, with view acquist
> Of true experience from this great event,
> With pride and consolation hath dismissed,
> And calm of mind, all passion spent.

III. SWINBURNIAN RODOMONTADE

Such moments of exaltation, however, were then rare with me. Sometimes I almost felt that I could share the so-called mysticism of Wordsworth before Tintern Abbey. But I mistrusted myself. I wanted so terribly to be a mystic that I did not dare to. I read some of the theological mystics but I was at the time repelled by their merciless self-discipline. Emerson was more to my taste. But I had sense enough to suspect his hypnotic vagueness. So I was fortunate enough to escape the psuedomystical anodynes that Mr. More justly attributes to the attenuated influence of the sage of Concord on various cults which so widely enervate American life today, and which bring unmerited reproach on the work of real mystics like St. John of the Cross, whom I was not to know for more than twenty years.

My prevailing mood was that of the genteel Victorian doubt, so beautifully portrayed in Matthew Arnold's "Dover Beach" — except when I adopted the Swinburnian swagger or steeped myself in the "naturalism" of Zola and Hardy, Ibsen and Shaw.

I was much preoccupied with the problem of personal immortality. I wanted to believe. But the skeptical passages in, for instance, Tennyson's *In Memoriam* appeared to me to be more convincing than his positive arguments which I now more fully appreciate. I contented myself with writing in defense of the mere desire. Then, as now, one often heard that the desire for survival is cowardly and selfish. I have, in all these subsequent years, been interested in the attitudes of human beings toward survival. My mature observations verify my youthful ones. In the main I find that selfish individuals are indifferent toward immortality because they live in a shallow present, that many who sneer at it are poseurs, and that those who desire it do so, not from fear, but from loves and friendships, and from devotions to lofty purposes which would acquire an eternity to fulfill, as Kant justly contended. Some have conjectured that primitive man first thought of immortality when he dreamed that his other self went a hunting, or when he saw the reflection of his filthy and hairy visage in a stream. As well say that man developed his first interest in astronomy when, in his terrified acquaintance with eclipses and other portents, he fancied, as a few surviving alchemists still do today, that the stars in their courses had a direct influence on his marriage and sickness and death. One of the most widespread superstitions of the pseudo-intellectuals of our day is that all of the religious concepts are born of abject fear. Malinowsky, who began his anthropological career by some firsthand study of the religion of a primitive people, the Melanesians, finds this to be a half-truth which is "worse than no truth at all."

I left Brown in a spirit of Swinburnian rodomontade. My class poem, "At Sunrise," urged loyalty to truth though the heavens fall. I portrayed this austere Truth as a delightfully voluptuous woman with "red-gold hair like dawn." It reminds me of a futuristic poem by Marinetti which I was to read years later. Away with all the old songs, cries in effect, the swashbuckler. Let romantic love in particular, be anathema. Turn from the stifling, perfumed caresses of Guenevere and Helen of Troy to the contemplation of pure, abstract Beauty. He then proceeds to personify pure, abstract beauty as a very concrete woman limned with all the sultry langors and undulations of a Cleopatra. Such is the revenge which some tradition or other will always have on the hair-brained antitraditionalist.

I did not know it, but I was, like Francis Thompson, pursued by "The Hound of Heaven."

> I fled Him, down the nights and down the days;
> I fled Him, down the arches of the years;
> I fled Him, down the labyrinthine ways
> Of my own mind; and in the mist of tears
> I hid from Him, and under running laughter.
> > Up vistaed hopes I sped;
> > And shot, precipitated,
> Adown Titanic glooms of chasmèd fears,
> From those strong Feet that followed, followed after.
> > But with unhurrying chase,
> > And unperturbèd pace,
> Deliberate speed, majestic instancy,
> > They beat — and a Voice beat
> > More instant than the Feet —
> All things betray thee, who betrayest Me.

CHAPTER III

AT HARVARD

*"Thou seekest a name befitting Him and findest none:
thou seekest in what way soever to speak of Him and
thou findest Him in all things."*

WHILE at Brown University I earned part of my expenses by putting
away returned books in the college library, working holidays in a book-
store, giving crude piano lessons to students almost as crude, and reading
gas meters. This last experience was particularly enriching, the informal
encounters with all sorts of individuals in the intimacies of their cellars.
But, despite the cooperative efforts of all the members of my family, I
could never have proceeded directly toward my doctorate at Harvard
had it not been for the assistance of my father's cousin, Austin H. King,
who also gave me my first prolonged acquaintance with the greatest of
all poets, Dante. In the words of one of the innumerable, beautiful prayers
of the Church: "Condescend, O Lord, to reward with a long life all those
who help us for the glory of Thy name. Amen."

I. YOUTHFUL SURGINGS

My first year at Harvard was rebellious. I had hoped to major in
English Literature and minor in Philosophy under the guardianship of
Palmer, Royce, James, and Santayana. I dreamed of reviewing the Renais-
sance in the light of an intensive study of Plato and of rereading the
romantic poets in the perspective of Kant, Fichte, Schelling, and Hegel.
But I was forced to study linguistics, to read Gothic, Anglo-Saxon, old
French, and Middle English (which I extended into a study of Middle
Scots).

I thank God for this. For my heritage of unconscious Protestant
prejudice and my neopagan idolatry of the Renaissance had left me
densely ignorant of the Middle Ages. In this graceless state of mind I
clung, for many months, to my old ways. I spent far more time writing
verses than in etymologizing and translating. I was disgusted when I had

21

to spend an entire semester on the origins of words of the first ten lines of the Norman French *Song of Roland*. And when, during the next semester, we were expected to read widely outside of class, but to pettifogulize (as I might have said then) with our professor over a handful of philological problems, though I roamed far abroad in the chivalric *lais* and romances, I was so frequently absent from our linguistic symposia that I had to be content with a rather disreputable grade.

I discovered some convivial friends from Canada and California, Missouri and Virginia, and we spent far too many hours wining, dining, and slumming. I liked to drift alone through the crowded and crooked streets of Boston, fortified well with alcohol, and consequently aglow with a Walt Whitmanian (or should I say Walt Whitmaniac?) admiration of all my fellow men, particularly the lawless ones. I associated this vaguely with the sentimental vestiges of my Christianity. I was battledored and shuttlecocked between the intemperate indulgence of drink and the equally intemperate abstinence, morbid remorse.

If I were a so-called naturalist I might here and often hereafter in this book Freudianize about various amorous adventures of which I experienced what a Havelock Ellis would probably consider a "normal" amount. But although my struggle with the concupiscence of the flesh has been sufficiently prolonged and grim to make, no doubt, a fairly saleable book, I cannot, since I am not a naturalist, but only a realist, regard it as of sufficient importance to inflate a volume which will be long enough as it is. From the practical point of view, moreover, what I do have to say about the deeper currents of my life will help a fellow sufferer to solve these problems far more than any amount of quasi-aesthetic or quasi-scientific pornography, which dwells lip-smackingly on the subject and coins all sorts of hypnotic terms like "conditioning" and "Oedipus complex" without offering any real solutions. I hope that my unfolding argument will do something to show that confession and Communion can minister to a mind diseased far more efficaciously than psychoanalysis, behaviorism, gestalt or hormic psychology, despite the fact that Freud demonstrated — to his own satisfaction though not to that of the best anthropologists — that Holy Communion evolved from a cannibalism which he quite irrationally associated in a scientific daydream with varying totems and taboos. Of my own detailed work in psychological laboratories and clinics I must needs write at some length at the proper point in my story. But while I am deeply grateful for the many valuable insights which I have derived from such sources, I have gradually learned that there is more real psychology in St. John of the Cross or St. Francis de Sales than in all the professionals of the last generation, from Alexander Bain, Ribot, Wundt, and William James, to Freud, Watson, McDougall, Koffka, and Köhler taken together.

I wrote many poems, during this year, some of which were highly praised by critics, both students and instructors. But at the ebb of the spring I suddenly fell silent. It was like a bereavement, a bereavement which haunted me for nearly thirty years. But one night, after several months sojourn in the Catholic Church, when I lay happily awake in bed, the octave of a sonnet leaped full-born into my mind. On the following day, on returning from Holy Mass, I finished the sestet with equal celerity.

When I fell silent at Harvard, I thought that my poetic sterility was caused by the damning influence of pedantic studies. Now I know that it was brought to pass by my own gracelessness. I was spiritually bankrupt. I thank God for it, because this dryness (as the mystic might call it) was a katharsis which prepared me for the discovery of the Middle Ages. And at the beginning of that vista of the Middle Ages, which then lay revealed before me, stands the second radiant milestone on my road to Rome.

II. ST. PAUL IN GOTHIC TEXT

I was set to reading Gothic because its literary monuments were then thought to constitute the oldest relics of those Germanic dialects which are the primal organ tones in the multilanguaged fugue of modern English. And because the only extant Gothic Literature is scriptural, we were assigned the *Epistles* of St. Paul. I had paid no attention to the Apostle of the Gentiles since my somnolent boyhood days in Sunday school. Swinburne, I remembered, had execrated him for reasons not then at all clear to me; for I was not, of course, at all familiar with the manner in which the theologies of Luther and Calvin envenomed the Pauline sublimities out of all perspective for the children of the "Enlightenment." Paul, who was shipwrecked and scourged, beaten with rods and stoned, in perils from his own nation; in perils from the Gentiles and finally beheaded, seems to have become particularly exposed, in subsequent centuries, to the blind hatred of apostates and their mistaught descendants. Now the stern necessity of fathoming his all but fathomless meanings, in a barbaric tongue, word by word, with a dictionary at my elbow, and cheek by jowl with the errant and erring translations of Wyclif, Tyndale, and the authors of the King James Version, awakened me to the fact that I was in the presence of a profound philosopher and an intrepid saint. What St. Paul means to me today will form later the principal theme of one of my chapters. At Harvard, quite unawares, I was preparing myself to understand a sermon of Cardinal Newman's which I discovered long afterward. Speaking in particular of the virtue of compassion as found in St. Paul, the Cardinal says:

It is the habit, then, of the great Apostle to have such full consciousness that he is a man, and such love of others as his kinsman, that in his own inward conception, and in the tenor of his daily thoughts, he almost loses sight of his gifts and privileges, his station and dignity, except he is called by duty to remember them, and he is to himself merely a frail man speaking to frail men, and he is tender toward the weak from a sense of his own weakness; nay, that his very office and functions in the Church of God, do suggest to him that he has the imperfections and the temptations of other men.

The notion of the "communion of saints" appears in many a Protestant profession of faith. But it is perfunctory, skeptical; it carries little or no weight to the Protestant. The saint tends to be either a legendary figure or a pretender who would usurp the throne of Jesus. It is only a Catholic, like the German theologian, Karl Adam, for instance, in *The Spirit of Catholicism*, who can write with the fervor and depth which transfigure the following passage:

Communion of Saints — what a glad and blessed light illuminates it! It is the hidden treasure, the secret joy of the Catholic. When he thinks on the Communion of Saints his heart is enlarged. He passes out of the solitariness of here and there, of yesterday and tomorrow, of "I" and "thou," and he is enfolded in an unspeakably intimate communion of spirit and of life, far surpassing his needs and dearest wishes, with all those great ones whom the grace of God has forged from the refractory stuff of our humanity and raised to His height, to participation in His Being. Here are no limitations of space and time. From out of the remote ages of the past, from civilizations and countries of which the memory is now only faintly echoed in legend, the saints pass into his presence, and call him brother, and enfold him with their love. The Catholic is never alone. Christ, the Head, is ever with him, and along with Christ all the holy members of His Body in heaven and on earth. Streams of invisible, mysterious life flow thence through the Catholic fellowship, forces of fertilising, beneficent love, forces of renewal, of a youthfulness that is ever flowering anew. They pass into the natural, visible forces of the Catholic fellowship, especially to pope and bishop, completing and perfecting them. He who does not see and appreciate these forces, cannot fully understand and expound the nature and working of Catholicism. And, indeed, it is simple, child-like faith alone which perceives these forces; and therefore that faith alone discovers the road to sanctity. For such is the prayer of Jesus: "I praise thee, O Father, Lord of heaven and earth, because thou hast hidden these things from the wise and prudent, and hast revealed them to little ones. Yea, Father, for so it hath seemed good in thy sight."

It was through certain members of the Communion of Saints that the barbarians of the Dark Ages, Goths and Vandals, Huns and Lombards and all the rest were mellowed to an understanding of St. Paul and his Divine Master.

III. EUROPE IN THE MAKING

Let us, for instance, try to envisage the situation at about the time of St. Benedict in the sixth century, A.D. Those who dare in their bigotry to blame the monks and the saints of this period for the darkness of ignorance at that time and later, could easily learn that the exact opposite is true if they would but scan four or five competent books. For a beginning, I commend the first chapter of Dom Cuthbert Butler's *Benedictine Monachism,* and the whole of a book by the recent convert, historian, sociologist, political scientist, Christopher Dawson, *The Making of Europe.*

I am ashamed to confess how abysmal was my ignorance in my early Harvard days and long after. To me the twentieth century, before the beginning of the "war to make the world safe for democracy," the war "to end all wars," was at the peak of progress facing the dawn of a heaven upon a Utopian earth. To me the solitaries of the fourth century and after were morbid, monkish visionaries, selfishly turning their backs on their fellows to cower in filthy caves and mortify the worshipful body. I did not know that St. Anthony, the "Father of Christian Monks," came forth from a score of years of seclusion, in a ruined fort on the verge of the river Nile, to minister to an army of aspiring eremites. I did not know that the cenobitical Benedictines were not content with mere prayer and with the preservation of ancient learning but also went out into the fields to teach the people the use of the plow and to organize market places which, if emulated widely today, would go far to annihilate the price fixing of avaricious capitalists. I did not appreciate how St. Benedict prepared himself and his followers for all this by retiring, for a space, from a civilization fully as degenerate as our own period of wage slaves, capitalists, Communists, Nazis, voluptuaries, indifferentists, and militarists, only to save this disintegration from turning into a perdition from which only such saints today will be able to save us. Perhaps they will come at last to a barbarized, idolatrous Communistic and Nazistic civilization of Europe and America from a Christianized India and China, Oceanica and Japan, Africa and Arctica.

In the fifth and sixth centuries, pauperized Italy, the corpse of "the grandeur that was Rome," represented a country of vast estates in which slaves had displaced the yeoman farmer class, a country of grinding taxation, divorce, and birth control, a country wherein the gluttonous and lascivious plutocracy depended on hordes of barbarian mercenaries. It was this civilization, so like our own today, that was inundated by Alaric and his Visigoths who thrice besieged Rome and finally sacked it; by the brutal Huns under Attila, the "Scourge of God" whom only an unarmed Pope could turn back; by Vandals from land and water who embraced that heresy of Arianism which was the most dangerous rival that Catholicism has ever encountered; by Alamans and by Lombards who for half a century devastated all Italy from sea to sea. This was the chaos which Christian monks turned into a cosmos which was to reach its climax in the thirteenth, "the greatest of all centuries."

It was at Harvard that I first learned that there existed a profound Christian culture in Celtic Ireland long before my barbarian Anglo-Saxon ancestors arrived at that stage of enlightenment. I went on to observe that, through the centuries, martyred Ireland, despite centuries of oppression, sustained, perpetually unextinguished, her light of faith.

A History of English Literature should indeed begin with those sad receding Celtic cousins of the Irish, the Britons whose children are now sequestered in Wales, Cornwall, and Brittany.

The three so-called races of the dawn of Europe's history, now inextricably and confusedly intermarried, were the Nordic (longheaded and blond), the Alpine (roundheaded and dark), and the Mediterranean (longheaded and dark). Between the first and the third, the Alpine wanderers drove a wedge, broad-based in Slavic countries, its point in the British Isles. Doubtless those Celts whom we call the ancient Britons were largely Alpine. Long before the times clearly celebrated in history the Celtic peoples came from eastern points beyond the Danube and swept over western Europe like an ocean devouring a continent. They overran France, for instance, where they came to be known as the Gauls, those terrible warriors who once threatened Rome itself, floundered through the Alps with Hannibal, and streamed back to St. Paul's Asia.

While the vanguards of this oceanic migration were crossing the English channel toward the Hesperides, the struggling masses of the rear of these unorganized hordes were probably as far away as the Danube. An unorganized army we may call it. For those divisions which followed the outriders seem to have swept over their predecessors as one wave crashes over another toward the seashore. Apparently one Celtic tribe was quite ready to half-assimilate, half-annihilate its fellows in the fore. At last the far-flung spray of these tumultuous groups conquered the all but forgotten people of dimmer days and settled down in comparative quiet in the British Isles. Their pagan culture was mellowed first by the culture of pagan Rome and then by the missionaries of Christ who had learned the Good News in the same "Eternal City." Though later humbled and scattered by Nordic invaders, these Celts, of whom one of their own bards wrote, "They went out to battle but they always fell," were destined to reconquer spiritually a large part of the western world in England, France, Germany, and even Italy with their glamorous story of King Arthur and his knights of the table round, and to accelerate among the Anglo-Saxons and the Norse the ineffable tidings that "Christ has risen."

In *The Making of Europe* Mr. Dawson eloquently expresses what my Harvard discoveries equally revealed to me regarding the significance of the Celtic genius for Christianity. "It was in the newly-converted Celtic lands of the far West," he says, "that the influence of monasticism became all-important. The beginnings of the monastic movement in this region dates back from the fifth century, and probably owes its origins to the influence of Lerins [in Gaul], where St. Patrick had studied in the years before his apostolate and where in 433 a British monk, Faustus, had held the position of abbot."

The growth of the monastic movement in Ireland, set on foot by St. Patrick and related after a time with a similar movement in South Wales, was "the origin of the movement of culture which produced the great monastic schools of Clonard and Clonmacnoise and Bangor, and made Ireland the leader of Western culture from the close of the sixth century." This development may well have been based in part, as Dawson suggests, on the native tradition of learning which the Irish without question possessed. So by degrees, "the imported classical culture of the Christian monasteries was blended with the native literary tradition, and there arose a new vernacular literature inspired in part by Christian influence but founded in part on native pagan traditions. . . . Thus there was no sudden break between the old barbaric tradition and that of the Church, such as occurred elsewhere, and a unique fusion took place between the Church and the Celtic tribal society entirely unlike anything else in Western Europe."

Mr. Dawson has more still to say regarding the early voyages of the Irish pilgrims, until "Every island of the northern seas had its colony of ascetics." Thus was that tremendous impulse given which led to the spread of Christianity everywhere by Irish and monastic colonies, such as those of Colomba at Iona, and of his namesake Columbanus at Luxeuil.

To the one was due the conversion of Scotland and of the Northumbrian kingdom, to the other the revival of monasticism and the conversion of the remaining pagan elements in the Frankish kingdom. . . . Very many of the great mediaeval monasteries not only of France, but of Flanders and Germany, owe their foundation to its work. . . . All through central Europe the wandering Irish monks have left their traces, and the German Church still honors the names of St. Kilian, St. Gall, St. Fridolin and St. Corbinian among its founders.

To both the Celtic monastic movement and the Roman Benedictine mission is here ascribed the appearance, in the seventh century, of the new Anglo-Saxon culture (between 650 and 680). Yet it was with no little difficulty, Dawson admits, that the Church succeeded in putting down the old pagan customs. Usually it was done "by providing a Christian ceremony to take the place of the heathen one. . . . The liturgy for Advent Ember Days, especially, is full of references to the seedtime, which it associates with the mystery of the Divine Birth. . . ."

The last point noted here is of particular importance. It is the fashion of journalists and professors of today who have that "little knowledge" of comparative religion which is "a dangerous thing," to inform their cynical audiences that Christianity is a patchwork of borrowings from pagan cults. It is never so except in the assimilative way here described. More often still, the reverse is true and, from ancient Persian-Roman Mithraism to contemporary Japanese Buddhism, it is the pagans who have borrowed, not always wisely, from Christianity. Finally, Christianity often uses the truths of a cruder religion as steppingstones to the absolute truth, as when today in Japan the Catholic missionary father commends the Shintoist for his reverence for his ancestors, and thence leads him to the necessary inference, to the discovery of that Ancestor of all ancestors who is the Uncaused Cause.

IV. ANGLO-SAXON POETRY

It may well seem to my readers that I have here turned utterly from the account of my pilgrimage toward Rome to write a treatise on the early culture of the British Isles. But I have already described my exterior life, convivial as it was. My interior life, on the other hand, now began to grow deeper and deeper with my contemplation of what was for me the New World of the Middle Ages. It can only be set forth, therefore, as a series of vignettes from the panorama of medieval literature which my instructors unfolded before my rapt gaze.

A great deal of this was non-Christian: the Anglo-Saxon epic of *Beowulf,* stirringly and stoically and fatalistically pagan despite the occasional Christian interpolations; the French, Provençal, German, and English romances of chivalry and of that Court of Love described with a gently, merrily irreverent liturgical idiom. But at the same time vistas most relevant for a book like this came from numerous passages of pious works which moved me deeply. And although I still remained an agnostic spectator, yet often I was carried away, for brief periods, by enthusiasms which, as I can see today, never quite faded out. Long after they had been experienced they still warmed me subconsciously, persistently, recurrently, even to the recent years when, at last, I surrendered to the Hound of Heaven.

It is therefore of no import here to dwell on my impressions of *Beowulf* for all its auroral spaciousness. The first relevant vignette I glean from the *Ecclesiastical History* of St. Bede the Venerable. It consists of the story of the conversion, about 627, of King Edwin of Northumbria. After tarrying with the noble but stark fatalism which inspired the heroic struggles of Beowulf with the demon Grendel, his witch mother and the dragon, this quiet antidote cheers us like the first golden shaft of the fully arisen sun. In reading it we may easily construct a picture of the grimly resolute, tawny-haired warriors listening gravely, in the long hall where the fitful, almost gloomy light of the fire threw capricious flames over their armor, to the dawnlike words of the mildly resolute monks with heads tonsured like the shaven heads of pagan slaves that they might glory in their slavery to the infinite Master and Saviour. At last one of the king's chief men, slow of thought and speech, "unlocked his word-hoard," as the old Teutonic poets used to say. With a seriousness at once childlike and profoundly mature, he advised his liege lord in a lovely parable which has been so often quoted. I offer the translation of Albert S. Cook and Chauncey Tinker.*

O King, the present life of man on earth seems to me, in comparison with the time of which we are ignorant, as if you were sitting at a feast with your chief men and thanes in the winter time, and a fire were kindled in the midst and the hall warmed, while everywhere outside there were raging whirlwinds of wintry rain and snow; and as if then there came a stray sparrow, and swiftly flew through the house, entering at one door and passing out through another. As long as he is inside, he is not buffeted by the winter's storm; but in the twinkling of an eye the lull for him is over, and he speeds from winter back to winter again, and is gone from your sight. So this life of man appeareth for a little time; but what cometh after, or what went before, we know not. If therefore this new doctrine contains something more certain, it seems justly to deserve to be followed.

It is in the work of St. Bede also that we can read the oft-quoted story of the first great Anglo-Saxon Christian poet, Caedmon (670 b.c.), a story which has always moved me as a beautiful harmony of homely simplicity and cathedral visioning. Caedmon, so the gentle chronicler tells us, was for many years a lowly servant in a monastery, a sort of male Cinderella among poets, unlearned, silent, almost stupid. When at table the harp was passed from hand to hand, he used to arise sadly and humbly and steal away before he was called upon to take his turn. But one night, as he was caring for the horses in the stall, there came to him an angel saying, "Caedmon, sing." "I cannot," he replied. Said the angel once more, "Caedmon, sing to me." "What shall I sing?" "Sing the beginning of created things." And at this celestial exhortation the poor herdsman "unlocked his word-hoard." Caedmon then assumed the religious habit in the monastery, as became the author of the long and splendidly poetic paraphrases of *Genesis, Exodus,* and *Daniel,* whose authorship various historians believe they must assign to him. I was stirred by their striking originality to which Milton may in a measure have been indebted. The stern God of Hosts and the celebration of battles dominates over the Old Testament stories, while Anglo-Saxon taste suffuses these poems with Germanic color. Thus in the *Exodus,* the marshaling of Pharaoh's hosts and their death in the Red Sea resembles a battle between Saxons and Frisians. I quote from the passage describing the walls of water closing over the pursuing Egyptians. The rendering is from Henry S. Canby's translation with its excellent reproduction of Anglo-Saxon alliteration.

*From *Select Translations from Old English Prose.* By permission of the publishers, Ginn and Company.

Then with blood-clots was the blue sky blotted;
Then the resounding ocean, that road of seamen,
Threatened bloody horror, till by Moses' hand
The great lord of fate freed the mad waters.
Wide the sea drove, swept with its death-grip,
Foamed all the deluge, the doomed ones yielded,
Seas fell on that track, all the sky was troubled,
Fell those steadfast ramparts, down crashed the floods.
Melted were those sea-towers, when the mighty One,
Lord of heaven's realm, smote with holy hand
Those heroes strong as pines, that people proud . . .*

The peaceful death of this great monastic singer is in every detail narrated by the Venerable Bede. He tells how Caedmon himself had foretold the hour of his departure "when the brethren are awakened for lauds." He then signed himself with the sign of the cross, laid his head on the pillow, and died as if falling into a light slumber, "And thus," Bede continues, "it came to pass that, as he had served the Lord in simplicity and purity of mind, and with serene attachment and loyalty, so by a serene death he left the world, and went to look upon His face. And meet in truth it was that the tongue which had indited so many helpful words in praise of the Creator, should frame its very last words in His praise, while in the act of signing himself with the cross, and of commending his spirit into His hands. And that he forsaw his death is apparent from what has here been related."

Naturally as the years have flowed past me since I first read of Caedmon's death, it has been my lot to witness or to be intimately cognizant of many deaths. And among these there has never been a Catholic death, not even that of a youth who suffered untold agony after an automobile accident, which did not have something of the calm of Caedmon's. All of them faced death unflinchingly. All of them rose above their infirmities as if they had some faint hint of the Beatific Vision.

Next there still looms large in my memory the figure of the eighth-century poet Cynewulf who, if he wrote a modicum of what has been attributed to him, was unchallengeably the greatest English poet before the advent of Chaucer. It was fascinating to attempt, as Stopford Brooke did in his engaging speculations, a reconstruction of the character of Cynewulf from the few hints of himself which he wove most intimately into his own epics, precious as they are with the revelation of a man who

*From *Select Translations from Old English Prose,* ed. by Albert S. Cook and Chauncey B. Tinker. By permission of the publishers, Ginn and Company.

had the widest sympathies, a loving and profound knowledge of the life of the poor and the homely, the rich and the splendid. In youth, if we may believe his words, written in remorseful maturity, he was (to my delight in those Harvard days) a sad dog. He furnishes another bit of evidence against the psychoanalytic notion that religious rapture is a morbid substitute for a starved life. For he was vigorous, rollicking, the beloved of nobles who showered him with "appled gold," the boon-comrade apparently of the rogues in the lower classes. In those days he wrote lyrics called "Riddles" about the swan, the wine-vat, the one-eyed garlic peddler, the Storm-Spirit in the Sea. At last came, thought Brooke, a period of troubled and uninspired transition, to which the poet refers in his *Elena*, a narrative in which he tells how the mother of the victorious and converted Constantine fared forth on a pilgrimage of thanksgiving to salvage from heathendom the cross upon which the Saviour died.

> I was stained with misdeeds,
> Seared with sins was I, with my sorrows tortured,
> Bound with bitter thoughts, burdened sore with troubles
> Ere the Lord gave love to me through a light-imparting Form
> For my solace, now I'm old. It is a gift unshareable.

When I read Cynewulf I loved to read about penance — without practising it. But the leaven was working slowly. And I could faintly reflect his rapture when, as is conjectured, he described his vision of the "light-imparting Form" in *The Dream of the Rood,* in which the poet pours forth his ecstasy over a tremendous apparition of the cross which spans the sky, appearing in one moment covered with blood, in another gorgeous with gold and jewels.

The next personage, in these Harvard days, who turned my thoughts reverently toward the Catholic Church was King Alfred the Great (871–901). To understand him, we must behold him in the perspective of the Viking depredations which ranged from Constantinople and North Persia to Mohammedan Spain, reached North America, and planted settlements in Russia, Greenland, Iceland, Normandy, Scotland, England, and Ireland. Western Europe had attained a cultural Catholic unity under Charlemagne. But this was, as Mr. Dawson says, a "premature synthesis." The Roman Church was to face one of those almost continual crises which, from the days of pagan Roman persecution, were to succeed each other: on through the long menace of Arianism, the politically motivated separation of the Eastern Orthodox Church, "the great Schism" manufactured by avaricious French kings, the heady wine of the Renaissance which brought corruption even within, the clashing, confused, dividing, subdividing and sub-subdividing sects of the so-called Age of Enlightenment of the eighteenth century, and the eruption, side by side, of romantic and naturalistic obsessions. Then followed the bankruptcy of nationalism in the "great war." Hard upon it came next the bloodthirsty Communism in Russia, Mexico, and Spain, and the artificially revived Nordic superstitions of Nazist Germany. Through nearly two millenniums these successive crises have consistently stormed the Rock of Peter only to prove that Christ has kept His promise when, entrusting His Church to the Apostle who became the first of the unbroken line of popes spanning two thousand years (the longest continuous existence of any institution), He said: "And the gates of hell shall not prevail against it."

The Nordic culture which today still inspires a dangerous idolatry among some American sentimentalists and atheistic German bigots and pagans, had always tended toward a proud insularity. Tended, I say, because, as we shall promptly see, the Nordic culture was not as purely Nordic as those who would make of it a racialistic religion uncritically presume. But certain it is that, from causes still obscure to historians, eastern Asia and Europe, particularly western Europe, were dazzled by the terribly magnificent explosion of the Viking invasions.

It was Ireland, the martyr of Christian nations, that endured the worst of the Viking attacks. Turgeis (832–845) sought to establish there a Norwegian state. He profaned the Church of St. Ciaran and therein enthroned upon the altar, as prophetess, his heathen wife. Ireland, mother of western European Christian culture, for the time, collapsed. Her fate, too, soon befell Anglo-Saxon Christian culture, particularly in Wessex and Southern England, under the never despairing Alfred the Great. And while the Vikings raged, the Moslems sacked St. Peter's and desecrated the tomb of the Apostles. To cap the climax, the wandering Magyars (a savage blend of Finno-Ugrian and Turkish) destroyed the now Slavic Christian kingdom of Moravia. Western civilization tottered on the verge of disintegration. As pertinently it is pointed out in *The Making of Europe*:

... during the earlier barbarian invasions Christendom could rely on its cultural superiority, which gave it prestige even in the eyes of its enemies. But now even this advantage was lost: for the centre of the highest culture in the West during the tenth century was to be found in Moslem Spain, and Islam was no less superior to Western Christendom in its economic and political development than in intellectual matters. . . . Fortunately for Christendom, the shattered culture of Western Europe preserved its spiritual vitality and possessed a greater power of attraction for the Northern peoples than either paganism or Islam. By the close of the tenth century Christianity had already gained a firm foothold in the North, and even such a typical representative of the Viking spirit as Olaf Trygvasson had not only become a convert himself, but set himself to spread the faith in characteristically Viking fashion.

In Ireland, in 1014, the Vikings were hurled back at the Battle of Clontarf. In England, the Danes conquered a part of the country only to melt into Western Christian unity and to freshen "the somewhat anemic and artificial civilization of the Carolingian world" in its decadence. Nordic culture, even in Scandinavia, its recent idolators to the contrary notwithstanding, lost its pristine purity. Into remote Iceland and Greenland what I have called the Celtic spiritual reconquest penetrated, and with it, according to Olrik, even the old Skaldic poetry. Vigfusson, although overstating his case, nevertheless demonstrated the existence of a Celtic-Nordic culture in the western islands and Celtic influence on the greatest poetry of the Edda and on the prose saga. As Mr. Dawson has it, "Some of the noblest families of Iceland had Celtic blood in their veins," and so he concludes: "The Viking ideal was by itself too destructive and sterile to be capable of producing the higher fruits of culture. It acquired its higher cultural value only after it had accepted the Christian law and had been disciplined and refined by a century and more of Christian civilisation."

V. KING ALFRED

But I am ahead of my story. As I remarked before, King Alfred did much to increase my admiration of Catholic character. Alfred was the grandson of that Egbert who had done so much to make Wessex the center of a unified England under one king. Trained in books and warcraft, in youth an eager traveler to Rome, Alfred strove like Charlemagne to be a benignant patron of the Church and of scholars and literary men, most of whom were, perforce, of the clergy. We all love to read of his concealment (in the glowering days when the Danes had scattered his army and swarmed everywhere) in the huts of the common people. The Anglo-Saxon chronicle of Alfred's day, written largely perhaps by the king himself, tells us in unvarnished and never despairing language the story of years of blighting vicissitudes crowned at last by a peace which the Danes, though established in England, were bound to respect.

Then the indomitable king, like all truly great men a dreamer as well as a doer, gazed about him at the charred ruins of monasteries and at his half-savage, ignorant people. It was a sight to bring utter hopelessness to all but Alfred. Quietly, heroically, he set about the rebuilding of knowledge and of churches. The preface to his first real literary work, a translation of *The Pastoral Care* by Pope Gregory the Great, tells with characteristic simplicity the story of desolation and issues its calm victorious exhortation to overcome the decay of learning.

Besides the collection of sermons from St. Gregory the Great, Alfred translated St. Augustine and Boethius, and sections from the churchman Orosius, who wrote a *Universal History*. To this last book I return today with renewed interest and with a great change of heart.

To Orosius, history was but a pageant of great civilizations, Athens, Sparta and Macedon, Carthage and pagan Rome, each arising to a pitch of pride only to crash down in ignominious ruin. The churchman's eye was fixed not so much on time as on beatific eternity. At Harvard, and for many years thereafter, I suffered from that delusion of progress with which so many, since the so-called Age of Enlightenment in the seventeenth and eighteenth centuries, have sought to assuage the pangs of their religious hunger with a pseudo-religion of temporal dreams. Now I know that Orosius was right. It is hard to see how anyone, after "the war to make the world safe for democracy," the world-wide depression, and the spectacle of avaricious nations guided by infamous statesmen, can still believe in our vaunted progress. And any clear-eyed person ought to be able to observe that the whirlwind which we reap today was sown with the Reformation and the birth of covetous nationalism and capitalism. We have used science to conquer disease — and to manufacture poisonous gases for warfare. We have accumulated vast wealth — for a very few in the midst of a fearful poverty. There has been no concerted progress.

In *The International Journal of Ethics*, in his essay on "Progress," John Dewey pointed out that while we have the instrumentalities for advancement, libraries, laboratories, museums, symphony halls, art galleries, and the like, we do not move forward because we lack the sincere good will to progress. The conclusion of this much-quoted sociologist and philosopher is only one of many instances indicative of a largely unconscious tendency on the part of the diverse sciences to return to what in reality accords with the teachings of the Catholic Church when she declares the insufficiency of a merely terrestrial life and the supreme importance, in the eyes of God, of the good will in the souls of men saturated with His sanctifying grace. Dewey's diagnosis is perfect. But the "good will" of which he speaks he knows not how to conjure up because he still thinks with his Protestant forebears, that the Middle Ages were superstitious and stagnant, that Christianity implies the total depravity of man, and that the so-called Reformation was the mother of democracy and the life of reason. It is only with the turn of our century that scientific history has begun to replace legend-fabricating propaganda. And John Dewey, like most college professors as yet, seems to go for his sources to the "naturalistic" romancing of men like James Harvey Robinson and Harry Elmer Barnes rather than to genuinely scientific and genuinely contemporaneous historians. The one thing needed is a return of the world to that true Christianity of the Catholic Church which alone can restore the moral force required for the proper rebuilding of our decadent civilization conformably to the divine ideal which she sets before us.

And so, with a reluctant adieu, let us leave King Alfred, quoting his beautiful prayer that is found at the conclusion of his translation of *The Consolation of Philosophy* by that Boethius whom Dante placed in the Heaven of the Sun. It is fragrant with the very attar of Catholicism.

O Lord, Almighty God, Creator and Ruler of all things, I beseech Thee by Thy great mercy, and by the sign of Thy holy cross, and by the virginity of Saint Mary, and by the obedience of Saint Michael, and by the love of all Thy holy saints, and by their merits, that Thou wilt guide me better than I have deserved from Thee; direct me according to Thy will, and according to my soul's need better than I myself can; establish my mind according to Thy will, and according to my soul's need; strengthen me against the temptations of the devil, put far from me all foul lust and all unrighteousness, and shield me from mine enemies, seen and unseen; and teach me to do Thy will, that I may inwardly love Thee above all things with a pure mind and a pure body; for thou art my Creator and my Redeemer, my Help, my Comfort, my Trust, and my Hope. To Thee be praise and glory now and for ever, world without end. Amen.*

VI. SCIENCE AND THE SUPERNATURAL

The Norman invaders of England, once Northmen, were unique in their amazingly facile way of sinking into the manners and the tongues

* Rendered by Elizabeth Deering Hanscom for Cook and Tinker's *Translations from Old English Prose*. By permission of the publishers, Ginn and Company.

of those whom they pillaged and upon whom they forced themselves as unwelcome neighbors. When they invaded France and seized from the weak descendants of Charlemagne the fair lands of Normandy, they quietly took foreign wives, learned to speak fluent French, and quite forgot their harsher Scandinavian accents. Up rose their new churches, their beautiful flowing architecture, a combination of Gothic and Romance, strong and graceful with its clusters of columns, its almost curved but slightly pointed arches, its rose windows, simple, yet "like the flower itself."

William Butler Yeats, alluding to the Normans, writes of "their beautiful haughty imagination and their manners full of abandon and wilfulness" and contrasts with it the Anglo-Saxon "earnestness," its "reserve of a counting house." We must be cautious with these phrases. But the Norman was certainly brilliant, whereas the serious Anglo-Saxon was slow to "unlock his word hoard." On the other hand, the Anglo-Saxon had an exaltation that was given time to grow before he began his slow speech, a larger quality than Norman volubility. So while the Norman told, with all the ease of improvisation, charming gossipy tales that grew longer and longer as they developed with the centuries, the laborious Saxon held his tongue until his song burst forth with a mighty glow that the Norman never knew.

The Saxons had long been growing more and more hesitant and uneasy with the Danes for neighbors and the Normans across the channel waxing more and more ominously neighborly. And the literature of the Saxons became ever narrower and narrower. Night shut down on it. The *Chronicle* marched steadily and somewhat heavily on. *Homilies* or *Sermons* and *Lives of the Saints* in alliterative prose or poetry multiplied. Often they were eloquent. But all were restricted, reiterative. Readers will find in them much about hell and many pictures of the Last Judgment. The grandeur and exaltation glowed on but in company with monotony, gloom. Now what if into this withered giant oak of literature were to be grafted the spray of a thousand delicate branches and all the foliage of spring? What would come of a wedding of heavy English majesty and Norman brilliance? Polish, simple, fiery loyalty, nimble adaptability, and sweet piety. From this union, certainly, did come our oceanic modern English. And this was the next Pisgah-sight which deeply moved me in my Harvard pilgrimage.

My main concern in those days was with the Arthurian stories in chronicle and romance, with the metrical romances about Alexander the

Great in the fabulous Orient, with warriors of Greece and Troy, English heroes like Guy of Warwick and Bevis of Hampton, and Richard of the Lion Heart. But from the interminable Anglo-Norman chronicles I never tired of gleaning examples of those "visions," which in Western Europe stimulated the terrific imagination of Dante, and appeared in the saints' lives and miracles. I often had a wistful desire to share what seemed to me then to be the lovely but childlike credulity of the chroniclers. As I said before, I did not then believe even in the miracles ascribed to Jesus. It was not until years later that I was to learn that contemporary scientists have become so much less urgent in their defense of a rigid, unbroken, mechanical, cause-and-effect chain that it would be perfectly possible for a scientist today to admit the possibility of occasional supernatural intervention. What will be the outcome in science of the controversy between Sir James Jeans and Sir Arthur Eddington, on the one hand, and Max Planck and Albert Einstein, on the other, remains to be seen.

But as I now know from my study of neo-scholastic philosophy, the philosophical conjectures of natural scientists themselves are frequently very amateurish. And it is, therefore, pathetic to observe how naïvely they are sometimes followed by the epistemologically bankrupt contemporary followers of Descartes, Hume, Kant, and Mill. The genuinely philosophical attitude toward these matters has been well summed up recently by Father André Bremond, S.J., in his *Religions of Unbelief*:

We must bear in mind the essential difference between *science* which has for its object the laws of phenomena but remains abstract and hypothetical as to the existence of things, and *philosophy* which starts from the fact of existence as such, and seeks the causes of that existence. Not only, then, does the theist not conclude the existence of God from any scientific fact or theory, but he is sure that scientific investigation and reasoning, if it be careful not to transgress its own rules, cannot possibly interfere with his own conclusions.

. . . it often happens that certain scientists, and unbelievers of the "scientist" type, do transgress those rules and make their negation of God dependent on scientific determinism, taken as an absolute and necessary law of things. For them the sequence of events of any observable order is ruled by the same necessity as mathematics; and as mathematics excludes all consideration of efficiency and finality, so does the knowledge of nature. Consequently, if it happens that the very progress of scientific investigation throws some doubt on the absolute character of determinism in physics, and points to indetermination and spontaneity in the inmost heart of nature, the dogmatic unbeliever and scientist will have some reason to be genuinely distressed. The believer, on the other hand, will have some reason to rejoice, not for himself but for the sake of the unbeliever; not that science has proved the existence of God, for it can neither prove nor disprove it, but because science itself has removed a prejudice which was for some of its devotees an obstacle to the rational belief in the existence of God.

As a Catholic I am today fully convinced of the authenticity of the miracles of Christ on grounds which I can more appropriately discuss here and there in later chapters. Moreover, I am quite ready to entertain the probability that some of the later miracles, such as for instance those described by the Anglo-Norman chroniclers, were real miracles. And I will present some evidence for my belief that miracles occasionally occur today. Few non-Catholics are aware of the severe scientific scrutiny to which the alleged miraculous cures at Lourdes are now subjected. While faith-healing sects often deny the validity of the sciences and bandy about the wishes that are fathers to their thoughts, at Lourdes an unpaid bureau of physicians, of any faith or unfaith, investigate the case histories and subsequent careers of the afflicted who appear to be healed. Some of these "cures" they find to be either the result of natural recuperative processes or hysterical manifestations. But there is an average of about one in every two thousand which remains inexplicable on purely materialistic grounds, although even then the physicians confine their observations to merely medical problems and make no pronouncement of miracles. When the idolatrous atheistic novelist, Emile Zola, visited Lourdes, he was greatly shocked at the spectacle of some of these unaccountable phenomena and declared roundly that if he witnessed a million of them he would still not believe them to be miraculous events. In a novel in which he made use of an episode at Lourdes he *imagined* that the woman whom he *saw* cured succumbed soon after to the resurgent disease. As a matter of fact he died before she did. Non-Catholics would be the most amazed persons if they read of the scientific and philosophical techniques for the verification of what the theologian calls "extraordinary graces" required by Benedict XIV in his treatise on canonization.

I pass on to another of my most memorable experiences with medieval religious literature. If it was a single author (perhaps Hugh of the Royal Hall) who wrote *Sir Gawayne and the Green Knight, Cleanness, Patience,* and *The Pearl,* he was indeed a great poet. However this may be, it is the last of these poems which I desire to add to my autobiographical anthology. It is a poem with a childlike faith which I loved and still love, but which I could not and cannot share, a poem which, I suspect, contains a measure of wisdom which will never be mine — this side of eternity. It is a most tender lament of a father for his little girl, Margaret, "My precious perle wythouten spot." The poet says that he lost his pearl in the grass and that he wandered about the spot inconsolable, unable to leave it. Blossoms and fragrant spices will always come from it. One day in the high season of August, when the corn was falling under the keen sickle, he came once more to this lovely arbor in the midst of myriads of flowers "seemly to see, sweeter to smell." There, overcome with the aromatic odors, he sank prostrate and slumbered. Then came a sweetly ministering dream: cloven cliffs of crystal, a forest on a hill, a silver stream whereof the gravel was of pearl, "Birds sang sweeter than citole or viol." The banks glittered with beryl. The pebbles in the pool were emeralds and sapphires, gems so rare that they shone like stars on a wintry night. More marvels arose. There came a child, "a gracious maiden full debonnaire," in a white robe. He longed to see her face. And when she lifted it, ivory white, he stood stock still, not daring to speak, "as steady as a hawk in a hall." For it was his daughter, her winsome grace made royal with pearls.

Down to the bank she went, "fresh as a fleur-de-lys in May," crowned with pearls in floretted patterns with no other fillet except her golden hair which fell in soft waves upon her neck. At last her father spoke: "Art thou in sooth my pearl, so long lamented, through many weary nights?" She lifted her gray eyes and answered seriously: "Your pearl was never lost. Call not your fate a thief, O gentle jeweler. You lost no pearl but a mortal rose that flowered and faded according to its kind. Now the rose has become an immortal pearl which rests safe in a coffer and that is this gracious garden." Long he talked with her and listened to her healing words. Then he followed her within sight of the Celestial City and the procession of the saints. Ill it pleased him to be an outcast. But he was at peace when he remembered that she abode with Prince Christ.*

VII. DRYDEN AND CATHOLICISM

If I were writing a comprehensive autobiography instead of an account of my lifelong pilgrimage to Rome, I would tarry a long time with

---

* In making this much abbreviated paraphrase I have occasionally turned from the original Northern Middle English to plunder a graceful phrase from Jessie Weston's translation in *Romance, Vision and Satire*.

Chaucer. I now see how profound his Catholicity was. But in my Harvard days I did not detect it. I would love to dwell on many another beloved man of letters. But my theme compels me to leap over the centuries and close this chapter with my experience with John Dryden.

I had read Dryden pretty thoroughly and with considerable relish at Brown. But I then shared the conventional opinion that he was, for all his genius, a mere turncoat, and that his Catholicism was but the peak of his insincerities which even he, sycophant that he was, lacked courage to renounce at the end of his life, after his long and ignominious series of desertions. A very careful review of his work made by me at Harvard, when I never dreamed of becoming a Catholic, when I was in fact still aflame with the notion that the Renaissance and Reformation, particularly the Puritan Reformation, were mighty steps toward the attainment of a sacred liberty, yet convinced me that Dryden was a much greater poet than I had realized and, throughout most of his life, stalwartly sincere.

"All knowing ages," said John Dryden, "are naturally sceptic and not at all bigoted, which, if I am not deceived, is the proper character of our own." Although it is far from true that all "knowing ages" are consistently skeptical, it is certain they have in them a disposition to inquire which is not incompatible with strong faith, and which is the antidote for bigotry that only blights and warps. As to Dryden's age, the second half of the seventeenth century, its skepticism was too often gangrened with cynicism and badly blighted with puritanical bigotry. The Catholics, particularly under James II, were in fact the only ones who could be called tolerant as a class — perhaps because they could not be otherwise. "Glorious John" was a child of the age, a drifting, extraordinarily open-minded personage, in his earlier period changing color like a chameleon, inclined to flatter, but fundamentally sincere, courageous, magnanimous. Although he began by yielding hastily and uncritically to the lewdest and most artificial habits of the day, he rose august above them to interpret the most Olympian impulses of his epoch.

Dryden came of a family full of strong Puritan currents but also with "noble" connections. Indeed his own temperament seems from the first to have had much of the Cavalier in it, albeit with a curious alloy of middle-class vices and virtues, flunkeyism and a fine sturdy industry, shrewdness, and moral earnestness. His abounding generosity moved him to refuse to raise the rents of his little estate when rents soared. This same generosity buoyed him up to move among the most scurrilous enemies with lofty reticence and withal a hearty readiness to admit on occasion the justice of their assaults — although, when he felt justified, his poetical rapier thrusts were annihilating. Compounded of a Cavalier chivalry, purged of its Quixotism by the Puritan homeliness of his nature, he was admirably tempered for that sanity which is so characteristic of the essence of Catholicism.

It is not surprising that such a large nature, as in the case of all the greatest poets, should develop very slowly. Critics take impish delight in dwelling on the unwitting buffoonery of the ponderous serious fancies which, under the influence of Cowley and Sylvester, he stuck all over his early verses. At eighteen, for instance, he wrote as follows of Lord Hastings, who died of smallpox:

> Each little pimple had a tear in it,
> To wail the fault its rising did commit.

But it was Dryden himself — whose middle-class sturdiness steeled him to a steady growth, while Cavalier poets like Suckling, Lovelace, and Rochester, with perhaps more native brilliance, quickly burned themselves out — it was Dryden, with his severe self-criticism, who was to be the first to expose his own faults.

But Dryden seasoned slowly. Even his poem on the death of Cromwell, written after leaving Cambridge University at an age beyond that at which Keats died a distinguished poet, is not particularly promising. It is more interesting because it preceded much praise of Charles II and is often cited, from the days of his venemous rival Shadwell, as proof that Dryden was a garish weathercock, swayed by every gust of public favor. For he published, in the very next year, his welcome to the Stuart monarch, a much better poem, incidentally, associating the Restoration of Charles with the coming of May in the lovely line, "You and the flowers are its peculiar care." But Saintsbury has noted that, though the earlier poem is a clever eulogy cunningly evading all allusion to the evil traits of Cromwell, it is also marked "by the entire absence of any attack on the royalist party," and deems it possible that "a certain half-heartedness may have been observed in Dryden by those of his cousin's party," for "no kind of preferment fell to his lot."

We may here once more emphasize the truth, too seldom stressed, that Dryden's alleged changes of front are usually nothing but a hearty sympathy for whatever subject he had in mind for the nonce, and that many of his alleged "insincerities" were naught except his eager skepticism-tinged aspiration to absorb a variety of divergent views in order that he might sift the best from them all. Dryden's biographer concludes sensibly:

Now it must be remembered that, either as the losing party or for other reasons, the royalists were in the great civil war almost free from the charge of reckless bloodshedding. Their troops were disorderly, and given to plunder, but not to cruelty. No legend even charges against Astley or Goring, against Rupert or Lunsford, anything like the Drogheda massacre . . . or the hideous bloodbath of the Irish women after Naseby, or the brutal butchery of Dr. Hudson at Woodcroft, in Dryden's own country, where . . . [these Puritan] soldiers chopped off the priest's fingers as he clung to the gargoyles of the tower, and thrust him back with pikes into the moat which, mutilated as he was, he had managed to swim. A certain humanity and absence of blood-thirstiness are among Dryden's most creditable characteristics, and these excesses of fanaticism are not at all unlikely to have had their share in determining him to adopt the winning side when at last it won.

Dryden's first period of production came to a close, when he was thirty-five, with *Annus Mirabilis,* of "The Year of Wonders," the first poem that shows unequivocally his genius. The "heroic quatrains" sang of the exciting but far from uplifting year of 1666, of the Dutch War and the Great Fire of London. And it is not surprising, therefore, if he lapses now and then into the conceits of his callow youth.

Before the composition of the *Annus Mirabilis,* in fact by the time he was thirty, Dryden had brought out his first play and followed it up with several others. Thus he began, on the threshold of the Restoration, that long assignation with the stage in which he pandered and blundered, but worked doggedly until he not only acquired a temporary affluence but also a spiritual growth of permanent value which expressed itself at last in his masterly dramatization of the tragic amour of Anthony and Cleopatra in *All for Love.* Dryden's theatrical career was continuous until the popular, fanatical delusion of a "Popish Plot," the sort of mob-insanity that still reverberated in the United States during the candidacy of Al Smith for the presidency, aroused the poet to his greatest destiny, the composition of satires. And even after this regeneration from original sin he persisted in his work for the stage at intervals to the last year of his life when, a poor man, he wrote some lines for a drama of Fletcher's revived at a benefit performance for him.

It was his early association with the stage, no doubt, that brought

Dryden the acquaintance of Sir Robert Howard who became his father-in-law. Dryden's slanderers were later to make much of the lady's dubious reputation, declare the marriage unhappy, and assert that Dryden himself was a libertine. But the charge against him has never been substantiated; there are evidences of real marital affection; and the only definite shadow was the tragedy of his wife's later insanity which cast its gloom upon him and was among the many other adversities which purified Dryden's later life for the great religious faith which he was to espouse. As to Dryden's moral looseness in his plays and his stylistic heaviness and artificiality, it is worth noting that he became his own most unsparing critic in his dignified acquiescence to Jeremy Collier's onslaught in later years with the noble words: "It became me not to draw my pen in defence of a bad cause, when I have often drawn it for a good!"

It would be fascinating to tarry, as I once loved to do, with Dryden's theatrical career. But the real Dryden who led me along the path of truth turned to satire.

The tide of the poet's prosperity had turned. And his misfortunes were about to metamorphose him from a popular and kaleidoscopic writer into a powerful and profound artist. With his fame and fortune there had come, as usual, enemies. These fine noblemen, these king's favorites and mistresses, were likely to change the whims that they dignified as friendship and patronage at any moment. And who was more likely to veer than the dissolute Earl of Rochester? Fancying that Dryden had a hand in a passage in Sheffield's *Essay on Satire* which girded at his "want of wit," Rochester hired some ruffians who ambushed the great poet in Rose Alley and beat him brutally. Rochester's cowardly and bestial form of attack was quickly followed by an equally crude verbal onslaught by Thomas Shadwell, a third-rate dramatist, who was to be made in Dryden's place poet-laureate after the master's dismissal by the Whigs. The latter had at this time brought in the puppet, William of Orange, to replace James II, a Catholic and the last of the shrewd but faltering Stuarts.

A mosquito fog of poetasters, criticasters, and lordlings now buzzed angrily about "glorious John," so that his life, from the time of the "Popish Plot" to the Revolution, was teeming with vicissitudes. He had received attacks entirely unprovoked. But presently he was to enter the lists fearlessly, to strike back with a force that humiliated his currish foes, and at last to engage with a powerful figure worthy of his steel, a personage no less than the Luciferean Lord Shaftesbury. Perhaps it was just those pettier attacks which aroused our poet, hitherto a mere man of letters, to emulate all the greatest singers by a synthesis of dreaming and doing. Dryden reconciled dreaming and doing in the satire, the genre for which he was born.

By 1687, or soon after the accession of James II, Dryden became a Roman Catholic. This, beyond all other episodes in his life, has been a great source of the accusations of insincerity which have been urged against the poet. The weathercock, it is thought, turned with the coronation of a Catholic monarch. No animadversion could be more crass. The brief and stormy reign of the well-meaning James II was a time only for unselfish loyalists, not for sycophants. No really shrewd and unscrupulous courtier — and Dryden's stage career proves his capacity for shrewdness — would have sold himself, in 1687 in England, for power and affluence, to the Roman Church. No, nothing could be more audaciously logical than Dryden's conversion to Catholicism, nothing could be nobler. On the eve of the revolution he declared his complete independence of the really popular party which would have been more than glad to commandeer his pungent pen. Dryden might easily have been poet-laureate for William and Mary in place of the leaden Shadwell, had he chosen to place his brilliant talents at the disposal of the Whigs (who sadly needed an eloquent poet and mordant pamphleteer) by taking a few far from exacting oaths of allegiance that would not have disturbed a conscience of the common variety in any age. Cynics have said that shame at last prevented a hitherto shameless adventurer from making another rightaboutface. But Dryden was poor, his years were declining. Poor and sick — but hardy in spirit. For Dryden was now the author of such masterpieces as *Absalom and Achitophel* and *The Hind and the Panther*. Dryden, by the grace of God, had discovered himself.

With *Absalom and Achitophel* Dryden stepped out into the discordant arena and dealt the Whigs a blow of far-reaching consequence. He had for years dreamed of emulating Spenser in writing an epic about the glamorous figures of King Arthur or of the Black Prince. But now, doer as well as dreamer, he chose a contemporaneous subject that was epical in its largeness, a religious and political crisis of the day, of a nation making ready to cross the Rubicon. Nothing short of the destiny of his country's very soul now moved our poet, and moved him to write, in these febrile hours, with unparalleled temperance, justice, and magnanimity. His symbolical use of a Biblical story of world-old popularity was a stroke of great genius. Who could seem more like King David — in his weaker and more indulgent moods — than Charles II? His illegitimate son, the Duke of Monmouth, a winning person and popular, conspiring to wrest the throne from his own father, was like another Absalom, lovely of body. The Earl of Shaftesbury, noble yet Satanic, was Achitophel the sinister and puissant counselor to the headstrong youth.

Dryden's position has sometimes seemed warped to democratic enthusiasts. That some sort of aristo-democracy like Dryden's is the ideal no one can now doubt. For in these days of mediocre politicians and highly talented but avaricious bankers and merchants, with the irrational pseudo-democracy or demagoguery of our day so desperately on trial, it is less difficult, than a generation ago, to fathom Dryden's perspicacity. Shaftesbury, in his country's eyes, was something of a hero, something of an enemy. Dryden's virile portrait of him, so bold in its general brush strokes, so cunning in *chiaroscuro*, is — for an attack coming from a Tory — singularly fair minded in its recognition of Shaftesbury's better qualities. In fact, it does great credit to Dryden's chivalrous generosity, yet it is irresistible in its well-controlled but mortal cut and thrust. It is one of the supreme satirical passages of the world.

> Of these the false Achitophel was first;
> A name to all succeeding ages cursed;
> Sagacious, bold, and turbulent of wit;
> Restless, unfixed in principle and place;
> In power unpleased, impatient of disgrace:
> A fiery soul, which, working out its way,
> Fretted the pigmy body to decay. . . .
> A daring pilot in extremity,
> Pleased with danger, when the waves went high
> He sought the storms: but for a calm unfit,
> Would steer too nigh the sands to boast his wit.
> Great wits are sure to madness near allied,
> And thin partitions do their bounds divide;
> Else why should he, with wealth and honor blest,
> Refuse his age the needful hours of rest?
> Punish a body which he could not please;
> Bankrupt of life, yet prodigal of ease?
> And all to leave what with his toil he won,
> To that unfeathered two-legged thing, a son. . . .
> In friendship false, implacable in hate;
> Resolved to ruin or to rule a state; . . .
> Then seized with fear, yet still affecting fame,
> Usurped a patriot's all-atoning name.
> So easy still it proves in factious times
> With public zeal to cancel private crimes.

Here is none of the butterfly shimmer of fun in Dryden's clever comedies about naughty flirtatious couples. The poem is not at all amusing; it is as tragically grave over the dilemmas of Dryden's nation in its Age of Anarchy; it is close knit in its intellectual lucidity and massive in its relentless march.

VIII. POET OF "THE HIND AND THE PANTHER"

On Dryden's forge, the pentameter couplet at last came to deserve its epithet, "heroic." For the first time we find it free from rough dissonances and noisy braggadocio such as are common in Donne's verse. It is smooth as Waller's without being so effeminate, more quietly strong than Sir John Denham's, and so powerfully controlled that Thomas Gray could well liken each couplet to a pair of spirited and thunderous coursers held in span only by the hands of a titan driver.

In the following year when Shaftesbury, acquitted of high treason, was honored by his followers with a medal on one side of which were stamped his lineaments, on the other the grim Tower of London obscured by a cloud, the intrepid satirist returned to the attack with *The Medal*.

That same year Dryden condescended at last to answer his literary persecutor Shadwell, because Shadwell now raised what was to Dryden a larger issue than his own fair name by penning a most scurrilous reply to *The Medal*. The master satirist rejoined with his crushing satire, *MacFlecknoe*, which possesses to an eminent degree that quality which Saintsbury perceives in all of Dryden's poems of the period, "a cool and not ill-humored scorn."

In this poem, Flecknoe, a bedraggled poetaster, is supposed to choose Shadwell as his spiritual son (MacFlecknoe) and as heir to his dullness. The garrulous father acclaims his son in a passage which requires consummate art. For it is the task of the author to make Flecknoe, in language which the poetaster intends to be laudatory, damn Shadwell with corrosive scorn. In Dryden's satire, we see, as Taine has it, "from all sides through the streets littered with paper, the nations assembled to look upon the young hero, standing near the throne of his father, his brow enveloped in a fog, the vacant smile of satisfied imbecility floating over his countenance." Thus, then, Flecknoe lauds Shadwell before the vast audience.

'Tis resolved! for nature pleads, that he
Should only rule, who most resembles me.
Shadwell alone my perfect image bears,
Mature in dulness from his tender years;
Shadwell alone, of all my sons, is he
Who stands confirmed in full stupidity.
The rest to some faint meaning make pretense,
But Shadwell never deviates into sense.
Some beams of wit on other souls may fall,
Strike through and make a lucid interval;
But Shadwell's genuine night admits no ray,
His rising fogs prevail upon the day.
Besides, his goodly fabric fills the eye,
And seems designed for thoughtless majesty;
Thoughtless as monarch oaks, that shade the plain,
And, spread in solemn state supinely reign.

Mockery usually seems of necessity undignified and is likely to rebound on the scoffer as well as his victim. But in the close of this passage mockery rises to a unique majesty till we think of its creator like a stately knight-at-arms setting his mailed foot on the neck of a slanderous villain and then scornfully granting him the right to live out his servile and squalid life but with no power to do injury to the just.

Dryden's fine control of sustained and sinewy argument had matured still further in his *Religio Laici* in which he defended the Church of England against Catholic and Presbyterian. The Anglican Church had reached the position of acute peril in which she still remains, at war with the Church of Rome which she had left, and at war with the Puritan sects on the other side which had left her. Dryden is but one of the long procession of Anglicans on to Newman, and then to men like Father Vernon Johnson and Doctor Frederick Joseph Kinsman in our own day, who have abandoned this impossible position to surrender to Rome.

On the very eve of the overthrow of Catholic King James II, Dryden immortalized his conversion and defended the Church of Rome in a fable and didactic poem, *The Hind and the Panther*. His arguments were now suffused with an emotional loftiness and an eloquent warmth to which he had never before attained. As we read this poem we are not surprised to remember that he refused allegiance to King William III. With adamantine humility he resumed — a poor old man deprived of pensions — his professional literary work at a time at which he had undoubtedly hoped to be free. He wrote plays or patched up others; he translated from the

Latin Classics and paraphrased stories from Boccacio and Chaucer; he
composed a new prologue for Fletcher's *Pilgrim*, revived as a benefit performance for the author of *Absalom and Achitophel* now fallen into hard
straits. And finally, within a few weeks of death, he celebrated the advent
of the new century with a masque which could not be produced before he
breathed his last. For this toil, so much of which was uncongenial, the
unconquerable poet assuaged himself by pouring out his mellow prefaces
of literary criticism in what he loved and had the supreme right to call
"that other harmony of prose."

The portrait of Dryden in his old age is not so impressive nor yet so
forbidding as that of Milton which I outlined in the previous chapter.
Perhaps only a Catholic, who knows what is meant by the "sanctifying
grace" which God infuses into the soul of a believer in the one completely true faith, can understand. It is a picture of unflinching integrity
and blessed resignation, of moments of peace and honor which could not
be denied even by a hostile age. It was well that the youths at Will's
Coffee House admired this plump fine-looking man, with a downward
look and a tendency toward reticence, but an imperial manner which,
when it gently praised some fledgling poet, seemed to confer a coronation.

The Hind and the Panther is uneven in quality, but it is the most
warmly sincere of all Dryden's poems. In his prose-prelude he tells us
that it was written over a rather prolonged period — "during the last
winter and the beginning of this spring; though with long interruptions
of ill health and other hindrances." That he expected to woo more or less
unpopularity is manifest from his remark that: "The nation is in too
high a ferment, for me to expect either fair war or even so much as fair
quarter from a reader of the opposite party." Like all Catholics who have
entered the arena he knew that his Church had always been persecuted
and that it probably always would be. King James's declaration of toleration had but aroused a surly and menacing attitude well described at the
end of a fable which the Hind (The Catholic Church) tells the Panther
(the Anglican Church) to whom she has given shelter.

The beautiful opening sounds the theme of that persecution which
Catholics were constantly undergoing. It sings of the purity of a Church
unstained alike by foes without and betrayers within. It extols her power
to grow without change and to enrich herself while yet remaining faithful
to her general tenets.

A Milk-white Hind, immortal and unchanged,
Fed on the lawns and in the forest rang'd;
Without unspotted, innocent within,
She feared no danger, for she knew no sin.
Yet had she oft been chas'd with horns and hounds,
And Scythian shafts; and many winged wounds
Aimed at her heart; was often forced to fly,
And doom'd to death, though fated not to die.

He describes the Panther with many a recurring touch of magnanimity and tenderness that shows that he did not part with fickle facility from the convictions of his *Religio Laici*.

The Panther sure the noblest, next the Hind,
And fairest creature of the spotted kind;
Oh, could her in-born stains be washed away,
She were too good to be a beast of prey!
How can I praise or blame, and not offend,
Or how divide the frailty from the friend?
Her faults and virtues lie so mixed that she
Nor wholly stands condemned nor wholly free.

But he has less sympathy, for the Calvinist (the Wolf), the Anabaptist (the "bristled Boar"), the Quaker (the Hare) and other nonconformist sects. All these he condemns for their reliance on the ever changing caprices of arrogant and lazy individual opinions, out of which no harmony can ever grow. In contrast, he lauds the authority of Catholicism, as a sure guide, and closes with the diapason of a touching prayer.

What weight of ancient witness can prevail,
If private reason held the public scale?
But, gracious God, how well doest Thou provide
For erring judgments an unerring guide!
Thy throne is darkness in the abyss of light,
A blaze of glory that forbids the sight.
O teach me to believe Thee thus concealed;
And search no farther than Thy self revealed,
But her alone for my director take
Whom Thou hast promised never to forsake!
My thoughtless youth was winged with vain desires;
My manhood, long misled by wandering fires,
Followed false lights; and when their glimpse was gone,
My pride struck out new sparkles of her own,
Such was I, such by nature still I am,
Be Thine the glory and be mine the shame!

Attacking next the evanescent, flickering interpretations of Scripture by the various conflicting "reformers," Dryden, in an eloquent passage, urges Catholic tradition, as upreared by the Apostles, Fathers, and Councils, against the irresponsible and mutually jarring appeals to the Bible alone by ancient schismatics and modern Protestants. With a thrust not to be parried he writes:

> For did not Arius First, Socinus now
> The Son's eternal Godhead disavow?
> And did not these by gospel texts alone
> Condemn our doctrine, and maintain their own?
> Have not all heretics the same pretense,
> To plead the Scriptures in their own defence?

So, then, in a similar passage, the Hind challenges the Panther by contrasting the work of the great Catholic Councils with the Protestant flounderings. It is indeed a strong temptation to quote here at length from his well-reasoned pages that once cast their light on my long pilgrimage to Rome. Powerful, in particular, is the Hind's proud defense of the four god-given attributes of his Church: the oneness or perfect unity, the holiness or sanctity, the Catholicity or universality, and the unbroken ancestry from the Apostles with whom the Master Himself walked the earth. Thus does she challenge the Panther with her picture of the Catholic Church:

> One in herself, not rent by schism, but sound,
> Entire, one solid shining diamond
> Not sparkles shattered into sects like you,
> One is the Church, and must be to be true;
> One central principle of unity.
> As one in faith, so one in sanctity . . .
>
> Thus one, thus pure, behold her largely spread
> Like the fair ocean from her mother bed;
> From east to west triumphantly she rides,
> All shores are watered by her wealthy tides.
> The gospel-sound, diffused from pole to pole,
> Where winds can carry and where waves can roll,
> The self same doctrine of the sacred page
> Conveyed to ev'ry clime, in every age.

Unity, sanctity, universality — these three marks can surely not be denied to the Church and least of all, apostolicity, which obviously no modern sect can claim. As for the oft-repeated objection on this score, Dryden in one line demolishes it:

> Tis said with ease, but never can be proved,
> The Church her old foundations has removed,
> And built new doctrines on unstable sands —
> Judge that, ye winds and rains; you proved her,
>   yet she stands.

Certainly Dryden did more than any earlier influence to give to my yearning toward Catholicism an intellectual cast. I think I was by now convinced that the Catholic Church was the only one I could dream of joining. But, alas, I was still an agnostic on all matters of religion, not in the Spencerian sense of the "Unknowable" (to which attitude, by the way, as the poet-convert, Alfred Noyes shows in *The Unknown God*, Spencer himself was now and then theistically inconsistent), but in the humbler Huxleyan sense of "I don't know whether or not God exists." Sometimes I wonder why I did not then pause stock still to await the unhurrying footsteps of the Hound of Heaven. But when I further reflect and gaze along the spacious avenues and crooked byways of the following years, I can now see that God desired for me a much longer apprenticeship. I always feared, almost to the point of morbidity, that I would succumb to wish-thoughts. And so I was yet to revel in many tawdry externalities before I could cast them off. There were more spiritual bankruptcies ahead. There were more panaceas to acquire laboriously, to see through, and to slough off with an ever renewed disillusionment.

CHAPTER IV

THE RELEASE

"The peace of the celestial city is the perfectly ordered and harmonious enjoyment of God and of one another in God."

MY ERUDITE friend, Professor Frederick J. Teggart, in *The Processes of History*, declares that human advancement occurs when two cultures or idea systems come into violent contact with each other. The result he calls a "release." The two cultures develop critical acumen and enrich each other. A culture in isolation languishes. After the menace of the Danes had ceased, Anglo-Saxon literature became stagnant. It was only after Norman invaders settled down among the Anglo-Saxons that there came to merry England a new sunburst of song. This clash of two cultures may or may not be bellicose. But in some sense or other it must be violent.

I have for many years been particularly impressed by the fact that the Roman Catholic Church has had as many resurrection-like releases, from the days of its first Easter as the reburgeoning lilies of the field. The "Judaizing" Christians and the pagan Roman persecution, the various occultistic Gnostics, the dreadful menace of the Arians (the deadliest crisis, as I have already suggested, that ever shook the See of Peter), the Manichæans, and many more of the earlier heresies which began at once; then the crashing wave after wave of the barbarian invasions, and not least momentous, the Mohammedan siege down the centuries — all these were met by illustrious Church fathers and doctors, martyrs and saints, just as the terrorism of Communists and Nazists are resisted today.

Well-informed Catholics know that holy Mother Church, while always maintaining her fundamental doctrines in their pristine purity, has often in her ritual, nonessential practices, undergone a "sea-change into something rich and strange," though without any sacrifice of her divinely guaranteed integrity. It was not until the dawn of the thirteenth century that Eudes de Sully, Bishop of Paris, introduced at the climax of the Holy Sacrifice of the Mass the practice of elevating the Host, when the bread has become the body of our Lord, in order that the kneeling congregation may gaze and adore and murmur the phrase with which the Apostle St. Thomas banished his last doubt, "My Lord and my God!" It was not until the thirteenth century, in order to invoke Christ's blessing, and in order to make reparation for the frightful insults against the Host, that the Church enriched its liturgy with the celestial rite called the Benediction of the Blessed Sacrament, wherein the priest celebrant sumptuously robed, ascends the steps of the high altar, takes with hands now covered the burnished sunlike monstrance, in the crystal center of which reposes the "Bread of Angels" (*Panis Angelicus*), and turning makes with it over the bowed heads of the worshipers the sign of the cross. The hideous heresy of the Albigenses evoked the genius of St. Dominic, who, with the aid of the rosary which, it is said, was given him by the Blessed Virgin Mary, converted thousands. When argosies, sailing in from the opulent, mysterious Orient heaped the piers from Venice to Flanders with silks of Samarcand and spices and cedars of Lebanon; when, with this wealth, corruption weakened the Church within, then arose St. Francis of Assisi, the troubadour of God, wedded to Dame Poverty, who with his gray-clad mendicant brethren purged Catholicism with a fiery recrudescence of Apostolic simplicity. When Pope Pius prayed with the rosary to St. Mary of Victory, Don John shattered the Turkish fleet at Lepanto and wiped out forever that centuries-long Mohammedan menace which all but destroyed the Church of which Christ had promised that "The gates of hell shall not prevail against it." Let even a pope become too worldly and a St. Catherine of Siena is there to rebuke him without fear.

I. UNIVERSITY OF CALIFORNIA INSTRUCTOR

Whatever Teggart might believe about my Church history, I know he maintains that individuals, as well as groups, may experience the release, and that while a release always means advancement, it may mean not progress but ruin. I had spent my childhood, youth, and early manhood in my native New England. I was now, as a young teacher in the University of California at Berkeley, to come into a genuinely violent contact with the cordial and hilarious culture of the towns that girdle San Francisco Bay. It was to me an utterly new world, a tingling paradox of regeneration and degeneration. It was a release with a vengeance. It was a release in which I skirted the abyss. But in the end, by God's will, it brought me, along with various scars, a great enrichment.

After groaning a good deal under the austere teaching at Harvard I had entered the Department of English in the University of California with the callow and resolute dream of making my students love literature. I was not, of course, very much their senior. And while I was on the campus I all but lived at the fraternities and sororities.

My evenings, for months, I spent in San Francisco. I had a notebook full of the names of picturesque restaurants of many nationalities which I proceeded to visit in a most solemnly methodical manner. I liked, particularly, to take eastern friends to a Mexican Cafe where, with unholy glee, I watched them writhe over the gustatory torchlight procession of tamales, frijoles, and so forth, which I myself heartily enjoyed to engulf and extinguish with huge goblets of red wine. I went slumming in the dance halls of the Barbary Coast watching sailors and grisettes lurch around together. This was my notion of seeing life steadily and seeing it whole. I was made a member of The Athenian Club at Oakland where I learned much hitherto unplumbed worldly wisdom from businessmen and doctors and lawyers. As a member of the Bohemian Club in San Francisco, I hobnobbed with poets, novelists and musicians, painters, sculptors, and architects.

English composition was mainly what I was hired to teach. But grilling and grinding as this was, it gave me an opportunity to study intensively such prose masters as Arnold, Carlyle, Ruskin, and Newman. It was then that the illustrious convert-cardinal became, for the rest of my life, a great favorite. I love to think of Cardinal Newman in that lyrical portrait of him in which Matthew Arnold almost forgot, for the moment, his own agnostic pangs: "Who could resist the charm of that spiritual apparition, gliding in the dim afternoon light through the aisles of St. Mary's, rising into the pulpit, and then, in the most entrancing of voices, breaking the silence with words and thoughts which were a religious music — subtle, sweet, and mournful."

I could not, however, forget the smug warning with which Arnold anticlimaxed his romantic sigh, his remark that Newman's entrance into the Catholic Church was an "impossible" step. Fear of wish-thoughts restricted my admiration of Newman to a rather exotic reverence for his style although I did render a good deal of allegiance to his views on education. I wanted also to believe in what he calls "illative" reasoning in his *Grammar of Assent*. But I feared that it was antirational. And I was not wholly wrong. I am glad today that I waited many years before venturing to understand St. John of the Cross, who was at last to prove to me that there is a valid kind of intuition which may, quite realistically, be characterized as suprarational. In those days Newman would have confirmed me in my romantic weaknesses, for he is not a very skillful epistemologist. But there is such a thing as the "illative sense." And it is valid, I think, if we take it to refer, for instance, to that extraordinary convergence of argumentative strands, historical, biographical, biological, psychological, sociological, philosophical, theological, which should be pursued, in isolation, inductively and deductively, but all of which may, by some sort of illative interpretation, be grasped comprehensively as converging in a colossal web to establish the supremacy of Catholic truth.

II. SPOKESMAN FOR THE PROLETARIAT

After teaching for a few years with gusto the so-called social prophecies of Carlyle and Ruskin, it occurred to me to inquire on what grounds these gentlemen were honored as visionaries of the future. Well, since their future was my present I saw that I might assess them by studying the social unrest about me, particularly the labor movement, at first-hand. Herein I sought what I hoped would be an incomparable substitute for religion.

With my best friend, Charles Seegar, through whom I then learned to understand the most revolutionary contemporary music, and with whom I had scores of more or less hairbrained but always illuminating adventures, I hobnobbed with Industrial Workers of the World, members of the American Federation of Labor and Socialists of the Right Wing and the Left.

Our most instructive comrade was a German house painter, mordant and lovable, named Emil Kern. Emil had reclaimed a bit of sand-dune land on the outskirts of San Francisco whereon he had built for himself and his cat a snug little cottage. On occasion, he would prepare for his pet a fearsome mixture of chopped liver and oatmeal. Since the cat relished the liver and loathed the cereal, Emil was able to measure quite accurately the amount which his furry familiar would consume in the course of a week or so. Thus he was able often to adjourn with Seegar and me to Berkeley where we all attended together the classes of our colleagues in Economics, Anthropology, Sociology, Psychology, and Philosophy.

Emil Kern was broadened by incessant roaming over wide territories and intimate experiences with almost all phases of the labor movement. He was well read in Kant and Hegel and in economic theory. He was a devout and learned disciple of Karl Marx to whose theories, except for their materialistic and atheistic metaphysical implications, he completely converted us for a time. He was hardheaded. He was tenderhearted.

Soon after our first acquaintance he invited me to address a certain Radical Club of which he was president. At that time I discovered and espoused exuberantly the so-called Feminist Movement. "The Subjection of Women," by John Stuart Mill, had converted me to suffrage. After living in two universities which are only nominally coeducational I was romantically carried away by the unequivocal situation at Berkeley. The writings of Ellen Key had filled me full of very dubious notions concerning the liberalizing of the marriage bonds. Olive Schreiner had stirred me to champion the economic independence of women. Charlotte Perkins Gilman, in days when disillusioning apartment houses were few, had taught me an exhilarating irreverence for the existing home. And Margaret Sanger had hypnotized me with her well-meant but devilish sophistries on "birth control" — sophistries which, I was to learn later, are quite as unsound biologically as they are morally. For, among their many other unscientific evasions these contraceptionalists have a most convenient habit of ignoring uterine tumors and cancers, just as they have a very infantile economic conception of the relations between production and consumption and employment. Armed cap-a-pie with all this hysterical modernism, I descended triumphantly on the Radical Club only to become a laughingstock when I was fairly flayed alive by Kern's caustic epilogue to my apoplectic discourse. My cup of humiliation was filled to overflowing by the presence of a young lady toward whom I had assumed the somewhat difficult role of paternal adviser, teacher, and suitor. A year or two later the young lady rejected my offer of a fool's paradise for a stage career. I had a very similar experience later with a dazzling Russian revolutionary.

In those days Seegar and I were badly bitten with a lust for martyrdom which Kern ridiculed from morn till dewey eve. Like most social radicals we were unable to winnow out our genuine humanitarianism from our paranoidal conceit. Kern showed us quite clearly that our influence would only be injurious to the cause of social justice. Whatever the harm we might have done to others, certain it is that Kern saved us from a tragicomic disaster. For he trained us in a shrewd and sane dialectic that enabled us, with a decent self-respect, integrity, and serviceableness, to weather, undeceived yet undisgraced, that futile war which was to "end all wars" and to "make the world safe for democracy."

It was a disheartening spectacle to observe scientists and philosophers saturated with the mob-delusions so cleverly implanted by war lords with their lust for power, politicians with their servile office seeking, and bankers and wealthy merchants with their avarice. It was later to be recalled to mind in connection with the silly unrealities of the "Democracies [including Russia!] versus Fascism," which deluded the Popular-Front professors of the 1930's. When I left the classroom of such a doctrinaire professor, after hearing his discriminating analysis of Dr. Goddard's statistical studies on the heredity of the feeble-minded and then immediately seeing him swallow with complete credulity the newspaper caricatures of Lenin, without ever dreaming of studying the other side in a genuinely scientific spirit; when in the classrooms of my philosopher friends I heard some hold Hegel responsible for the soulless German militarism and others "prove" that Germany was damned for renouncing his lofty precepts and metaphysics; when I listened to the voices of the small professorial minority whispering that Germany was as pure white as the majority believed her pure black, while on the other hand one of my colleagues dropped Bernard Shaw from a course in contemporary English literature because of some flippant remarks made by him about the war, I was within an ace of turning my back on university life as on any seething colony of irrational bigots. But I was, of course, quite as irrational as they.

Although I had a leaning toward pacifism, and appreciated the fact that nonresistants were often more courageous than warriors, I soon came to accept the war as a reality that had to be met point-blank. I would have accepted the call to the army had it come just as Canute is said to have forced his courtiers to accept the fact that the surf would drench the feet even of a king. But my obsession was as bad as anybody's. To me all horizons were ruddy with the dæmon of a proletarian revolution that would bring socialism and international peace. I thought that professors, preachers, and artists were properly of the proletariat, not of the bourgeoisie. I believed in the class-war as the only war worth while. And I concluded that preachers, professors, and artists should rally under the dawn-red standard of awakened labor. I did hope that the class-war might be bloodless. I believed in the primacy of love. I was not so much a Marxian as I was a "Christian Socialist," blissfully unaware as I was that the latter creed is self-contradictory.

III. A SUMMONS TO THE INTELLECTUALS

My quixotic fervors finally found expression in a book called *The Intellectuals and the Wage-Workers,* a manic performance of which I became heartily ashamed almost as soon as it was published.* About the only unequivocal merit that it had was that it did much to cure me of my own fantasies.

In scheme the volume is rather interesting. I hoped to condemn and convert my pusillanimous comrades out of their own mouths. Hence my book bristles with citations from contemporary philosophers, historians, psychologists, ethnologists, sociologists, economists, and biologists. These quotations jostle cheek by jowl with many passages from the proletarian propaganda of various nationalities. Both of these currents of thought I conceived to be more or less unconsciously converging. With their complete confluence we should float with full proud sail into the port of Utopia.

In order to make clear my mental condition at this point on my road to Rome, it is necessary to quote from *The Intellectuals and the Wage-Workers,* giving both a few of its lucid intervals and a few of its bizarre dreams.

The first chapter, "Equality," opens with a statement of the general thesis of the book. "With the development of the Industrial Revolution, the growth of modern middle-class democracy, the consummation of the *laissez-faire* competitive states, the relations between artists or scientists and patron or public have become more and more equivocal. In England, Doctor Samuel Johnson's famous letter to the Earl of Chesterfield sounded, over a hundred and fifty years ago, a kind of emancipation proclamation of the artist against the genteel servitude of patronage. Nevertheless patronage has continued. Artists, educators and scientists are still too often mere flunkies. And whereas patronage under Renaissance aristocracy was sometimes rationally planned, patronage under middle-class democracy is almost invariably capricious, utterly divorced from a healthy institutionalism. Very rarely does the captain of industry, with a modicum of discrimination, assume the artistic *noblesse oblige* of the lord of earlier days. For him, at best, aesthetic values are the dessert of life or those afterthoughts, some little attention to which will prove that he is thoroughly respectable. The discoveries of science he

* New York, The Sunrise Turn Press, 1920.

values only as they lead obviously and instantaneously to further industrial exploitation. [I was then ignorant of the fact that certain great corporations, like the Bell Telephone Company, have allowed certain physicists full freedom to experiment in search of the truth for the truth's sake, having realized that applied science is but a parasite on pure theoretical science, that had there been no Faraday and no Herz (who cared naught for matters practical) there would be no smaller men like Marconi and Edison, that utilitarian results are not so often gained by direct search for them as by the incidental or even accidental suggestions which come in a laboratory wherein all that is desired is the widening of our knowledge of the most remote depths of the universe.] So today artist, educator and scientist stand half-parasite, half-pariah. And their voices are heard scarcely at all in the great tumult of class-war and the growing murmurs of social reconstruction. Let us not pity them, however, for — until they dare to realize that the dignity of research is intimately bound up with the joy in life, the workmanly pride, the moral autonomy for which society should allow release in the most oppressed 'unskilled' laborer today — our artists, educators and scientists have no insight whatever, no courage, no integrity."

There was something, however, to be said for the latent possibilities of reconstructing the existing social order, and so I continued: "The critic sees this element of truth in the reactionary point of view: that the stability of aristocracy gave the leisure necessary for development of that kind which makes at least a few of the economic necessities beautiful. He sees that if the middle-class regime were not unstable it would have great art, science and religion. Our factories would rise like temples of a miraculously new style in architecture. [I was then unaware of the steps which then and much more now, have been taken in that direction.] Our laborers would not be the slaves of machines and we should need no Samuel Butler to dream of an evolutionary conquest of men by machines endowed by man's own blind cunning with some hideous, impassive intelligence. Machines would be our slaves — the only slaves in human society. The critic finds that Ruskin and Morris were partly right and partly wrong in their diagnosis of the Industrial Revolution and Victorian laissez-faire. They did see that short-sighted buccaneers of the market-place were wantonly befouling our lives. They did see, what was far more important, that we must organize in guilds and educate ourselves to share more rationally our social duties with the State. . . . Ruskin and Morris were wrong, however, in thinking that it was because ma-

chinery was invented and factories planted beside the sweetly garrulous
and hitherto unsullied streams, because the air was made grim with
canopies of smoke, and because the new powers of steam dragged men
and children from their homes, that art and morality and religion fell.
Today the critical intellectual asserts that some of these things, though
evil, will, if treated with defiance and mastery, prove convertible into
incalculable good. To destroy machinery and factories would be to destroy a valuable current that might be turned toward progress. Morris'
News from Nowhere is thus in many respects on the same intellectual
plane with the earlier outbursts of the Luddite rioters of England and
the weavers of Germany. We needed the subtle experimentation of the
labor movement of post-Chartist days — that hard-headed period of the
labor movement which Sidney and Beatrice Webb love to praise — to
purge and to elaborate the vision of Ruskin and Morris. Just here, too,
the critic will try to increase vital and logical relations by winnowing
and fusing the best in the irregular palinodes and pæans of men like
Ruskin [who was almost Catholic except for a solitary difficulty, his
miscomprehension of papal infallibility and leadership] and William
Morris [who was drenched with the Middle Ages, the golden age of
Catholicism] with the larger and more logical, if too fatalistic, materialistic and atheistic analysis and forecast of Karl Marx. The democratic
bourgeoisie has so ordered things, say Marx and his continuator Engels,
that life is full of capricious vicissitudes. Petty capitalists are crowded
into the proletariat. Bankruptcies abound even among the capitalists.
Panics and that condition absurdly and deceitfully called 'prosperity'
alternate with implacable certainty yet caprice. [It is amusing today to
look back at the solemn asseverations of 'orthodox' economists who used
to assure me that the formation of the federal reserve banking system
made impossible any future depression in the United States.] International wars follow as larger expressions of the growing socialization
of the means of production in trusts coupled with irreconcilable anarchy
of control by a fortuitously elevated minority of uncritical minds who
plunge into foreign investments as soon as domestic investments cease
to stir their feverish imaginations. Always the world is full of paupers,
tragic failures and a minority of *nouveaux riches*. Now the latter, as
Ruskin and Morris knew, are always vulgar and often cruel. And before
they can develop aesthetically and ethically their money evaporates and
we have to devise a new travesty of art and science for a new crop of
nouveaux riches."

Unwittingly I was nearer Rome than I dreamed, as any reader of *Quadragesimo Anno* of Pope Pius XI will readily see. But it is equally obvious that I had much to learn and unlearn. Although I was no sentimental equalitarian, although I was quite aware that men are created biologically unequal and develop, from differing environments, painful inequalities of moral insight, yet such was the enthusiasm of belated adolescence that I crudely overstated my case. I did not understand, as I do today, the great and gracious Catholic truth that all men are created equal in the sense that they are all the children of God, that God does not expect from the moron or the invalid what He expects from the normal and the healthy, and that He does not expect the same reactions from the babe born with a silver spoon in his mouth and the infant who comes into the world with a pickax invitingly near his elbow, or a child whose first wail echoes through a squalid alley in the slums.

I will not tarry over the second chapter "Proletarianism," longer than to say that it is an amusing and exasperating *petitio principii* in which I tempted everyone to join the "workers" by making my definition of my term a catalogue of all virtues. Nor will I linger over the chapter on "religion." It contained a sympathetic but uncompromising attack on materialism and atheism as suicidal to the highest potentialities of the labor movement. It correctly discerned a genuine if perverted religious fervor in radical proletarianism.

But my efforts to describe religion were pitiful. It was characteristic of my agnosticism, coupled with a pathetic wish to believe, that I found much satisfaction in a hypothetically benevolent and tenuous saying with which William James summed up what he took to be the essence of religion: "If any phrase could gather its universal message, that phrase would be 'All is *not* vanity in this Universe whatever the appearances may suggest.'" I was so full of the dogma-phobia of Locke, Rousseau, Hume, Voltaire, and other champions of the so-called Age of the Enlightenment that I was utterly befuddled.

I remember lunching in those days with a priest at the Faculty Club. My warm sympathy for Catholicism, which had never flagged since my earliest years, was for a moment stilled by a sentence of his about dogma which seemed to me utterly crass and reactionary. I entertained for a time the hope of becoming a Catholic through the route of the short-lived "modernistic" movement in the Church and was deeply shocked when Pope Pius X quelled it. I owe my wholesome disillusionment as to Modernism to that urbane and palely visionary atheistic philosopher, George Santayana, who remains sufficiently mindful of the Catholicism of his childhood to write about it, at times, with deep reverence and understanding. In *The Winds of Doctrine* he, who I expected would be its champion, certainly gave to "Modernism" in the Church an unanswerable *coup de grace*.

Well would it have been for me if I could then have read the following paragraph from Monsignor Fulton J. Sheen's *Moods and Truths*:

It is false to say that we can be absolutely free from law and authority, for freedom from law and authority is an illusion. The real problem is not whether we will accept law and authority, but rather, which law and authority we will accept. Even though this is a free country, I find that if I do not obey the authority of my government, then I shall have to accept the authority of the undertaker; if I do not accept the authority of the traffic lights, I shall have to accept the authority of the jailor. In religious matters, if I do not accept the authority of the Church, then I must accept the authority of public opinion. Public opinion is the common stalk of thought and sentiment created by human society, and in the realm of religion outside the Church it is practically always a compromise. . . . It approves Christ only as much as Christ approves it.

I suppose I thought that Catholicism advocated the blind acceptance of dogma (the utterance of authority). It was only years afterward, when I was quite ready to be received into the Church by priests who were in no hurry whatever to receive me, that I realized that I was expected to weigh Catholic authority in the balance with rival authorities, with relentless reason. It was only then that I perceived that the born Catholic is similarly taught by the catechism to the full extent of his capacity and with a view to the growth of that capacity — if he chooses to remain mentally alert. I suppose I thought also that Catholicism claims to have a complete answer to every question and therefore fed us with many solutions, incomplete and insincere. This is because I did not know what the Church meant by that concept of a "mystery," which I discussed in an earlier chapter and to which I will return in due time. As to consistency, a really prolonged study of Catholic doctrine ought to convince a genuinely open-minded and adventurous person, as I will try to show in later chapters, that Catholicism is the only completely and perfectly consistent doctrine of any scope in the world.

It is also the only doctrine compatible with real freedom — responsible, rational freedom — as I gradually found out when I became first too liberal to remain "a liberal" and afterward too radical to remain "a radical." Whether you are within or without the Church you are unceasingly challenged to challenge its claims to teach a pure revelation of the precepts of a God who can neither deceive nor be deceived. Faith and reason, as we shall see, interact intimately. Faith is supreme. But faith does not flout reason. Faith, then, is not below reason. Faith is above reason. For faith is grounded upon the reason like an audacious soaring cathedral whose foundations grip and pierce some adamantine rock. Faith is not the emotional debauch which many Protestants and decadent Hegelians and loosely philosophical idolators of "the religious experience" presume it to be. Faith is not the superstition that many superstitious agnostics and atheists presume it to be. Faith is an act of the intellect requiring assent of the will. It is grounded on reason. And faith is a gift of God.

In the remaining chapters of *The Intellectuals and the Wage-Workers* I can find only two strands of thought which are relevant here. The first is a good example of the type of sophistry that made my steps toward Rome stagger. The second, despite all its admixture of romanticism, brought me more closely within all hail of the home in which I had never dwelt but for which I have, until lately, been homesick all my life.

As for the first consideration. I was much interested in the psychology of the proletarian slogan of "direct action," that is to say, economic action which flouts the apparently more orderly procedure of politics. Of this I chose two examples, "sabotage," or covert violence, and the general strike. The earlier forms of sabotage, such as injuring the employer's machinery by putting emery in the oil cups, were and are crude, cowardly, and unredeemably base. But there were more refined forms which seemed to me to possess a certain benign tinge. Such, for instance, was the *bouche ouverte,* advocated by certain French Syndicalists, when they urged the underpaid salesman to tell his customers the truth about certain goods which his employer expects him to garnish with lies. Again, on the French railroads there was a network of rules which were presumably made to safeguard the limbs and the lives of the operators. Yet they were camouflage. For to obey them would be to tie up traffic hopelessly. They were made to be ignored. But the Syndicalists exhorted the rebellious laborer to take the employer literally and to obey.

Now, I realized that sabotage always suffers, even in its more highly sublimated forms, from the sinister tinge of hatred in its motivation. But I was partisan enough to presume that whereas capitalistic sabotage was sullied by the dominance of possessive impulses, proletarian sabotage was bound to move progressively toward creative zeal, away from destructiveness.

Again, because my researches brought to my attention certain really laudable episodes in some general strikes, I gave to a sentimental interpretation an added air of the miraculous. I knew, for example, how at Wheatland, California, where an abject mass of unskilled workmen had assembled under unspeakably filthy living conditions to gather hops for the rancher, in two days these "illiterates" had listened to addresses in seven languages and were organized for a nonresistant defiance that became violent only after the example was set by the sheriff's posse which represented the Law and the State. I studied the even more extraordinary organization of an even more multilingual chaos at Lawrence, Massachusetts, which certainly belied the hopes of some American employers of stamping out unionism by the importation of ignorant immigrant hordes.

Of the Swedish general strike, when the proletarians of the press refused to print what they believed to be lies leveled at other laborers and raised the defiant cry against editors and owners, "Either you'll print the truth or you'll print no paper at all," I dreamed that just here I discerned the dawn of a momentous reform which would be a balm to those of us who are heartsick over the degradation of the "prostitute press." To my quixotic imagination the Swedish printers had acted an *Areopagitica* which would take an honorable place in the history of freedom of thought alongside Milton's sonorous pamphlet.

A much more wholesome enthusiasm which I heralded forth in my book was born of my encounter with the contemporary British Guildsmen, some of whom rather inaccurately and very infelicitously dubbed themselves guild-socialists. This experience was most fortunate because it brought me much closer to the conception of social justice set forth in the two superb papal encyclicals on the reconstruction of the present social order. Indeed there were some Catholics among the guildsmen. The architect, Arthur J. Penty, had made out a slightly reactionary but very vigorous case for them in *A Guildsman's Interpretation of History*. The misguided, who condemn Christians as too otherworldly to ameliorate our terrestrial social evils, were here shown by him that the most ascetic of the followers of our Saviour, the early ones like the monks of the desert, were not otherworldly but rather renounced the world in order that they might conquer it. In other words, they turned from the centrifugal and less essential part of their own natures to learn that deeper

centripetal secret of their own personalities which gave them their beautiful lowliness and their sublime invincibility when once more they
mingled with men.

Guildsmen sometimes called their schemes a synthesis of Syndicalism
and State-Socialism. These guildsmen believed that we should expand
craft unions into nationwide industrial unions. The American Building
Trades, for instance, are organized into bickering groups of masons,
plumbers, carpenters, and so forth, whose internecine avarice weakens
their efforts to resist the encroachment of the "bourgeoisie." These guilds,
in the view of Syndicalist-minded groups, should be nationwide and would
ultimately absorb, often no doubt as leaders, those who are now employers. But the guild itself would then, according to Syndicalist concepts, be the sole owner of any given industry. While the guild idea here
was laudable, the denial of man's natural right to productive no less than
to consumptive property was essentially wrong and fundamentally identical with the error of Socialism.

These same guildsmen, however, separated from Syndicalism in holding that it relied too exclusively on direct or economic action, and that
political action, the hope of State-Socialism, is equally important. It
would follow that the guilds should send delegates to a national Guild
Congress where economic issues, so often befogged in current politics,
would be threshed out. But some of our interests are less economic than
geographical. Therefore we should elect territorial representatives who
would form a Parliament. Finally the dilemmas which might sunder
these two bodies could be solved in a Joint Committee, which would
hold the sovereignty, and which would be made up of super-delegates
from both the other two national groups.

For a long time I held that the program of this group — a program in
part Syndicalist and in part Socialist, and not representing all classes of
guildsmen — was one of the best available. But I now see that it fell
far short of the program of Pope Pius XI. It remained blind to the importance, from every angle, of a certain amount of individual ownership
for everybody, so far as possible. That is the Catholic idea underlying the
Occupational or Vocational Group System of Pope Pius XI.

IV. SOCIAL ENCYCLICALS

It will be observed that I have not made this autobiographical sketch
strictly chronological. Most books of this character begin with an account

of the authors' lives and then turn more or less exclusively to an exposition and defense of Catholic doctrine. I have tried to weave both strands together throughout. When a later insight has clarified an earlier conviction or rectified it, I pursue the topic up to my present. And although I first read the two papal encyclicals on social justice only six years ago, it seems most fitting to paraphrase, at this point, parts of them which have influenced me the most. For this purpose I employ not only the encyclicals themselves but the long preludial commentary which Father Joseph Husslein, S.J., has prefixed to them in his volume called *The Christian Social Manifesto*.

The *Rerum Novarum* (1891) in which Leo XIII, "The Pope of the Workingmen," discussed the condition of labor, was an acute diagnosis, a daring prophecy, a very constructive program, and a ringing refutation of the slanderous remarks that the Catholic Church cajoles the poor and truckles to the rich. Very rare have been the moments when any of the long line of popes, from crucified Peter to Pius XII, have ever, even for the safeguarding of the temporal security of the Church, made the least concession to princes, plutocrats, and demagogues. Yet, unwelcome as his missive must have been to many powerful and greedy and paranoidal men, Leo was widely beloved by myriads within and without the Church. Thus W. T. Stead, a non-Catholic, penned his eulogy in the *American Monthly Review of Reviews* (August, 1903): "When the Pope died, the greatest among us passed away, greatest in station, greatest in fame, greatest in the wisdom of the statesman. *Leo XIII was the Nestor of the human race.*" He "spent his life — the whole ninety-three years of it — in an honest, weariless attempt to bring heaven down from the skies, so that even here and now the toil-worn children of men should realize something of the peace and joy of Paradise." And so, at his obsequies, "Protestant, Freethinker, and Catholic sorrowed as brothers at the tomb of their common father."

Both Pius X and Benedict XV upheld their illustrious and saintly predecessor. But it remained for their equally illustrious successor, Pope Pius XI, "after due prayer, counsel, and deliberation," to support and supplement Leo XIII, forty years afterward in his communication to the Universal Church, *Quadragesimo Anno,* which is an equally piercing and powerful analysis of conditions today and an unanswerable presentation of the one solution.

The work of these last four popes on political and economic questions cannot be overestimated as one of the many testimonies of the divine resilience of the Church. After the heroic Pius VII had survived the abuses inflicted upon him by Napoleon, it came to pass that the self-elected temporal champions of the papacy, Metternich for instance, the slaves of usurious bankers and of their own blind nationalism, created new problems even more perilous than those with which the arrogant Bonaparte confronted the Church. Now resurgent Italy, impatient to cast off the yoke of conquerors, associated the papacy with tyrannical Austria which no doubt defended the Church mainly for ulterior purposes. It must also be admitted that the policies of the Vatican, though uncorrupted, were wavering. And herein lies some explanation of the fanatical anticlericalism of certain Italian, French, Spanish, Portuguese, South and Central American, and other nationalities even to our own day. But in due time Rome spoke, in the voices of our last four popes, in accents defiant of all the insults that might be heaped upon them. Once more it became transparently clear to all greedy nations and to all tyrants that for Christianity the only political philosophy to be tolerated is that which respects the spiritual autonomy of every individual, whatever the type of ruler, monarch, or president, who seeks to realize it.

The Christian Social Manifesto gives a sweeping history of labor conditions from ancient times. It traced the iniquitous profit system from compulsory herding of drudging, uncreative labor; from the explorers' rape of the mines of Africa, Asia, and the New World; and from the slave trade which proceeded in defiance of the warnings of Christianity and spread to the looting of the Church's own guilds, monasteries, and cathedrals (as we have seen it in Russia and Mexico, in Spain and Germany, today) until, in the paraphrase of Father Husslein: "The wealth of the institutions which formerly had been devoted to religion and the poor, now ultimately went, in the main, to swell the fortunes of individuals," and "a new class of predatory rich was created in many countries."

Christianity did not fail. Men rejected it. The new discoveries of science, Pope Leo strikingly emphasizes, widened the breach between the exploiting minority and the hordes of the propertyless, whether toiling at the machine or relegated to the growing armies of the unemployed. Whereas, in the Middle Ages, the Guild Master, when he was worthy of his state, listened to the precepts of the Church instructing him how to provide for the vocational education, the health, and the spiritual development of his apprentice, now the cold-blooded banker and the coupon clipper replace even the captain of industry. Thus Pope Leo XIII traced the seeds of certain revolution to "the enormous fortunes of individuals and the poverty of the masses" and the inevitable "general moral deterioration" following religious laxity.

Now, the Church should say naught about problems *purely* political, economic, or industrial. But she must speak out, said Leo, upon matters which have spiritual implications. "Whatever in things human is of sacred character, whatever belongs, either of its own nature or by reason of the end to which it is referred, to the salvation of souls, or to the worship of God, is subject to the power and judgment of the Church." This implies that many problems relating to wages, prices, conditions for women and children in factories, profits, dividends, injurious methods of production, preventable business crises, poorly regulated seasonal occupations, hours of labor, the public good, have ethical as well as economic connotations and therefore, in the words of Pope Pius X, are not entirely "susceptible of settlement extraneous to the authority of the Church." Since "the relative rights and the mutual duties of the wealthy and the poor," in the phrase of Leo XIII, are blurred by the self-interest of Capital and Labor, we may thank God for having given us His Church. As Pius XI has it: "It is not, of course, for the Church to lead men to transient and perishable happiness only, but to that which is eternal. Indeed the Church believes that it would be wrong for her to interfere without just cause in such earthly concerns; but she never can relinquish her God-given task of interposing her authority, not indeed in technical matters, for which she has neither the equipment nor the mission, but in all those that have a bearing on moral conduct."

Pope Leo XIII provides us with a long and devastating historical dissection of "liberalism," *laissez-faire*, blind individualism. In referring to the results achieved by the *Rerum Novarum*, Pius XI does not deny that some ameliorative measures antedated Leo's enclycical. "But after the Apostolic Voice had sounded from the chair of Peter throughout the whole world, the leaders of the nations became at last more fully conscious of their obligations, and set to work seriously to promote a broader social policy" than that of "those tottering tenets of Liberalism which had long hampered effective interference by the government." For example, Pius XI notes the international labor code inserted into the final treaty which closed the Great War. "Many of the conclusions of the national representatives agreed so perfectly with the principles and warnings of Leo XIII as to seem expressly deduced from them."

In particular Pope Leo XIII leveled his thunderbolts against the eighteenth-century and nineteenth-century destruction of labor organizations and against "rapacious usury." When plutocrats gorged themselves with monetary surpluses which had none of the industrial creativity of capital, this was the usuary against which the Church had always fulminated. But even in his own day, Pope Leo insists, the interest on loans and the profits on goods are so unreasonable in their demands that the same sordid usury is squeezed out "under a different form but with the same guilt." Against such wolfish tactics the Church urges for the worker the right of organization.

Karl Marx saw in the dreadful impoverishment of the masses the potency of revolution bred of despair. With this cynical meliorism the Church has nothing in common. Pope Pius X, in his *Motu Proprio* on Christian Democracy, urged that: "Catholic writers, in taking up the cause of the poorer classes, should be careful not to use language that may arouse in them hostility against the upper classes." For "Jesus Christ desires to unite all men in the bond of charity which is the perfection of justice and binds us all to strive for the good of each other." To those who urge the gospel of hate this seems like soft-soaping. But nobody is more trenchant than Pope Pius XI in his Philippic against the "immense power and despotic economic domination concentrated in the hands of a few" who are frequently not even "owners, but only the trustees and directors of invested funds" which they administer "at their own good pleasure . . . pure financiers, men who by their influence may perhaps to a large extent decide the fate of nations, make war or declare peace, as their own interests prompt . . . men who pay least heed to the dictate of conscience." To those myopic people who like to call themselves "rugged individualists" Pius XI has this scarifying answer: "Free competition is dead, economic leadership has taken its place. Unbridled ambition for domination has succeeded the desire for gain; the whole economic life has become hard, cruel, and relentless in a ghastly manner."

No less resolutely Pope Leo XIII dealt with the solution offered by Marxian Socialism, with its materialistic theory. According to this practically every human activity, economic, moral, poetic, religious, is the inevitable result of the particular soulless tool of production which, by some evolutionary torsion, which Marx did not probe incisively, appears to dominate a given age. One is tempted to turn the tables and ask Marx what particular soulless tool of production begot his own soulless theory. It has been shown by contemporary anthropologists, that the Marxian notion, claiming universal communism to have been native to the primitive uncorrupted mind, is a piece of silly Utopian pseudo-science, based to a degree on the work of Lewis Morgan, who contributed greatly to our knowledge of the Iroquois, but who went on to apply a procrustean pseudo-evolutionary theory, *a priori,* to the many primitive peoples concerning whom his knowledge was entirely inadequate and based on wrong assumptions. The popes, in backing the validity among all peoples from time immemorial of both communal and private property, are quite at one with recent anthropology.

This is only one of many instances — some of which I have cited already with many more to come — in which scientific opinions, not as yet verified, after temporarily taking a position apparently opposed to the Church, have with fuller information swung back to the view which the Church has always unflinchingly championed. There never has been and never will be any conflict between rationally established scientific formulations and the traditional Christian dogmas. Leo XIII quite correctly accused the Marxian Socialists of "working on the envy of the rich" and so seeking to abolish most if not all individual possessions — in the venomous phrase of Marx, to "expropriate the expropriators." The Church holds against Marx that this process is not a blind evolutionary necessity. There are increasing signs that most of what have been called theories of evolution will, before the end of our century, be scrapped by our sadder and wiser scientists along with astrology and alchemy. But nothing that can be scientifically demonstrated to be true will the Church ever fear or hesitate to accept. All truth is ever welcome to her.

Leo XIII pointed out that "It is surely undeniable that when a man engages in remunerative labor, the very reason and motive of his work is to obtain property, and to hold it as his own private property." The Church holds that ownership is a natural right for everybody. Socialism is not radical enough. It would replace the subjection of Labor by Capital, in the words of Father Husslein, by "a far more complete and hopeless slavery of all men to an omnipotent state, or rather to the all-powerful and relentless Red clique in power." After all, Marxian Socialism is but an inverted Capitalism. Its dreams of a transition, through the "Dictatorship" of an hypostatized abstraction, "the Proletariat," to a romantic "Classless Society," grow obviously more untenable with each new brainstorm of the Utopia-mongering intelligentsia, so accurately labeled by Arnold Lunn in *The Science of World Revolution* as "the eternally surprised intellectuals."

V. PROPER DISTRIBUTION OF OWNERSHIP

In equal opposition to both Marxian Socialism and rationalistic abuse of wealth, Pope Leo XIII attacked the ownership by the few and urged a widely distributed ownership by the many. Unlike even socialistically inclined guildsmen, Pope Pius XI would not abolish the wage system. Yet he was keenly aware of its evils. With characteristically Catholic temperance and sanity he suggested that, for the time being, "the wage contract should, when possible, be modified somewhat by a contract of partnership, as is already being tried in various ways to the no small gain of both the wage earner and the employers. In this way wage earners are made sharers in some sort in the ownership, or the management, of the profits."

Pope Pius XI, moreover, from the vantage point of his later regime, was able to go more deeply into the various brands of post-Marxian socialism. He visits a stern censure upon the attitude of some of the critics of Bolshevism: that, namely of treating it too lightly, or the even greater "foolhardiness" of those Czarists and gluttonous capitalists "who neglect to remove or modify such conditions as exasperate the minds of the people, and so prepare the way for the overthrow and ruin of the social order." In other words, the violent plutocrats themselves are the parents of the communists who revel in bloodshed and would deprive man of his most inalienable deeply needed right, the right to worship his Creator. Of those milder reformers who would, while still calling themselves socialists, deplore violence and even, in some cases, espouse Christianity, the Holy Father felt that they would do better to reject the term "Socialism," which for them has become all but meaningless, while retaining an aura of evil connotations most distasteful to them, and instead frankly espouse the Church.

Catholicism, he reminded us, is quite ready to agree with those who attack, not "the possession of the means of production" but rather "that type of social rulership, which, in violation of all justice, has been seized and usurped by the owners of wealth." On the other hand, the oft-repeated hopes of those who think that Christians and Socialists should combine are hollow. "Those who wish to be apostles among the Socialists should preach the Christian truth whole and entire, openly and sincerely, without any connivance with error. If they wish in truth to be heralds of the Gospel, let their endeavor be to convince Socialists that their demands, in so far as they are just, are defended much more cogently by the principles of Christian faith, and are promoted much more efficaciously by the power of Christian charity." It must be remembered that by Charity, the Catholic signifies not the superficially palliative brand, but he means the lives by all on the principle that we must love our fellow men because we love God. The Pope does not deny that some Catholics by their antisocial conduct have brought on their Church grave reproach. But these sinners do not represent the faith which they so besmirch in the undiscriminating public eye.

The popes, as we have seen, stand foursquare in favor of private ownership which they regard as a natural right. God Himself has decreed that parents should have the means to provide for their own children. This natural right, maintained Pope Leo XIII, "is one of the chief points of distinction between man and the animal creation." For man deserves "to have things not merely for temporary and momentary use, as the other living beings have them, but in stable and permanent possession. He must have not only things which perish in the using, but also those which, though used, remain for use in the future."

I may here point out that this consideration shows that the Church appreciates the value of capital. But contrary to the superstitious libels of communists, the Church is and always has been the consistent foe of capitalism when signifying an undue concentration and selfish abuse of wealth. So understood, capitalism is condemned for originating in an attempt to deprive laborers of their rights. It was this, we may interpolate, which under the aegis of such monsters as Thomas Cromwell and Lord Burghley made of the so-called Reformation an excuse for their own cupidity, despoiled not only the monasteries but the guilds, and enclosed the commons upon which simple folk had allowed their animals to graze. It was such capitalists as Thomas Cromwell who justified themselves by slanders against the Church that still live, as I well know from my early education and as I still discern today among my colleagues in all typical so-called nonsectarian universities. Assuredly there was and still is corruption in the Church; but the Church, in her theological and moral teachings, is not and never has been corrupt.

Socialism, the bastard child of Mammonism, proposes to commit the same crime as its parent, the crime of excessive confiscation. Pius XI warned that "neither Leo XIII, nor those theologians who have taught under the guidance and direction of the Church, have ever denied or called in question the twofold aspect of ownership, which is individual or social according as it regards individuals or concerns the common good."

To define in detail the individual and social duties of capital, "when the need occurs and the natural law does not do so," is the function of the government. "Provided that the natural and divine law be observed," the government may specify more accurately precisely what it will regard as licit or not in the use made of their possessions by property owners. But materialistic moderns, having denied God, go on to deny natural law and tend to make the State omnipotent. Let the State beware of grinding taxation. On the other hand, observed Pius XI, "When civil authority [without swallowing all a man's property] adjusts ownership to meet the needs of the public good, it acts not as an enemy but as the friend of private owners; for thus it effectively prevents the possession of private property, intended by Nature's Author in His Wisdom for the sustaining of human life, from creating intolerable burdens and so rushing to its own destruction. It does not therefore abolish, but protects private ownership, and, far from weakening the right of private property, it gives it new strength." The Socialistic Omnipotent State, on the contrary, believing that neither nature nor God, but the State has instituted all existing rights of property, holds that the State can, by bullets or ballots, abolish them. The most telling argument of the Church is that the ownership of private property contributes to man's spiritual development.

In *What Is Wrong with the World*, in which Chesterton so sturdily championed Distributism, the typically Catholic golden mean, equally opposed to the greedy serpentine Scylla of a rationalistic capitalism and the blindly omnivorous whirlpool-Charybdis of communism, wrote: "I am well aware that the word 'property' has been defiled in our own time by the corruption of the great capitalists. One would think to hear people talk, that the Rothschilds and the Rockefellers were on the side of property. But obviously they are the enemies of property; because they are the enemies of their own limitations. . . . It was the negation of property that the Duke of Sutherland should have all the farms in one estate; just as it would be the negation of marriage if he had all of our wives in one harem. . . . Property is merely the art of democracy. It means that every man should have something that he can shape in his own image, as he is shaped in the image of heaven. But because he is not God, but only a graven image of God, his self-expression must deal with limits that are strict and even small."

The right of private ownership, which distinguishes between the extremes of capitalistic oligarchy and socialistic collectivism, is, as the popes demonstrate, further established by the family. Marriage is man's right which no human law may destroy. The family is the primal society. It is not surprising, then, that communism, after rejecting private property, should proceed toward the ruin of the family by making divorce possible for every fleeting whim and turning over the child to the custodianship of its Leviathan, the State. The State should intervene only as a helper when great needs require succor.

The Church holds that all men are equal *as children of their Father who is in heaven.* As St. Paul put it: "There is neither Jew nor Greek; there is neither bond nor free; there is neither male nor female. For you are all one in Jesus Christ." All men, said Pius XI, are equal in the sense that all "have been redeemed by Jesus Christ" and all "will be judged, rewarded, or punished by God according to the exact nature of their merits and demerits." But *economic* equality is a delusion. If the poor often suffer, so do the rich in their equally tragic way. The human equality of man, in the Christian sense, is too realistically envisaged to preclude the existence of classes. But all classes, employers and employed, have obligations. This does not mean that a worker, forced by hard times into an unjust contract, is bound by it. He may well refuse to return something for nothing. And the just employer would recognize far more obligations of his own than those which are the categorical imperatives of the toiler. Thus, as Leo XIII insisted, the worker's dignity must be respected; he must have time for his religion, his strength must not be overtaxed; his wages must not be cut down "either by force, fraud, or by usurious dealing. The employer may have wealth, but not the right to use it as he pleases." Yet from this it does not follow, as Pius XI added, that "the right of ownership and its proper use are bounded by the same limits; and it is even less true that the very misuse or even nonuse of ownership destroys or forfeits the right itself." Pope Leo XIII quoted the dictum of St. Thomas Aquinas that "Man should not consider his outward possession as his own, but as common to all, so as to share them without difficulty when others are in need." Thus we come again to the one final solution of all our social tragedies, to the maxim of the love of our neighbor for the love of God. The Church, from its Apostolic beginnings, has steadily preached and practised this solution. The occasional defections of her betrayers within, like those of the Gallican clergy under Louis XV in France, cannot stain her integrity. They only confirm her indestructibility.

Since holy Mother Church maintains that a mother should be with her children and not absent long hours in a factory, she desires for man a "family wage" which, as Father Husslein describes it, "will enable the breadwinner of the home to support his wife and children in frugal comfort according to what is reasonably implied by these words at any given period, and which will further permit him, by the exercise of the proper foresight and economy, to lay aside at least as much as may be normally needed for the future." But what if a business does not earn enough to pay a just wage? The employers should plan and strive together to overcome their difficulties, with the aid of public authority. "In the last extreme," says Pope Pius XI, "counsel must be taken whether the business can continue, or whether some other provision should be made for the workers." The guiding spirit of this decision should be "mutual understanding and Christian harmony between employers and workers." Here is one of the legitimate functions of the State, since the State should exist for the good of all.

The "Pope of the Missions" also commended the establishment by certain employers in Northern France "of a general family fund within the industry," in the words of Father Husslein's commentary, "from which each head of a family receives subventions in proportion to the number of children born to him." Nevertheless, for the employer's sake, the condition of his business must be the determining factor. But besides all this, it is proper that a worker should receive remuneration commensurate with the value of his individual contributions, not merely a minimum "just wage," but an "adequate wage." And now that more forward-looking employers are beginning to realize in the words of one of them, "that low wages for Labor do not necessarily mean high profits for Capital" and "that an increasing wage level is wholly consistent with a diminishing commodity price level," we should look forward to what Father Husslein calls a "constructive wage," the product of "union and management cooperation," a cooperation which would make possible for the worker what Pius XI terms "a modest fortune" and would "uplift men to that higher level of prosperity and culture, which, provided it be used with prudence, is not only no hindrance, but is of singular help to virtue."

Along with the adequate wage the papal outline of Social Reconstruction demands "a proper distribution of ownership, and a resolute application of the System of Occupational Groups." Here and there, to the delight of some of the more sensible leaders of large corporations, employees have bought stocks and bonds from their own industry. But as yet they have been unable to acquire and to retain anything like a decent amount. President Treagle of Standard Oil, New Jersey, realizes that recently "the ownership of big business has been passing from the hands of the few into the hands of the many," that "monopoly becomes impossible as public ownership of industry expands," and that "the spreading ownership of industry is a natural development of the joint stock company which is substituting the everyday man and woman for the big business baron." It is for the rapid expansion of this tendency that Pope Leo XIII most earnestly hoped, just as he wished that in agriculture the soil would come more and more to belong to the man who, in John Locke's phrase, mixed his labor with it. Out of all this, that saintly Pope foresaw a quickened love of one's fatherland. But the best expression of distributive ownership would be cooperative societies for banking, production, and consumption of which the last has already scored a conspicuous success in many countries, particularly in Sweden, and of which most interesting examples have developed, of late, in Quebec and Nova Scotia, under Catholic inspiration.

The adequate wage, the distribution of ownership, and the Occupational Group System! Let us approach this last great papal ideal for Social Reconstruction through a survey of the Catholic attitude toward labor unionism. First of all, note that Leo XIII emphasized, as fundamental, self-help. And for bridging over calamities, sickness, death and its consequences, he discerned that among the various institutions "the most important of all are Workingmen's associations." He recalled the value of the old guilds even for civilization at large. He proclaimed associations to be a natural right, a view which he grounded on a passage in *Ecclesiastes:* "It is better that two should be together than one, for they have the advantage of each other's company. If one fall he will be supported by the other." This necessity for self-perfection through organization applies alike to Capital and Labor, though the State, despite its sacred duty to protect natural rights, must intervene when injustice looms. But too often in modern days the State has sinned against such groups, particularly against Ecclesiastical communities, destroyed their rights, robbed them. On the other hand, the Church has disapproved of some groups both of Labor and Capital. The principle, however, if justly carried out, is sacrosanct. Labor unions are really safeguards against revolution even if they have often abused their power of collective bargaining. Many suppressions of labor unions, as for instance after the French Revolution, were the result of the excesses of Red Radicalism. Hence the need of Christianizing these organizations.

To Christian trade-unions, so often misunderstood, Leo XIII consequently devoted much attention. They were introduced by the clergy
and by self-respecting European Catholic toilers when the only other
unions were socialistic. Like the old guilds, they have emphasized spiritual as well as temporal goods. And they are especially important since
the overwhelming majority of the children of God are poor. The recent
congregations of young laborers, the Jocists, in Belgium, France, and
other countries, is full of fair promise. Pius X saw that some laborers
must needs join neutral unions — neither Catholic nor socialistic — and
permitted this, provided such men allied themselves with some purely
Catholic organization for religious, moral, and educational edification.
These members of such organizations may well be, as Father Husslein
suggests, handfuls of leaven in the masses of neutral unions. This was
the belief of Pope Pius XI. Under the inspiration of *Rerum Novarum*,
pure Catholic trade-unions, though less numerous than Socialistic ones,
have flourished — at least until the days of Hitler and his ilk. In the
United States, Catholic workers have not had the same problems. They
have been welcomed in our unions as an antidote for socialistic tendencies. But they have been sadly starved in their Catholic training — and
tragically unaware of it.

We come now to the System of Occupational Groups. Pope Pius XI
held that today "social life has lost entirely its organic form," it has disintegrated, become atomic — a sad contrast with the industrial life of the
Middle Ages at their best. In the days when the Catholic guilds flourished
the State was not hounded with "an infinity of affairs and duties," outside its normal scope. Today we must depend on organizations larger than
the old guilds. Hence the need for the Occupational Group System. The
old guilds were adapted to small-scale industry. Ours must cope with
industries vast and protean. Like the more radical of British guildsmen,
Pius XI cherished no hope of returning too literally to the economic
past. "The demand and supply of labor," he observed, in our day "divides
men on the labor market into two classes, as into two camps, and the
bargaining between these parties transforms it into an arena where two
armies are engaged in combat." As a remedy he advocated that *"well-
ordered members of the social body come into being anew. Occupational
Groups, namely, binding men together, not according to the position they
occupy in the labor market, but according to the diverse functions which
they exercise in society."*

This implied the organization of all laborers in any given trade or industry, and similarly the organization of all the employers in that same trade or industry, so that their combined representatives could form a joint board for regular consideration of all their mutual problems and interests, with no less constant advertence to the common good. For, added the Pope: "as nature induces those who dwell in close proximity to unite into municipalities, so those who practice the same trade or profession, economic or otherwise, combine into Occupational Groups. These groups, in a true sense autonomous, are considered by many to be, if not essential to civil society, at least its natural and spontaneous development."

Industrial society would thus be bound, first, by "the effort of employers and employees of one and the same group to produce goods or to give service," next, by "the common good which all groups should unite to promote, each in his own sphere, with friendly harmony." Would this not necessitate a sort of Guild Congress like that which I described in my previous section? But Pius XI was strong, where the guildsmen were vague. He saw to it that due provision was made for private property, with its temporal and spiritual benefits, under a system of distributive ownership. Unlike the guildsmen too, he approved, in the words of Cardinal Gasparri, the continuation, "as far as practicable," of "the simultaneous establishment of separate unions for employers and workers, while creating, as a point of contact between them, joint committees, intrusted with the duty of discussing and settling, in a peaceful manner, in accordance with justice and charity, the disagreements that may spring up between the members of the respective unions." In a word, while the Pope, in his Encyclical *Quadragesimo Anno,* simply desires that "those who practice the same trade or profession, economic or otherwise, combine into guilds or organizations," he does not express preference for combined or separate organizations of capital and labor. The stress is upon the steady operation of a joint committee. This spacious program would end strikes, lockouts, all class-war, all insane business-crises. It is the pinnacle of rational Democracy and Christianity. But for all this we need the will to progress which can be set aflame by religion alone. We must, as Pius XI urged repeatedly, pray above all things for the blessing of God, the Father Almighty, the mercy of His Son, and perchance a new Pentecostal visitation of the Holy Spirit, to saturate us with sanctifying grace and with faith, hope, and charity.

VI. THE POET OF "THE FAËRIE QUEENE"

My preoccupation with the labor movement did not stem my literary activity. At Harvard I had written as my thesis for the doctorate, *Spenser's Influence on English Poetry to the Death of Keats*. In Berkeley the poet of poets remained a subject for continual meditation until, seven years after my arrival there, I published with the University of California Press a volume called *Edmund Spenser, A Critical Study*.* I thought even then that Spenser, for all his Low Church Anglicanism, had a good deal of unconscious Catholicism in him despite the fact that his political animus led him to launch several obscene attacks against Rome. I believe that he brought me closer to the Church, particularly through the loftier and broader phases of his too often local, ephemeral, and intolerant moralizing.

Once we admit with Lowell that "the true use" of Spenser is "as a gallery of pictures which we visit as the mood takes us, and where we spend an hour or two at a time, long enough to sweeten our perceptions, not so long as to cloy them" — once we admit this, then we are vexed at the very things for which he burned out his large and generous life. A picture gallery, to dally in only! No wonder we should grow restive. Like Hurd, Lowell makes the mistake of thinking Spenser was forced into an artificial double scheme, a sensuous poem plus a moralistic or allegorical veneer. He quite erroneously thought that the customs of the day demanded such a procedure. According to him:

Allegory, as then practiced was imagination adapted for beginners, in words of one syllable and illustrated with cuts, and would serve both his ethical and pictorial purpose. Such a primer, or first installment of it, he proceeded to put forth; but he so bordered it with bright-colored fancies, he so often frilled whole pages and crowded the text hard in others with the gay frolics of his pencil, that, as in the Frimani missal, the holy function of the book is forgotten in the ecstasy of its adornment. Worse than all, does not the brush linger more lovingly along the rosy contours of his sirens than on the modest wimples of the Wise Virgins?

Lowell is here a charming but pathetically characteristic descendant of Calvinism, the excesses of which foredoomed it to swing to an equally un-Catholic opposite extreme.

* The following pages are condensed with a number of modifications from this book.

It is perfectly and manifestly absurd to suggest, as Lowell does, that Spenser's art lingers more lovingly over Immodest Mirth (Phædria), let us say, than over Charity; that the sentimental and lascivious Malecasta is made more fondly alluring than Britomart (Chastity) standing over her in her virgin smock with her blazing falchion upraised. But let us not pause to quibble over matters of detail. Protestant-reared generations have always found it hard to realize that Acrasia (Sensuality) in her Bower of Bliss portrays a vice which is but a virtue poisoned by excess and which must, by all the demands of truth, be portrayed as superficially alluring before it leads to temperate Sir Guyon's recoil from succumbing to it. Excess, warping the good, is really privation. Spenser was not far from the Thomistic view of evil. It is amazing to find Lowell declaring some allegorical alloy a necessary expedient in an age whose willful and indulgent poetry he himself knew so well. Surely he had read Shakespeare's unblushing *Venus and Adonis*.

A list of Spenser's audacities in the interest of moral rectitude may well leave the scoffer dumbfounded. I do not forget or condone for one moment his servile proneness to fulsome flattery. Yet let us remember the young and obscure poet already raising his voice against his queen's attempt to curb Puritan preaching and "prophesying." Let us remember with this, too, his ironical portrait, in "Mother Hubberds Tale," of the ignorant and corrupt type of priest whom Elizabeth — and her rulers, like the infamous Lord Burghley — would have molded for their proto-totalitarian Protestant State. Moreover, it was almost madness to satirize in this Tale, which was actually "called in," the rumored French marriage of the queen when the bold words of Stubbes on that topic were answered with a brutal and felonious punishment. It was most quixotic to stir up the old contempt for the French suitor by the delineation of Braggadochio in the second book of *The Faërie Queene*, even though accompanied with the colorful if silly tribute to Elizabeth as Belphoebe. Here indeed was true patriotism in a poet most absurdly called unpatriotic — the only worthy patriotism, that which both blames and exalts. It was as reckless as it was wrongheaded to devote one stern and lofty book of *The Faërie Queene* to a defense of Lord Grey's vile and violent policy in Ireland and to a defiance of his foes *after he was disgraced at court*. It was very indiscreet and loyal to praise Harvey, an old friend, in the days when Nashe and other redoubtable university wits were launching brilliant satires at the fallen literary dictator with the rapidity of a machine gun. It was undiplomatic and truehearted to eulogize Raleigh in *Colin Clouts*

Come Home Again when he was in precarious standing with the capricious and vengeful queen with all her duplicity. It was tactless and most faithful to remember in the *Prothalamion,* written in honor of Lord Essex, that at Essex House once dwelt Leicester, now dead, but even dead a rival to a man as jealous as the younger lord whom Fortune had brought into possession of Leicester's desmesne. It was somewhat undiscerning but dangerous and courageous to wage unceasing war on Lord Burghley, the most ruthless of pioneer capitalists, not, be it remembered, because of merely personal grievances, but because Burghley was a Philistine with all the vices of the tribe.

Most audacious was the colossal scheme of *The Faërie Queene* which, for all its imperfections, was a complete expression of the Phaetonlike genius of the English renaissance. It was a scheme which has been taxed enough with its defects. For Spenser planned a new form of epic, not a glorification of the heroism of the past, but an epic of prophecy which was, by its allegory both moral and political, to dictate the future to a country that was leaping to a rivalry with the world powers of the centuries.

The *first* book of *The Faërie Queene* is nearly perfect in its fulfillment of the requirements of an epic about the future. It glows with a hyperbolical hope that the Red Cross Knight (St. George, the patron saint of England), if he will but avoid Duessa (Falsehood) and her misrule, and the overweening power of the giant Orgoglio (The Roman Catholic Church), and the House of Pride (Anglican corruption), lest he fall into the toils of squalid Despair and commit suicide — that St. George may, with the help of Prince Arthur (Leicester) destined to marry Gloriana (Elizabeth), the Queene of the land of Faërie (England), and with the teachings of Una (Holiness), grow strong to slay the Dragon (Evil) and recover Eden, that is to say, restore the Golden Age, create Utopia.

The *second* book, which explicitly tells us that Faërie Land is real, because it is England, is not quite so sure in touch. And we may attribute this slightly more abstract, slightly paler attitude partly to the febrile influence of the pious and opulent but morbid Tasso. However, thanks to the influence of the vivacious Ariosto, it is full of spirited and delightfully grotesque actions. And it is firm in the general outlines of its structure. Prince Arthur, the superhero of each book, again fulfills his function of rescuer at the critical moment when Sir Guyon (Temperance) is in dire peril. Beloved is Medina (the Golden Mean) set above both Perissa (Wantonness) and the Puritan Elissa (Prurience).

In our warped appreciation, we soon grow heavy eyed and call *The Faërie Queene* tedious and unreal. Yet what if we find that Spenser, despite the generalizations of the textbooks, is close to life in his highest moments and (strange paradox) closest to reality just when he is most allegorical? Thus Florimell, in Book Three, who has absolutely no allegorical meaning, is but a shadow beside Britomart who is Spenser's most vividly conceived woman, a character especially loved by the poet himself, so real that we see both her noblest and most trivial gestures, yet nothing if not allegorical; for she is Chastity, who humbles the lewd and sentimental Malecasta, who thwarts the lustful purposes of Busirane, who slays the virago Radigund. Every appearance of Florimell is the almost invariable signal for the rending of the structure of *The Faërie Queene*. The adventures of Britomart take form in some of the strongest and most lasting arches of the great crumbling edifice. The characters of Spenser, when firmly drawn, have at once allegorical meaning and reality, being drawn from models out of contemporary life: court ladies and knights and fierce Irish kerns, mobs of London and of Cork, kings of Spain and France.

The *third* book, to a large extent, is irresponsible and discursive romance unalloyed. This was not due merely to the difficulties of the heaven-storming structure. But Leicester, whom Spenser admired so blindly and sincerely, died. Corruption persisted; Burghley remained unresponsive to the vast dreams of the idealists. Disillusion came. And so the story of Florimell's remote insipid sorrows and meaningless adventures lured the poet far afield to seek solace for his fading hopes of making of England a Utopia. Now the poet finds that he cannot hold to the real without becoming sordid and bitter. And this is precisely what happens when he is not purely romantic, when he no longer clings to allegory. In lieu of the larger sins, the worthy foes of heroes, we now find groveling monstrosities, like Slander and Ate (Dissension). Cynicism, so unnatural to Spenser, creeps in with the numerous and evanescent amours of the jilted Squire of Dames. Petty cowardly knights, like Paridell and Blandamour and Turpine, throng and jostle and jangle. As Professor Grierson says: "The later cantos of *The Faërie Queene* reflect vividly the unchaste loves and troubled friendships of Elizabeth's Court." Thus Book Three, which set out to be an epic of dictatorial forecast, grows ever more and more despondent. The moral allegory becomes capricious and bitter. The political allegory deals no longer with prophecy, but with the successes in the past of Leicester, or with the disgrace of Lord Grey.

The *fourth* book is invertebrate. Its alleged heroes appear only in episodes. The ending is but a beautiful digression hastily rounded off with a conclusion of the scattered and irrelevant adventures of Florimell, and the sons of Cymodoce. The book purports to deal with Friendship, but its dominant figure is the hideous antitype, Ate (Strife), a personage drawn with the lurid extravagance of a hand that trembles with rage.

The *fifth* book is sternly unified, mainly by its mood of proud and implacable scorn. It is an avowed "treatise" with an austere avoidance of all the sumptuous pageants which have flowed through the earlier books. It is a bold defense of his dead, humiliated commander, whose friendship, even in memory, could bring the poet little but reproach from the sycophants who obviously had a monopoly of the queen's ear. We must not, therefore, resent too much its narrow hero worship of a man at once noble and yet so savage as to seem almost lycanthropic.

The *sixth* book is serene at times on the surface. But its hero, Sir Calidore (Courtesy), disappears on his quest, for a long space, only to re-emerge as a shepherd renouncing public life. The most exquisite passages, the meditations of the old rustic, Meliboe, and Calidore's love suit to the shepherdess, Pastorella, are merely a renaissance version of the philosophy of the ivory tower. Arthur, the superhero, reappears, as he was supposed to do at the critical moment of every book, but here only in combat with the grotesque jack-in-the-box, Disdain, and in behalf of a silly wench named Mirabella. At the end of the book comes a cry of anguish and the last complete portion of the no longer heroic poem closes without denouement or cadence. No such futility would Spenser have felt if he had lived in the age of real heroes, the Catholic thirteenth century, instead of in an age wherein he was, for a time, beguiled by the fake heroes and heroines of the so-called Reformation in England.

What I have ventured to call an epic of prophecy, a prophecy of events which were never realized, can today be reinterpreted as the futile attempt of an idealizing Protestant to glorify heroes of a Reformation which never reformed, men and women who, in England, France, the Low Countries, Germany, and Bohemia alike were inspired primarily not by the spirit of religion but by avarice. And so it came to pass that Spenser's bewildered Jeremiads did far more than I realized in California to purge me of the Puritan sophistries and calumnies with which I was saturated by many unscientific histories which I read in my childhood and youth.

In another country or in a later age Spenser would inevitably have gone the way of a Cardinal Newman. And I can see today, as I only fitfully glimpsed then, how much his groping dialectic did to guide me in the right direction. Disillusion, if it is touched ever so lightly with insincerity, is likely to breed cynicism. But a disillusion like Spenser's always proves to be a *katharsis* to admit a resolute and reasoned faith. So it was with Spenser. With the *Fowre Hymnes* (to Love, to Beauty, to Heavenly Love, and to Heavenly Beauty), at least the last two, and with the fragmentary cantos on Mutabilitie (supposed to be intended for a seventh book of *The Faërie Queene*), the poet of poets turned to an orient light, a reconquest of himself, an ineffable Prospero-mood. For Spenser's swan songs were to be almost mystical, a yearning not despondent but victorious for the Beatific Vision, athrill with the Theological Virtue of Hope. He was pacing, still restlessly but within all hail of peace, among the stars, gazing earnestly beyond them, seeking the very throne of God, where

> With the great glorie of the wondrous light
> His throne is all encompassed around,
> And hid in His owne brightness from the sight
> Of all that looke thereon with eyes unsound:
> And underneath His feet are to be found
> Thunder, and lightning, and tempestuous fyre,
> The instruments of his avenging Yre.

With the cantos on Mutabilitie, which of all his work moved me the most, Spenser detached himself from the petty vicissitudes of court life and looked with undazzled eyes on cosmic changes. Referring to the contest of the Titaness Mutabilitie with Dame Nature, Aubrey De Vere wrote: "According to the philosophy of Spenser it was impossible that Mutability should enjoy a final triumph, because her true function is to minister through change to that which knows no change. . . . When the creation has reached the utmost amplitude of which it was originally made capable, it must stand face to face with the Creator, and in that high solstice it must enter into the Sabbath of His endless rest." We here content ourselves with quoting the final stanza, representing perhaps the very last lines that Spenser ever penned:

> Then gin I thinke on that which Nature sayd,
> Of that same time when no more change shall be,

And steadfast rest of all things, firmly stayed
Upon the pillours of eternity,
That is contreayr to Mutabilitie:
For all that moveth doth in change delight:
But thence-forth all shall rest eternally
With Him that is the God of Sabbaoth hight:
O that great Sabbaoth God graunt me that Sabbaoth sight.

VII. A GLINT OF PEACE — SAN RAFAEL

There remains for this chapter but one more memory, the most precious of all, which glows as constantly as a sanctuary light. My father had died a death as quiet as his all but sinless soul. My mother was with me in Berkeley. It came to pass that she was offered an opportunity to teach French and German at the Dominican College in San Rafael. Every Saturday I went over to meet her, and there I walked by the hour with Sisters of the order of the saint whose name I was to assume, thirteen years later, on the Pentecost when I was confirmed by Bishop Gerald Shaughnessy, S.M., in the Cathedral of St. James, in Seattle. In a lovely out-of-door setting the girls of the Dominican College played Milton's *Comus*. I can hear today the silvery laugh of Sister (now Mother) Mary Raymond and see, "with that inner eye which is the bliss of solitude," her consecrated, happy face. Occasionally the benignant figure of Archbishop Hanna uprose before us, "like an apparition." His few words to me were never of religion and the Church in denotation, but in connotation they were sanctifying. Under the spell of the Sisters I discovered, but little comprehended, the writings of St. John of the Cross, who has now become, after our Lord Himself, my ideal; and I reread with more insight the poems of Coventry Patmore and Francis Thompson, both of whom Ellen Virgin had, long before in Providence, taught me to admire. (I had indeed, a few years before, contributed to *The Dial* an essay on the poet of *The Hound of Heaven* which had brought me a perfect spiritual bouquet of letters from Alice Meynell.) Verily, my Lord, "with unhurrying chase, And unperturbèd pace, Deliberate speed, majestic instancy," was pressing close upon me. But still I fled, even though "Fear wist not to evade as Love wist to pursue." The music of *The Hound of Heaven* was as yet more to me than its meaning.

CHAPTER V

THE SHADOW OF GOD

---

*"Who doubts that he lives and remembers, and under-
stands, and wills, and thinks, and knows, and judges? For
indeed even if he doubts, he lives; if he doubts, he
remembers why he doubts; if he doubts, he understands
that he doubts; if he doubts, he wishes to be certain; if he
doubts, he thinks; if he doubts, he knows that he does not
know; if he doubts, he judges that he ought not to give
his consent rashly. Whosoever therefore doubts about anything else, ought not to doubt about all these things; for
if they were not, he would not be able to doubt about
anything"*

SHORTLY after my country joined in the Great War I was called East
to serve on the War Labor Policies Board of the Federal Government.
Washington was then so crowded that living there was out of the
question; so mother and I established ourselves in Baltimore. This
presented me with an opportunity which I had long sought, the
opportunity to work in some of the scientific laboratories of the Johns
Hopkins University. For government duties were very slight, involving
only an afternoon or two a week of research in current trade-union
journalism in the library of the Department of Labor and a slight
part in the preparation of a brief history of the Socialist International
for the untutored members of Colonel House's Commission as they
set out for Europe.

I. AT JOHNS HOPKINS

At the same time I received an invitation from a San Francisco friend,
Mr. Max Rosenberg, to study psychoanalysis with Dr. Trigant Burrow,
who was then a member of the staff of the Phipps Psychiatrical Clinic
of the Johns Hopkins Medical School. I had already devoured most of
the volumes of Freud, Jung, Adler, Jones, Brill, Holt, and others. But
it was clear that the only proper way to study psychoanalysis was to

submit oneself to the grilling like any patient. This I did, two hours a week, for a year and a half. A little later came the opportunity to deliver lectures on child psychology, from time to time, before various organizations in New York. The memory of those lectures makes me shudder in abject humiliation. The only compensating experiences were the many Saturday mornings which I spent with my friend, Doctor Robert Lowie, in the American Museum of Natural History studying the exhibits of various cultures: the almost Homeric spears and helmets of the native Africans who developed with such amazing independence, in isolation, a highly advanced iron technique; the intricate scrolls of the tattooing of mummified Maori heads; gorgeous and delicate Hawaiian feather capes; particolored Crow Indian quill coats; ancient Peruvian rugs whose textile intricacies baffle the contemporary specialist with machine and microscope; Hopi Indian, Esquimau, Australian, Melanesian devices — a veritable Alladin's cave revealing stark and drab our pettiness in vaunting our superiorities over these so-called "backward" peoples. Finally Dr. Adolf Meyer, the head of the Phipps Psychiatrical Clinic, asked me to help, in a literary way, with his manuscript on abnormal psychology, a task in which I was very unsuccessful in repaying for the broad-gauged wisdom in that field which I gleaned from him.

The time had come for me to leave Berkeley and take once more the open road. I had faithfully attended nearly all the courses in Philosophy and Ethnology in the University of California together with General Psychology, the History of Psychology, Social Psychology, Genetics, Animal Behavior, Paleontology, the Methods of History, "Studies in Jeffersonian Democracy," Sociological Conferences, General Economics, the Labor Movement, Business Methods, and so on. What I sadly needed was laboratory discipline. This I was to obtain, principally in biology, at Johns Hopkins.

So I turned my back gaily on my beloved Berkeley, little knowing that I would spend five years at Johns Hopkins, never to return to the University of California except for a brief visit on my way back to Seattle from the Middle West, after teaching one summer in the Department of General Literature at the University of Chicago.

II. STUDIES IN PSYCHOANALYSIS

I was very fortunate in having Doctor Trigant Burrow as my analyst. Reared in a choice French-Irish Catholic family, he retained some charming trace of it. He is a physician trained at Johns Hopkins, a doctor of philosophy, and he studied psychoanalysis in Switzerland with Jung. I was very fortunate, I say, for unlike most of the followers of the "new" psychologies, he was not at all sectarian.

In the first place, he was much more consistent than the founder of psychoanalysis and most of his chief disciples. Freud had abandoned hypnotism as a method of psychotherapeutics because, as he wisely held, it savors too much of suggestion; that is to say, the analyst insinuates, no doubt unintentionally, certain notions into the mind of his subject and as a result both of them come to believe that the ideas in question are really an integral part of the patient's personality. But neither Freud nor most of his followers ever quite succeeded in eradicating the itch to suggest. Too often, for instance, they took the lead in interpreting the student's or patient's dreams. By contrast Dr. Burrow insisted that the only one who could validly clarify dreams would be the dreamer himself. Consequently he would sit quietly by while the student recounted and then undertook to unravel his vision. Dr. Burrow merely interrupted now and then, with the most subtle acumen, to charge his all too glib subject with evasion or with attitudinizing. Reflection disclosed to me that he was always right. Numerous were the times when, after various abortive attempts at soul searching, I sat dumb for the greater part of our austere symposium. Doctor Burrow would never break the silence. And I would slink out, with never even an adieu, my tail between my legs. I began to find it impossible to remember my dreams. I adopted various mortifications to rouse myself from a sound sleep, whereupon I would lurch miserably to my desk fresh from the dream and scrawl an account which often, because of my somnolent desperation, proved on the next morning to be quite illegible.

Doctor Burrow maintained that the supreme time to interpret a dream was immediately after it occurred — and before completely awaking. I never made much of a go of it with my nocturnal imagination. But in recent years I have had some fruitful adventures in analyzing my dreams during that hypnagogic state which intervenes between sleeping and waking. I was interested to read, in *The Mind and Its Place in Nature,* an avowal by that eminent philosopher, Doctor C. D. Broad, that he has had the same experience.

It is certain that one of the most striking capacities of the soul is its ability, unlike matter, to carry at least some of its past along with it. Both Freud and Bergson seem to believe that the human spirit retains all the content of the waning and perished years. That daring and refreshing philosopher, William Pepperill Montague, from whom I was later to learn many things at Columbia University, is hopeful that this will some day be proved experimentally. I believe that while working with Dr. Burrow I collected some evidence, not experimental to be sure, but at least empirical, that all our memories do remain intact. Often my Baltimore reveries or daydreams were suddenly illumined by an episode from a very remote past. I was able to verify some of these objectively by consulting cautiously, later in Providence, with my oldest and lifelong friend, Bill Otis, who always loved to revel with me in reminiscences. It is not necessary to conjure up the fantastic myth of an unconscious mind. Nevertheless, we may say that forgetfulness is probably relative, while memory is absolute. I agree with Bertrand Russell (in *The Analysis of Mind*) that consciousness (which with Knight Dunlap I consider synonymous with attention) is a matter of degree. But let us remember that consciousness is not the soul, which (with William McDougall and with Catholic philosophers) I now know to be a substance. No, consciousness is merely a function or activity of the soul.

Trigant Burrow never accepted the theory in *Traumdeutung* that all dreams are fulfillments of wishes, an hypothesis that forces Dr. Freud into fantastic extremes in his efforts to interpret unpleasant dreams so symbolically as to render the more distressing of them more plausible as desires vicariously come true. I think that the late Dr. Rivers, physiologist, ethnologist, psychologist, presented us in his *Conflict and Dream* with a more inclusive and workable foundation. He argued that all dreams are conflicts of wishes, attempts to solve the dilemmas of the day, and, when properly interpreted, sometimes most helpful attempts. In some dreams the conflict is solved and the Freudian view justified in these cases and to that extent. I was interested recently to discover that as early as the thirteenth century, St. Albertus Magnus, pioneer scientist, took a similar view of at least one of his dreams. But in many of them the conflicts remain drawn battles, though even these, if understood, might well aid the dreamer.

Today it gives me pause to compare and contrast psychoanalysis with the Sacrament of Penance. The ways of Sigmund Freud and his followers have often been compared with the confessional. Some psychoanalysts try to outflank this unimpeachable truth. Nevertheless the confessional, except for its unfortunate brevity, is far superior because it has a goal far more clear and exalted. Psychoanalysis, at its best, leads merely

to a rapport with the physician and through him to a readaptation to a
human society that is as often degrading as elevating.

I much admired Doctor Burrow's scientific heterodoxy at this point.
He held that society at large, with its hypocrisy, selfishness, and wars,
has a neurosis. By society he meant all the human beings enslaved by
standardized opinion. If he had known and accepted the Catholic
philosophy of history which was perfected by St. Augustine and applied
to our time by such writers as Hilaire Belloc, Christopher Dawson,
Jacques Maritain, Karl Adam, and Peter Wust he would have understood this social neurosis to be the climax of several centuries of
degeneration through a process of secularization, of turning away from
God for nationalistic, racial, and class idolatries which began in the fourteenth century, reached a cancerous climax during the days of the so-
called Renaissance and the so-called Reformation, and has achieved
today a hideous *reductio ad absurdum* in the imperialistic, oligarchical
capitalism of France, England, and America, the Bolshevism of Russia,
the Fascism of Italy, and the Nazism of Germany. For Trigant Burrow
the so-called neurotic seemed to be a desperately sincere person who is
sorely hurt by the more or less unconscious insincerity around him, a
sensitive soul yearning to be true to itself, a person who realizes vaguely
that mere adaptation may be moral and aesthetic degeneration. This is
refreshing by contrast with psychoanalysts who have advised shrinking
youths to achieve manhood by picking up a lady of pleasure on the
board walk at Atlantic City Beach. I think there is much truth in
Doctor Burrow's conclusions.

I attended Dr. Meyer's clinics for a year or more. I often heard insane
men and women say things redolent with beauty. But I am afraid that
it would be perilous to minister, in Doctor Burrow's manner, to some
minds diseased. I have studied the methods of a number of psychoanalysts and I have had close acquaintance with some of their patients
pronounced cured. Most of these — if not all — remained pathetically
dependent upon their physician and whenever possible hovered about in
his neighborhood. In one case, for instance, an affluent depressive actually
bought a summer home in the neighborhood of her psychoanalyst and
contrived to see her physician informally at frequent intervals.

By contrast, the confessional is all very impersonal. The priest does
his best to remain ignorant of the identity of the one who kneels in
the darkness on the other side of the grating. It is hardly necessary to
tell readers of this book that the confessor, unlike the psychoanalyst,

receives no pay. Indeed, although the Church is supported wholly by the voluntary contributions of her parishioners, a poor man may receive all her benefits without offering a penny. And the goal is a rapport, not primarily with society, but with God. No doubt some Catholics confess too infrequently or lightheartedly. But while Confession carries forgiveness, some temporal punishment is accepted by way of the enjoined "penance." Yet it does not follow that by it all the temporal punishment is wiped out, which must be paid for in Purgatory if not otherwise eliminated in this life. Confession is sacrilegious unless suffused with contrition and steeled to the purpose of an amendment which should sooner or later prevail. After Luther abolished the Sacrament of Penance he was horrified at the demoralizing outcome and sought vainly to patch up the matter by urging voluntary confession. The true Catholic, be he simple or sophisticated, does not go to unveil himself to a priest with pleasure unalloyed. He goes with a blend of fear and of God-fearing yearning. But when he is absolved and says his penance and emerges from the church he is moved to lift up his eyes unto the hills.

Psychiatry will never become a successful applied science or art until its practitioners outgrow their superstition that all religions are superstitious, and replace their shallow idolatry of "adaptation to society" with a recognition of the truth of St. Augustine's sentence, "Thou hast made us for Thyself and our hearts are restless until they find rest in Thee." My later experiences, since I became a Catholic, together with my earlier clinical studies, have aroused in me a growing conviction that many if not most neurotics are fundamentally tormented God-seekers who suffer either because the God in whom they believed was crudely or grossly imagined, or because they have betrayed God, or because they believe, or think they believe that there is no God at all, or because they want to believe in God and do not dare.

In another field of psychology I had the opportunity to watch some of the resourceful experiments of John B. Watson, the archbehaviorist. Dr. Watson's narrow and bigoted materialism did not prevent me from esteeming highly his brilliant pioneer work with infants from their birth to an age of a few months. It was thrilling to watch a child fenced off in a world of its own, immune from the suggestions of adult-attendants outside his purview because surrounded by a *chevaux de frise* of arc lights whose beams poured over the comfortable area. Into this environment strolled white mice, chattering monkeys, and barking dogs, all received by the uncontaminated child with radiant delight. Surely Dr.

Watson is correct in saying that a child's unlearned emotions are few. He deems them to be fear, anger, and love. Some of his followers would hyphenate the first two. In *The Autonomic Functions of the Personality*, Dr. Kempf has shown that some, if not all of the manifestations of fear, are followed by an angry recoil so closely that the two might be considered merely phases of the same affective reaction. I felt then, moreover, and still feel, that a Christian would not here abuse the findings of the behaviorists if he inferred from them that something like love is the most primal of all. To be sure, it usually appears to be a very elemental creature-comfort-love. And real love, as St. Thomas Aquinas makes abundantly clear, is not an emotion but an act of the will, often reinforced, no doubt, by feeling-tones. Nevertheless, my own daily, and I hope judicious, observation of my own adopted infants confirms me in the conviction that there is a perfect continuity of maturation that binds the baby's smile, in the bath or when caressed, with Plato's rarified vision sweeping Godward and with St. Paul's magnificent pæans in praise of Charity, the love of our fellow man because of our love of God. And more lately I have found further confirmation in Professor Mortimer J. Adler's excellent neo-scholastic critique of psychoanalysis called *What Man Has Made of Man*.

All of my active work in psychological laboratories was done at Johns Hopkins with Professor Knight Dunlap and Professor Buford Johnson and, in the summer school of Columbia University, with the assistants of Professor Robert Sessions Woodworth. I worked out most of the standardized experiments, took many of the tests, and did a little statistical investigation. To Knight Dunlap I owe more than I do to any other psychologist. And I owe a vast debt to Professor Woodworth's genial and closely coherent eclecticism.

III. OUT OF THE DEPTHS

Toward Easter, during my second year in Baltimore, my mother died. I had been, I suppose, a rather typical only child, oscillating between fierce rebellion and a very loving loyalty. Mother died of pneumonia. She gave up life only after a terrible struggle. For days I had almost hallucinatory reminiscences of the rasping, convulsive breathing of the last hours as I shared with doctor and nurse the task of holding the oxygen tube to her lips. She died with a frown on her face. But she died, so Ellen Virgin told me later, in what Catholics call "the baptism of desire." During her California days she had arrived at High Church Anglicanism. I often attended services with her out of filial piety. But Anglicanism — even High Church Anglicanism — left me cold. Agnostic though I was, I was constantly assuring her of the fact that her logical place was with Rome. In Baltimore, a week or two before she had the slightest intimation of her last illness, she asked Ellen, without ever telling me, what steps were necessary for reception into holy Mother Church. That was twenty years ago. I have her rosary.

During my long years of wistful agnosticism I had occasionally prayed in a crude sort of way. Indeed I never knew how best to pray or precisely what prayer meant until I joined the Catholic Church. When I worked with Doctor Burrow I endeavored to put his hostile views of religion as an escape from life to the full test. I ceased to pray utterly. I read no religious works. I banished ruthlessly all religious meditations. As my mother lay dying, an instant before the death rattle, the doctor touched my arm and said, "Let us pray." I knelt politely at his side. But I uttered not a single prayerful syllable, aloud or inwardly. I was not a pessimist shaking my fist at high heaven. I thought I was sure that there was neither a hell nor a heaven. Even in my agony I felt a vague wonderment that a physician and a scientist should care to do such a childish thing. For, a year or so before this happened, I had adopted atheism, at least as an hypothesis which I proposed to put to a rigorous and a prolonged test, a test which I refused to relax (as far as I can remember) even for an instant by the side of my dying mother — a test which I refused to relax even when, soon afterward, I lay expecting death for myself at every moment.

From the beginning to the end of his philosophical writing, Josiah Royce was never tired of dilating on what he called "the reflexive turn." As we strip away conviction after conviction, under a merciless dialectic, we come at last to bedrock. We even doubt that we doubt. But to doubt doubt is to affirm doubt. This is the reflexive turn. In an early work, *Studies in Good and Evil,* Royce garnered from John Bunyan's autobiography, *Grace Abounding,* a vivid anthology linked with illuminating comments to show how Bunyan cured himself of a neurosis, a sort of Dr. Jekyll and Mr. Hyde personality, by an "inner dialectic" not unlike that practised with their patients by psychopathologists. William James describes Bunyan as suffering from "secondary hallucinations." The old Puritan seemed constantly to hear voices within him tempting him to perversity of will. One most persistent and sinister voice goaded him on to give up the struggle, to surrender to certain damnation. At last he apparently yielded. Down dropped his spirit like a stricken bird. Catholic doctrine avers that despair is a sin against the Holy Ghost. But evidently this was not despair. It was more like a *De Profundis*. For no sooner had he touched the depths than within his soul there germinated the beginnings of a new and steelbright faith. In one of his last works, *The Sources of Religious Insight*, Royce thus describes the reflexive turn:

Cynics and rebels, ancient sages and men who are in our foremost rank of time, can agree, and have agreed, in maintaining that there is some goal in life, conceivable, or at least capable of being, however dimly, appreciated — some goal that, if accessible, would fulfil and surpass our lesser desires, or would save us from our bondage to lesser ills, while this goal is something that we naturally miss, or that we are in great danger of missing — so that, whatever else we need, we need to be saved from this pervasive and over-mastering danger of failure.

> Oh, love could thou and I with fate conspire
> To grasp this sorry scheme of things entire,
>   Would we not shatter it to bits and then
> Remould it nearer to the heart's desire?

Thus Fitzgerald's Omar expresses, in rebellious speech, the need of salvation. "What is your greatest hour?" so begins Nietzsche's Zarathustra in his address to the people. And he replies: "It is the hour of your great contempt" — the hour, so he goes on to explain, when you despise all the conventional values and trivial maxims of a morality and a religion that have become for you merely traditional, conventional, respectable, but infinitely petty. Now, if you observe that St. Paul's Epistle to the Romans, despite its utterly different religious ideas, begins with an analogous condemnation of the social world as it was, or as it always naturally is, you may learn to appreciate the universal forms in which the need for salvation comes to men's consciousness, however various their creeds.

While Doctor Burrow's devastating diagnosis of the social neurosis seemed to have left me graceless, at my lowest point, I was soon after that period to experience a metempsychosis of faith. As I stared into my dead mother's staring eyes I was, unknowingly, on the verge of the reflexive turn.

In recent years it has been most illuminating to me to contrast that Protestant resignation of Bunyan's, verging as it does on the dreadful sin of final despair, with the loving resignation of a Catholic of the same era, St. Francis de Sales. This is well described by Dr. Michael Müller in his book on the benignant and heroic Bishop who developed, through a stormy youth, to struggle in Geneva almost singlehanded against the brutal and bourgeois Huguenots of the days of the so-called Religious Wars:

Calvin had preached an absolute predestination to heaven or hell. Theologians in Paris had debated the question passionately — the question as to whether God determined the eternal happiness or eternal damnation of men according to their future conduct in life or regardless of it. As an intelligent youth — he must have been about nineteen — Francis took a lively interest in this quarrel. . . . Some sort of psychological depression, usual enough in adolescence, had led him to answer in the unfortunate sense and he condemned himself to hell. His natural desire for self-affirmation fought against such a terrible fate, though his piety, at the same time, urged submission to the supposed decree of the Almighty. . . . From the psychological point of view there were two solutions, either a sharp turn to the left — enjoy this life seeing that the next is already lost; or the subduing of self-love by love of God. Francis's deep-rooted piety selected the second way out. He acquiesced in his damnation; he was ready to go to hell if it was pleasing to God. "Yea, Father, Thy will be done . . ." But with this inhuman sacrifice the spell was broken. . . . It came over him like a wave of light that damnation was really a very unworthy glorification of God. . . . And so the frightful struggle ended in a triumphant optimism. . . . From the theological point of view, Francis had turned to Molinism. . . . Through this acute tension . . . he gained . . . a deep understanding of the tormenting nights of the soul, and a deep sympathy with them. Men acquire the gentleness with which to heal suffering in others, only by the personal experience of similar suffering.

I took my mother's body to Providence to have her buried at my father's side. Toward the close of the first day in my native town I was stricken with a serious attack of fever. Convinced that I had pneumonia I summoned a hotel clerk in order that I might dispatch several telegrams before delirium set in. Within twelve hours an ambulance took me to the Rhode Island Hospital. Pneumonia it was. I owe my life in large measure to the instructions given by my mother's physician when I shared the vigils with her nurse. My mother had failed rapidly because she refused to take the light collations of food frequently required. Remembering this, despite my exhaustion and distaste, I always allowed the nurse to turn my head and feed me through a glass tube. I looked at my fingernails and watched them grow more and more purple. When the crisis came and the nurse gave me frequent injections of camphor, I remembered that my mother began to receive these a few hours before she died. I felt that it did not matter if I died. And simultaneously I felt that I ought to be enough of a sport to cooperate with the doctors and nurses to the uttermost. I had no fears. I had no explicit hope of immortality. I did not believe, or clearly believe, in God. And yet my attitude was curiously like that of the Christian who, believing in free will, should exert himself to the uttermost and yet say with full resignation: "Thy will be done." I began to feel that there was something almost devotional in the experience. One of my doctors, so I later learned, gave me up. I celebrated my convalescence when it was sufficiently advanced by reading Evelyn Underhill's *Mysticism*. While this volume had an unfortunate overture based on the philosophy of vitalism (which she herself today would now discard for a more or less scholastic realism) it was quite free from the unscientific anti-intellectual or sentimental or occultist fancies which taint most of the ventures in this field in non-Catholic circles. But, at that time, I could make neither head nor tail out of it. About nineteen years afterward I picked it up again and reread it with much profit. But by that time I had been a Catholic for six years. And I was also reading St. John of the Cross.

After this I made a regular practice, when the Summer School at Columbia ceased, to go to Providence for a month or two. I could not bear to see Ellen Virgin. I was still an unbeliever, but now once more an eager agnostic. Once more I began to read psychological and philosophical works by authors more or less favorable to religion. I was not interested in visiting my mother's grave. But I met one who was near enough like her to be almost her reincarnation.

This was Ethel whom I found in Providence in dire trouble and whom I married. For ten years we lived together in devotion most tender, and yet with the same rebellious streaks, on my part, that marred my relations with my mother. She who had adored her father mothered me and I fathered her. We were a pair of babes in the woods. She died in Seattle Hospital after days of terrible agony. It then occurred to me that I would like, if possible, to have a Mass said for her. Father William J. McClory, a Dominican, agreed. When our first interview terminated I told him that I had, for most of my life, been much attracted by Catholicism. "Well," said he quietly, "I hope that some time God will give you the grace." That was all. Had he been an evangelistic Protestant he would have haunted my doorstep. But he was a Catholic priest and therefore knew the futility of coercion, no matter how gentle. I often wondered what he meant by "grace." I did not see him again for a long time. But when I did, it was as a member of his parish, at the Church of the Blessed Sacrament.

IV. POSTDOCTORATE IN BIOLOGY

At Johns Hopkins I became more and more deeply immersed in biology. Night and day I experimented in the laboratories and in my home. I read practically nothing but books on biology. I had perused many volumes on the subject in California and had there become pretty well overawed by the mechanistic point of view that purpose, animal, human, or divine, was an illusion. Now, in actual contact with the facts, I began to see purpose everywhere. I was, of course, familiar with Kant's attack in *The Critique of Pure Reason* on the teleological argument for the existence of God; I could see with him that, while there was evidence of a benevolent purpose at work in the world, there was also considerable evidence for one that was malignant. But I began to believe that the benevolent purpose was more pervasive. I had read Darwinians who contended that their master had dethroned Paley's "Argument from Design" by proving that evolution was a matter of "natural selection" and so, of chance. I could see that a great deal of evolution was degenerative. Yet it appeared to me that Paley had made the mistake of his age in conceiving of the Master Designer as too mechanical and too utterly apart from the nature which is His creation. God must, of course, in some sense transcend nature. But could not God also be in some sense, at least at times, immanent within nature? If He did work from within, then I could better understand the working of at least a groping Person or Superperson. For assuredly He could not be less than His greatest creation, personality — if indeed He was the Creator of all.

I was as yet unacquainted with St. Thomas' superb doctrine of *analogia proportionalitatis,* and with his conception of God the Conserver as well as Creator, which completely nullifies the alleged refutations of the proofs of the existence of God which are so widely taught in the non-Catholic universities of the moment. Because of this inadequate background I became something of a disciple of Bergson although I dreaded and despised his idolatry of "intuition." I read with enthusiasm William James's account of a God "in trouble," a God all good but not all powerful. In all innocence I was experiencing a crude version of that Manichæanism which for a time enthralled St. Augustine. I did not see the difficulty to which H. G. Wells rather naïvely left himself open in his *God the Invisible King,* where he compels himself to infer that over and above such a finite God there must be a much more powerful and neutral something which he called the "Veiled Being." It was only later that I discovered that every advocate of a finite God is but a shame-faced atheist.

The fact that some animals, like the brachiopods, appear to have remained stagnant, and that others, like the cephalopods, have in some respects evolved backward did not bother me. I had already ceased to believe in progress, at least as a universal phenomenon. I already agreed with John Dewey that man, though he has the means, still often refuses to exert the will to progress, a will which Professor Dewey, because he still confuses real Christianity with the Lutheran-Calvinistic heresy of "the total depravity of man," does not know how to provide. I was at one with the old Catholic historian, Orosius, whose position I sketched earlier in this book. I saw that the proof either of man's salvation or of God's existence was not dependent on the demonstration of human progress, that such a view was a mere vestige of the bankrupt Deism of the eighteenth century.

V. MECHANISTS AND VITALISTS

I was considerably influenced by the theory of emergent evolution as a compromise between mechanism, which argues that life is merely a very complicated kind of matter, and vitalism, which insists upon some spark of force in protoplasm which is not matter at all.

The most ardent mechanists, who seem to be decreasing in number, consider that men, animals, plants, suns, moons, planets, molecules, and atoms are all made of the same stuff, that their differences are due merely to the number of their electrons, protons, positrons, neutrons, and so forth, and that one "law" governs or one fundamental scientific principle can or ultimately will explain or at least describe the movements and reciprocal influences of these particles or "wavicles" which make up the whole universe. They seem quite unaware, as I now realize, that what they call a "law" fails to include a real relation or a relation to be desired between terms, one of which is the lawmaker or law enforcer, and that without these terms the law would have no existence, no actuality. The mechanist's so-called "law," if valid, ought to predict or at least to describe as statistically possible, the movements of a future Shakespearean complex of "wavicles" writing a fiftieth-century *Hamlet*. Moral freedom is an illusion. Purpose is an illusion. God is an illusion. Souls are illusions. Of course, the mechanist admits that, for instance, he does not yet know enough about the electrons and protons of the human brain to expound memory in terms of their motions and patterns. He can only offer us, as Arnold Lunn wittily says in *Science and the Supernatural*, "blank checks on eternity."

Indeed the mechanist cannot explain the much simpler phenomena of color purely in terms of the movements of the electromagnetic waves or quanta which, while they differ only quantitatively, arouse in the brain the peculiar and qualitatively different disturbances which we call seeing blue or yellow. And how is he to explain the translation of molecular vibrations into heat? The molecules of a "red-hot" needle are not themselves hot. Their violent oscillations arouse a similar excitement in the molecules of certain cells in our skins, which dispatch in turn a "nerve current" or progressive disintegration of the cells of some of our nerves to the molecules of the brain where heat is said to occur. But heat is not movement in the sense of local motion. In a word, nature does not have the perfect homogeneity which the mechanist assumes. Nature is not purely quantitative, a uniform substance, completely explained when measured by light-years, microns, and chronometers. It is full of qualities. Blue is not warmer or colder or longer or thicker or swifter than heat or sound or sweetness or fragrance or yellow. These qualities and many more are physically irreducible to each other. Finally, let me repeat it, the mechanist seems unaware of the fact that a "Law," even if spelled with capital letters, is a mere relation between two real entities with no reality *in its own right*, and that a "Force" is nothing but a convenient scientific fiction, as even the materialistic Lord Bertrand Russell admits.

The biological mechanist usually ignores these difficulties and centers his attack on what he regards as the essential similarity between the behavior of living and nonliving things. He will point out that a drop of ethyl ether on a glass slide will squirm about much like an amoeba. He loves to talk about the various "mechanisms" of human behavior. Yet his efforts, for instance Sir Arthur Keith's, to demonstrate exact analogies between metabolism and candle flames, interstitial growth and the accretion of crystals, radioactivity and reproduction, molecular changes and irritability or sensitivity, the inertia of a piece of matter and memory are based on an oversimplification of the vital phenomena.

The great complexity and subtlety of these vital phenomena led to the rival doctrine called vitalism. Curiously enough, while many an eighteenth-century mechanist was theologically minded (usually a more or less naïve deist unconsciously oriented toward atheism), some of the earlier vitalists justified themselves on what they considered to be the grounds of strictly neutral science. Today, on the contrary, mechanism has often attempted to be consistent with nothing short of uncompromising materialism, fatalism, and atheism, whereas vitalism has included a belief in freedom and has left room for a faith in some sort of a soul, albeit a groping, rather irrational one, and some sort of a God, albeit a blind and fumbling one. This, at least, seems to be the conclusion toward which Bergson gravitates in his most recent work.

How would the mechanist explain the apparent differences between atoms and suns, on the one hand, and "protobion" (ultramicroscopic primordial bits of life-jelly) and human beings, on the other? But vitalists challenge more than they can explain. They defy the mechanist to account for memory merely in terms of the movements of molecules, atoms, electrons, protons. They want to know what is to be said mechanistically about "mental images" like those of Wordsworth when he saw the absent daffodils with "that inner eye which is the bliss of solitude." Is purpose, they wonder, the mere illusion which mechanism declares it to be? And freedom, well, a certain amount of freedom, in the sense of self-determinism, seems to them to be an obvious fact, though they crudely blur together the animal's trial-and-error self-determinism with the free will of the rational human being with its clear inner experience of a choice often prevailing against the greatest obstacles or counterattractions. Is it not true, so vitalists are content to observe, that animals and even plants, if they fail to do a thing in one way, try another and yet another and yet another? The more complicated the living creature the more resourceful he appears to become in controlling his environment. Now freedom is one of the cardinal tenets of traditional Christianity. When Calvin abandoned it for predestination he turned his all-powerful but merciless God into a fiend, and left man to all the slavish irresponsibilities of a fatalistic immorality which, still further muddled by Rousseau's sentimental anti-Calvinism, reached its apotheosis in the bourgeois Manchester School of Economics and the equally bourgeois Marxian glorification of a mythological proletariat. But vitalism does not provide man with any real free will. And its vague hints of élans and entelechies and psychoids are sorry substitutions for the scholastic "substantial forms" and "prime matter."

The vitalist certainly does face facts which the mechanist either ignores or merely promises to explain some day when he has learned more. But the vitalist falls back for his own explanation on seminaturalistic, semireligious hypostatizations, such as "vital force" or "entelechy" or "psychoid," which are neither scientific nor religious, which he adds to the well-known analyzable water, mineral salts, carbohydrates, fats, and proteins of material life-stuff. So the mechanist accuses him of being a mystery-monger who would paralyze all scientific advances. We can isolate carbon or chlorine or any other chemical element in protoplasm. But nobody has ever isolated an "entelechy." The mechanist, in turn, has a very crude theory of knowledge, which he imagines to be a mere mosaic of sensations and images. He fails utterly to describe with any real scientific clarity the role of intellection. Some day he will rediscover the *intellectus agens* of St. Thomas Aquinas. And on that day he will cease to be a mechanist forever, and become a real scientist.

The theory of emergent evolution is at least praiseworthy as an attempt to select the soundest pronouncements from each of the two futile rivals. It has appeared in a growing and bewildering variety of versions.

VI.   EMERGENT EVOLUTION

Consider a molecule of water. It is composed of two atoms of hydrogen and one atom of oxygen, and nothing more. Yet it can accomplish many things that neither hydrogen nor oxygen can do. The theory of emergent evolution accounts for this by declaring that water is equal to more than the sum of its parts; it is equal to its parts plus the form of organization to which they have attained. A molecule of grain alcohol and a molecule of ethyl ether contain the same number of the same kinds of atoms: carbon, hydrogen, and oxygen. But in behavior these molecules show little resemblance. They are different kinds of *organisms*. An atom is an organism compounded of electrons and protons. Even electrons and protons appear to be peculiar condensations of energy, perhaps organized wave-clusters of wavicles, if we follow Schrödinger's development of the quantum theory. Or, if we agree with Professor Einstein and Professor Alfred North Whitehead, that science and philosophy should describe reality in terms of events, then we might say, as Whitehead does say, that everything is an organization of events. The advocate of emergent evolution is on the right track. But he should learn to know the factual scholastic distinction between "organism" and "substantial form."

I am tempted to pause here to observe that a growing number of scientists are developing a morbid fear of the substances which perform these events. Either they would deny their existence or consider them outside the field of science. Substances they wrongly conceive to be definable (as Monsignor Sheen notes in his *Philosophy of Science*) as a "chunk of matter" or "stuff." This is largely due to the baneful influence of the philosophy of Descartes which has eventuated today in non-Catholic circles in a widespread, unavowed skepticism or solipsism, which is often oddly and inconsistently compensated for by a violently dogmatic adherence to Marxian dialectical materialism or some other totalitarian metaphysics. But for St. Thomas Aquinas a substance was conceived more precisely as that which exists in itself (*per se*). For Catholic philosophy the natural scientists can know a substance (the human soul, for instance) only through its accidents (quantity, quality, and so forth), which depend upon it for their existence. "Science," proceeds Dr. Sheen, "by its very method and nature can touch only the accidents of the substance which is quite a different thing." Therefore scientists may *ignore*, but they should not *deny* that which belongs to the field of *metaphysics*: substance, causation, and so forth. But, in this part of my book I am concerned primarily with the hints which science furnished me toward the finding of God. I did in fact once believe, with my first resurgence of theism, that science, unaided, would probably bring me to God. This, for reasons upon which I have already touched and to which I will return later, I now reject. But I still believe that science carried me a long way in my God-seeking and can always be "a friend and aider of those who live in the spirit."

It will be noted (to return to our thread of discourse) that the theory of emergent evolution, instead of making a sharp distinction between the living and the nonliving, carries its distinctions of organismic complexity back into the realm of matter. It makes much of what it calls "levels." When electrons and protons organize themselves — or are organized — to make an atom, a higher level results. New properties, new qualities, new capacities *emerge*. There is some dispute among the different champions of the theory as to whether we should say that new *qualities* emerge or whether we should infer that, at each higher level, the behavior of the emergent organism is partly explainable in terms of new *laws* which could never be foreseen if we knew nothing except all that is to be known about the simpler levels. Some believe in both. In any case they would contend that the atom has more "freedom" than electrons and protons and that science should give up its old rigid determinism or fatalism. In this they are supported, at least so far as animals are concerned, by the gestalt psychologists who have lately been gaining ground on the behaviorist.

At a level higher than the atomic, the molecule appears to be even more versatile. Again, when molecules organize — or are organized — to achieve the exquisite symmetries of crystals, new capacities bud forth. And when molecules associate — or are gathered together — in that organism known as the living cell we have a level higher still.

It is futile, think the champions of emergent evolution, and here they agree with the vitalists — it is futile for the mechanist to attempt to explain the intricate form of life, with its elaborate integration, on the basis of purely physicochemical laws which explain the behavior of its constituent molecules only. To be sure, the materialistic explanations should be pushed as far as mechanism can go. The vitalist is ill advised, according to the theory of emergent evolution, when he argues that the constituents of life are anything more than electrons, protons, atoms, molecules, crystals, and colloids. But the mechanist is wrong in attempting to account for the subtle co-ordinations of protoplasm *entirely* in terms of the performance of its artificially isolated parts.

Life has also *some* laws of its own; life has, perhaps, its own qualities. And when the first children of some living cell clung together, instead of separating utterly as when their parent divided itself, into two children, when these cells in turn subdivided and still clung together, when in further subdivisions these increasing cells parceled out their tasks and cooperated as specialized tissues and organs, then, at this multicellular stage, came a yet higher level with the emergence of novel and still more wonderful propensities. Beyond this point the various versions of this theory diverge. Some would say that conscious life is at a still higher level. Others surmise that even the simplest animals and plants are conscious to some humble degree. Some would trace a certain vague sentience even in the particles or wavicles of inorganic nature. Some think that the life of reason is at a distinct level above that of mere consciousness.

In his *Time, Space and Deity*, in a theory which I endeavored for a time to embrace in my God-seeking, Samuel Alexander has made the bold suggestion that a nonexistent Deity would be the ultimate emergence. But this atheistic theism puzzled me. I wondered what could have set electronic wavicles organizing themselves in higher and higher levels in search of a nonexistent and never-to-exist Godhead which would always be just around the corner, existable but never existing. Evidently I was minded to search for that First Cause in which so many scientists have forbidden us to believe. Years were to elapse before I was to learn that St. Thomas Aquinas was no fool when he argued for a divine First Cause, an *Uncaused Cause,* that Unmoved Mover, that Necessary or Absolute Being who said to Moses in *Exodus* "I am who am" and who, though humbly clothed as Jesus Christ in human nature, yet spoke out as God to the shocked Pharisees and Saducees: "Before Abraham *was* made, I *am.*"

Alexander's theory and, in fact, all the theories of emergent evolution fail to escape, as William McDougall has shown in his *Modern Materialism and Emergent Evolution,* the difficulties of the older materialisms which, under the scrutiny of recent mathematical physics, are moribund. How is the theory of emergent evolution able to explain unpredictable novelties, expanding freedom, and the progress through higher and higher levels in terms of mere vaguely conceived forms?

The difficulty with materialism has always been to explain how an irrational Lucretian swirl of atoms has developed rational creatures; how purposes, however few and finite they might prove to be, evolve from purposeless mechanism. To reply that purpose is an illusion is simply to refuse to face facts. It is just as perverse as the attitudes of those idealists, so justly condemned by the mechanistic materialists, who insist that evil is not fact but illusion. How do values, the enjoyment of beauty and the detestation of ugliness, the aspiration to be righteous and to conquer sinful impulses arise in a universe of blindly neutral wavicles obedient only to mechanical "law"? Professor Whitehead thinks that values are somehow universal. But among scientists he is a voice crying out, most abstrusely, in a wilderness of colleagues who at least deserve the credit of making themselves clear. The twentieth century inherited from the nineteenth a disheartening schism of materialist and idealist each of whom presented his warped system with an utter disregard of the facts which preoccupied the other. I fear that the theory of emergent evolution, though it certainly helped me to reconcile some of the differences between mechanism and vitalism, has done little to heal this deeper schism. Are purpose, values, freedom, and reason abrupt emergents, explainable *solely* in terms of more and more complex forms, "forms" conceived in a curiously crude diagrammatic external way, like mere silhouettes instead of seen, as Aristotle saw them, as internal, actualizing principles or sources?

Whence came this incessant and ubiquitous form-making tendency? Here the apologist for emergent evolution usually becomes vague, although Lloyd Morgan, one of the most consistent champions of the doctrine, expresses a "pious" (but not "scientific") belief that there is inherent in all things a *nisus* or striving which is felt pushing us on from within and at the same time drawing us from beyond. This *nisus* he identifies with God. Lloyd Morgan seems here almost to have discovered Aristotle's *Actus Purus,* Pure Actuality. But if he had, he could have *proved,* instead of guessed at, the existence of God. This *nisus* of Morgan's seemed to me, in my Johns Hopkins' days, to be an improvement on Professor Alexander's adumbration of a nonexistent God always just around the corner. I preferred it also to Professor Whitehead's cloudily expounded universe in which everything everywhere is seeking values at higher and higher levels — though some things appear to point or be pointed in the wrong direction. And I preferred it since, to agree with Whitehead, we should be in danger of acquiescing in a universe, not of things but of substanceless events, to banish from our language, all nouns and keep only the verbs.

VII. GOD AS UNMOVED MOVER

At last I had reached a position where it appeared to me that there might be a rough parallel between the reflections of these scientists and the saying of St. John of Patmos that "God is Love." Not that the beloved Apostle added empirical evidence to the naturalists or vice versa. But it occurred to me that if the universe is more fundamentally engaged in harmonious form-making than in disruption, this process might be accounted for by the inference that it is saturated with a Love which must transcend it as well as be immanent within it. And so here I was, groping unwittingly toward St. Thomas Aquinas' fourth and fifth arguments for the existence of God. A Love so powerful as to saturate personalities could hardly, I thought, be less than personal. Thus I began to hope for the existence of a God who, if not all powerful, was at least loving, good, and personal or superpersonal. But if, as it seemed possible, this form making might be on the increase despite the mutual repulsions of like charges of electricity, the disintegration of radioactive atoms, disease, death, and hatred; if this harmonious tendency were prevailing, could it be that God is, if not omnipotent, at least — as May Sinclair suggests in her learned but rather fanciful volume, *The New Idealism* — at least omnipotential?

But if God proved to be omnipotential, why would He be so? Would it not be more consistent to say that God is omnipotent? Here, however, up loomed the dreadful problem of evil. For this I had then no answer. Yet, in the face of it, came the strong push of positive arguments. Did facts, after all, force me to believe in an omnipotent God? Without knowing it, I was on the verge of finding the God for whom St. Thomas Aquinas had argued so well in his first three arguments, the demonstrations of God as Unmoved Mover, Uncaused Cause, and Necessary Being. But I did not yet know how to distinguish between an Unmoved Mover (a Pure Actuality, supremely alive), and some sort of inert God who, according to Professor Ralph Barton Perry's interpretation of Aristotle's God in his *General Theory of Value,* repels us with "a frozen stare," because I had not grasped the tremendous contrast which the Aristotelian-Thomistic philosophers have perfected between mere motion and actuality (*actus* as above *actio*). I did not know that the question as to the eternity or finitude of the universe, so long debated in philosophy and the natural sciences, is wholly irrelevant to the question of an Unmoved Mover who, whether or not He first initiated finite motions in time, is certainly sustaining them now and always must, if He does not allow them to relapse into nothingness.

Like practically all non-Catholics I had no comprehension of the Thomistic meaning of creation, a failing which, so far as his attack on Catholic philosophy is involved, wrecks the argument of as fine a philosopher as Professor Arthur O. Lovejoy (the most influential of my non-Catholic masters) in *The Great Chain of Being,* as is conclusively shown by Professor Anton C. Pegis in his *St. Thomas and the Greeks.* Furthermore, I did not note that the present supercilious attitude toward "cause" presupposes the fallacious theories of knowledge of Kant and of Hume, or confuses (as Eddington does) cause with condition, or forgets that to mathematics, a science of abstract quantity, cause is irrelevant because mathematics *as such* is not concerned *directly* with motion. I did not realize that many who reject the epistemologies of such skeptics or quasi-skeptics as Hume and Kant still cling to the baseless presuppositions of these eighteenth-century philosophers who made knowledge consist merely of sensations and images, and ignored intellection. I did not know that the attacks on the third argument (for the Necessary Being) were based on a complete failure to comprehend St. Thomas Aquinas' adroit avoidance of the two extremes of agnosticism and anthropomorphism in his profound doctrine of analogy. Nor did I realize that the efforts, from the days of John Stuart Mill to the days of our champions of the theory of emergent evolution, to dispose of the Principle of Sufficient Reason, raised a swarm of insoluble difficulties. I did not, in short, know that the very arguments of atheist and agnostic against the proofs of the existence of God would, if consistently applied, destroy all our right to believe in the validity of those very natural sciences upon which these iconoclasts so arrogantly take their stand. Such are only a few of the results of a long uninvestigated prejudice among most non-Catholic philosophers based on the notion that St. Thomas Aquinas said things which he did not say, and failed to make certain observations which he made so well that — if they had been carefully observed, from the days of some of his most stubborn and blind contemporaries and decadent followers to the day of Descartes — would have saved the world from that debacle called modern philosophy, and would have furnished the blind adherents of the crazy economic, political, and metaphysical sophistries of our generation with a sure cure for their delusions.

CHAPTER VI

ORIENTATION

"In every place, O Truth, thou givest audience to such as consult thee, and at the same time thou dost answer all their demands, be they ever so diverse. Thou givest them clear answers, but everyone doth not clearly understand thee. For all men consult thee about what they will, but they do not always hear what they will by way of answer. He is thy best servant who endeavoreth not to hear from thee that which he desireth, but rather desireth that which he heareth from thee."

IN MY last summer in Columbia University, I met for a second time Frederick Morgan Padelford, dean of the Graduate School at the University of Washington. I had long admired his important contributions to the unraveling of the political allegory of Spenser's poetry and we had discussed them together, years before, at a memorable meeting in Berkeley. Upon his asking me about the tasks upon which I was now engaged, I recounted my errancies and told him that since my lean patrimony was rapidly evaporating, I must needs return to teaching, though not, I hoped, in an English department. Whereupon he informed me that I was, he suspected, just the man they were searching for at his university to introduce certain courses as a sort of antidote to specialism.

My perennial interest in literature and the fine arts had long ceased to be merely a historical one. For about five years I had focused my adventures in research on the theory of beauty and art. I was just finishing a book on this subject, a sprawling thing, which, a few months later, I threw into the wastebasket. I was engaged for the coming year as a lecturer in aesthetics in the Department of Philosophy of the Johns Hopkins University. But when the next summer came, I departed for Seattle to initiate a department, somewhat lamely entitled Liberal Arts, in the most hospitable and forbearing University of Washington under whose oriflamme I hope I shall spend my remaining days.

I. PHYSICS VERGES TOWARD SCHOLASTICISM

My first course was entitled: An Introduction to Modern (it should have been Contemporary) Thought. I undertook to weave together the relevant findings of the contemporary sciences in a system which would reveal man's place in a Nature perchance neutral or alien or friendly. The course was to reach its climax in a very "liberalistic" apology for religion, which for me, as for Professor Montague, was to be defined as "the acceptance of . . . the possibility . . . that what is highest in spirit is also deepest in nature, that the ideal and the real are at least to some extent identified, not merely evanescently in our own lives, but enduringly in the universe itself." I had a phobia for anything which I deemed to smack of the supernatural. I believed that the sciences alone could furnish the empirical data to be smelted into a rational religion. My last ecclesiastical disillusionment had been in Baltimore at the hands of the Quakers. I had long loved this gentle sect. So I was shocked when I found that they had followed the ways of all the hundreds of Protestantisms and were riven apart as two sects, they who I thought were the only undisputatious ones. Today, as a Catholic, I understand it perfectly as the inevitable aftermath of the Reformation. But, at that time, I was quite sure that no church would ever do for me. There was one and only one for which I had a remnant of respect. I had an ever deepening reverence for Rome. But I was repelled by the concepts of revelation and dogma both of which, of course, I sadly misapprehended.

I now fell prey to that pious hope of certain eminent physicists like Professor Millikan, of wistful pastors, and of the few followers of Mrs. Eddy who are not too squeamish and lily-livered to glance at a scientific work: I began to hope that the new theories of matter and energy were dissolving all material things into spirit. I reveled in the earlier Bohr-Rutherford models of the atom, three hundred millionths of an inch in diameter, visualized as a delicate system of electrons (whose dimensions in relation to the whole atom were as a fly to a cathedral), of protons and electrons in a nucleus, and of planetary electrons sweeping around them — atoms, in other words, as systems of negative and positive charges of electricity, ethereal electricity instead of the coarse-grained, impenetrable, shin-bruising matter which had been the bugbear of my Shelleyan youth! I was a bit disconcerted when now I found Schrödinger ignoring the nucleus and mathematicizing the electrons into clusters of waves, each one fitted with three spatial dimensions of its own, so that for, say five

electrons, you had to have a fifteen-dimensional space. Still, it was exhilarating to find Sir James Jeans, in *The Universe Around Us* and in *The
Mysterious Universe,* declaring that twentieth-century physics was dissolving the material cosmos into waves, some "bottled up" and labeled
"matter," some "unbottled" and dubbed "radiation." It was fun to think
of matter turning into energy and of energy remetamorphosed as matter.

Surely in such a flexible, good-natured, and effervescent universe there
ought to be some room for a few souls! And when Sir Arthur Eddington
declared the subject matter of physics to be merely sets of metrical
"pointer-readings," skeletonic blueprints, as one might paraphrase it, of
reality, and when the great astrophysicist passed on to the panpsychistic
theory that all reality is fundamentally mind-stuff, I was ravished. To be
sure I was a bit nonplussed when he went on to say that his "mind-stuff"
was neither exactly stuff nor exactly mind. But along came Sir James
Jeans with the asseveration that reality is in its essence apparently of the
nature of pure thought and that the existence of God is an impressive
likelihood.

By pure thought, to be sure, he meant something like spotlessly
theoretical mathematical thought. And I could not warm up quite enough
to a heaven peopled with square roots of minus one to intone with the
cherubim and the seraphim, an awed "Sanctus, sanctus, sanctus."
Nevertheless, I could imagine that the brilliant astronomer's conception
of God as an Omniscient Mathematician would have fired the fiery soul
of the William Blake of the drawings and the prophetic books. I myself
could and can see a kind of Platonic grandeur in it. And it evoked happy
memories of my hours in Berkeley with the dialogues of that poet-
philosopher who was one of the glories that were Greece two thousand
years ago.

Today I am convinced that the new physics is groping toward a rediscovery of the Aristotelian-Thomist conception of "prime matter," pure
potentiality, which to exist must be actualized by some substantial form
which makes it, as the case may be, an electron, a proton, a hydrogen
atom, a uranium atom, a carbohydrate molecule, a protein, a fat, a
crystal, a living cell, a multicellular organism, or a human body. What is
this "electricity" of which, according to the new physics all matter is
basically constituted, if it is not that *materia prima,* that pure potentiality, that just not-nothingness which is the antithesis of God, the Pure
Actuality? But just now, unfortunately, the tendency of mathematical
physics is, as we have seen, to ignore or deny the existence of what

scholasticism called "substance," that which exists *per se*, and to dissolve the universe into "events." These latter the scholastics would have classified (1) in part under the heading of that "accident" which they called "action" and which they believed to inhere temporarily along with other accidents like quantity, quality, time, etc., in a substance or to be associated with it, and (2) in part under the heading of "motion," a broad term including not only local movement and physicochemical changes, but thought-movement, moral degradation, or regeneration, all transitions from potentiality to actuality, not a being, either accident or substance, but a becoming. I was even then strongly inclined to adhere to my early notions and to agree with the scholastics (of whom I was just beginning to discover that they did *not* spend all their time wondering how many angels could stand on the point of a needle), that souls, if there were souls, were substances. My enfeebled conceptualizing deterred me from going all the way with Bertrand Russell in his meditations on a phrase like *Tom walking* to the effect that the "walking" was much more "real" than the "Tom."

Science has been known many times in its history to go to extremes and then to veer around to their opposites. It certainly took many lusty leaps in seven-leagued boots to pass from a universe made of solid, indestructible, impenetrable atoms to an Einsteinian universe of thingless events. Again the physicist's idea of energy, as made up of discontinuous puffs, still alternates with his contradictory notion of continuous vibrations upheld by the "classical wave theory." Sir William Bragg has confessed that he uses one of the rival hypotheses on Monday, Wednesday, and Friday and the other on Tuesday, Thursday, and Saturday. Sir Arthur Eddington has admitted that in order to account for the passage of light from a distant star through space and his telescope he requires the wave theory, but that in order to understand the action of the photoelectric cells of the plate which mirrors the star he must needs "switch on" the quantum-hypothesis. Nonetheless, Neils Bohr and others have taken steps toward wedding the pair of quarrelsome bedfellows. And I have enough reverence and trust to believe that the trick may yet be done.

I was much interested, as I have already noted, in the possibility of a scientific support, by the quantum theory, of the traditional Christian belief in freedom. Some scientists would have even extended freedom to the atom or its constituents. Others found this electronic freedom so dizzily capricious that they turned toward a Tychistic theory of an absolutely haphazard universe. And there seemed to be comfort in the gauntlet which the new theory of energy hurled down at the feet of the iron monster, mechanical determinism. But I grew more and more wary of seeking much direct support of any religion worth the name in the breathless onrush of the science of the past decades. In her *Philosophy and the Physicists,* Professor L. Susan Stebbing relentlessly observes that "Every scientist turned philosopher tends to find support in his special studies for the metaphysical theory which *on other grounds* he finds attractive." In this connection, too, read carefully *The Degrees of Knowledge* by Jacques Maritain. I would say of the scientists what Swinburne wrote with the theologians in mind: "Hope thou not much, and fear thou not at all." It is becoming increasingly clear that Heisenberg's "principle of indeterminism" proves neither the reality of freedom nor the ubiquity of chance; it merely reveals the limitations to which the natural sciences are committed by the kind of abstraction to which they must needs conform. In his exhaustive treatise on *Electromagnetics* Professor Alfred O'Rahilly, certainly a mathematical physicist with whom his peers will cross swords at their peril, pronounces these words of warning:

Physicists all talk about the same things, but they are not yet agreed what it is they are talking about. . . . Any faddist or group with a particular philosophy at present finds physics a happy hunting ground. Every popular or ostensibly philosophical book on modern physics is a farrago of materialism or idealism or some new-fangled "ism," dogmatically propounded with the prestige of "science." The ill-educated layman succumbs to the propaganda; most professorial philosophers, overawed by elementary algebra, try to convert the stuff into the grist for their particular mill. The others, reviving the Averroist hypothesis of two truths, admit that it may be all right in science, but hold that it is wrong in philosophy.

In spite of the general impression to the contrary, what has been lacking is the *internal* criticism of physics. There has merely been a variegated invasion: mathematicians fresh from the logical analysis of geometry and hungry for new systems of postulates, idealists anxious to tickle the bourgeois with paradoxes, pragmatists desirous of emulating in physics the achievements of the behaviorists in psychology.

Against the alien intrusion it has been maintained [throughout Professor O'Rahilly's book] that the symbols of physics represent nothing but numbers, that they throw no light whatever on any philosophical problem, that their genesis and verification lie in the laboratory at the level of everyday unsophisticated experience. . . . So far as electromagnetics is concerned directly or indirectly, all those imposed irrelevant elements — relativity, fourfold world, dimensions, coincidences, pointer-readings, operatives, imaginary observers and clocks, local time — have been rebutted and rejected in the fore-going pages. The philosophical neutrality and the pragmatic character of physics has been upheld. This conclusion is, of course, opposed to all the recent attempts to foist a particular brand of philosophy into scientific lines of physics: the Berkeleyanism of Sir James Jeans, the symbolism with a background of mental activity upheld by Sir Arthur Eddington, Einstein's subjectivist theory of Space and Duration, Professor Dingle's solipsism, the logical positivism of the Vienna School.

Some philosophers today, after sneering at the Thomistic proofs for the existence of God whereof, so far as I can see, they have either never read the original or, if so, have read it uncomprehendingly, do not hesitate to replace God with the "lines" or the "field" of a "vector," mere metaphors, as Professor O'Rahilly shows. Verily the atheist is the most idolatrous and superstitious of men.

Yet I still think that sciences have furnished the religious apologist with some fruitful possibilities. I agree with Professor Shaler Matthews, a theologian in the University of Chicago (in his *Contributions of Science to Religion*), though with only a modicum of his assurance, that here and there the sciences seem to fill in the outlines of some of the vastly draughted pictures of Holy Writ. I do not mean to be patronizing. I respect and enjoy what science is doing (quite apart from any relation with religion) to enhance the material comfort and the spiritual dignity of man. Finally, I am sure that in the majesty of its vision and in its multifarious versatility and in its all but incredibly delicate precision, science emancipates imagination and reason to a point where, with a proper degree of humility toward science and sanity toward religious speculation, it ought to be of considerable indirect service to the lover of God in grandly depicting the heavens which declare His Glory. So thought Roger Bacon and St. Albert the Great, men whom our contemporary scientists are coming more and more to recognize as their kinsmen and their peers. In modern times there developed the phobia that the love of God would becloud scientific neutrality. Is the contempt of God any less prejudicial?

II. PRIME MATTER AND SUBSTANTIAL FORM

Today, as I look backward over my long years of reading in the fields of twentieth-century physics and biology from the perspective of my more recently acquired knowledge of scholastic philosophy, medieval and contemporary, it has become clearer and clearer that recent theories of relativity and electric fields and quantum mechanics are bound to converge with current theories of emergent evolution in a rediscovery of the hylomorphism (the matter-form theory) of "cosmology," the first section of that borderland subject which is called "natural philosophy" in the *philosophia perennis* of Aristotelian-Thomism and which immediately precedes a second section, called "rational psychology." This latter, indeed, deals with many problems completely ignored by the physiological-psychologists of contemporary laboratories, introspective, behavioristic, psychoanalytical, hormic, and gestalt. To a clarification and confirmation of scholastic hylomorphism our natural scientists are bringing facts which will solve several stubborn difficulties for the Schoolmen — facts which center on the exact relations between "prime matter" and "substantial form," the problem of the disappearance ("reduction"), of one form, the emergence ("eduction") of another. Pertinent illustrations occur when the form of water disappears as it is disintegrated into hydrogen and oxygen, and the forms of hydrogen and oxygen vanish while the form of water reappears as these atoms are reintegrated into a molecule of H_2O.

While Professor O'Rahilly is certainly right if he means in his assault on the amateurish "scientistic" philosophers that metaphysics (specifically ontology and the more fundamental principles of epistemology) was, is, and forever will be untouched by the ephemeral changes in the particular natural sciences, it is nonetheless time, as contemporary Thomists like Jacques Maritain and Father Robert Edward Brennan, O.P., heartily and gratefully concede, to admit that natural philosophy (cosmology and rational psychology) is subject to more or less revision, as a borderland subject, from the researches of physics, chemistry, astronomy, geology, plant and animal anatomy and physiology, and empirical or experimental physical and physiological psychology. Natural philosophy will not have to yield up its fundamental concept of hylomorphism. But the advancing particular sciences will, as already noted, fill out some of its vaguer outlines. At the same time, if and when astrophysicists, mathematicians, and biologists shake off their prejudiced ignorance and go open-mindedly to school to Aristotle and St. Thomas Aquinas (to their philosophy not to their largely irrelevant scientific observations), and to contemporary "live Thomists" in contrast with those whom Father Walter Farrell, O.P., calls contemporary "dead Thomists," then the scientists will be rewarded by the purification of their now often most fantastic and fatally misleading concepts of time, space, matter, life, mind, etc. This will emancipate them from much of their romantic irrationality, materialistic or idealistic, deistic or pantheistic or atheistic.

While I was pondering these drifts in the summer of 1940, there appeared a book which partly confirmed my conjectures, a book approved by Einstein, *The Soul of the Universe*, by Gustaf Strömberg, an astrophysicist of the Mt. Wilson Observatory of the Carnegie Institution at Washington. It applies the latest experimental findings to a scrutiny of the ultimate essence of matter, energy, life, soul. The author's purpose is to investigate the phenomena of physics and biology "from within." He stresses the fact that in the world of the nonliving we discern not only electrons, protons, positrons, and whatever variants of these beings the physicist is continually detecting, but electric "fields," radio waves, and the "pilot waves" of quantum mechanics which are evidently immaterial "structural properties," form makers.

Now let us turn to the hylomorphism of the *philosophia perennis* of Aristotle, St. Thomas, and the contemporary schoolmen. Here we learn that God is Pure Spirit, the Former of forms; that the bodies which all the sciences from astronomy to zoology study — stars, planets, men, animals, plant, grains of sand, molecules, atoms, electrons — are each one composed of two incomplete substances, prime matter and substantial form. Primordial matter, because it is pure potentiality in its essence, can never exist as *materia prima*. It must be actualized by an informing substantial form, Aristotle's "entelechy" to which the great vitalistic biologist, Driesch, and a growing number of the advocates of emergent evolution have come more and more frequently to allude. According to the Aristotelian-Thomist, *materia prima* must be actualized, I repeat, by an informing substantial form (not an accidental form like shape) to *exist* as hydrogen or uranium, a violet, a turtle, or a man. Matter, prime matter, pure potency is, as Father D'Arcy felicitously phrases it in his *Thomas Aquinas*, "just what is *not* nothing; it is indistinctness, the principle of indefiniteness, multiplicity, barbarism waiting to be civilized, a formless void distinct from nothingness only by its capacity to receive form." Matter, sheer matter, which the too idealistic Eddington and Jeans have, with characteristic scientistic exaggeration, been trying to conjure out of existence altogether, is the principle of indeterminacy, a *real* being (i.e., independent of being known in human thought, not a *logical* being), but yet a being which cannot *exist* until it is wedded to a determining source or principle, form. Form is the actualizer (and existence is defined, is measured by the degree of actuality, *actus*), form, which molds matter from within, be it a poem in print or a painting, or the poet or the portrait painter, or a pebble or a proton in the nucleus of an atom. Form is the beginning, the source, that which makes otherwise nonexistent matter into *this* thing. All bodies are compounds of potentiality and actuality. God is *Actus Purus* the Former of forms. Since He is not, in any sense, potential, He must be distinct (*pace* pantheists like Alexander and Dr. Strömberg) from the bodies which owe their being to Him because He makes them where once there was nothing. He is, as theism knows, God the Father Almighty, Creator of heaven and earth.

Now let us return to Dr. Strömberg. Since he finds it "necessary to postulate" immaterial form makers, structural properties, "guiding fields and guiding waves to explain the structure and motions in the inorganic world," he reckons it "even more necessary to do this for the much more complicated structures and changes in the living world." We can see iron filings converging into a composition in a magnetic field; similarly, he holds, living wave systems must activate various molecular aggregates to bring about living organisms. For Dr. Strömberg there must be a distinction not only between living and nonliving wave structures but also between their sources; he finds an absolutely essential distinction between the animate and inanimate. Nonliving wave structures originate for him, somehow, in electrons and protons which are material. But immaterial living sources are designated "genii," a term which he himself associates with the entelechy of Aristotle.

Despite an inconsistent bias toward pantheism, Dr. Strömberg inclines toward a recognition of the supremacy of intellectual life and the immortality of the soul. Were he at all familiar with the *philosophia perennis* he could disentangle some of the inconsistencies to which he himself humbly and fearlessly pleads guilty; and he would cease to pay his faltering respects to his all but meaningless "World Soul, Cosmic Consciousness, Cosmos, God, or whatever term the reader may prefer."

For the Schoolman it is all clear enough. Each thing, tiny or immense, relatively simple or highly intricate can have but one form. A form actuates prime matter as this or that kind of thing, an electron, a hydrogen atom, a protein molecule, a lily, a gazelle, a man. Form, then, furnishes the essence. Matter is the individuating principle which measures off, as it were, a pin from another pin, a man from another man. Clearly, in the hierarchy of things which the sciences study, individuality attains to higher and higher significance. In man individuality achieves a kind of uniqueness. Here occurs the chief puzzle for the Thomist, one for which the sciences in due time will probably bring no little aid. Form gives the essence. It makes prime matter human; it does not seem to make it Peter, Paul, or John. Matter, so the Angelic Doctor sturdily insisted, is the individuating principle. A substantial form and prime matter, as co-substances, unite to make *materia secunda:* an electron, a hydrogen atom, a protein molecule, a lily, a gazelle. But in the case of man, as is proved in the second part of natural philosophy (rational psychology), various sorts of *materia secunda* (proteins, carbohydrates, fats, water, mineral salts), which come together as a body, are actualized as human nature by a substantial form which is a rational soul, simple (i.e., not composite) and therefore deathless. Yet religion tells us that this soul, which lives on after the body disintegrates, lives on as an individual, Peter, Paul, or John. How can this be since the matter which is the individuating principle, has rotted away? What is left but mere humanness, not Peter, Paul, or John? In his *Summa Contra Gentiles* (II, 80), St. Thomas answers as follows:

It is not any and every diversity of form which makes a difference of species. The fact of souls separated from their bodies making a multitude follows from their forms being different in substance, inasmuch as the substance of this soul is different from the substance of that. But this diversity does not arise from the souls differing in their essential constitution, but from their being differently commensurate with different bodies; for one soul is commensurate with one body and not with another. These commensurations remain in souls even when their bodies perish, as the substances of souls also remain, not being dependent on their bodies for their being. For it is by their substances that souls are forms of bodies; otherwise they would be united with their bodies only accidentally, and soul and body would not make up an essential, but only an accidental, unity. But inasmuch as they are forms they must be commensurate with their bodies. Hence it is clear — that their several different commensuratenesses remain in the departed souls and consequently plurality.

Thus held St. Thomas in the face of anxious Augustinian critics who feared that he was laying himself open to onslaughts of materialists and pantheists. Students will find other important references, for instance in his *De Ente et Essentia* (c. 6) and the *Summa Theologica* (I^a, q. 3, a. 3, and q. 85, a. 7). Many a reader will doubtless wish for more light, and I am one of them. Be that as it may, the Angelic Doctor stuck to his guns in the face of his perhaps too spiritualistic opponents. And the impossibly extreme dualism into which later writers like Descartes fell, a sort of

belated Augustinian dualism, that led the despairing to separate as absolute materialists or absolute idealists, both hopelessly untenable views,
seems to justify the moderate dualism of Aquinas. He did not flinch from
concluding that the human soul must be in an unnatural state after it left
the body. But as a theologian he could take comfort in the revelation of
the resurrection when God will reunite the soul with the body — a body
glorified in the case of the just — to make a fittingly incorruptible mate,
with all its positive perfections and none of its frailties.

Anyway, for the Thomist, as we must always be careful to remember,
a human "I," a complete "I," whether before or after death, is not a mere
soul (spirit), as some idealists think, a mere material body, as materialists
insist, or a soul *and* a body as extreme dualists like Descartes most fatally
surmised. A human "I" when in its normal state, whether on earth or in
hell, purgatory, or heaven, is a body-soul.

It is very significant to note that a *genuine* mystic like St. John of the
Cross, steeped in all the dialectic of Thomism, cleaves so consistently to
this moderate dualism that he often makes remarks which anticipate the
Freudian and the Behaviorist — but how much more sanely, without falling into their shallow inferences! — by more than three hundred years.
"It often happens," observes this much more precisely and comprehensively scientific Mystical Doctor in *The Dark Night of the Soul,* "that, in
their very spiritual exercises" beginners find that "without their being able
to prevent it, there arise and present themselves in the sensitive part of
the soul impure acts and motions." This I once found out to my great
distress until I learned from St. John — and the carnal images have now
vanished for years — not that these were caused by thwarted sex desires
(I had no occasion to suffer from any such inhibitions), but by the fact
"that when spirit and sense are pleased, every part of a man is moved by
that pleasure to delight according to its own way and manner. For then
the spirit, which is the higher part, is moved to pleasure and delight in
God; and the sensitive nature, which is the lower part, is moved to the
pleasure and delight of the senses, because it cannot know or lay hold
upon any other, and therefore it lays hold upon that which is nearest to
itself, which is the impure and sensual. . . . There are some souls so tender
and frail naturally, that when there comes to them some spiritual consolation or delight in prayer, the spirit of luxury is with them immediately,
inebriating and delighting their sensual nature and in such manner that
they are, as it were, immersed in the enjoyment and pleasure of this sin.
. . . The reason for this is that, since their natures are, as I say, frail and

tender, their humours and their blood are excited by any disturbance."
To a Thomistic moderate dualist, like this great Carmelite, whose mind-body theory synthesizes the best out of three of our crude contemporary hypotheses — interactionism and the double aspect theory (neutral monism) and epiphenomenalism — it is perfectly clear that since body and soul "form one subject, they ordinarily both participate in that which one of them receives, each after its own manner; for, as the philosopher says, everything that is received is in the recipient after the manner of the recipient."

III.   WITH THE STARGAZERS

I think that it is possible for Catholics, without offending sober scientists by any sentimental gush or smugness, to share with astronomers their reverence for the starry firmament and to be nourished by their noble awe. Professor Moulton of Chicago has remarked that an irreverent astronomer would have to be a mad astronomer. Professor Harlowe Shapley of Harvard, in his long list of bodies from electrons to meta-galaxies of stars in *Flights from Chaos,* leaves a blank at the bottom and at the top which we believe are meant to be filled in with some spiritual beings, infinitesimal at the bottom, perhaps infinite at the top. Professor Einstein, in his *Cosmic Religion,* writes in the same vein as Moulton. St. Thomas Aquinas knew it long ago, but devoid of all the modern misconceptions. And long before him the Psalmist affirmed it in his exultant cry, "The heavens declare the glory of God and the firmament showeth his handiwork."

The sleepless stargazer's colossal narratives of suns so remote that radiations from them reaching us only now, having traveled about one hundred and eighty-six thousand miles a second, after leaving their source millions of years ago, even before the first primordial life appeared on earth, to antedate by aeons the first man — such marvels make us feel our insignificance and may well, if we are theists, discipline us in the virtue of humility. At the same time, without inconsistency, the reflection that infinitesimally tiny men (on a little wizened planet swimming around a middle-aged dwarf star, our sun) can plumb such all but unfathomable spaces — such a realization ought at the same time surely to increase our awe over the contemplation of the souls of these pygmy-bodied but intrepid and most subtle watchers of the skies. And as St. Francis de Sales knew long ago, we could learn that a genuine humility is saved from a degeneration into impious depression by its fusion with reverent confidence.

In the neighborhood of two hundred million times a million years ago, according to the cunning calculations of scientific wizards like Sir James Jeans, the present matter of the universe may be conceived of as coming into existence through the agency of waves of radiant energy poured into space and condensing into the electrons and protons which were to form atoms. Both Sir James Jeans and Sir Arthur Eddington are not averse to believing that both science and the God-inspired *Book of Genesis* must begin with the saying, "And God said, 'Let there be light.'" It is interesting also to reflect that certain of these scientists — though others like J. B. S. Haldane are inclined to dissent — discern a definite beginning to the universe as opposed to some earlier theories of an indefinite beginningless ocean of matter.

It would seem, then, that some scientists, unlike their predecessors, would not be wholly indifferent to the contemplation of a First Cause, an Unmoved Mover, who for St. Thomas, is "the Father Almighty, Creator of heaven and earth." But as we have already noted, the first three Thomistic proofs, the metaphysical arguments for God's existence, are equally valid, as the Angelic Doctor himself made clear, whether or not the material universe had or had not a beginning in time. For St. Thomas Aquinas established the independence of philosophy from the divine Revelation which Dogmatic Theology studies. He proved the existence of God without appeal to authority. From these proofs, without the aid of authority, he went on to deduce the fact that such a God would of His very nature reveal Himself to man and reveal to him such undiscoverable secrets as he needed for his salvation, among others the beginning of the created universe in time.

It is interesting, however, to follow the controversies of these scientific sages as to the likelihood or the unlikelihood of an ending of the universe consonant with the doctrine of the Last Judgment. Some, like Sir Arthur Eddington for example, find in the doctrine of entropy, or the dissipation of energy, evidence of the foredoomed, far-seen dissolution of the millions of galaxies, each with its billions of stars, made or in the making. The Catholic Abbé Lemaître, by Einstein's acclaim one of the greatest of contemporary astronomers, has devoted much attention to the theory of expansion of these enormous islands of the universe which are flying apart with terrific velocity. This too, if unstemmed, would spell ultimate disintegration. Others, like J. B. S. Haldane and C. D. Broad, regard entropy as more or less localized and, at best, a statistical formulation. Professor Millikan, one of the chief discoverers of the tiny cosmic rays which come into our atmosphere wholly from the outside, once maintained that they come from interstellar spaces, not from the sun, and that they are the "birth-cries" of a building-up process which is counteracting the tremendous waste. His localization of these rays was disputed both by Professor Compton and by Sir James Jeans. The latter ascribed them to the "annihilation" of matter into energy which would then be so diffused as to lead to an ultimate cosmic death of all matter, to the shattering of the architecture of the universe. On the other side, Professor Richard Tolman, after constructing various mathematical models of the universe, has chosen, as the most plausible, one which is engaged in a titanic rhythm of expansion checked by contraction which would save it from heat-death. Of course, the Catholic, who has what to some scientists seems to be an exasperating answer to everything, would doubtless rejoin that even this grandiose rhythm might ultimately flicker out. The sciences themselves have emphasized conservation more than destruction and they have never demonstrated that waste, which so shocks the poets and novelists who play with scientific speculation, is an ultimate characteristic of reality. The pious Catholic awaits further enlightenment confident that the cosmic drama is not the tragic farce which Lord Bertrand Russell imagines it to be in that histrionic rodomontade which he inconsistently entitles "The Free Man's Worship." Yet all intelligent Catholics ought curiously and fearlessly to follow the sculpturings of the physicists, mathematicians, and astronomers — as far as they can legitimately lead us — in clothing with colorful flesh the tremendous skeleton of metaphysics. Sir Francis Bacon somewhere wrote that the really learned scientist truly reveres God because he so admires His creative acts that he desires to know more of their splendid details. Whether or not he wrote this with his tongue in his cynical cheek and his worldly fingers crossed, he spoke the truth.

IV.   THE EARTH AND ITS INFANCY

I have also spent many inspiring hours with the geologists admiring the rhythms of that earth which seems fairly to breathe, until it almost appears, as it did to the panpsychist Fechner, to be a living ample-bosomed mother.

Earth-rhythms with their majestic systoles and diastoles, like bars of music which take thousands of years before the accents are repeated, seem almost ideally devised for the emergence of those tiny but even more subtly rhythmical creatures called living beings. The majestic slowness of terrestrial rhythms, which is now calculated, since the discovery of radioactivity, to have pulsated for some two billion years, is the theme of "uniformitarianism." This may be defined as the theory of gradual, broadly harmonious, steady earth changes which in geology has replaced "catastrophism," the doctrine of sudden, violent, and very rare transformations. The more recent view, then, dovetails more nicely with St. Thomas Aquinas' fifth argument. It shows that, since so many unintelligent things act as ordained toward an end, we are bound to infer that their enormous processes are directed by some vast Intelligent Being. In the nineteenth century Lyell followed Hutton by clinching the argument that earthquakes, volcanoes, and the rise and fall of land in relation to sea are but superficial manifestations of changes which are very, very slow. A geological textbook is like the lifeless symbolical score of a tremendous palpitating symphony. The Catholic Church, of course, does not concern herself with geological theories as long as a Creator is acknowledged. But the individual Catholic may find, at least provisionally, in the more rationally grounded of these, details which quicken his appreciation of the glory of God.

The terrible and grand picture of the earth in its infancy has haunted me like a passion. Truly here the scientist has filled in the outlines of the Scriptural account with impetuous and luridly colorful brush strokes and awful chiaroscuro. Chamberlin (opposed, but not too radically for our purpose here, by Jeans and Jeffreys) thought that our planet had at the outset about one tenth of its present mass and consequently could hold on to little or no atmosphere. But it was large enough to develop rapidly a thin flow of air, partly from a terrific barrage of larger planetesimals (meteorites) heated and half dissolved by friction with gaseous molecules, and partly from the heat generated by the larger planetesimals as they churned into the solid but unstable outer layers. After a while the pressure and grinding of surface solids, settling by gravitation toward the center of the earth, produced, by friction and consequent heat, liquid and gaseous matter. This, rushing upward again, as livelier molecules partly defiant of gravitation, like the contents of a pot boiling over, would greatly enrich the atmosphere as volcanoes still do today. As the solid part of the earth grew larger and the compression greater, the nonmetallic rocks locked up a great deal of heat inside. While the major part of the earth remained solid, masses of molten rock would collect here and there, force their way upward, and gush out through a crack. Craters widened, ashes fell, and volcanic mountains arose, dread masses which could have destroyed a Pompeii and a Herculaneum, yet withal vast reservoirs for that atmosphere without which life (as we know it) could not endure. In this atmosphere, at last, water-vapor molecules formed, and condensing around particles of wind-blown volcanic dust, as water vapor always does condense on floating particles and so becomes rain, fell in showers into the small hollows between banks or drifts of solid, close-packed planetesimals to form those pools which were the pygmy parents of our subterranean springs, long rushing rivers, broad lakes, and multitudinous seas. Thus came the hydrosphere which, with the lithosphere (the solid layers of the earth's surface) and the atmosphere, constitutes the triumvirate of substances necessary to life.

That the earth has a dense central core, solid yet as plastic as steel, has been shown likely by various investigations such as the work of Einstein and Gale on tidal deformations. The lithosphere whereon we dwell is not, as La Place thought, a mere precarious scum, coating an interior of fiery liquids and gases. This completely compounded crust was, likely enough, the last to solidify. Within it cooled huge blocks only to sink and melt and lash the seething mass to an appalling intensity of heat. Even after the solid crust was fairly well established, volcanic eruptions must have been ubiquitous and incessant. Meteors were surely far more common before life began, tearing through the fearful gushes of steam which permeated the atmosphere. Dense clouds, thousands of times more massive than those today, lowered, teeming everywhere with the blazing trails of myriads of hurtling planetesimals. Slowly tranquillity came. As the crust grew more solid, steam was forced out to cool into water. Pools formed. Rains fell soothingly. The stage was being prepared for the first ultramicroscopic lumps of life.

At all events the processes grew ever more and more complicated. Marvelous minerals formed in the crust: hard quartz (silicon dioxide), brown, pink, and purple, including agate, rose quartz, onyx, and amethyst; feldspars, pink, white and buff, gray and red and green (compounded of silicon dioxide, aluminum oxide, and other oxides often of potassium, calcium, or sodium); calcite, the marble maker (which first combines with bones of dead animals to make limestone); plates of mica (made of silicon dioxide and of aluminum or iron and of potassium, calcium, or magnesium). These and other minerals made and still make the fire-forged (igneous) rocks, such as granite and others. Afterward came the sedimentary rocks, first powdered from igneous stone by weather and water, and then resolidified and sometimes kneaded up with animal bones. These are limestones, shales, sandstones, and the like. Thirdly, earth-crust movements and hot lavas made and make of igneous and sedimentary rocks the metamorphic stones, as when limestone becomes marble, granite turns into gneiss, and shale is transformed into slate. Lastly over all, spreads the loose debris of mantle rock which, when mixed with decaying animal life, becomes our fruitful soil. God might be opposed; He could not be thwarted. Out of evil, which for a time He may permit, He always brings good all the greater.

V. TERRESTRIAL RHYTHMS

Our "respiring" earth, according to the British geologist, Gregory, shrinks gravitationally toward a shape approximating a tetrahedron and then rhythmically bulges at the equator because of its axial rotation until it tends toward the shape of a sphere. In this process of rhythmical contraction, expansion; of grandly repeated contraction, expansion, vast continents and oceans slowly appear alternately, and alternately disappear. This earth of ours has not been permitted to remain a steadfast place. For good or evil on occasion, but in God's Providence for absolute good in the long run, it aspires toward its end in its own tormented but orthogenetic way. It is thought that Greenland once extended to the British Isles; that Australia was once bound to Africa over what is now the Indian Ocean; that the Indian and Arctic Oceans were once confluent over Russia and Persia; that South America once tapered northward, broad at its base; that North America was once but a mere archipelago, and again a mere sausage-shaped peninsula; that the pristine Mediterranean Sea was an enormous ocean (christened by geologists Tethys) while the Atlantic Ocean was a mere gulf.

These great terrestrial rhythms of expansion and contraction, coupled with the secondary and more superficial rhythms of gradation and diastrophism, denudation and deposition, culminate, by God's Providence, in that sorting out ("segregation") of nourishing carbonates and veins of useful iron and copper, precious silver and gold which furnish an environment fit for man, to enrich him and to try him that by his own will and by God's grace he may become Godlike.

When the earth crust first quieted down, the earliest continents were naught but dreary, bleak, mountainless, valleyless ranges of rugged granite rocks. But the secondary rhythms, just alluded to, involve the underground movements which combine with the surface sculpturings of air and water, of ice and snow and flying sand to mold the long ranges of mountains and shape the so-called rift valleys. Huge "earth-blocks," which are the oldest parts of the terrestrial surface, resist billows (horizontally moving "crumpled bands") of land; and both unite with widespread "sheets of sediments" in ever changing proportions. Some of the hoary earth-blocks are all but impregnable and stand like the coigns of an immense diamond, terrestrial monuments, as Scandinavia, Labrador, the highlands of Eastern Brazil, a part of India, tropical Africa.

Crumpling lithospherical waves were probably once almost universal. And even today these crumpling bands predominate. Yet, because of the gradual thickening of the crust, they are delimited to certain areas, and the upthrust of earth-blocks has become more important than the horizontal wrinkling. The older crumpled bands are exemplified by the Appalachian Mountains. The most impressive of the ever crumpling waves is the far-reaching Eurasian Alpine-Himalayan Chain, meandering at places where the land-waves were driven somewhat out of their straight line of horizontal march by the ineluctable defiance of the giant earthblocks. Here ran the Pyrenees, Alps, Carpathians, Balkans. Then came a range now under the Black Sea, and after it the Caucasus from which branched two southward loops. One loop crossed under the western Mediterranean, through the Balearic Islands, to the Sierra Nevada of Southern Spain, and thence bent back across the African Atlas Mountains, across Sicily, and, as the Apennines passed on through Italy to rejoin the Alps. The other of these two loops twisted off on the western side of the Balkan Peninsula. Thence it swept on from the Caucasus as a series of swirls, the westernmost of which turns through Persia to the Suleiman Mountains and then northward to fuse with the main branch in the mountain knot of the Pamir. From this point the great chain passes eastward through the Himalayas where it has been thrown back by the earth-blocks of the Chinese plateau and forced to swerve southward under Bengal Bay to rearise in Sumatra, Java, the Malay Archipelago and, apparently, running, at the last into the Circum-pacific Mountains in New Guinea.

The other series of geologically recent crumpled bands is the Circumpacific fold mountains. These girdle the mighty ocean discovered for our brief generations by Balboa. The Alpine land-billows, breaking against their earth-block forelands, were given their impetus by forces just below the surface of the land behind. The rise of the Circum-pacific oval was caused, at least in part, by the collapse of the land in front, a subsidence which made the great ocean-bed. The Rocky Mountains, Sierra Nevadas, and Coast ranges, the Andes of South America — these rippled on across a now submerged Antarctic Continent, over New Zealand, and on to Japan, and so to the Aleutian Islands between Alaska and Kamchatka. These ranges are — or in part were — the crown of the bed of the Pacific.

Between the coigns of antique rocks and the folded bands we often find spacious plains of young and sedimentary rocks, whose frequent metamorphoses from land to ocean and ocean to land, have remodeled again and again the sweep of the continents. Between the venerable Appalachians and the barbaric young Circum-pacific chains of western North America, over the Mississippi Valley and the great prairies, the sea has repeatedly swept from the Gulf of Mexico to the Arctic Ocean. The deposition of sediments by this retreating inland sea united the now existing North America, while east of the Appalachians and west of the Circum-pacific ranges vast continental areas of land went slowly foundering downward and constituting the beds of our two greatest geologically contemporaneous oceans.

Let us concentrate for a space on the spectacle of gradation and denudation which, despite its devil's tantrums, is, on the whole, equally magnificent to poet, scientist, and saint. All these alike love to contemplate the pageant of the Millenia with their holocausts recorded by fossils sometimes found aloft on mountain peaks. But God will not be foiled in His majestic plans. While the shrinking of the earth's barysphere (central core) has transformed our planet from spheroid to quasi tetrahedron; while axial rotation has remade it rhythmically as a spheroid, ever smaller and smaller; and while the consequent rhythmic uplifts and subsidences of the crustal lithosphere have made and remade oceans and continents of blocks, crumbling folds and sedimentary sheets; during all these hundreds of thousands of years, wind and water, cyclones and floods, flying sand, tough little roots of plants and ominously sluggish irresistible glaciers have been reshaping mountains, burnishing deserts, and cutting out spacious valleys, the Mississippi, the Nile, Niagara Falls, and the Falls of the Yosemite in a gradation which is continually balanced rhythmically by the diastrophism which to us, as we crawl about on the scarf-skin of our planet, discloses itself furtively by earthquakes and volcanoes.

Our sun's radiant waves splash over the curved whirling surface of the earth with a certain inequality of heat and light which stirs up and quiets down the atmosphere and hydrosphere in their statuary work. Winds circulate. Water freezes and expands in the cracks of the lithosphere. Vigorous plant roots, nourished by the carbon dioxide of the air, reach downward. Heat and cold of day and night work their will. Minerals suck up oxygen and water and carbon dioxide. Winds sweep clean over beach and mountain and desert, polishing them till they are thick sown with jeweled scintillations. Water falls as rain to swell a Mississippi which every twenty-four hours carries a million tons of mud and silt into the Gulf of Mexico or sinks downward to hew out such subterranean cathedrals as the Mammoth Cave in Kentucky. Glaciers, with their captive boulders, grind out broad, deep valleys and sharpen and steepen the great divides. Ocean waves gnaw at the coasts and cut out sheer cliffs and overhangs. And yet, though continents wane, they rise in new formations to make new habitats for those who breathe the air. The Earth rotates, its equator bellies out, and land-waves buckle up as mountain ranges.

VI. STRUGGLE OF LAND, AIR, WATER

The more superficial lithosphere is everywhere rather loosely organized. And streams easily bear away masses of it which color them brown or tawny. Sometimes the waters plunder soil and subsoil sufficiently to leave bare the stark closely coherent rocks. But even these have their cracks into which water seeps, freezes, and expands to break off chips which are ready enough to yield to gravitation. Tough roots squirm; they insinuate themselves into surprisingly forbidding recesses. So down the cliffs roll stones and rocks and boulders.

Oxygen, water, and carbon dioxide from the air combine with minerals to make the lithosphere more susceptible to plants and water. Winds pick up the finer particles and roll them along. Or if these particles are delicate enough, they are swirled up higher as dust clouds. Most sand runs low to make the ever changing rounder dunes along the shores, the windward side ever crawling over the top, rounding it, and dropping to the other side until the whole dune seems to crawl forward, slow and ghostly. But winds have reddened the air with Sahara dusts, high flung as far north as the Baltic Sea. And winds have carried from our Southwestern deserts to our Northeastern Great Lakes a million tons of sand.

Streams converge to form rivers. The Mississippi begins in Minnesota at Little Elk Lake, 1680 feet above sea level. It angles through a maze of glacial lakes and miniature waterfalls until at Minneapolis it drops sixty-five feet over a distance of three quarters of a mile. Then onward it swells through various rapids cutting deeper and deeper between rocky bluffs at Cairo, Illinois, where it meanders ever more and more widely until, below Memphis, it becomes the crookedest river in America. It captures hundreds of contributory streams, thus sweeping along the much greater Missouri which brings its own garrulous children from the Yellowstone National Park, that "place of fountains," and from various other areas. From the East glides the beautiful Ohio, enriched by rain-falls over the Alleghany Plateau from New York to Alabama. Many of the armies of contributory rivers are swelled by water vapor from the Gulf of Mexico, which always receives the lion's share of it back again along with an exhorbitant usury from far-distant mountains and valleys. The opulent Mississippi spreads rich soils over the alluvial lands until it covers about twenty-three millions of acres.

In remote mountains, glaciers grind into the sternest stuff and convert large masses of broken rock into biting teeth which gnaw out the spacious U-shaped valleys. Then these glaciers melt away along their merciless paths to leave their massive rock-debris on land. They have spread over and rounded the stately cones of mountains once ablaze like Rainier. All the continents, except Australia, have these regions of eternal snow which gathers on the loftier peaks and accumulates to depths of hundreds of feet of ever compacting ice until the unstable mass can no longer remain quiescent and so commences to slide slowly down the slope, inexhaustibly renewed, in our relatively cold age, by the perpetual snows above. If a glacier hews out an arctic valley, it often tumbles icebergs into the sea. Farther south, it dissolves as rushing rivers. The ice-cap of Antarctica stretches out for several million square miles. It flows downward from a height of nine thousand feet to make the "Great Ice Barrier" from which hordes of huge icebergs dash out to confront the hesitant mariner.

To meet and reinforce these eroding land-disturbances, oceans snarl against the shore. Many times they have swarmed over ranging con tinental areas as shallow seas. And always they undercut the coastal cliffs, using rock-fragments as crunching tools until these also are worn by the furious process down to mud and drying grit. Here and there, especially at the verge of more sheltered seas like the Gulf of Mexico, rivers push out long low flood plains through which they thrust themselves diagonally over the coast and build up masses of sand and gravel.

But from desert dusts, river mud, and the finer stuffs of the cliffs and smooth beaches the sea exacts an avaricious toll.

To an ancient Zoroastrian, a Persian dualistic poet, all this would seem a fitting stage for the ghastly and incessant war between Ormuzd, the god of good and light, with his legions of angels and good men, and Ahriman, the god of evil and darkness, with his cursing, quarreling hordes of demons and sinners. But how exultantly would Roger Bacon, St. Albert the Great, and Duns Scotus the Subtle Doctor have reveled in all this information had it been theirs! How astounded they would have been to find some naïvely cynical, post-Cartesian, post-Humean philosopher like Bertrand Russell using it to shock the bourgeoisie with the belatedly adolescent atheism of his "Free Man's Worship"! Many a new geological discovery tallies in favor of the Christian scholastic and against Persian dualist and Russellian atheist.

Why is it that erosion does not culminate in the complete submergence of all the lithosphere making it necessary for man to sacrifice two of his greatest spiritual talents, the toolmaking of stone axes, telescopes, and cathedral organs, and the language in which he composes his poems, philosophies, and prayers? What safeguards him from resorting to the more limited aquarian life of his mammalian relatives, the whales, lest he perish? In a certain sense, if we are to believe some geologists at the University of Chicago, gradation contains its own antidote. God here, as always, brings good out of what might appear to be the evil misuse of His originally wholly good creations. Herein the subtle equipoise of the gradational-diastrophic rhythm becomes manifest. Many of the heavier substances on land are more soluble in water than the lighter compounds. Thus they are washed down more readily to the sea. This theory would account for the fact that shallowly submarine continental platforms are lighter than ocean bottoms to which most of the heavier substances would gravitate in the passage of time. As sea beds concentrate and settle more and more they press against the coasts and combine with the equatorial distortion which is due to the diurnal rotation to cause those horizontal land-waves which, as we have seen, are wrinkled up and diffused as mountain ranges.

But the results of this diastrophism would, in turn, become ruinous if unthwarted. Now while these lithospheric surgings preserve us from complete inundation, yet they pass on to an invasion of the atmosphere which thereby becomes more and more attenuated. We know nothing certain about the causes of climatic changes. But the following recent speculations are worth pondering. Minerals exposed to the air impoverish it by absorbing much of the oxygen and carbon dioxide so necessary to the nourishment of life. Again, as the air wanes, the climate becomes colder and colder. For the atmosphere is a blanket which holds heat waves from both sun and earth in a sort of reservoir of enshielding warmth. Thus, as the air grows thinner, the ice sheets steal southward to Kentucky and frantic life flees before them or huddles coweringly in the caves provided by gradation. As the air, moreover, surrenders its carbon dioxide to the sucking minerals, the leafy plants lose their raw material for the making of their foods. And we animals are parasitical on these plants which give us directly — or indirectly through other animals who eat them — all the food as yet available. But, like gradation, diastrophism is thought to provide its own antidote. The wrinkling earth, grown hot with friction, shudders, melts, and belches forth volcanic liquids and gases which, however terrible they may be for men too unwary here and there, enrich the atmosphere once more with carbon dioxide and water vapors. The atmosphere grows thick and warm. Rain falls and makes rare soils to clothe the valleys and prairies. Invading seas bring rich deposits and leave them behind after diastrophism has hurled back the floods. These inland seas have destroyed much life. But these imperialistic waters have strewn abroad the multiform salts which make of our deserts veritable chemical laboratories.

Altogether, out of the struggle of the land, the air and the water, out of these prodigious rhythms, there has prevailed for hundreds of thousands of years an environment which has led the biochemist, L. J. Henderson to propound, in *The Order of Nature,* a bold hypothesis which has been challenged but not dismounted. For him not only is perduring life fit for the environment, but also the environment, with its water, its carbonic acid, and its various benign materials, is amazingly fit for life. A great many of the scientists of an earlier generation, and a fair amount of them today, treat life as if it were a mere accident born of the meaningless convulsions of matter and energy, and so lend specious plausibility to the saturnine poetry of a Robinson Jeffers. Such self-styled naturalists, scientific, poetical, and philosophical, seem to think that the word *chance* (which is but a confession of ignorance) explains something if it is spelled with a capital "C." The notion of a teleological (purposeful) order in nature has been scoffed at as the mere fantasy of old women, sentimentalists, and theologians. Yet a physicist like Sommerfeld, concerned largely with lifeless matter and energy, can aver today that even his science requires the concept of purpose to grow luminous. And Professor Henderson finds in the thrilling interplay of organic and inorganic forces an evidence of teleological order, design. "The chance," he submits, "that this unique ensemble of properties should occur by 'accident' is almost infinitely small. . . . Therefore the properties of the elements must for the present be regarded as possessing a teleological character."

Henderson does not hazard the generality that design is to be found throughout the whole universe. He does not consequently urge the existence of a cosmic design which must needs be the work of a kindly God. This issue, as a scientist working in a limited field, he quite properly leaves open. But he is convinced that, in the terrestrial drama which he analyzes, it is not accident which prevails, but cooperative order. The layman and the philosopher may be interested in this modest asseveration. They may use it as a fragment of empirical evidence to add to many other testimonies, harvested from many fields. Taken in their aggregate, these evidences have been held by more than one thinker to lead us "through nature to God." Metaphysics has no essential need of such scattered speculations. Yet it can use them, if the scientist himself can verify them, somewhat as the historian uses pictorial illustrations.

At all events, perhaps the most exalting aspect of earth rhythms is that process which so cunningly and sumptuously prepares for the sustenance of life, that development called segregation. In the deeper, simpler rocks, minute specks of widely scattered metals are swept upward with volcanic magma and fused with other elements into minerals. The magma cools into igneous or fire-spawned rocks. But within this, hot volatile vapors collect the metals until these spurt up in gaseous form into the upper regions of the magma and into neighboring rocks. Then hot acid or alkaline water brushes the metals in solution out into cooler regions as ore bodies. Rain sifts in and deposits them more richly. The ore is sluiced into fissures as concentrated veins, poured out as beds, or coated over the grains of sedimentary strata. Phosphorous, the great fertilizer, is useless as long as it is sown as widespread bits embedded in igneous rocks. Nitrogen, one of the most essential atoms in living cells, though abundant in the air, is inaccessible to life until rains wash it into the soil and are assisted by benign bacteria in concentrating it into nitrites and nitrates. So, too, rain sweeps carbon dioxide into the ground where it combines with silicates to form carbonates which the soaking rain then dissolves to hasten a useful decay of the crystalline fire-forged stone, still exposed in bleak lofty places, into the secondary stratified rocks of loam regions, rocks full of the rich residue of life where mining and agriculture flourish. How silly, in this context, seems John Stuart Mill's argument against The Principle of Sufficient Reason when he says that lovely flowers spring *merely* from the dirt and dung, *ergo,* a result may be "superior" to its cause!

Most of the sedimentary rocks, to be sure, are the deposition of the encroaching seas: the sandstone, which cements firmly and makes excellent building material; the muddy clays, which prevent rains from seeping too far below the roots of the plants, while these thereupon decay and with rotting life make rich soils. Clays also level out under wind and water to form smooth prairies. Limestones, fashioned in part of animal skeletons, also fertilize the soil and lock up large amounts of subterranean water. Lastly the coals, bred in swamps in low humid lands, where waters feed and submerge plants and deluge and mix them with mud until the resultant peet is compacted — these coals, oil bearing and anthracite, have formed for thousands and thousands of years to aid man through the babyhood of civilization. And now man himself, who as yet can scarcely mouth his A B C's, learns from Divine Revelation to regard himself as a favored son of God. Or, in historical epochs like our own, wherein his material progress outstrips his spiritual adaptation and makes him drunk, he dares to brag that he has no need of God, and to replace the superstitions of religions corrupted with magic by even grosser superstitions — the worship of such unreal abstractions as "Humanity" or "The Aryan Race" or "The Proletariat."

VII. MULTIPLE RHYTHM OF LIFE

Life, even from the point of view of its merely material constituents, stirred my reverence, wondrously made up as it is of hydrogen, oxygen, nitrogen, carbon, sulphur, phosphorous, silicon, magnesium, potassium, sodium, chlorine, iron, manganese, copper, and iodine. According to those physical chemists who still hold to some of the deductions from the Bohr-Rutherford theories, some predatory atoms, such as oxygen and chlorine, steal electrons from their neighbors. Prodigal atoms, like hydrogen and sodium, readily yield up one or more of these negative charges. In other families, "the noble gases," helium and neon for example, atoms live together in a benevolent anarchy which neither gives nor takes nor shares. Others, like silicon, phosphorus, carbon, and nitrogen, can give or take or share their electrons. Phosphorus plays a great part in one of the unique achievements of life, the reproduction of children. Nitrogen is of paramount architectonic importance. But carbon stands supreme as the master builder. All these atoms organize in societies, called molecules: water, salts, carbohydrates, fats, and proteins. Protein molecules, to the formation of which nitrogen and carbon ally themselves to play the chief part, are often composed of thousands of atoms. Invisible though they be, they are, from the point of view of the smaller molecules, as large as Himalayan mountains are from the point of view of man. As large proportionally as mountains, but immensely more intricate in design than mountains or even suns, they have for years defied complete chemical manipulation at the hands of the most brilliant investigators. All these molecules then associate as cells which can perform prodigies which sharply differentiate them from the nonliving.

Besides its multifarious rhythms, life can reproduce its kind, it contains a catalyzer, a chemical which can break down other compounds without destroying itself. Life grows not by accretion, the sticking on externally of bits like itself as crystals do; it grows interstitially, that is by absorbing into its interior alien stuffs which it transforms later into itself. In other words the life-principle, the vegetal soul or animal soul or immortal intellectual soul of man, is, as the scholastics always knew, capable of "immanent" as contrasted with the merely "transient" action of inorganic beings. All animal life can learn from experience. The highest life, human beings, can reason, can prove the existence of God and, better, can know Him by love as the End toward which all things are oriented.

Some biologists believe that life comes only from life; and they leave its origin a scientific mystery. Others say that life began, in much warmer and more humid days, in pools or on their edges as ultramicroscopic lumps of carbonaceous jelly. No such life is found today even in filterable viruses. Although biochemists have made organic products, like urea, they are still (despite an occasional premature promise) very far from the synthetic manufacture of even an infinitesimal blob that lives. And even if they did the trick, they would not prove thereby that God did not intervene directly in the organic process at that earlier period when, long after He had created matter from nothing, he saw fit to animate, perhaps a single ultramicroscopic lump, perhaps a number of separated mites of carbonaceous jelly.

Meanwhile Catholics can await, as Catholicism (in contrast with early Lutheranism, Victorian Anglicanism, contemporary Fundamentalism, and

Christian Science) has always done, with perfect equanimity, the findings of future experimenters. It does not matter to Catholics whether biogenesis or spontaneous generation (abiogenesis) turns out to be the brute fact. In the interim we may believe provisionally, if we care to, that after God had created elemental matter and allowed it to go its own evolutionary way for aeons, He intervened to breathe into it what scholastic philosophers called "vegetable souls" and "animal souls" by which they mean merely certain principles of vitality. By the word "principle" the Thomistic ontologists signify nothing at all mysterious but merely "that from which anything proceeds or takes its rise in any manner whatever." Vitalists, particularly those as cautious as Hans Driesch, have been right in their insistence that this "vital principle" is not to be ignored. And for my part, the more I pondered the arguments of such a neo-scholastic metaphysician as Father George Joyce, S.J. — (who in his *Natural Theology* showed himself to be as well informed on the facts and theories of non-Catholic scientists and philosophers as they are ignorant of the work of his school) — the more I pondered over this amazing discovery of a distribution of knowledge, quite the opposite of that which I had been brought up to expect, the more superstitious appeared the myth-mongering vagaries of mechanistic materialists such as Doctor J. B. S. Haldane. Doctor F. R. Thompson (in his *Science and Commonsense*), himself a Catholic and a distinguished mathematical entomologist, has exposed among such biologists as Doctor Haldane something of the same uncritical mathematicism and amateurish metaphysics which Professor O'Rahilly, as we have just seen, has found among so many of his fellow physicists.

Be all this as it may, the Catholic must at least insist that God intervened to breathe into man, made somehow like all plants and animals from the dust or slime, a soul which is spiritual, made in His own image, a soul which glorifies that material body which Jesus reverently called a temple. There is today a considerable number of biologists quite ready to admit that man is a mutation, that is to say, a more or less abrupt evolutionary jump. Although they differ widely as to the degree and vitality of mutations, all their attempts to disinter fossils which would serve as a series of missing links to establish an absolute continuity between man and his highest animal relative, the anthropoid apes, and some undiscovered primate ancestor have failed, despite the touching credulity of many paleontologists and their extraordinary imagination as draughtsman of pictures of such mythical creatures.

An overwhelming mass of plain facts confronts the quasi scientist who attempts a theory of the evolution of man from the animals in terms of absolute and exclusively physical continuity. What if man's *body* did evolve from some animal ancestral to all the primates? The materialist must produce some important missing links in animal *behavior* as well as in animal anatomy. These behavioristic links are equally lacking in the data of paleontology and of the comparative psychology of the living primates. As Gilbert Chesterton pointed out with characteristic vivacity and sanity in *The Everlasting Man,* the only thoroughly tangible traces of those who are dubbed with the bizarre sobriquet "prehistoric" men, reveal them as capable of drawing excellent colored pictures of bison and reindeer, a gift so far above animal genius as to confirm the Christian in his belief that man is a spiritual being. Neither is any animal at all capable of real laughter, that most subtle and versatile evidence of human rationality. And despite the ingenious experiments of Kohler who induced his cleverest chimpanzee, Sultan, to haul a banana into his cage by biting off slivers from a solid stick and fitting it into the hollow end of a bamboo rod — despite this experimental exploit of the famous gestalt psychologist, no scientific virtuosity has inspired any animal to make a tool even as simple as a needle of bone, to say nothing of a violin. Let Wundt, in his *Folk Psychology,* fancy that man's contact with limber branches which bent and snapped back against his face led to the invention of a bow. Even so, it took amazing genius, sustained reasoning, to complete the process of construction. And who will belittle that most amazing invention of the very primitive native Australian, the boomerang?

If certain birds, as Hudson thought, show something like a rudimentary aesthetic appreciation of the dance, what of the great aesthetic inferiority of the much higher apes? The best achievement in this respect was the delight which one of Professor Yerkes' anthropoids found in arranging orange husks apparently in certain patterns on his body. What evolutionist will trace the Darwinian "descent" of the interweaving scrolls of the savage Maori's tattooing back, step by step, to this anthropoid origin? Who will trace, in any plausible, *really* scientific detail, the behavioristic steps between the ape of the gestalt psychologists who, by trial and error, constructed a tottering stairway of boxes to clutch a banana hung aloft and those Christian architects who, in defiance of gravitation, with no reinforced concrete, no steel, upreared the soaring cathedrals as prayers incarnate in stone? Who will link the brilliant lyrical fragment of the meadowlark or even the prolonged outburst of the

canary with the Gregorian chant of Catholicism, the "music," as Sister
Mary Teresina phrased it in a thesis for my seminar, "that prays"? What
animal ejaculation bears the remotest resemblance to a concept, a universal idea, like "red," "animal," "man," "truth"? As some philosopher
said, "When I meet an animal who says to me, 'I am a pig,' I will take
off my hat to him." Animals flee before fire; men harness it and, if need
be, produce it.

The attempts of earlier anthropologists and social psychologists like
Levy-Bruhl to demonstrate the existence of "prelogical" human societies
have succeeded only in attracting our attention to the rationality of the
most primitive men. The facile pseudo-evolutionary generalizations of
Lubbock and others regarding the alleged ignorance of God among the
simplest folk have yielded before researches, from the days of Andrew
Lang to Father Wilhelm Schmidt now, to the discovery that the most
primitive men are universally — or all but universally — monotheistic.
They know one God, the Father Almighty, at times somewhat too an-
thropomorphically conceived, but far more sublime than the polytheistic
pantheons of more civilized, more decadent peoples.

VIII. THE MARVEL OF INDIVIDUAL MAN

There is no problem in biology which is more fascinating than the
emergence of the human individual who, according to the work on
heredity by Abbot Gregor Mendel and his followers, appears at first to
be no more than a mere knot in the web of life, in the myriad converging
threads of inheritance from a host of ancestors, a creature of so many
fragmentary reincarnations that he reminds us somewhat of the dreams
of a placidly melancholy Buddhist.

Yet some of these individuals, these exfoliations from the genes parceled out from parents, grandparents, great-grandparents and all the other
forebears, have attained to such degrees of integration, indivisibility, per-
manence, and uniqueness that they actually aspire to eternize their future
beyond death.

But the merely biological chance of a human individual's coming into
existence, when one remembers that the prodigious number of germ cells
(spermatozoa and ova) in his parents is calculated at about one in five
millions of billions. Remember also that the chances of the existence of
either of his parents were equally slim. Moreover, let us not forget that
the father and mother might have found other mates. Then go back over

the earlier generations and compute his chances until your head reels
with impotence. How unlikely that this particular "I" should ever have
been! To cap the climax, Herbert S. Jennings, one of the leading contemporary investigators of genetics, confronts us (in *The Biological Basis
of Human Nature*) with another staggering series of facts and reflections.

There existed in the two parents . . . the actual beginnings of thousands
of billions of . . . personalities as distinct as you and I. . . . Our instincts
and education impel us to regard a human personality as the highest and
most real of entities [*sic!*], having attributes of worth possessed by nothing
else. What are we to say of this infinite number of personalities whose existence was foreshadowed and prepared in exactly the way that gave origin to
you and to me: who depended only on a chance meeting of particular germ
cells for their full fruition, yet never advanced further? Nature, it appears,
plays in the same infinitely wasteful way, whether with the spores of fungi
and the eggs of fish, or with the potencies and beginnings of human
personalities.

Yet biologists themselves know, from their study of what they call
"the cycle of life," that in the long run nothing is, in any absolute sense,
wasted. It is hard for me to understand how, after all this and the reflections soon to be quoted, Professor Jennings remains among those scientists who say of God, "I have no need of such an hypothesis." As a scientist he does not; but as a philosopher he does. And Professor Jennings
has great philosophic gifts.

Moreover, it is Professor Jennings himself who rejoins to the materialist's prejudices: "There are facts of biology that raise doubt as to
whether it is diversity of gene combinations that gives origin to distinct-
ness of selves." He cites the case of identical twins, produced by the same
pairs of genes, yet distinct selves. The efforts of materialistic doubters
of the reality of human personalities have failed to banish this dilemma.
I myself spent the best hours of a long summer in the Adirondacks, swimming, rowing, and playing all manner of games, with twin girls aged
eight. From them I learned much more about the reality of the unique
human soul than I ever found in philosophical texts. In addition, Jennings cites the case of two eggs which, instead of playing their part in the
production of two individuals, unite to develop one. "From such facts,"
he proceeds, "it could perhaps be argued that the existence of myself is
in some way one of the determining factors for what shall be produced
by other germ cells, whether having the same combination of genes, or a

different one." Observe that Professor Jennings, though he has been and in his later years still seems to be an atheist, nevertheless leaves room here for divine intervention. Thus, he continues:

To work this out in detail, one would apparently have to hold that the human self is an entity existing independently of genes and gene combinations; and that it merely enters at times into relations with one of the knots formed by the living web. If one peculiar combination or knot should not occur, it would enter into another. . . . The relation of the self to genes would be like its relation to the environmental conditions: the particular combination acting upon it would help to determine its characteristics; *but would not determine its total existence as a self.* [My italics. I am interested especially in Professor Jenning's use of the word "total" since for the Thomist, let us remember, a self or ego is a body of prime matter actualized by a substantial form or soul. The human ego is a body-soul. The soul, in the case of human beings, is infused into the body by God at the moment when the wandering sperm melts into the ovum.] . . . Neglecting all difficult details as to when and how the temporary union of the self and the body is made, it could be held that there is a limited store of selves ready to play their part, that the mere occurrence of two particular cells which may or may not unite has no determining value for the existence of these selves, but merely furnishes a substratum to which for reasons unknown they become temporarily attached. And therefore there would be no cancellation of billions of inchoate human personalities, such as that to which the other view leads. And what interesting corollaries might be drawn from such a doctrine, as to the further independent existence of the selves after the dispersal of the gene combinations to which they had been attached!

It will be observed that Professor Jennings' speculations, scientist though he is, leaves the way perfectly clear for the Catholic conception of the human soul as a simple indestructible substance with which God informs a material body. And the Catholic conception is the only one which accounts for the obvious facts of the unity of human consciousness and for the extraordinary power of the human being to escape in thought the limitations of space and time.

In general, science has been content to describe (not explain) things, in so far as they have been regarded as nonliving and nonmental, in terms of kinetic and potential "energy," their intensity, direction, acceleration, all observed externally. But if things are alive they must also be described, in terms of their relations to their own past and future, *as more or less determined from within,* capable of immanent activities. A plant seems to be concerned primarily with structure building to which function is secondary. I am here much indebted to a study which Professor Montague contributed to *Essays in Honor of John Dewey*. As he puts it, the plant subordinates *doing* to *being* and confines "its effective intercourse with the environment mainly . . . to the domain of immediate contact." The multicellular plants, at least, are usually stationary, not mobile. The animal, albeit retaining a good part of these vegetative proclivities which in fact dominate within the eggshell, and though even afterward it devotes itself (in ways more versatile than those of the plant) to mere vegetative feeding, assimilation, and "the growth and maintenance of a physical organism," nonetheless, over and above all this, the animal soul or animal principle controls "its reactions to the individually acquired past." Its memories of earlier experiences, its learning-processes, make it "far more of an individual than the plant. It has an acquired private life over and above the inherited life common to its species." It is likewise concerned, much more than a plant is, with remote objects. Its behavior is much more selective, self-determined, *volitional*. But the animal is fain to devote its private and individual life to society, to the preservation of his species. And although the animal has a will, he has not a free will.

Now in man, by contrast, in so far as he attains to personality, we descry a further "emergent level." There is still today no better definition of personality than that of Boethius, "an individual and autonomous or incommunicable substance of a rational nature — *individua substantia rationalis naturae*." Man develops from a seed (embryo) like some vegetables. He learns like the animals. He propagates his kind. But, *mirabile dictu,* he "ceases to be a mere slave of perception. Images of absent objects which, in the waking life of the brute occur only as parasites of the present situation, in man become preoccupations, with reference to which the present situation is subservient or altogether disregarded. In the animal, there are no images of absent objects that occur spontaneously and apart from perpetual bidding except those dream-images which come when the senses are closed and perception itself is in abeyance. Man alone can dream without sleeping, for only in him are the images of memory and imagination strong enough to endure the rivalry of perception. Man's thoughts are waking dreams. They are like stars steadfast and bright that not even the daylight can pale them." He alone contemplates the firmament. He alone has ideas which give rational knowledge. He can feel not only pity for one whom he could not help injuring; he can be remorseful over the victim whom he harmed through negligence or passion. He is conscious of a free ego which can deliberate even when the issue is trivial, which can reinforce a weaker against a more alluring motive, which can conquer acute and prolonged temptation, which knows itself to be a cause, which can distinguish clearly between free volitions and conations which are not free. Man has, in short, a sense of duty, a rational will which yearns ever restless for that Infinite Good who will be perfectly revealed in the Beatific Vision.

Thus man, in so far as he rears himself above mere animal individuality toward personality is the "absent-minded animal" whose thinking is so lyrical and abstract in contrast with those brutes whose sensitivity is so pathetically concrete and practical. When the new and higher level of personality emerges, in man alone, it brings emancipation from mere servitude to species, and to the web of life and its societies.

Man can look, as St. Ignatius shows so vividly in the opening of his *Spiritual Exercises,* beyond humbler creatures like animals and plants toward his goal, their Creator, God. Plants are the slaves of space. Animals transcend space but are enslaved by time. They are oriented toward God, too, as also are stones and stars, but unconsciously, determined from without. Man alone can look beyond space and time into eternity. Man alone, in Browning's phrase can "greet the unseen with a cheer." Man alone can make things which survive for millennia. Is it then impossible that the God-implanted soul which makes these things will survive their dissolution and the disintegration of man's own body? There are powerful, perhaps not conclusive, but very powerful (if properly understood) philosophical arguments for immortality. The human soul can be shown, by its intellectual behavior, to be of necessity a simple (i.e., uncompounded) substance and therefore indestructible. When the existence of God is proved, as it can be, without appeal to authority, it can be shown that such a God would never thwart the universal human desire conscious or unconscious, confessed or swaggeringly disavowed, for eternal survival. But above all and unanswerably, Divine Revelation (which, as I was later to learn from my Catholic instructors, need not be believed on mere say-so and hearsay but upon an irresistible chain of reasoning for one who, forgetting the Protestant travesty of philosophy and theology, goes to the Roman masters of Ontology, Theodicy, and Apologetics) approached through scholastic metaphysics, the most precise and sweeping of all the sciences, and through history which man has just learned with the turn of our century to write scientifically — divine Revelation assures us that human immortality is a certainty. Verily we may exult with Browning when he makes the students of their beloved "grammarian" carry their dead teacher up the mountain, singing, leaving the low valleys to take him to a peak where lightnings play, singing, not lamenting, because

He's for the morning.

CHAPTER VII

A VICTORY FOR GOD'S GRACE

"Too late have I loved Thee, O Beauty, so old and so new."

ONE summer about fourteen years ago, I was delighted to see, in my class called "Realism in Philosophy and Literature," two gentlemen in clerical garb.

There came a moment when I had to declare myself on a point in epistemology: in what sense is any general idea or concept or universal, like "humanity," real? Now Plato would say, I suppose, that the idea, "humanity," is more really real than any imperfect individual with a snub nose or an aquiline nose or a broken and lifted nose called Tom or Dick or Harry. Plato might be called an exaggerated realist because he would say that the idea of "humanity," more perfect even than the Hermes of Praxiteles which is more perfect than any concrete human being beheld by the illusion-haunted mind of man — Plato might say that the chaste universal, "humanity," has an existence quite independent of any finite soul like yours or mine. So, too, held Boethius, in one mood; but in another mood Boethius was apparently of the opinion that the idea "humanity" exists only as a name in the finite minds of individual human beings.

This second or nominalistic notion I did not like very well. But I felt constrained to defend it. For, although, as I now see, it cannot be held consistently without consciously or unconsciously surrendering to skepticism — the denial of the possibility of all knowledge — yet, since the days of Martin Luther, it has acted like a subtle poison on almost all non-Catholic modern thought, whether by way of acceptance or by way of a too violent rejection.

I observed, during my lecture, that one of the clerical gentlemen, with a face outlined like a cherub and complexioned like a glowing seraph, and with that unmistakably Celtic expression of those tribes which spiritually reconquered western Europe, was smiling and nodding a most enthusiastic negation. When class was dismissed I halted him. "Father," said I. "No, mister," he replied. For, as I found out later, he was but a

143

young scholastic, a student in Gonzaga College preparing to take holy orders as a Jesuit. "Well, Mr. McGoldrick," resumed I, "you seem to dissent from my view concerning universals. I wish that we might discuss it more fully." He was good enough to spend an evening with me during which he brought me over to the theory of moderate realism advocated by Aristotle and St. Thomas.

Let me phrase the rival formulations as Jacques Maritain, the eminent convert from Bergsonism to Catholicism, does in *An Introduction to Philosophy*. Nominalism contends: That which our ideas present to us as a universal has no real existence whatsoever. For Platonic realism: That which our ideas present to us as a universal really exists as a universal. Moderate realism, which I now came to espouse, temporizes with typical Catholic good sense and sanity as follows: That which our ideas present to us as a universal does not exist outside the mind as a universal; nevertheless, that which our ideas present to us as a universal exists outside the mind individuated. "For example *the* human nature *found alike in Peter, Paul, and John really exists, but it has no existence outside the mind except in these individual subjects and as identical with them; it has no separate existence, does not exist in itself.*"

When my spiritual adviser left me that evening I remarked that I had often felt very near to the Catholic Church. He laughed merrily. "Oh," said he, "you'll be a Catholic some day." When summer school ended, he disappeared. I did not see him for some five years when, as Father James B. McGoldrick, S.J., Dean of Seattle College, he returned to the University of Washington to complete a doctorate in Educational Psychology. Two years afterward he received me into the Church of Rome.

I. WHAT IS BEAUTY?

Meanwhile, I changed the title of my postgraduate seminar in "Realism" to "Recent Aesthetic Theory and Literary Criticism." I also offered for undergraduates a course which I christened "An Introduction to the Study of the Fine Arts." It had a threefold function: to engender a rudimentary appreciation of the dance, architecture, sculpture, painting, design, music, and imaginative literature; second, to compare the ways in which in the various arts the same problems were variously solved; third, to sketch the philosophy of form, technique, meaning, the sublime; the relations between beauty and truth; the comic; the relations between beauty and morality; and the religious significance of beauty and art.

I published a number of articles on these topics in *The Journal of Philosophy, The International Journal of Ethics,* and *Modern Philology.* I wrote a second book on Aesthetics which I have never published and never will — in its present form. But as I look back over my researches and meditations during those seven years I can understand why Father McGoldrick prophesied so confidently my ultimate conversion to Catholicism. For, ignorant though I was of Thomistic philosophy, yet in my own groping efforts to solve what was for me the critical problem, the relation between beauty and reality (the metaphysical significance of the aesthetic experience), I was forced into a sort of rough-hewn approxima- tion to the dialectic of the scholastics of the thirteenth and the twentieth centuries. I saw that there were broadly two logically possible solutions: either the experience of beauty is, as many neo-Buddhistic philosophical thinkers from Schopenhauer to Santayana have thought in our spiritually bankrupt age, a trafficking with illusion, a pseudo-spiritual drug taking — or this aesthetic experience penetrates to the very heart of that which is most constructively real in the universe. I saw that as a matter of his- torical fact the greatest works of art in all the most inspired ages have been produced by men who have held more or less explicitly to the latter conviction. And so my philosophical meanderings, already directed more and more by Plato and Aristotle, turned more and more directly toward thinkers as yet little known to me, toward St. Augustine and St. Thomas Aquinas and their followers, down to our contemporary, Jacques Mari- tain, toward the one and only continuous and cumulatively progressive *philosophia perennis.* I then discovered that scholastic Ontology and Natural Theology enunciated quite clearly what I was only stammering. And so I have spent many of the happiest hours of my last six years in the leisurely and prayerful composition of this book.

At this point, then, let me try to retrace some of the speculations which led, as far as the aesthetic phase of my life went, to my conversion in 1933.

Many artists, in all fields, have taken a hopelessly skeptical attitude toward the definition of beauty, because so many distinguished efforts have ended in apparently contradictory results. I began to see that these formulations of famous artists and philosophers were erroneous, not in what they affirmed, but in what they omitted. Each one emphasized ob- sessively a single facet of beauty. Some were exclusively subjective, some were intolerantly objective. Beauty, I realized, must be defined partly with qualities in objects, partly with spiritual states in the beholder, be he an artist or just an appreciator. Beauty stood before me confessed as an almost mystical marriage with reality, a profoundly religious experience. My task was to distill the attar from all the definitions. Or, to change the figure, finding that the definitions were not contradictory, but simply fragmentary, I sought to dovetail them all together picture-puzzle-wise.

All these considerations led me to construct a definition which, to my best knowledge, synthesizes all earlier attempts: An object is beautiful if it has unity and variety of form and contents, and congruous expressiveness or meanings, which arouse in the beholder a free intuition, a sentiment which centers in love, impulses to become one with it and impulses to manipulate its materials with a reverence for their unique properties.

By form I meant, in part, the arrangement of the contents or details (sounds, colors, lights, shades, lines) with a variety in unity compounded in harmony, symmetry, balance, or contrast, and evolution or emphasis or climax. Now I have already stated that my empirical survey of the most recent scientific discoveries had led me more and more to the conviction that the universe, despite all its dreadful dissonances, is fundamentally engaged in harmonious form making. I suggested that this conclusion might be deemed parallel with the belief of St. John of Patmos that God is Love. Or we might suggest that the universe is fundamentally form making because its Creator saturated it with His Love. The artist therefore would often be remolding forms into superforms. He would be working in rapport with God. Dimly, too, I realized, what my later reading in Aristotelian-Thomistic philosophy has made quite clear, that form is not a merely external thing, a silhouette alone, an "accidental" form, shape, but a substantial thing which saturates, which *informs* "prime matter" with which it fuses. Vaguely I realized that God, though not like the divine phantasm of the pantheist to be identified with the universe — that the true God, while transcending His creation, is nevertheless "informatively" and "operatively present" in every part of it. The artist, I began to see, was more or less consciously aware of this and as he remodeled some of God's things he was but reverently imitating their ultimate Creator and Conserver.

For me the meaning (what I prefer to call the expressiveness) of an object is its capacity to arouse associations in the mind of the contemplator. Poets dominated by the romantic tendency have been particularly luxurious in piling up these connotations which in things of beauty must, of course, be congruous with their design, form. Think of Wordsworth's meditations on the distant song of "The Solitary Reaper."

No Nightingale did ever chaunt
　　More welcome notes to weary bands
Of travellers in some shady haunt,
　　Among Arabian sands:
A Voice so thrilling ne'er was heard
In Spring-time from the Cuckoo-bird
Breaking the silence of the seas
Among the farthest Hebrides.

Will no one tell me what she sings? —
　　Perhaps the plaintive numbers flow
For old, unhappy, far-off things,
　　And battles long ago:
Or is it some more humble lay,
Familiar matter of today?
Some natural sorrow, loss, or pain,
That has been, and may be again?

Remember, in the "Ode to a Nightingale," what magic the one word "forlorn" had for John Keats.

Forlorn! the very word is like a bell
　　To toll me back from thee to my sole self!

What a treasure of meaning, too, the old Renaissance tune of "A Toccata of Galuppi's" led Browning to conjure up: St. Mark's Cathedral, the old rulers, the Doges wedding the sea with rings, the masquerades and balls of brilliant frivolous lords and ladies, the pathos of their brief glittering lives and of their mortality!

Dear dead women, with such hair, too — what's become of all the gold
Used to hang and brush their bosoms? I feel chilly and grown old.

From this meaning or connotation or expressiveness or suggestion, this capacity to arouse in our souls a particolored pageant of memories, we may pass to the first aspect of the spiritual state of the beholder, that kind of cognition (or intellection) which is characteristic of the aesthetic experience. Benedetto Croce has called it "expression" or "intuition," which he describes as a free spiritual experience. So important did this seem to the Italian philosopher, and so great was his idealistic prejudice against matter, that he defined beauty and art both exclusively in terms of this sort of intellection which he correctly described as free. This aesthetic intuition is free, because it is not bound by the dreaded pain of error or by the yearning for truth. Witness beautiful fairy tales. Of course, a work may be true as well as beautiful. Ruskin, no doubt, wrote validly when, in his essay on "The Pathetic Fallacy" in *Modern Painters,* he declared that the greatest poets pay their allegiance to both beauty and truth. But the artist is free to idealize as much as he pleases. This freedom has led many ill-advised contemporaries to emulate Schopenhauer in defining beauty as illusion. But such an interpretation would be rather misleading if, as I have suggested, the beauty lover and the beauty maker are living in the ways of God in their form making. Even when they are not uttering truths about God they are in rapport with Him, with the way He works. And the possession of freedom as a spiritual attribute is, as we have seen, a fact essential for the Catholic because he believes in God's mercy and in the possibility that we may cooperate with the infusions of His sanctifying and actual graces, that we may contribute to our own eternal salvation, to our ultimate abiding with Him.

We have next to ask ourselves what is the affective or emotional aspect of our experience of beauty. I came to characterize this as a sentiment which centers in love, itself an act of the will, as we have seen. I used the word "sentiment," after the fashion of certain contemporary psychologists and philosophers, Shand, Stout, McDougall, and others, to denote a complex or symphony of emotions focused on a specific object. These constellations of emotions evidently vary somewhat in the presence of various beautiful objects. But their common denominator lies in the fact that whatever the feeling may be, they are always organized by love, which I describe as Plato and as Christian doctrine do. Hence the further religious significance of beauty. For Plato, the love, whether of a man for a maid or for a fountain, a friend or a cause, is a passion so magnanimous that it expands to include the contemplation of God. Doubtless Wordsworth had something like the lack of this in mind when he described the prosaic peddler, Peter Bell, as one for whom a primrose by the rill "a primrose was and nothing more." On the other hand, such Platonism could hardly have been far from Tennyson's thoughts when he told the "little flower in the crannied wall" that, if he could only know all about it, he would be able to fathom the mysteries of God. The Christian act of charity asserts the same truth from an opposite and far more profound approach when the Catholic, apostrophizing God, prays, "I love my neighbor as myself because of my love of Thee."

We come now to the conative aspects of spiritual activity called by the scholastic philosopher "appetition." For the aesthetic experience these strivings are twofold: impulses to become one with the object, and impulses to manipulate its materials with a reverence for their unique properties. The former set of impulses has been called *Einfühlung* (empathy) by several Germans like Lipps and Lotze, and in England by Vernon Lee, all of whom have been inclined to define beauty solely in terms of this concept. It is indeed very important. In the case of sympathy you are quite as fully aware of yourself as of the object of your solicitude. When, by contrast, your impulses are empathetic, you become one with the beautiful object by forgetting yourself, you are somewhat like the mystic who, in his adoration of God, loses himself to save himself. Thus empathy is one of the best of disciplines for religious reverence.

The second sort of conation, striving, or appetition, the impulse to manipulate the materials of the object (bronze or brick or marble, brazen French horns and air waves, glass or granite or steel and reinforced concrete) with a reverence for their unique properties, involves the principle of technique. This, too, is so significant that there are those, like Mr. Marriot, who have been on the verge of maintaining an extreme antithetical to Croce's, the ultramaterialistic attitude that the nature of the matter employed determines the composition of the beautiful. Now technique is skill. And aesthetic technique is reverent skill. You do not endeavor to make one kind of stuff do what another can better perform. Donatello did not use rugged stone for his statues of the almost pathetically youthful shepherd-poet David who slew the giant, Goliath, with a sling. For one version, Donatello resorted to smooth delicately veined marble, for another to smooth bronze with its mellow glooms and gleams. This reverence for matter as well as for spirit is of the essence of all genuine Christianity. For did not Jesus call His body a temple? In the sublime opening chapter of the Gospel according to St. John, which is the usual conclusion of the Holy Sacrifice of the Mass, there occurs a sentence about the "Word" at which every Catholic makes a genuflection: "And the Word became Flesh."

Some of my friends have quite reasonably objected to the last part of my definition on the ground that it would not apply to the lover of nature. How, for instance, can he who finds the sunset beautiful manipulate its materials? If they had extended their objection to the art lover as opposed to the art maker they would have found the answer. The art lover, the mere appreciator, unlike the artist, does not manually manipulate the materials of the beautiful object in the making. But he does manipulate them imaginatively. The nature lover does precisely the same thing. Francis Thompson will help us with one of his magnificent descriptions of the mind of Shelley.

He is still at play, save only that his play is such as manhood stops to watch, and his playthings are those which the gods give their children. The universe is his box of toys. He dabbles his fingers in the day-fall. He is gold-dusty with tumbling amidst the stars. He makes bright mischief with the moon. The meteors nuzzle their noses in his hand. He teases into growling the kennelled thunder, and laughs at the shaking of its fiery chain. He dances in and out of the gates of heaven: its floor is littered with his broken fancies. He runs wild over the fields of ether. He chases the rolling world. He gets between the feet of the horses of the sun. He stands in the lap of patient nature, and twines her loosened tresses after a hundred wilful fashions to see how she will look nicest in his song.

I was getting my preparation for the appreciation of a lyrical poet far greater than Shelley, St. John of the Cross, the Mystical Doctor, and of how, after he had so ruthlessly detached himself from nature and man, he could at length return to all created things with the pure and tender rapture of a child, because on every mountain peak and in every lily cup and in the gentle laughter of a nun he could discern the triune presence of the Ineffable Trinity.

> Our bed is of flowers
> By dens of lions encompassed,
> Hung with purple,
> Made in peace,
> And crowned with a thousand shields of gold.
>
> In Thy footsteps
> The young ones run Thy way;
> At the touch of the fire
> And by the spiced wine,
> The divine balsam flows.
>
> When Thou didst regard me
> Thine eyes imprinted in me Thy grace;
> For this didst Thou love me again,
> And thereby mine eyes did merit
> To adore what in Thee they saw.

II. DRAWING CLOSER TO GOD

I had begun to read a fair amount of Catholic Philosophy. Yet I was still hoping to reach my conclusions without dogma, the utterance of authority, and without the acceptance of Divine Revelation, but rather by empirical proof. I subscribed for a year to *The New Scholasticism*. As far as Catholic Theology was concerned, I cared only for Natural Theology in so far as it seeks to prove the existence of God and the soul without appeal to dogma.

I went a good deal to the St. James Cathedral to sit in the organ loft with the organist, Dr. Franklin Sawyer Palmer. Doctor Palmer, nephew of the celebrated Harvard philosopher, George Herbert Palmer, was an organist who had studied widely in Europe and an expert dermatologist whose interest in skin diseases led him to inspect a most revolting and baffling case which was treated at Lourdes. He went to scoff and remained to pray. But, of course, there were many more cogent reasons which made him a Catholic. He taught me to understand and to love Gregorian Chant. He was my godfather at my baptism several years later. In turn I was asked to be one of his honorary pallbearers. It was the first Catholic funeral I had attended since the one I witnessed as described in my first chapter. Out of my intense love of him and my morbid memories of many funerals conducted by various Protestant denominations, I entered the cathedral cold with dread. I left at the conclusion of the Requiem High Mass in a state of radiant exaltation.

At last came my providential meeting with Mary. With her I began, though with no suggestion from her, to attend Catholic churches quite regularly. Our first visit together was on a Good Friday afternoon when for the first time I witnessed the great ceremony commemorating for three hours the three hours of agony of our Saviour on the cross. I met her friend, Father William J. O'Brien, an incomparable compound of good-fellowship, sanity, and piety. From him I learned many things. He it was who married Mary and me in the rectory of the Church of Immaculate Conception.

I redoubled my study of Catholic doctrine. I expressed a desire to talk with Father McGoldrick, and so Father O'Brien brought to pass our reunion. Father O'Brien was driving Mary and me home one afternoon when he suddenly descried my old Jesuit acquaintance and swerved after him posthaste. This was the beginning of a series of discussions with Father McGoldrick. Our talks remained very discursive for a long period. But it occurred to me that I was beginning to understand what Father McClory meant long before when he expressed the hope that some day I might get the "grace."

Sanctifying grace is God's greatest gift to us in this life, earned for us by the infinite merits which our Lord treasured up for us by His Redemption. It is the fountainhead of the three supreme virtues, Faith, Hope, and Charity, which are supernatural because they, too, are not won by our wills but freely given us by our heavenly Father. Of this grace I began to feel the glow in church kneeling beside Mary, turning from the altar to look at her uplifted face with its angelic piety and turning with renewed fervor to behold the celestial drama of the Mass which I was just beginning to comprehend. Father McGoldrick, too, with his profound charity and ardor, seemed often God's messenger both sharpening my logic and relaxing, like a physician, the proud tension which had so long held my mind impervious to God's great gift. As Father Many puts it, in his *Marvels of Grace:*

What must have been in the minds of the angels as they gazed upon the great God of heaven and earth, who from His throne on high, by a single act of His will, had launched countless worlds into space? What must have been their thoughts as they saw Him descend from His Throne of glory, cross their ranks, annihilate the immense void that separates heaven and earth, abase Himself to the point of nothingness, and take on our nature, not in the state of its original innocence, but in that miserable state to which sin had reduced it? What could possibly have been the motive of so stupendous an abasement as this? . . . Jesus had but one end in view in humiliating Himself in this fashion. It was to elevate us to Himself by grace. . . . What was more, He did not believe He had done enough to secure for us so inestimable a gift. He willed to subject Himself to the most outrageous opprobrium and to experience human miseries to the uttermost, and all this to prove that even a God-man could not suffer too much for grace.

Something of this I began to sense when, on the unforgettable Good Friday afternoon, I listened to the cameolike sermonettes of Father Vincent Carey, O.S.B., and to the prayers and music which centered around the seven last poignant sayings from our Lord as He writhed in the agony which only one who was both God and Man could suffer on the cross. With the coming of grace, then, I saw that we could actually share in the divine drama. As St. Basil has it, "Through the medium of grace, which is loftier than anything we could desire, we become 'gods.' " God

Himself tarries within us. We become gods by virtue of our submission to His holy will. From my later and clearer insight into the nature of beauty I could realize how, by yielding to the infusion of ineffable grace, we could, emulating at a far distance saint and mystic, lose ourselves to save ourselves. As St. Thomas has it, "Grace, making the soul pleasing, disposes it to the personal possession of God." Christ, before His Ascension, promised us the Holy Ghost for our guest: "I will ask the Father, and He shall give you another Paraclete, that He may abide with you forever." St. Leo exclaims: "That God should call Man His son, and that man should call God his Father, is a gift surpassing all others." Or, as St. Augustine says: "The Son of God, the only-begotten according to nature, by a marvellous condescension has become Son of Man that we, who are the sons of men by nature, might become sons of God by grace."

"Human nature," writes Father Many, "is, so to speak, the résumé of all Creation. Indeed, all the kingdoms of creation are represented in man: the minerals are represented in his body, the plants in his vegetative life, the animals in his sensitive life, the angels in his intellectual life. Hence man is, to use the terminology of the ancients, a little world, a 'microcosm.' " Thus God created in us a multifarious unity and, by Himself becoming Man, He recapitulated "all things in His adorable Person." "I am the vine," said Jesus to his followers, "you the branches." The grace He gives us is our sap. As St. Augustine summed it up, "The head is the only Son of God; the body is His Church." This is the priceless union that grace brings. This is the inspiration of our charity toward our neighbors. "If you have charity," exults St. Augustine, "you possess all things."

"He that shall lose his life for Me," said our Blessed Lord, "shall save it." My period of worship has been relatively brief. But, even in the face of a fair number of sharp vicissitudes, I can echo the acknowledgment of St. Teresa of Avila: "I have never known real sorrow from the day I decided to serve with all my power my Lord and divine Consoler."

III. THE CHURCH ALERT AGAINST ILLUSIONS

At about this time my typically non-Catholic superstition that all Catholics are of their essence superstitious was profoundly shaken when I read *The Spiritual Life,* by the great and humble Sulpician, Father Adolphe Tanquerey, who warns against such a search for sanctifying grace that it would seek to be coupled with a desire for visions, super-natural words and divine touches. "The great mystics are unanimous in teaching that one must neither desire nor ask for these *extraordinary* favors. These are not necessary means to the divine union; nay, at times they are rather obstacles owing to our evil tendencies." St. John of the Cross, in particular, points this out. He asserts that "the desire for revelations deprives faith of its purity." This ought to be clear since a prayer for revelation might at any time be, as I soon found, a faltering doubt masquerading as faith. Father Tanquerey warns us that such a desire develops a dangerous curiosity which becomes a source of illusions, fills the mind with vain fancies, and often proves the want of humility and of submission to our Lord, who, through His public revelations has given all that is needed for salvation.

Of the arguments for the Divinity of our Lord and his consequent infallibility as a public Revealer, I will have much more to say than I have said as yet. This I shall do when later I sketch my experience with the proofs of the historical authenticity of Jesus. As for private revela-tions, I was delighted with my discovery of Father Tanquerey's outline of the Catholic rules for the guidance of the apprentice to asceticism, in order to winnow the true from the false. These rules demand an attesta-tion of freedom from psychoneuroses, the possession of sound judgment and education, the freedom from habits of exaggeration, from mental weakness after disease or long fasts, the endowment of "*solid* and tried *virtue*" rather than "a more or less sensible fervor," the depth of sin-cerity, of humility, and of reticence in the company of persons other than the spiritual director, the measure of obedience to the adviser, the question of self-discipline and endurance of "passive trials" during "the first stages of contemplation."

But these rules do not alone suffice. The subject matter of the alleged revelations must be examined. Anathema are "the alleged revelations of spiritualists which deny several of our dogmas" and are "opposed to the unanimous teaching of the Fathers and Theologians." We should also at least suspect an alleged revelation "claiming to settle the controversy between the Thomists and the Molinists. God is not wont to pronounce on such questions." The examiner would "likewise reject visions *opposed to morality and decency*." Nor should we lend credence to "commands," purporting to come from God, which are "impossible of realization, for God does not command the impossible."

The spiritual adviser must therewith turn to the effects of the supposed

illumination on the soul of the recipient. "According to St. Ignatius
and St. Teresa, a divine vision causes at first a sense of wonderment and
of fear, soon to be followed by *a sense of deep and lasting peace, of joy
and of security.* The contrary is true with regard to diabolical visions."
It is thus that "the devil brings about the downfall of souls." Accord-
ingly, "true revelations strengthen the soul in humility, obedience, patience, and conformity to the divine will; *false* ones beget pride, presumption, and disobedience." Confirmatory signs, like miracles and other
important manifestations, are to be received humbly, if they are apparently granted, but also in a spirit of reverent insistence on verification.
If these signs are not vouchsafed, we should not despair. "The parish
priest of Lourdes requested our Lady in apparition to make a sweet
briar to bloom in the midst of winter; the sign was not granted, but
she did cause a miraculous spring to well forth which was destined to heal
both body and soul."

We may analyze the origins of some errors that have appeared in some
alleged revelations sincerely believed in. There are false statements im-
putable to contemporary imperfections in the knowledge of the sciences.
"St. Frances of Rome asserts that she beheld a heaven of crystal between
the empyrean and the starry heaven." Nor will an institution as prudent
as the Catholic Church leave the directions of the spiritual adviser of the
mystic or pseudo-mystic unscrutinized. Historical errors are also detected.
"Thus among the various accounts of the Passion [the Crucifixion of
Christ] many little details are either contradictory . . . or in opposition
to the best historical authorities." Again, at times, "a revelation may be
unwittingly *altered* by the seer himself when he attempts to explain, or
still oftener by those to whom he dictates his revelations. St. Brigid
realized herself that at times she retouched her revelations the better
to explain them. . . . It is acknowledged today that the scribes who wrote
the revelations of Mary of Agreda, of Catherine Emmerich, and of Marie
Lataste modified them to an extent difficult to determine."

Holy Mother Church imposes on herself a most judicious reserve. "The
Church accepts no revelations except after long and careful investigations, and even then she does not force them on the faithful." In this
practice she is loyally emulated by her saints. "Thus Blessed Julienne of
Liége, chosen by God to bring about the institution of the Feast of
Corpus Christi, did not submit her project to the theologians until
twenty-two years after her first vision; fully sixteen years elapsed before
the Bishop of Liege instituted the feast for his diocese, and it was six

years after the death of the Blessed Julienne herself that Pope Urban IV made it a feast of the entire Church," which always delays "long years before pronouncing, and decides only after the matter itself and its bearing on Dogma and Liturgy have been carefully considered." We should all secure, before we "pronounce with certitude . . . convincing proofs which are well summarized by Benedict XIV in his work on canonizations." A spiritual director should withhold all admiration for a penitent professing a vision lest he lead the seer thereby to believe too hastily that his experience is veridical. Yet the spiritual director should seek the confidence of his consultant by kindly treatment.

We see therefore — what I have set out to show — how the Catholic Church is the last institution to encourage superstition. What she exhorts all to do is to pray, and we all, Catholic or Protestant or Jew, Moslem or Buddhist, unbeliever or pagan, have the inestimable opportunity to comply with this exhortation. My own prayers, as Protestant, as agnostic and as heterodox theist, were often neglected and always too heavily weighted with egocentric desires, some of which were too trivially worldly. And yet I may add that the Catholic Church does not prohibit, it even encourages, a reasonable number of worthy temporal requests in our orisons and other devout meditations and longings. But I had to approach closely to Catholicism to learn how to pray.

When, out of regard for my mother alone, I attended the services in her Anglican Church and smothered my boredom, and when out of respect for her alone, I kneeled prayerless, when the congregation kneeled for the few moments requested at intervals of us, my knees ached and my torso writhed. I can now, in my happiest moments, kneel alone in a chapel before the Blessed Sacrament and pray for a half-hour, an hour or two hours, and arise refreshed like a strong man about to run a race. I recommend to all unbelievers, as a sincerely executed experiment, the frequent repetition of this practice.

IV. WHAT IS THE ASSENT OF FAITH?

After a long period of reading and of discussions with Father McGoldrick, I was seized one night with a great enthusiasm and I suddenly exclaimed: "Father, will you baptize me?" He answered, "No." He *seemed* to think, however, that, just as I had given evidence of faithful, prolonged, and fairly intelligent study, I had also something of the appearance of one who had been illumined by the first faint dawn of some

actual grace which God will give any earnest seeker as a prelude to or
reinforcement of that sanctifying grace which conversion and the reception of such Sacraments as Baptism, Penance, and Communion will
bring. At all events, whatever precisely Father McGoldrick did think in
his heart, he now initiated a long period of systematic instruction in
Catholic doctrine replying to my thronging inquiries and objections with
indefatigable patience and ardor.

The Church desires that none of her children be creatures of blind
faith, a faith below reason. Even the simplest of those who are born
and bred under her shadows, receive not only initial instruction and the
lifelong inspiration of her rich and glorious Liturgy, together with the
grace-drenching Sacraments of Baptism and Confirmation once, of Confession (Penance) and Communion (Holy Eucharist) as often as they
seek them, of Extreme Unction at death, and, in accordance with their
choice of vocations, of Matrimony or Holy Orders, but they are further
exhorted to use their reason without fear and to bring their difficulties
without shamefacedness, as often as they wish, to their spiritual adviser
or to any other reverend father who inspires in them confidence or
hopefulness.

To begin with, faith is asserted to be grounded on reason and to crown
it. According to Father Gabriel Brunhes, Professor in the Higher Semi-
nary at Dijon, in his work entitled *Faith and Its Rational Justification,*
the Catholic might begin with man's coming face to face with God manifested in the person of Jesus, seeing how Christ's preaching and miracles
amazed the people. He might behold the inspiring trust of the centurion
who pleaded for the cure of the grievous palsy of his servant, but who,
when Jesus set forth to return with him replied: "Lord, I am not worthy
that Thou shouldst enter under my roof; but only say the word and my
servant shall be healed," He might listen to the superb reply of Peter,
standing among the bewildered disciples when Jesus asked of them,
"Who do you say that I am?" when this one impetuous follower exclaimed: "Thou art Christ, the Son of the Living God." Then, down the
centuries, the Catholic or the student of Catholicism would do well to
survey the vast procession of converts, simple and erudite — a highly
intellectual positivist and eminent literary critic like Brunetière slowly
surrendering with his searching intellectualism, or a great contemporary
poet and statesman, like Paul Claudel, surrendering to the truth with
his "hostile prejudices" burned away in a lightning flash of understanding. Yet no less remarkable, as credentials, are the faiths of very simple

folk, sustained for a lifetime. Baptized in childhood, "not highly cultured, and with no knowledge of apologetics," they yet "have a luminous faith, and show themselves to be most intelligent in matters of religion." Curious, again, is the adherence to the *Credo* of many a corrupted and often excommunicated or self-excommunicated sinner, so that numbers of them repent and re-enter the Church even though in their temporal life they are very healthy and happy.

From my prolonged non-Catholic education I had imbibed, perhaps very stupidly, two curious superstitions: (1) that faith is wholly a matter of emotions and private convictions to be coddled along by the kindly pragmatic psychology of a William James, or blasted by the relentless veracity of a psychoanalyst or a behaviorist; (2) that if you accept the Catholic faith, you must accept authority blindly and servilely.

Here, on the contrary, are the facts as I discovered them to be. As an outsider I was expected, on purely rational grounds, to be ready to defend these theses: (1) that there is a God; (2) that Christ actually existed, whether God or man; (3) that He claimed to be and actually was and is Divine; (4) that He founded a church, one Church; (5) that He endowed that Church with His own authentic messages; and (6) that He guaranteed to that Church the insight to interpret those messages through ever changing ages to the end of time. Then, and only then, so I learned, would I be prepared to believe in revelation and authority, in a God who can neither deceive nor be deceived. I was astounded to realize by continued and widely varied experience how successfully these six propositions can be defended against what more and more clearly proved to be the ignorant and perverse misapprehensions of both non-Catholics and apostates. I have found the latter to be invariably sufferers from more or less slothful ignorance or carnal laxity or, most frequently, from that very pride, that most subtle and terrible sin which hurled Satan out of heaven.

To approach a psychological description of faith, we may well employ the definition of the Vatican Council, assembled to study that tendency called "Modernism" which arose nearly a generation ago within the Catholic Church, and which, for a time, tempted me. "Faith," pronounced the majestic Council, "is a supernatural virtue, by which, prepared and aided by the grace of God, we hold as true what He has revealed, not because of the real truth of things perceived by the natural light of reason, but because of the authority of God Himself, who reveals them, who can neither deceive nor be deceived." Whether we find reasons to solve problems or whether we scrutinize mysteries with only a partial, even if ever increasing, understanding, we realize "that God invites men to a life of friendship, of intimacy, with Himself." Faith is our response "to the advances of divine grace."

Faith, then, is compounded of intellect, will, and sanctifying grace. It is not irrational; it is always somehow or other, deeply grounded in reason, that is, if it is genuine faith, even in its simplest and most abrupt outpourings. Catholic philosophy is the only philosophy which, as any student of its epistemology can quickly learn, makes out a sound case for certain as opposed to more or less probable knowledge. The first impulse of faith may or may not be highly conscious. But lest anyone who shares my early superstitions should misinterpret these phrases let me quote once more directly from the Vatican Council with my italics: "If anyone shall say that the One true God, our Creator and Lord, cannot be certainly known *by the natural light of human reason through created things let him be anathema.*"

Faith, then, is not emotional; it is intellectual. It naturally requires, especially for the man who confuses "intellectual honesty" with arrogance, an "assent of the will." But to become a *virtue,* which is a habit, faith must rise to a supernatural elevation. True faith, as a virtue, is classified by Catholic doctrine as theological, that is, as a virtue whose object is God. It is won or maintained only after a hard fight by a humble reason, and requires the grace of God. How profoundly and supremely rational in its basis is the Catholic faith we shall comprehend when, in a later chapter, I will dilate on the oneness, holiness, catholicity, and apostolic continuity of the Church of Rome. In order to do this I will have enlisted, not one or two of the ways of knowing with which the other philosophers are to some degree obsessed, but all of the methods: skeptical, empirical, *a priori,* pragmatic, mystical, and authoritarian. Meanwhile I will merely point to the staggering coherence and astounding comprehensiveness of Catholic doctrine which becomes more and more evident to the faithful as they continue in the practice of this theological virtue. Truly, in these respects, Catholicism is a supreme and matchless synthesis of all but uncountable strands. Often the skeptic accuses it of plagiarism from other religions. It is not plagiarism, because the warp and woof of these tendencies are transformed into the perfect variety-in-unity of its sumptuous web. God did not turn His face away from simpler or even more decadent religious insights. In all religions, as St. Paul implies, He has "never left Himself without witness." But He founded only one Church. Consequently it is this Church alone which can incorporate and clarify, without danger of error, the flickering visions of all the other religions. As St. Thomas Aquinas assures us in his *Contra Gentiles:*

Final beatitude consists in the vision of God. But man can attain to that only by putting himself to school with God. Now this instruction, to be suited to human nature, cannot be given all at once, but must be given by degrees. Do we not constantly see a teacher give his pupil the conclusion of an argument while the pupil does not at once understand all the steps of the demonstration? The teacher's authority, then, comes in by way of proof. Without the use of a summary method of this kind, sciences of the greatest usefulness could not be popularized. The pupil begins by believing so that he may more easily reach in the end full knowledge of his subject. Not otherwise does God deal with us, for the beatific vision is but the fulfilment of the gradual instruction given here below.

It is widely believed by contemporary psychologists that, because scholastic philosophers often make use of the term "faculties," they are proponents of an outdated science of mind or behavior. If these gentlemen would but patch over some of the gaps in their historical knowledge they would soon discern that St. Thomas and his followers never held the silly belief of much more modern men, that the soul is compartmentally divided into faculties in the later denotation of the word. The Schoolmen knew as well as we do that in the mind cognition (intellection) and conation (appetition, striving, or impulse which includes desire and will), though often acting in opposition to each other, are not substances or parts of substances but varying operations of a soul which is itself a unified substance. The scholastic philosophers have always known, as non-Catholic psychologists are only just now rediscovering, that "affects," such as emotions, are largely physiological, which sometimes inhibit sometimes reinforce the two strictly psychical operations. But they felt (as do all psychologists today, no matter what terms happen to be in fashion) that these two aspects of spiritual activity (cognition and conation) may be studied in abstraction, that is by artificially focusing our attention on one of them.

Having dealt with the role of intellection (cognition) in faith we may, with Father Brunhes, direct our gaze to the function of the will in the genesis of this supernatural virtue, the will by which we become "morally responsible for the attitude that we freely take toward our spontaneous inclinations [appetitions]."

When Jesus warned us: "He that believeth . . . shall be saved, but he that believeth not shall be condemned," he meant "that those to whom the Gospel has been proposed" — expounded adequately for their capacities, I presume — "are responsible for their attitude toward the divine message, and hence, that free will plays an essential part in the genesis and preservation of the faith." As the ardent St. Augustine has it: "It is love that asks, it is love that seeks, it is love that acts, it is love that gives assent to revelation, and it is love, too, that sustains that assent once it is given." Or, in the words of the more austere St. Thomas, "Faith is an assent given by the intellect to divine truth under the command of the will moved by the grace of God." The mere fact that reason justifies faith leaves us still without a motive for it. Brunetière said that he was moved by poignant eagerness to "give oneself up to the truth." Newman confessed that he was stirred by anxiety lest he lapse into "sinning against the light." The once eccentric and brilliantly rebellious Péguy developed such an abundant appreciation of the authority of God that he decided that it would not do "to play the fool." Madelein Semar, the mystic, was driven to abandon the negations which she long shared with Renan and Nietzsche by *le beau désir* for progress in holiness. The will inspires in us, as Father Brunhes puts it, "renunciation, charity, prayer beginning with aspiration to higher things; then, when the idea of God has risen upon the horizon, prayer properly so called — moral activities which require the right use of free will. The end of this ever more and more passionate progress is certitude."

It is the will which goads a Newman to proclaim that "Ten thousand difficulties do not make one doubt." With some of these "difficulties" we will wrestle in the next chapter. It is the will, at its best so practical, which, as we are told by Father Brunhes, "serves to enrich and furnish" the "abstract ideas" of the intellect "with an experimental knowledge." And the will's decisions "stimulate the curiosity of the intellect and . . . help it to focus the attention on the consideration of the object of study." The will's intervention — in contrast with temptations of vagrant wishes — is not a hindrance but a help to the quest for certitude, through the removal of internal obstacles, like passion and prejudices, and through the conquest of physical evils, such as droughts and diseases, or at least through the steeling of fortitude in the presence of external obstacles, such as earthquakes and cancers, which, for the present at least, are invincible. And the often astonishing intervention of our wills in the teeth of the most shattering catastrophies prepares us for the understanding of the infinitely more amazing intervention of God "in the historical order in order to guarantee the utterance of His messengers." Will, especially the loving will, is a marvelous discipline. We owe to St. Augustine the declaration that "If anyone pretended to see into the will of a man with whom he was not friendly, everyone would laugh at his impudence and folly. . . . If anyone wishes to understand the will of God, let him become His friend."

With this reflection on the intervention of God we may return to the contemplation of the service which His gift of sanctifying grace renders to faith. Without this intervention man's will might be his ruin and he might, as St. Prosper warns us, "find himself at the bottom of that abyss into which the abuse of his free will has cast him." According to the Vatican Council:

Although the assent of faith is by no means a blind movement of the mind, nevertheless, no one can adhere to the teaching of the Gospel, as he must do to attain to salvation, without an illumination and inspiration of the Holy Spirit, who gives to all sweetness in adhering to and believing truth. Hence faith is in itself a gift of God, even when it does not work by charity, and the act of faith is a work of salvation, because by it man submits himself freely to God Himself when he consents to and cooperates with grace which he could resist.

Man cannot too often pray, "O Holy Spirit, sweet guest of my soul, remain with me and see that I ever remain with Thee." For, as Father Brunhes shows, the Holy Ghost, if often invited by us, "never ceases to perfect the knowledge which comes by faith, in order to the realization of such progress as we have summarily described when dealing with the intellect and the will." The articles of faith become for us ever more and more intricately and intimately integrated. And amidst all our trials, their "loveliness, sweetness, and power" become ever more and more manifest and persuasive.

V. LIBERTY OF THE CHILDREN OF GOD

As regards the free will possessed by man and applied in his act of faith, no scholastic philosopher has ever been so naïve as to think that the issue is between absolute determinism and absolute indeterminism. They have always recognized the fact that we are determined by natural influences, both hereditary and environmental, to a very large extent.

Let the students of genetics, physiological psychology, and sociology decide among themselves the apportioning. The scholastic philosopher and Catholic theologian await the results of their investigation and will gratefully and respectfully accept every fact which the naturalists can, by their legitimate methods of proof, experimental and statistical, establish as such. These discoveries, indeed, will be of the utmost service to philosophy and theology, for even though the natural sciences cannot, so to speak, topsy-turvyize the findings of the much more fundamental science of being, metaphysics, they can enrich enormously its outlines with their specialized research, just as metaphysics, which is no dictator but a servant, can clarify the fundamental concepts from which the natural sciences must exfoliate.

As for those looked upon as to a large degree mentally helpless, we are getting our first startling glimpses of an interior life in these warped creatures of which we little dreamed. More lately, Father J. S. Cammack, S.J., in his *Moral Problems of Mental Defect*, has reviewed exhaustively and quite objectively all the facts and theories available, and has shown us conclusions which would stagger the amateur eugenist social reformers, and politician sterilizers could they become patient and unsentimental enough to travel with him on his serenely erudite journey. Who, then, are the real contrasts on earth to the saints, who enjoy the greatest amplitude of liberty? They are the ones who have allowed themselves to be determined more and more by their own feverish, clashing wishes for the things of the world taken as ends in themselves. They are the most servile of all slaves though they may rule entire nations. They are the most superstitious and pitiable of magic mongers and idolaters.

Let the unnaturally naturalistic, absolute determinist think twice. Does he believe, even in the slightest degree in love? In a love perhaps powerfully "conditioned," as the contemporary physiological psychologist may quite properly declare. But does this empirical psychologist believe that any human being ever loves with the slightest spark of spontaneity, or that one single human being has ever, however slightly, however naïvely, "idealized" his beloved? If this psychologist does, he must believe in freedom.

The reality of human freedom has been guaranteed by the Christian Revelation which, in turn, as we note elsewhere in this book, can be proved by the unaided reason without authority. But I have learned, from St. John of the Cross, a purely philosophical argument for freedom that is the most conclusive of all. It is introspective. Yet it can be tested and verified by anyone who tries. For although I have gone but a very little way with St. John of the Cross, I have gone far enough to know that anyone who learns to say, with even a modicum degree of sincerity to God, "Thy will be done" — such a person, more and more as he proceeds on such a way, will learn with ever growing clarity and richness the meaning of an immortal phrase, the "glorious liberty of the children of God." He will find himself in a state distinctly the opposite to that of those "Illuminists" and "Quietists" of all ages against whom St. John of the Cross continually crusaded. He will find that though his "faculties" are more or less "at rest" they "are working, not actively but passively, by receiving that which God operates in them." Oh, yes, they will be working "passively"; but they will be working with more fiery, vivid, and victorious energy than they ever worked before. For the "resting" soul is most industriously purging off every luxurious and conceited craving that arises to distract it from the ministrations of the Hound of Heaven. It is a hard job to be even relatively undistracted amid "the blooming, buzzing confusion" of the sensations which assail us, alike in society and in solitude. It is a hard job to sweep the memory and the imagination clean. Sometimes, so strenuous is the process, that it will render the frail flesh all too susceptible to supposed "ecstasies" and "trances" and "raptures." But if we follow the Mystical Doctor, we will not allow ourselves, like the sentimental religious self-deceivers, to gloat over these abnormalities which arouse the not always unjust suspicions of the psychopathologist. For these overwrought moods may be of the devil, not of God. And if they are of God they are to a certain extent exposures of our own cringing weakness, our unworthiness to be the recipients of messages from a Lover so tremendous. Thus the "faculties" of the soul, although in one sense at rest, will have more to do than they ever did before.

VI. HUMANISM MINUS RELIGION

Coming now to the humanists and their assertions that they can make a religion out of their love of their fellow men without believing in God, a passage from Arnold Lunn's *A Saint in the Slave Trade* will impress any honest man who has ever been a worker with organized, "scientific" charity or a recipient of its services:

'They analyzed helpfulness recently,' writes Father Ronald Knox, 'in the psychological laboratory at Pharsalia, Oregon. The analysis showed, I am told, the following results:

Love of interference............	32 per cent
Pride of workmanship............	22 per cent
Desire for gratitude.............	11 per cent
Desire for admiration............	11 per cent
Self-importance	10 per cent
Reaction from suppressed contempt	9 per cent
Genuine moral altruism...........	5 per cent.'

Philanthropy, in the exact sense of the word — love of man — is seldom found excepting in a religious setting, for it is one thing to work for the benefit of humanity, as many secularists have done, it is quite another matter to love men. Indeed, there would seem to be some necessary connection between the first and the second great commandments, for the saints aflame with love of God have found it easier than other people to love their neighbors.

Now I have endured a very substantial amount of suffering, most of which I have deemed irrelevant to parade in this book. And I have been a close and agitated witness of many more physical evils, more dreadful than any which ever palsied my own mind and body. And I have read and heard with horror graphic narrations of physical evils even more overpowering. And yet today I do not agree with either Nietzsche or with what Arnold Lunn dubbs "the humanist premise that happiness in this world is the only sane criterion of conduct." But I agree with Mr. Lunn that if, just for the sake of argument, we should accept the humanist premise "we should reach the paradoxical result that Christian conduct satisfies the criterion of the humanist and that humanist conduct does not. Happiness, in other words, evades the man who consciously pursues it, whereas experience confirms the paradox of Thomas à Kempis: 'When you have got so far that tribulation is sweet to you and savors of Christ, then indeed it will be well with you, and you will have discovered Paradise on earth.' " À Kempis knew what the surrender to grace meant.

I am not implying that you must have a cancer or poverty coupled with a copious brood of children or that it is necessary for you to be on your deathbed or to be bereaved of a beloved little daughter to be happy. Many have lived in a state of grace and happiness without any of these disasters. Yet I know of certain persons steeped in grace and possessed of the Catholic faith — three dying of a cancer, two parents on the verge of poverty with a tumultuous abundance of children, two men on their deathbeds, and three bereaved of a little daughter — all of whom sustained their happiness and whose grace-born faith became, if anything, stronger than ever. Not a one of these individuals could be branded as stupid, stolid, or callous. And although I have read much psychopathological literature and have had a very solid clinical experience, I have not found in a single one of these cases a single trace of morbidity or vapid sentimentality or a single tendency toward unrealism or a single adumbration of mental abnormality.

By contrast we may quote with Mr. Lunn a passage from one of his controversial opponents, Professor Joad. It has reference to Bertrand Russell, who shared with Professor Whitehead the authorship of the famous and learned *Principia Mathematica*. Bertrand Russell is an enthusiastic atheist with an antidotal enthusiasm for what he vaguely calls values and what he rather sentimentally accolades as love. Having reached a skeptical attitude even toward the sacrosanct science of physics, he has healed his outraged disillusionment by writing giddy books on what he takes to be justice and happiness. The following is a specimen of his ripe wisdom from his *Education and the Good Life:* "In teaching my own children . . . I shall not teach them that faithfulness to one partner through life is in any way desirable or that a permanent marriage should be regarded as excluding temporary episodes." Some further knowledge of his sociological scherzo may be gained from the quotation from Professor Joad who, though he opposed Christianity, is clearly much less in agreement with Lord Russell on the nature of happiness than he is with Catholicism. Writes Professor Joad:

It is notorious today that heavenly rewards no longer attract and infernal punishments no longer deter with their pristine force; young people are frankly derisive of both, and, seeing no prospect of divine compensation in the next world for the wine and kisses that morality bids them eschew in this one, take more or less unanimously to the wine and kisses. Unfortunately the pleasurable results anticipated from these sources fail to materialize. That unchecked indulgence in the more obvious types of pleasure is unsatisfying is the unanimous teaching of those who have had the leisure and opportunity to try them in all ages. It is the more unfortunate that it is a truth which nobody believes to be true until he has discovered it for himself.

Professor Joad's allusion to the "pristine force" of references to "heavenly rewards . . . and infernal punishments" will arouse in the cynic the old sneer that Christianity is supported solely by its bullyragging methods and that its exhortation to lead the good life is sordid and groveling. This has been true of many Protestant faiths of the past and of some of their less timid and equivocating descendants of today. But no enlightened Catholic is guilty of preachments so base. The spirit of Catholicism, in this respect, may be readily epitomized by quoting (with my italics) an Act of Contrition of the type always made by penitents in preparation for confession and desirably again immediately before receiving absolution: "O my God, I am heartily sorry for having offended Thee. And I detest all my sins, because I dread the loss of heaven and the pains of hell, *but most of all because they offend Thee, my God, who art all good and worthy of all my love.* I firmly resolve, *with the aid of Thy grace,* to confess my sins, to do penance, and to amend my life."

Returning to Professor Joad's jeremiad against the carnality of our day and its consequent satiety we must in fairness admit that the judicious humanist, if he suspects this to be launched at him, will parry the thrust by asserting that he, too, is well aware of the futility of the sybaritic life, that he seeks happiness by unveiling scientific truths, by adoring and making beautiful things, by increasing the happiness of others through the spread of social justice. I have met intimately many distinguished humanists, atheistic or agnostic, who have placed their trust in science, art, or social reform as a tonic for happiness. But I have never met one who was really *happy,* whose more or less evanescent complacence over his refined *pleasures* was not frequently blasted by some awful, inward emptiness and solitariness. I have met many believers who have been scientists, artists, and reformers. But they were not lovers and seekers of happiness. They were lovers and seekers of God. Such truly happy souls can understand the grace-saturated Oblation of St. Thérèse of the Infant Jesus offering herself as a victim of holocaust to God's merciful love, that she might become a very martyr of His love.

CHAPTER VIII

DIFFICULTIES

"The depth of the word of God engages to the full the study thereof; it doth not refuse understanding. For if all things were closed, there would be nothing whereby what is obscure might be revealed. Again, if all things were hidden there would be nothing whereby the soul could gather nourishment and get strength to enable it to knock at what was closed."

Not long after I had become a Catholic I began to meditate, from my new perspectives, over the problem of evil which had so long deterred me from accepting any version of orthodox Christianity. So comprehensive was my newly acquired dialectic, so strong my faith, so deep my trust in God, that I was impressed, not with the feeling that Catholic doctrine which had proved itself to me to be so coherent and exalting could possibly be riven apart by this dilemma, but that I was in some state of stupidity bordering on the sin of sloth.

So I went to confession. Father Christopher Sloan, my confessor, encouraged me with a brief but lucid homily which gave me new energy to tackle the problem more resolutely, and emphasized the point that I was not suffering from a doubt but from a difficulty.

Not having at that time found in Newman the passage containing the sentence, "Ten thousand difficulties do not make one doubt," I departed to make my penance not without a persistent notion that the distinction between a difficulty and a doubt might be a quibble. And I venture to add even today, that while the statement is certainly true so long as the will yields to no doubt and the intellect remains firm in faith, by the grace of God, knowing, too, that this best conforms to reason, yet Cardinal Newman does not carry me all the way with him in his use of the concept. There is, in that eloquent and noble writer a certain lurking tinge of anti-intellectualism of which I am still afraid. But whatever the case might be, I knew that holy Mother Church did not want me as her child on a basis of blind faith. Consequently I set out first to see if I could find any real distinction between these terms. Now a doubt, I perceived, is a suspension of judgment, a withholding of assent when confronted by two or more propositions each of which is about equally weighted by probabilities, or when all of them are endowed with evidence too meager. I thought then that I might call a difficulty a case in which one of the warring propositions was buttressed by much more testimony than its rivals could mass for their support.

For the seven years following my confession I have progressed more and more richly and clearly in the understanding of the Catholic solution of the problem of evil, so that where once I was quickly baffled I devote today an entire term of a graduate course to the topic ending always with the thought that I wish I could afford the time to carry on my exposition for at least a year. The problem of evil is indeed a mystery. But the "difficulties" which it arouses are not clouded by any of the logical contradictions that would force upon an intellectualist the duty of doubt. The Catholic solution establishes quite clearly the fact of God's Providence even though it does not always enable us to understand all of its manifestations in detail. But, as we have already seen, a mystery, as Catholics understand it, is not an opaque curtain before which we must stand in despair. It is a glass through which at first we see but dimly. Men are not so wise as the God in whom Catholicism believes. But suppose we continue undaunted to reason rigorously and resolutely and to pray continually, ardently, and humbly. May not the Holy Spirit vouchsafe us some slowly elongating vistas, even though we never arrive at complete comprehension until we gain, with God's grace after death, the Beatific Vision? I have reasoned and prayed incessantly for light. I now know that even as a reasoned explanation, apart from what God has revealed to His Church, the Catholic answer can satisfy completely any pure logician emancipated from his moods. I know that I am penetrating ever more and more deeply toward the core of the mystery. And while in a spirit of reverent curiosity, reverent because I love a God whom I know to be infinitely good and powerful, I still pursue the quest, I do so because I feel that He wants me to do so in order the better to deserve salvation through ministrations to my faltering neighbors. If for Catholics the problem of evil is a mystery, in the sense just defined, for all other philosophies their alleged solutions are words signifying nothing and do but veil some one of the protean versions of latent despair. Indeed all non-Catholic solutions imply some one of the numerous contemporary epistemologies which lead straight to skepticism or solipsism, and so to the denial of the objective validity of that potentially omniscient "Science" which latter-day "rationalists" and "naturalists" (as they most inaccurately label themselves) seek to enthrone in the place of God.

I. PROBLEM OF EVIL: CATHOLIC ATTITUDE

We will first measure the answer of the materialistic atheist. He says that there is no problem of evil, though he thoroughly cognizes its reality. A problem of evil arises only when we have to justify its existence along with that of a God both all powerful and all good. But for him no such God exists. The universe is a dervish dance of wavicles which have probably always whirled on in chance gyrations. "Chance" is the keynote. We can but content ourselves in our brief lives with conquering as many evils as we can. Now, the atheist has merely substituted for the difficult problem of evil the much more difficult problem of good. Let him explain to us just how the rational evolves from the irrational, the moral from the nonmoral. Each atheist, in his own way will be found to substitute for God some abstraction, some unreal figment: "Humanity," the "Proletariat," the "stateless Society of the Future," the "Social Will," the "German Spirit," "Chance," "Law," "Force," "Progress," a "Vector," the "Ideal." A superstition is an attempt to explain an event or a series of events in terms of an inadequate cause. The atheist, therefore, is the most superstitious of men. Idolatry is the practice of cherishing a means as an end. All atheists, in so far as they are in touch with realities at all, remain content with idolatry.

Atheists think that Christianity is immoral because it encourages us to lie down supine before evil, deluding ourselves with the faith that God will reward us for our petitions and our humility. As a matter of fact the most humble of the saints, those most relentless in self-mortification, have fought evil always and indefatigably with joyful intrepidity. Saints have annihilated many more evils, and not infrequently with the aid of science, than atheistic scientists (who divide their time between curing diseases and inventing poisonous gases) have ever done.

The early Christians erected the first real hospitals, many of which were sadly neglected and abused by their Protestant confiscators. And today I invite any truth seeker to visit in turn, first state-controlled, then Catholic institutions for the sick, the orphans, the aged, the destitute, the insane, or the delinquent. Assuming that the scientific equipment and attendants are adequate in the public institutions — they have been so in all the Catholic hospitals, homes, and reformatories I have visited — our truth seeker will find in the Catholic institution another curative influence which cannot be obtained with all the wealth and worldly wisdom on our planet; he will find a most efficient and unsentimental and deep and pure love of the wretched such as can be inspired only by the love of God. Let the truth seeker also examine one of these Catholic institutions, in a country like France or Germany or Spain or Mexico or Russia, first when it is in the hands of nuns and priests and afterward when it has been confiscated in the name of "progress" by some Masonic-liberal or communist or Nazist or other anticlerical government. If he has not been able to do this himself our truth seeker can find it done for him in a small but now rapidly growing number of really scientific historical writings, for instance the perfectly neutral researches which Professor Allison Peers made in Spain. Such a study, I guarantee, will completely cure any normal observer of the last vestige of addiction to any atheistic "Religion of Humanity."

Contemporary Catholics, at sacrifices little dreamed of by most non-Catholics, maintain hospitals and orphanages everywhere in metropolis and jungle and on the desert. Father Damien went to live among and to preach to and to die with the lepers. St. Peter Claver, in presurgical days, sucked the pus out of the ulcers of negro slaves. Holy priests and Sisters of Mercy throng the battlefields fearless of bullets and shrapnel. St. Ignatius Loyola and many other truly holy men and women do not close up houses of prostitution and administer prophylactics to wayward men; they convert, in large numbers, both the erring prostitute and the roué.

If science is looked upon as combating evil, then it may be well to take note again that the list of illustrious Catholic scientists, from Copernicus in the dawn of modern science to the Abbé Lêmaitre today, is very, very long. I have space here for only a limited though fairly representative list: Copernicus, founder of modern astronomy; Vesalius, the first master of human anatomy; Descartes, the inventor of analytic geometry; Galileo, eminent in mechanics; Lavoisier, almost a patron saint of chemists; Schleiden and Schwann who perfected that cell theory which enables the many zoological and botanical sciences to work in concert; Galvani and Ampère, pioneers in the study of electricity; Lamarck, eminent in vertebrate zoologist and evolutionist; Johannes Mueller, physiologist; Pasteur, the illustrious bacteriologist; Abbot Gregor Mendel, who placed the study of heredity on a scientific basis; Father Wilhelm Schmidt, who has so signally helped the young science of anthropology to come of age; the Abbé Lemaître, acclaimed by Einstein to be one of the greatest of contemporary astronomers.

Occasionally one hears some skeptical wish-thinker hint darkly and delightedly that Mendel was secretly an unbeliever. How strange, then, that he was made an abbot by his fellow monks! Again one is told that holy Mother Church sought to hinder the anatomical researches of Vesalius. She did — when in a moment of too lyrical enthusiasm he tried his hand at *human vivisection*.

As a fact the only scandal at all plausible which ever arose in the long history of the very friendly relations between the Catholic Church and the scientists was the trial of Galileo. And even here, the biologist, Huxley, though himself an unbeliever and a sturdy foe of ecclesiastics, admitted in one of his letters that, in the debate between Galileo and the Cardinals, the Cardinals had rather the best of it. Galileo did suffer at the hands of individual pedants. But they did not speak with hierarchical authority. He was in fact most generously endowed in his researches by the leaders of the faith. He was condemned at last, partly because he declared that he had proved that which had not been proved and had used arguments which scientists themselves rejected when the real proof was forthcoming; and partly because he made a rash and very amateurish incursion into biblical exegesis, a study which requires a technique and erudition in which he was totally lacking, a study which is just as scientific, in its way, as the physics for which he was so genuinely equipped. The statement that Galileo whispered a denial of his public recantation was fabricated by a historian for the first time about one hundred years after the trial took place. Galileo, after his condemnation, was not burned at the stake as two persons of my acquaintance once told their classes. His religious faith never wavered a hair's breadth. In this connection it would be very enlightening to many indignant scientists to read his correspondence, including letters to his daughter who was a nun.

And now it is high time for us to inquire into the nature of evil. To begin with, we must review the other theories of evil which, along with atheism, challenge the supremacy of the Christian believer.

First, then, evil is the opposite of good and of perfection. Hence the old Manichæan heresy which once beguiled me in a more modern masquerade dress, the heresy of a supreme and positive Evil which, if regarded as the cause of all evil, is untenable. Even Satan is not the cause of all evil, however much he may further it in cajoling the free will of man gone astray. For the scholastic philosopher evil is no negation of being in the crude and saccharine and cowardly and often selfish sense in which the "Christian Scientist" attempts to explain it away as "error of mortal mind." But it is a negation of good. It is true, as the ontologist shows, that goodness *is* being — being regarded from the point of view of its desirability. It is true as both Natural and Dogmatic theologians say, that everything which God created is good and that no one except God can, in the strictest sense, create, make anything where before there is nothing. Evil, then, for the Christian, is the absence of perfection; it is a privation. Blindness is the absence of sight, though nonetheless tragic as such. Evil may be physical, physiological, or moral, an earthquake, a cancer, adultery — if we accept the broad, clear, lax view of the modern worldling who is usually much more horrified by earthquakes and cancers than by adultery, and who often is somewhat more repelled by adultery than he is by avarice, envy, and satanic pride which, in fact, are not seldom extolled as virtues by capitalists, communists, Nazists, and Fascists. But, in the strict sense of the word, there is no evil except that which comes from misuse of God's good things by perverse angels and men. Physical catastrophes and diseases are often terribly tragic; yet the only unequivocally evil kind of evil, the only untransformably evil kind of evil is spiritual evil or sin: sloth, gluttony (intemperance), lust, wrath (particularly murderous wrath), envy, avarice, pride (in the worst sense), blasphemy, violation of the Sabbath, disloyalty to worthy parents, to legitimate superiors, and to dependent inferiors, theft and any dishonesty, hypocrisy and lying, despair, the being accessory to another's sin, final impenitence, and many more.

Some sins are called by the Church deadly or mortal and destroy the sanctifying grace in the sinner's soul until he repents. Others, called venial, are not so serious in themselves but are, by that very fact, insidiously venemous. God, we may be sure if we believe in Him, will not be as exacting on the sick, physically and mentally; on the poor, the ignorant, the naïve, and the foolish; as on the healthy and the wealthy and the wise. Our Lord made that point very clear in His comments on the rich man, the camel, and the eye of a needle. Yet many an aged and poor and sick Catholic would be the last to plead of our Lord extenuation. And many of the saints have courted poverty. As for sickness, St. Peter Claver often shared his coat with a shivering leper yet lived a good many vividly active years notwithstanding. Let me quote from Chesterton's biography of St. Francis of Assisi a passage about this man who once enjoyed the pomps of life and knew no fear of warfare:

It was while St. Francis was drifting, one may even say mooning, about the streets of Assisi and the fields outside the city wall, that an incident occurred to him which has not always been immediately connected with the business of the dreams, but which seems to me the obvious culmination of them. He was riding listlessly in some wayside place, apparently in the open country, when he saw a figure coming along the road towards him and halted; for he saw it was a leper. And he knew instantly that his courage was challenged, not as the world challenges, but as one would challenge who knew the secrets of the heart of a man. What he saw advancing was not the banner and the spears of Perugia, from which it never occurred to him to shrink; not the armies that fought for the crown of Sicily, of which he had always thought as a courageous man thinks of mere vulgar danger. Francis Bernadone saw his fear coming up the road towards him; the fear that comes from within and not from without; though it stood white and horrible in the sunlight. For once in the long rush of his life his soul must have stood still. Then he sprang from his horse, knowing nothing between stillness and swiftness, and rushed on the leper and threw his arms around him. It was the beginning of a long vocation of ministry among many lepers for whom he did many services; to this man he gave what money he could and mounted and rode on. We do not know how far he rode, or with what sense of the things around him; but it is said that when he looked back, he could see no figure on the road.

The Tychist, in a cynical mood, might remark that this anecdote is good grist for his mill. Naught but a universe of blind chance, he might say, could breed such a lunatic as St. Francis. May he who reads, the complete life of the holy man of Assisi — the while fearlessly and honestly searching his own soul — pronounce judgment. There are not wanting psychologists who will endeavor to fasten the stigma of insanity on many saints. Though it be but a *tu quoque* argument, I must say that in my long study and reading of psychiatry I have found a fair number of its practitioners who were themselves either on the borderline or, perchance, a wee bit over.

To the nineteenth- and earlier twentieth-century scientists the universe appeared to be governed by mechanical law and chance. That was a paradox too gordian for me, even in the days when I was inclined to lean their way. They believed that a scientific pilgrimage always found its goal in some mechanical exact causal law. Their proudest vaunt was for Newton's Law of Gravitation. But now, after about two centuries, it

appears that even Newton's law is not exact. In earlier chapters we have
noted a disposition of scientists toward the substitution of statistical for
exact laws. This is certainly along the line of progress. But when philosophers, already led astray by the false epistemology of Hume and Kant,
are tempted by the new scientific outlooks to deny the reality of cause
they are committing intellectual suicide. I should like to see formulas
and figures suggesting the probability that chance or irrationality could
ever beget reason. It has long been said that a metaphysician is a blind
man in a dark cellar looking for a black cat which isn't there. A waggish
professor of philosophy added an Alice-in-Wonderlandlike jibe that the
theologian finds the cat. I believe that the philosopher's merry quip
applies much more neatly to the statistics-idolater and his Molochlike
Chance.

II. ABSOLUTE IDEALISTS AND DUALISTS

For a number of years in Berkeley I tried desperately to surrender
myself to the stupendous but arid dialectic of the Absolute Idealist and
his more colorful and more vague brethren, the pantheistic poets. There is
only one individual, so it seemed. It is the Universe, the Absolute, which
a wistful theological disciple occasionally whispered that we might call
God. You and I with our superstitions, adulteries and scarlet fevers, fleas,
mountains and stars, droughts and tornadoes, are all fragmentary parts
of the Absolute. Be of good cheer, for Hegel tells us that the Real is the
Rational and the Rational is the Real. I was not surprised in 1914 to find
German Hegelians glorifying the German cause on the ground that it
was sound Hegelianism, American and English Hegelians damning the
"Huns" because they had betrayed Hegel, and American pragmatists and
realists damning our enemies because they were putting Hegel into
practice. No wonder that one of Hegel's most brilliant followers, Josiah
Royce, dwelt so long on 'the possibility of error' in *The Religious
Aspect of Philosophy* yet succeeded no better than his master in
explaining why the rational Absolute has within Itself so many tissues
of befuddlement. Is it strange that another Hegelian, Bradley, in his
Appearance and Reality, wrote rather sadly about the dance of the
"bloodless categories" in philosophy? And yet the idealist brings me the
glad news that I am free! How can I, a mere cog in it All, not an individual but a fragment, have the slightest flickering spark of freedom
without imperiling the whole majestic Reason-Machine of which I am a

part? Absolute Idealism, for all its parade of logic, is the violent antithesis of Tychism with its statistics-idolatry. Long before I became a Catholic I was almost instinctively restive in the presence of such extremes, and turned away sorrowfully to grope for the golden mean.

All this brings to mind that puny offspring of Absolute Idealism known as Christian Science, a view which would not merit any attention in a book like this were it not for the fact that I have been pestered by the inanities of friends who profess it or claim to profess it while frequently contradicting it in practice. Add to this the fact that, just now, it is a powerful influence for evil, although, like all its equally fickle predecessors, its life is not likely to round out a century. It will die, it will be forgotten, and, in due time, some magic monger will rediscover it and claim to be the founder of a new religion. It is a very materialistic denial of materialism. If it were at all consistent it would be a part of pantheism. To be sure, Mrs. Eddy, the founder, in a book of sermons the title of which I have forgotten, protests roundly against pantheism. But as she wavers gracefully on almost every page between monistic idealism and pluralistic panpsychism I am afraid that she was subject at times to Hegelianism although I have no assurance that she ever read Hegel or any of his followers for herself. In her *Science and Health* she calls evil naught but error of mortal mind. Well, as Juliet says, "A rose by any other name would smell as sweet." And I would add that gangrene by any other name would be as uncomfortable.

As I already said, I was so unpleasantly impressed with the reality of evil that the universe seemed to me either a battleground of a good god and a bad god who, with their retinues, fought each other to a perpetually inconclusive standstill, or a universe in which a good but not all-powerful god, with the very small aid of good men in their best moments, was slowly prevailing over the various evils, physical, physiological, and spiritual. This explanation seemed to my outwardly humble but inwardly arrogant apprehension to be, on purely empirical grounds (which I thought were the only respectable grounds), the more plausible hypothesis. But as the years rolled on, I began to ponder as to how such a finite God could have come into being and when and what the guarantee that He would not ultimately be overwhelmed by his opponents. Mr. Wells's "Veiled Being" did much to convince me of the shakiness of his own plea for his finite "God, the Invisible King." Moreover I began to see that if the universe were a chaotic battleground it would not respond as it does to the researches of the sciences. But both extreme Zoroastrian dualism and this theory of a finite God are unwittingly in full retreat toward atheism.

So, as I dallied with causes, I began to entertain a faint respect for two theistic arguments which St. Thomas Aquinas most highly esteems but which I had hitherto ignorantly despised, namely, the argument for the necessity of an Unmoved Mover and the argument for a First Cause. At this point I exorcised, after many years of servitude, the influence of the philosophy of David Hume.

Why in the world did not Hume, after he had reduced Descartes, Locke, and Berkeley to absurdity, apply his keen analysis more keenly to the very presuppositions of Descartes? Why does not Bertrand Russell do it? For a most charitable yet devastating exposure of all modern non-Catholic philosophy (which is really philosophical nihilism) read *The Unity of Philosophical Experience* by Etienne Gilson. More recently Willis Dwight Nutting, in *How Firm a Foundation,* has subjected the starting point of Descartes to a searching analysis which outstrips even Hume's. Incidentally Mr. Nutting exposes with merciless reasoning the irrationality of the modern prejudice against the supernatural to which Hume contributed so many sophistries. To this later point we will return when we deal with the historical authenticity of Holy Scripture.

III. PROBLEM OF EVIL: CATHOLIC EXPLANATION

We are now to return to that Catholic solution of the problem of evil to which I came slowly and suspiciously to render homage. Toward the question of physical and physiological evils, the attitude of the Catholic may seem apathetic. But I have already shown that it is not, as so many of its foes have accused it of being, supine or in reactionary opposition to scientific progress. Martyrs and saints, scientists of the Catholic Church and laymen have fought tooth and nail to overcome life's terrors. Having fought the good fight, they can look forward to a future in eternal salvation that beggars the evanescent present. Only worshipers of material prosperity and fleshly euphoria find the problem of physical evil a baffling enigma because even the most refined of them have forgotten or have never fully understood the spiritual standards. They have falsely equated unhappiness with pain, pleasure with happiness. Of all the horrors of our decadent age the most horrible and deadly are born of its unblushing complacent sinfulness. It is easy to show that many of our physical evils may be traced more directly to man's sloth, stupidity, myopia, and greed. We shall see the full significance of this when we treat of original sin. And now, even after the wonderful onward sweep of modern science, when avaricious men rape the woods without sufficient reforestation it is they, not God, who cause the floods which inundate, unfortunately in some cases, their successors, but in other cases, themselves.

The righteous man finds in physical evils a training for a virility with which he can win a high place in heaven, and which, as the life of a St. John of the Cross shows, can furnish, even in a state of disease and unmerited disgrace, enormous happiness on this earth itself. The Catholic believes that innocent sufferers, enduring their sufferings from supernatural motives, are recipients of special glories. The Catholic, to be sure, has usually as strong a wish to live as any normal man. But the average Catholic, as any watchful observer can prove for himself, has far less fear of death than others. Out of his long experience as a physician, the non-Catholic Oliver Wendell Holmes testified that the happiest deaths he had witnessed were those of Catholics. Very often the Catholic has no fear whatsoever. On the other hand, if he lives, he expects not only enjoyment, but also to find in sufferings precious opportunities to prepare his soul for Paradise. Pain may sting one to lofty action. Borne in conformity with the will of God, and in union with the sufferings of Christ for us, it may be the occasion of the most sublime acts of human love for God.

"It is necessary to remind ourselves from time to time," Mr. Lunn suggests, "that pain and evil are not necessarily synonymous, and that pain is the price which may cheerfully be paid for a nobler form of happiness."

But though pain-gripped man may win many merits for heaven, what of the helpless and soulless animal? Pains of animals are often most pathetic. But in the lower phyla they are, from the point of view of the biologist himself, all but negligible. And even among animals like the most complicated mammals their sufferings have been enormously anthropomorphized by sentimentalists. They suffer the worst, not at the hands of their foes in nature or of the really responsible and truly scientific among the vivisectionists, but at the hands of occasional bestial children and adults, and even then, not so much as they appear to do in the eyes of those who fancifully project their own mawkish and cowering personalities into them. To be sure, the decent huntsmen will do his best to prevent his stricken prey from crawling off to die in distress, even if its agony be but physiological rather than spiritual. But man, in as far as he transcends space and time with his memory and

forecast, man the only waking dreamer, is the only unequivocal sufferer
— except Christ who was both true God and true Man, and whose voluntarily accepted crucifixion is guarantee that God's permission of pain for
men and animals is not the trivial fancy mongering of a heartless
dramatist.

God, it has well been said, could not allow the evil He foresaw to prevent Him from creating the good He intended. Moreover, the evil He
permitted He could turn to a good end. "God is so powerful," St. Thomas
writes, "that He can direct every evil to a good end." Even the crushed
insect thus plays a worthy part in a universe in which, as the sciences
themselves show us, there is no discernible *ultimate* waste and for whose
rational inhabitant, man, as we learn from Christian Revelation, God was
willing to subject Himself in human form to ineffable pain and sorrow.

Man has been accorded a good deal of compensation, as we have just
seen, even on earth. Then, too, the more stolid the man, the less his pain.
Even children, when they endure intolerably prolonged and pathetic
fates, do not suffer all the biting intensity of the sensitive adults who
sorrow over them. Far be it from me to attempt a complete answer to the
mystery. But the Catholic God is certainly much nearer to us than a
vague Life-Force of a Bergsonian, or a pantheistic God which identifies
the murderer and the murdered, or a finite striving God — conceptions
which may bring God "physically near," as F. G. Machan says, but, as he
adds, make Him "spiritually remote," as ludicrously unreal as the hypostatized "Law" or "Processes" or "Force" or "Dynamism" or "Vector" or
"Chance" or "Ideal" of the atheist.

IV. RESULTS OF SIN FOR ANGELS AND MEN

Reason, purged of the modern superstition that a belief in the supernatural is superstitious, leads straight to the acceptance of a God who is
almighty and good, and to the acceptance of all real evil as being ultimately spiritual evil, sin, the workmanship of finite rational angels and
men. The explanation of the proneness of rational beings to sin rests on
our conclusions regarding their original nature.

The mention of angels brings a smile today to the lips of a self-styled
"rationalist," although the idea should not ring so oddly in the ears of
those who have so much to say about "evolutionary continuities." The
existence of angels is established by Divine Revelation which, as we have
seen and will see later even more fully, is in its turn firmly based on

proofs provided by the unaided reason quite independent of any authority. We know that they were created for the supreme joy of loving a Being to love whom is supreme happiness and that, in order that they might love, it was logically necessary that they should be created free, that is with the power to choose the worse as well as the better way. We know that some of them yielded to temptation, sinned through pride. Certain theologians think that their sin was specifically one which we human beings ought to be able to understand only too well, the sin of refusing to adore the Second Person of the Blessed Trinity, Jesus Christ, when He resolved to clothe Himself with Humanity in the prison of the womb of a little Jewish girl, to emerge amidst poverty and obscurity as the foster son of a proletarian; to suffer unjustly and to the highest degree every horror, physical and spiritual, that can be inflicted on finite beings; and by example to show his adopted brothers and sisters all over the world how, through humility and charity, these very evils may be used even by finite beings to become, by their own merits, more and more like unto God, our Creator.

Regarding human nature itself in the present order, four doctrines have been held, of which one only is tenable, whether considered from the viewpoints of science, philosophy, or religion.

The first view, often falsely confounded with Christianity by modern "naturalists" from Rousseau to Dewey, is that of Luther and Calvin. It represents man as totally depraved, so that he can do nothing but throw himself (with Luther) on God's mercy by an act of faith (since his works will avail naught for his salvation) or hope (with Calvin) that the divine whim has predestined him, in preference to his neighbor, as one of the elect. This view is scientifically worthless for it fails to account for the good deeds which are not infrequent in even the wickedest of men. Even the gunman is not so "totally depraved" as to be utterly incapable of occasional bursts of loyalty.

The second view, Rousseau's violent reaction against Calvin's violence, holds that man is by nature totally good; he becomes evil only under the warping repression of such tyrants as priests and kings. This view has obviously an enormous currency today. It has, for instance, done much, at least indirectly, to inspire, in educational theory, President Eliot's pernicious elective system and John Dewey's overemphasis of "interest" as opposed to "discipline." It plays its characteristically inconsistent part in that curious farrago of pseudo-scientific theories known as Marxian or communistic dialectical materialism. Its fatal defect is its failure to explain how priests and kings, who, after all, are also human beings and who, therefore, should be naturally good, have become evil. How did the first priest or the first king or the first "old man" of H. G. Wells's fake history come to have such an evil influence?

The third view, that of the unnatural "naturalists," conceives man as morally neutral, neither good nor bad, evolved in every respect from the animals. His ethical preachments and practices are explained as mere adaptational expedients, culture habits, "mores" which arise in great variety, differing in different societies, none of them demonstrably more righteous than their rivals. This view, popular among sociologists, purely empirical psychologists, and uncritical evolutionists, may be described as an ethical nihilism which runs parallel with the post-Cartesian skepticism or solipsism of so much modern epistemology. Its advocates, like the skeptics who declare all knowledge to be impossible, refute themselves by refusing vociferously and conspicuously to practise what they preach. To them their own moral preferences and principles, which are usually hedonistic, pleasure-idolatrous, are always sacrosanct. Give them a good chance and they will always impose their own "ideals" with a sort of totalitarian fervor upon as many others as they can, although they can give us no rational grounds for accepting their own peculiar *mores.*

The fourth view, most clearly set forth by Jesus Christ, and according to Him by St. John of Patmos and St. Paul, is the only conception of man's nature at all congruous with rationally grounded religion and really scientific psychology and sociology. This view holds that man, as we find him here today, though *essentially* good in origin, has not only a disposition to do the right thing but also, alas, a frail propensity to do the wrong thing, a threefold concupiscence. This is the price of the original sin of our first parents. When they decided to become godlike in a sort of get-rich-quick fashion, they left us a tragic inheritance: the concupiscence of the flesh (a proneness to lust, gluttony, and pleasant sloth, both physical and mental), the concupiscence of the eye (morbid curiosity and avarice), and, worst of all, the pride of life (envy and arrogance).

Leaving aside the *Book of Genesis,* in which by Divine Revelation we have the clearest account of the matter, the study of all folklore presents us with a varying, faltering, cloudy but universal conviction of this early disobedience and its consequences. And, if these consequences are serious, as indeed they must be, yet of Adam's sin the Church can sing, "O happy fault!" for it has led to our Lord's own ineffable human life of Redemption. We now can understand something at least of God's love for us.

Here, for instance, as an illustration, is an incident learned from an eyewitness, the Mother Superior of a certain Community of Saint Madeleine Sophie's Religious of the Sacred Heart. There was, in that Community, a certain humble lay sister stricken with cancer. At its inception she told her superior that when the period of most intense suffering came she would desire to offer that along with the sufferings of her Lord upon the cross, for His intentions. She implored Reverend Mother never to allow any physician to administer an opiate even though she herself lay too helpless in pain to say the word. The dreadful time came. Reverend Mother summoned their physician, a good Christian though not a Catholic, an hour or two before dawn. The sufferer could not speak. But when the doctor entered she fixed upon her Mother Superior a look so intensely appealing that its significance could not be misinterpreted. Summoning up all her own courage, Reverend Mother told the physician all the facts and apologized for calling him, at such an hour, to no purpose. He reassured her, and his answer was unreproducibly solemn. It was little more than a year thereafter, when he might have been seen, a convert to the Church of Rome, receiving Holy Communion in the chapel of that very convent school in which the holy Sister died.

God wishes all men to be saved and gives to all sufficient grace. The supreme evil, eternal separation from Him, can be attributed to man's own perverse will only, not to God. He does not arbitrarily predestine anyone to damnation.

That holy Benedictine, the Abbot Anscar Vonier, in his book *The Human Soul,* has provided us with a condensation of the Thomistic interpretation of the Catholic doctrine of reprobation that will furnish a perfect conclusion for our treatment of what, for the contemporary de-Christianized mind, is probably the greatest of the "difficulties."

It would be a most un-Catholic presentation of the land of the lost to picture it as peopled with spirits that cry for mercy, and cannot find it. Time for mercy is past, chiefly because the lost spirit does not want mercy.

Utter depravity of will is the feature most conspicuous in everything we know about evil spirits, both from Scripture and tradition. Their misery, or in other words, their punishment, is not greater than their moral perversity.

St. Thomas would say that the perverse spirit receives no grace because his will is intrinsically unchangeable. A less profound theologian would say, on the contrary, that the spirit's will is made unchangeable from not receiving grace. The Church tolerates both views, provided the fixedness in evil, in the reprobate soul, be adhered to.

St. Thomas looks for the causes of the unchanging reprobation in the will of the creature; other theologians look for them in the will of God, in the sense that God in His justice, is said to refuse graces to those that did not make use of them when they were plentiful.

In other words, St. Thomas makes the state of the created will the principal, or even the unique cause of the eternity of reprobation. If God is said to inflict an eternity of reprobation, it is in this sense: God has made spiritual natures so perfect, that a wrong use of their powers will bring about results as permanent as the right use of them.

No man of good will can ever be lost. Nothing could be more comforting than the words of Pope Pius IX regarding such as remain without any fault of theirs outside the true fold: "Those who suffer from invincible ignorance in respect to our Holy Religion," he wrote in an encyclical of 1863, "yet follow faithfully the precepts of the natural law written by God in the hearts of man, and being ready to obey lead an honest and upright life, can by virtue of divine light and grace gain eternal life. For God who sees, searches, and penetrates to the bottom of the minds, souls, thoughts, and habits of all men, God who is infinitely good and merciful, by no means suffers that anyone should be punished with eternal penalties unless he is responsible for voluntary sin."

It should be understood here also that original sin means only the loss of that supernatural state, that sanctifying grace, to which man by his nature had no right, and which was freely added. While the stain of original sin, therefore, deprives man of this, it is "not incompatible with a natural happiness after death," as Father Lattey says in his *St. Paul;* "it is only grievous personal sin that merits the actual pains of eternal punishment."

V. STILL FURTHER DIFFICULTIES

There was a time, during the long, dark twilight that I spent grappling with the ugly apparition of the problem of evil, that I was tempted to concede that the conception of Omnipotence alone, as an attribute of God, could be squared with His Goodness much more easily if we did not link Omnipotence with Omniscience. But God, as Father Joyce, in *The Principles of Natural Theology,* sums up the fact, must be infinite alike in the real and the cognitive order, and he concludes:

If the world is a place where God realizes in all its details an immense scheme of providential wisdom, in which the principal part is the training of free agents, He must know how such an agent will act when called on to choose between two courses. Were it otherwise — were He ignorant what the issue will be, His providence would not be, as reason and experience seem to assure us, a process of supreme wisdom, carried on in view of a definite end. He who does not know how subordinate agencies will act, cannot shape his means, save in a halting and imperfect way, to the attainment of his purpose. We must either admit that God knows the future free acts of His creatures, or admit that His providence is marred by frequent failure and often at fault.

I saw then, that if I rejected Omniscience I must needs fall back on some theory of finite God or on pantheism (the best version of which is Absolute Idealism) or on some brand of Atheism (preferably Tychism) or finally on some species of Agnosticism. I have already shown, here and there in this treatise, why all but one of these have failed me. I have not yet, however, dealt, with Agnosticism directly. This I will do now.

There are two kinds of Agnosticism. The first variation maintains that God is the Unknowable. If this is taken to mean merely, that He is not *completely* knowable, the Catholic will readily agree. We can prove God's existence, but since He is Infinite and Simple (Absolutely Unified) and we are finite and complex, we can only, say the Thomists, describe His "attributes" (*distinctio rationis cum fundamento in re*) by ascribing to Him in a supereminent degree the pure perfections which we know: Truth, Goodness, Intelligence, Freedom, Love, and all the rest. These and inconceivably more must be one in Him since He can be proved to be their Cause. It is not surprising, therefore, when we find Herbert Spencer, the most distinguished defender of the doctrine of the Unknowable, exposed by Alfred Noyes, in *The Unknown God*, wherein the distinguished positivist is shown by document to have lapsed — or soared — at times into a theism closely akin to orthodox Christianity.

As to the second sort of Agnosticism, the modest declaration, "I don't know," this was the view which I maintained, except for my brief incursion into Atheism, for about eighteen years. It is much more felicitously named, by my philosopher friend and colleague, William Savery, "Inquirism." I have observed that it is always unstable. Such an agnostic is always oscillating between quasi atheism and quasi theism. Professor Savery, for instance, has recently become, for the time being, a stalwart and stimulating Tychist. Thomas Huxley, one of the most illustrious proponents of inquirism, often betrayed himself with such strong theistic leanings that they can only be understood as evanescent beliefs in God. My readings and direct observations indicate that all inquirists, if carefully unmasked, disclose frequent and often final retreats from their interrogative attitude to some declarative judgment, atheistic or theistic. Agnosticism is really not a point of view at all.

So I come to my summary. From my researches in Natural Theology, the study of God with the unaided reason, I have been compelled to conclude not merely that orthodox Christian theory, for two thousand years unflinchingly and uncompromisingly upheld by the only apostolic Church, the Church of Rome, is incalculably superior to all its rivals; I have been compelled to conclude that Catholic Christianity is in fact absolutely the only answer to ultimate questions.

There is just one real difficulty — and it is only a difficulty, it does not justify a shadow of doubt. It is the question: Why did God, Self-Sufficient in His Trinitarian Perfection, concern Himself to create us at all. That is a mystery. But to one who reasons relentlessly and prays tirelessly, it becomes — I will not say transparent, but more and more brightly, blazingly translucent. "The Sovereign Good," says Father Leen, C.S.Sp., in his volume *The Holy Ghost*, "has in itself as such a tendency to communicate itself to others. God gives Himself in pure liberality . . . without any hope or possibility of there being a return in kind. He is, therefore, the Gift most Perfect in every aspect."

But how is it, one may further ask, that there remain even in heaven some stations higher than others, that a St. Bernard may come so much closer to God than the rest of us? Assured though we are by Divine Revelation that in heaven there is no envy, that in heaven each one is perfectly happy, yet it is natural to puzzle over this hierarchical arrangement. Here again is a theme for a stout volume. But we must content ourselves with a clue from Jacques Maritain's masterpiece of contemporary scholasticism, *The Degrees of Knowledge*. "God called forth things from nothingness in view of sharing His Own Being with them and having it made visible by them. A single creature could not by itself sufficiently shadow forth the Creator's perfection, hence existences were created in great number and variety, so that the perfection not imaged in one, might be set forth in another. Hence that goodness or perfection of being which, in God, is of utter simplicity and unity, is broken up and multiplied in creation." There could not, by logical necessity, be two Infinite Beings. Even God cannot create another God. Hence created reality becomes, as described in Shelley's magnificent image, a "dome of many-colored glass" which "stains the white radiance of eternity."

Long ago, one of the earliest and greatest of the Christian Mystics, called Dionysius, wrote in his *De Divinis Nominibus* a paragraph which was and is the last word on the mystery of creation. I will quote it with my italics.

The good is the cause of all love. . . . It is for it and because of it that the inferior beings love the superior by turning toward them, that equals have for one another a love of communication of goods, that superior beings have, with respect to the inferior, a love of providence, and that each being loves itself with a love of conservation. *The daring of truth will go as far as to say that He Himself, the Cause of everything by the excess of His goodness, loves all things, loves with true love, and is intent upon all things, creating everything by that love, giving to everything His perfection, maintaining them in being and turning them towards Himself.* . . . He is divine love, He is good with the goodness that comes from the Good. He is beneficent love for things which are, Himself subsisting infinitely in the Good. *He did not wish the good to remain sterile; He has prompted it to operate according to the infinite efficacy of His virtue.*

And just here the paradox of equality in the hierarchy becomes clear. In heaven, the Presence of God in each of His creatures, even the lowliest, is so clear and magnificent that a St. Bernard will love Him and know Him in the least illustrious of his comrades. Heaven is no place of inertia and the *Sanctus, sanctus, sanctus,* is no idle repetition, but an indescribably intense and lyrical activity. All of God's blessed in all their ranks and choirs will know each other in God and God in them: husband, wife, and child, repentant sinner and saint, all the saved out of all the ages in an eternal Now.

As I implied toward the beginning of this section, I was bewildered in my earliest Catholic days, not to the point of suffering critically in Faith and Hope, but with my inability to share my new insight in all charity with my neighbor, because of my lack of a sufficient knowledge of the magnificent Catholic theology of prayer. I should perhaps have noted, even at that point, that my difficulty was due even more to the immaturity of my prayers — the *relative* immaturity, I must say, because, God knows, they are still painfully immature today. Nothing can be more pitiful than the cynical atheist's anthropomorphic myth of a blasé God, a Russellian God, who, knowing in advance what His subject will pray for, and knowing in advance whether or not He will answer it, yet permits the farce to go on because it amuses Him. God wants us to pray in order that we may, by our own efforts and merits, make ourselves more and more godlike. One cannot pray with any intensity without changing his own character to a degree which he can achieve in no other way. As Doctor John Clifford Fenton says in *The Theology of Prayer:* "Prayer is an action which expresses our charity for God, and our hope in Him. But it is not an expression which has been arbitrarily imposed. It is the kind of action which, properly performed, tends to make us love God more fully, hope in Him with greater confidence, and serve Him with greater devotion."

Now, some of us can pour out veritable prose poems and theological treatises in prayer to God. But the greatest of theologians, St. Thomas Aquinas, mastered a prayer far more profound. Once, as he knelt before the Crucifix, he heard the assuring voice of his divine Lord saying, "Thou hast written well of Me, Thomas." And to the question, "What reward, then, dost thou desire?" came the instant answer of the Angelic Doctor: "Only Thee, O Lord." When you and I have learned to pray, *really* to *pray* like that, we may sometime thereafter be able to say, as did St. Thomas when exhorted by Brother Reginald to go on with the *Summa Theologica:* "I can do no more. There have been things revealed to me that make all that I have written seem like straw."

VI. ABORTION, BIRTH CONTROL, EUTHANASIA

More and more, by such meditations as the foregoing, did I prepare myself to receive on rational grounds the teachings of Divine Revelation, and to appreciate the scientific precision (just as precise, just as scientific in its way as physics) of the sublime analysis of these teachings in Dogmatic Theology. So long had the mere word "dogma" repelled my mind so bemused had I been by the many drifts of skeptical thought, that, within a few months of the age of fifty, almost on the threshold of the cathedral, I faltered. Those born and bred in backgrounds such as mine little know how subtly warped are their minds by the prejudices and misunderstandings which befog them, and how easy it is to blend humble uncertainty with arrogant and obsessive negativism. For the scholarly man outside the Church the path is fearfully long and steep and stony. He must needs traverse it with bloody feet, with aching eyes and agonized straining ears, with many sighs and groans, and with innumerable falls. But after long travail the time comes when we find out, in the words of Doctor Sheen (in *God and Intelligence*) that "meta-physical and theological continuity . . . far exceed biological continuity."

Revelation, though not dependent on Natural Theology, has, as we have seen, the most vital connections with it. The same is true of the connection between Revelation and Natural Law, expressed by the Natural Sciences as well as by Natural Theology which draws so much from them. As Father Henry Davis, S.J., has said in his *Moral and Pastoral Theology*:

Natural law is the basis, and — if we may so speak — the condition precedent even of divine positive law, because man must first acknowledge God and His dominion over the human will, before he realizes the obligation of a divine positive law. Natural law is truly the basis of all human law since man, as such, has no dominion over the will of other men. Rational human nature is the embodiment and the authentic instrument of the promulgation of Natural law, but the precepts of Natural law are revealed in consciousness, though at times obscurely, so that in human nature as it is, and in concupiscence, some Divine Revelation even of the Natural law is morally necessary.

But if the Revelation that has, as a fact, been given to man, is the Revelation of a supernatural destiny, and this includes all that Natural law commands, though the first principles of Natural law are easily known and the proximate conclusions therefrom, yet there are some conclusions, not at all remote from the first principles, which, for a time, it may be difficult to appreciate, more especially if false teaching and evil custom add their influence. Thus . . . fornication, theft, unnatural vice, have been thought not to be immoral, and in our own days, the practice of so-called birth-control is defended, outside the Church, by specious arguments, and we can well believe that it is defended conscientiously though erroneously. There are other conclusions which are both derived from the first principle and are immediately evident, but to establish them by reasoning is no slight difficulty.

The laws of nature are the laws of God. It may often be difficult to persuade a young pagan today to refrain from "birth control" because the one persistently faithful Church of Christ, the Catholic Church, so decrees. But even a "naturalist" like Bernard Shaw calls "birth control," that is to say, contraception, "mutual masturbation." No wholesome person, aflame with a real sense of beauty and in a moment of real love, could blunt and defame the abandon and the beauty and the love of the sexual embrace with any conceivable kind of contraceptive practice or device. The young ladies who allow the lure of momentary pleasure and the cowardly fear of pain or disgrace to prompt them, not to control, but to thwart nature, will learn that the laws of nature are the laws of God when the later years bring them a uterine tumor or cancer. The gynecologists tell us that it is not the childbearing but the childless women who tax their scientific technique beyond its capacity. As to the economic aspects of "birth control," the farther-sighted scientists seem to be coming more and more to the conclusion that race suicide will not eradicate but will actually increase unemployment and therefore poverty.

On the subject of abortion, no matter how plausible the supposedly "therapeutic" excuse in crucial instances, read the physician W. J. O'Donovan's account of "Death from a Medical Point of View" in *Man and Eternity*, the Cambridge lectures at the Summer School of Catholic Studies in 1936: "Official approval of killing before birth," writes Doctor O'Donovan, "will undoubtedly strengthen the determination of male neuropaths to have no children, and make married life not only a discord between husband and wife, but also a potential danger to the mother's life on every possibility of pregnancy, for abortion is not safe even in the most skilled and careful hands."

Euthanasia, "mercy killing," is a twin delusion. Its practice would do more and more to stultify the researches of science into the prolongation of life, the conquest of disease, Moreover, suppose yourself to be an elderly parent in a society consisting of a majority of elders as a consequence of the birth-control impetus given by Margaret Sanger and Marie Stopes. You are, let us say, in the prime of life, but somewhat ailing tonight. The family physician comes. There are whispers on the floor below among the members of the younger generation who have assembled for a social evening. When the physician ascends the stairs will he come to you to cure or to kill? You cannot know, for you will be living in a generation in which the dwindling minority of growingly selfish youth will have learned that it is "unscientific" to believe in a God, particularly in a God who said, "Thou shalt not kill."

No! The laws of nature are the laws of God. It is well to note here a passage from Monsignor Sheen's *God and Intelligence*. Some contemporary thinkers are fain to reiterate that the belief in Revelation paralyzed the attitude of scholasticism toward science. The actual fact is that Revelation clarified the power to interpret the rather meager science accessible to St. Thomas and his forerunners. Says Monsignor Sheen:

It is quite true that St. Thomas did not have such scientists as Bateson, Duhém, Poincaré and others to lay the experimental foundations of his philosophy. It is also true that the Aristotelian physics and astronomy upon which he relied have since been discarded. But after all, were Aristotle and the Angelic Doctor less capable of interpreting the findings of science according to firmly established and self-evident principles than are the philosophers of today? The point of great importance is not the experience on which they had to draw, but the *interpretation* of it. A conceptual realist like St. Thomas, working on the ordinary and evident facts of daily experience, is certainly more capable of interpreting them than is an extreme idealist [like Jeans or Eddington] even though the latter work on the "facts" of modern science.

VII. THE HISTORICAL CHRIST

There is, in short, such a close continuity for the well-instructed Catholic between reason and Revelation that, as I have often reminded you before, no child of the Church of Rome is required to accept the latter blindly.

Leaving aside the pre-Christian revelations, for to deal with them would require a whole separate volume of Biblical exegesis, let us turn to the supreme Revealer, Jesus Christ. Assuming our Lord to have existed — and this can be proved by modern methods of scientific history, as we shall see soon — we have to consider His Divinity. His own protestations, although they have been challenged by some pettifogulizers whose disagreements among themselves have reached the point of *opera bouffe,* are unequivocal. We next consider the possibility that He was insane or that He was mendacious. His superlative wisdom belies the charge of insanity. His humility in the home of Mary and Joseph for thirty years, His sufferings during His three years of preaching, and His prophecy of His own premature and most dreadful death are all against the theory that He was an ambitious liar.

In proof of the historical existence of Jesus there is a veritable library of Apologetics among which, to mention but a few recent ones, we find *The Credibility of the Gospels,* by Monsignor Batiffol; *Christian Apologetics, or a Rational Exposition of the Foundations of the Faith,* by Devivier-Sasia; *The Divinity of Christ,* by Monsignor Bougaud; *Revealed Religion,* by Hettinger-Bowden; *A Christian Apology,* fourth edition, by P. Schanz, the four most admirable volumes of *Fundamental Theology,* by Father John Brunsmann, S.V.D., and *The Mustard Tree, An Argument on Behalf of the Divinity of Christ,* by O. R. Vassall-Phillips, a convert and a distinguished Redemptorist Father. As a matter of fact the witnesses for the historical authentification and for the proofs of the Divinity of Jesus, from the earliest days, are far more comprehensive than the testimonies for the existence of many famous historical characters whose reality we accept without question. I must here content myself in part with passages from Father Léonce de Grandmaison, S.J., whose lifework is his monumental and many-sided *Jesus Christ, His Person — His Message — His Credentials,* a book which of late has become a great companion to me, an integral part of my life. Equally informative for us will be certain quotations from *Christ and His Critics,* by Bishop Hilarin Felder, O.M.Cap., whose two huge volumes are filled with citations from his opponents, the so-called higher critics of the Bible. After reading these, from Celsus to Strauss and Renan, and from Strauss and Renan to Loisy, one is tempted to say that the best arguments for the divinity of Christ and His revelations are the efforts of these fantastic exegetes to discredit Him.

Bishop Felder is not a bit too severe when he characterizes the work of the self-styled higher critics (predigested for the get-culture-quick faddists by writers like Emil Ludwig) as "An arbitrary fabrication of history completed in the name of a pre-conceived view of the universe." As I have already implied, a reading in this chaos of bickering rivals was a major influence in reconverting me to orthodox Christianity. "The moderns," as Bishop Felder sums them up, "consciously or unconsciously, proceed from the assumption that Jesus could have been only the representative and the incorporation of their own ideas and ideals. It is true, these ideas and these ideals are very varied in different critics. They show themselves in all the changing colours of the naturalistic, empiric, rationalistic, agnostic and monistic views of the universe." More imposing are the widespread confessions of defeat among the more honest of the more recent "liberals" and "radicals" themselves. Thus Julius Kaftan in *Jesus und Paulus* admits that "The portrait of Jesus, drawn by modern theology, is only supposedly real history." In *Von Reimarus zu Wrede,* Albrecht Schwertzer bitterly conceded that "The historical inquiry into the life of Jesus has not proceeded from a purely historical interest, but has sought to find in the Jesus of history an assistant in the fight for freedom from dogma." What an enslaving freedom is the tense, stubborn liberty of the freethinker! Bishop Felder collects scores of their semi-repentant surrenders to their own futility and concludes: "And just as only that study of Christ which confesses the Messiahship and divinity of our Savior can lay claim to the spirit of Christianity, so only can such a study claim to follow the scientific method. Every christological conception which regards Jesus as a mere man is, if historically considered, a fanciful monstrosity. Christ and Christianity cannot be measured and conceived by merely human standards. Whoever forms an estimate of this unique personality and phenomenon of history, without prejudice, partiality or prepossession, cannot but fall upon his knees and exclaim with the Prince of the Apostles: 'Lord, to whom shall we go? Thou hast the words of eternal life; and we have believed and known that Thou art the Christ, the Son of the living God.' " In a very recent and most beautiful book which he who runs may read, and, indeed, in reading, will feel more and more exultantly that he is running like an angel — in his *Jesus of Nazareth*, Bishop Felder sums up the work of his mighty volumes and adds a long appreciation of the character of our Lord that is itself a hymn-like confirmation of His Divinity.

As Grandmaison says, Jesus did not come like the Buddha in a half-legendary period, or like Mahomet in a remote district of Arabia. The Palestinian world in which He appeared stands in the full light of history, and new discoveries are constantly being made. He was born in the days of Augustus, and was contemporary with Tiberius, Philo the Jew, Titus Livius, and Seneca. The public persons mentioned in the Scripture accounts are intimately known: Annas and Caiphas, Herod the Great and Herod Antipas who mocked Christ, Pontius Pilate and the others, while nothing is better established than the history of the Precursor and of the immediate followers of Christ. St. Luke supplies us with year and place and every public detail of His coming.

On the Master thus located many texts speak to us offering us, together with the geography, the institutions, the literature, and the customs of a definite period, innumerable details. A compact group of the faithful, many of them powerful in speech and in works, give themselves to him unconditionally, openly professing that only by him do they go to God; and a whole world of particular beliefs, and a liturgical cult gifted with a prodigious force of expansion, has reference solely to him. Now between this spiritual blossoming and the God whom it proclaims not as an ideal or a symbol, but as a living person and as a fact, there is no longer thought to stretch the century which David Frederick Strauss postulated when he wrote his *Life of Jesus*, nor even the half-century demanded by the others. Twenty-five years after the date assigned by all to the violent death of this man "under Pontius Pilate," certain authentic and relatively considerable writings, the letters of Paul, take for their fundamental theme, Jesus of Nazareth, his life and death.

And even those twenty-five years were spanned, we have ample evidence, by oral tradition. Since Jesus never bade His Apostles to write, Tradition is as important, for Catholicism, as the Bible. The Tradition which Luther violently cast away in his reckless efforts to sunder himself absolutely from holy Mother Church is the same Tradition reverently treasured and most critically sifted by those great geniuses, the early Fathers, and by various early historians of the Church. To this Tradition I will return when, in my last chapter, I launch out upon an account of my growing acquaintance with the continuous apostolicity of the Church from the days of St. Peter and St. Paul to those of Blessed Frances Xavier Cabrini who died in 1917 and was beatified in 1938 for her holiness and for her world-wide work in the establishment of hospitals and orphanages.

The very fact that some of the first Jewish documents of the Christian era attacked so violently what is called the "Jesus myth" is significant because, as Father Grandmaison shrewdly suggests, "a merely legendary being is not hated, or disfigured or pursued by prejudice." And the greatest Jewish historian, a contemporary, Josephus, many of whose works are so well preserved, makes it clear in several passages (even if we omit one possible interpolation) that he had no doubt that Jesus lived.

The main value of early Pagan testimony lies in its grudging testimony to the pertinacity, unexampled heroism, and unimpeachable morality of the early followers of Christ. As to their pertinacity, Suetonius tells us how the Emperor Claudius "expelled from Rome the Jews who had become under the influence of Chrestus a permanent cause of disorders." Jews in general were often confused with Christians. And turbulent non-Christian Jews were often busy defaming their Christian brethren. As a matter of fact, the only sedition that has been veraciously imputed to Christians under the Empire was their refusal to burn incense to deified emperors and to various other gods who were included in the decadent liberal Roman pantheon. Christians, like Jews of high integrity, could worship but one God.

As mature ethnology from Andrew Lang to Father Wilhelm Schmidt shows, polytheism never precedes but is always a degenerate aftermath of a waning monotheism. This has been for me one of the most valuable of all the thronging discoveries of my reading during the past decade. At last I have come to understand just how, as belief wanes, the gods multiply as an overcompensation for a waxing doubt. And then, how easy and how apparently familiar and friendly it is to worship everybody's god! We see it today in the tendency of flabby liberalism to say that one man's religion is as worthy as another's. But Roman liberalism, like all brands of liberalism, could become quite intolerant when Nero, as lauded by Suetonius, punished Christians for their "new and evil superstition" by smearing them with inflammable substances (as Spanish "loyalist" Communists have done to Christians in our day) and setting them on fire to add to the garish gaiety of the grandeur that was Rome. Though less brutal, Tacitus was equally suspicious of the followers of Jesus, while still admitting their pertinacity. "Their name comes from Christ, who, under the rule of Tiberius, was delivered up to punishment by the procurator Pontius Pilate. Though suppressed at the time, this detestable superstition broke out afresh, not only in Judea where this evil had taken birth, but also in Rome where everything horrible and shameful in the world gathered together and found numerous disciples."

But at the same time, within a few years, Pliny the Younger who, as an experienced statesman abroad, knew far more about Christians than did Tacitus, paid a very striking tribute to the holiness and fortitude of the followers of Jesus whom he had met at first hand. While a legate of Bithynia he wrote a letter to his friend, the Emperor Trajan, admitting his hesitation over punishing Christians. Were they to be punished simply for being Christians? He had threatened, he had sentenced to death. But they multiplied. No real Christian would curse Christ. Charges of crimes brought against Christians were nullified even when two deaconesses were tortured. All that could be proved was that they had certain regular meetings, sang hymns to Christ *as God,* took oath, not to commit crimes, but to prevent them, and shared a common meal at evening gatherings. They were, in brief, guilty of naught but their "superstition." The philosopher, Seneca, had also written, in astonishment, of their unique courage and kindliness in the midst of excruciating tortures.

What, short of Divine Revelation handed on for the most part orally and in the face of all but insuperable obstacles, could account for that incomparable resilience and unquenchable charity which staggered even the world-weary pagan? I began to realize, as I studied these things, what the Tradition which Luther so arrogantly tossed aside meant and still means to those who are faithful to it. From the give and take of conversation we can learn to understand and believe as we never learn from books. It was and is, I now see, the living word, from Jesus to John, from John to Polycarp, from Polycarp to Irenaeus, and so on down to His Holiness Pope Pius XII, the living word which, with God's grace,

makes martyrs exultant in death and so aflame with love that it flows
out on their very torturers and slayers, who are not infrequently converted while they are at the most intense point of their hellishness. No
wonder that even today, J. C. Powys, disheartened by our own neopagan
spiritual bankruptcy, sees its precursor in ancient pagan days and, in
his autobiography, after writing of "those symbols of pure lust on the
sinister brick-red walls of ancient Pompeii," adds that "you have only
to enter one of the little Byzantine churches of the Rome we know
today to realize what a rainy dew of cuckoo flower freshness must have
fallen upon the jaded sexuality of the ancient world."

VIII. CREDENTIALS OF THE NEW TESTAMENT

We may now follow Father Grandmaison in an examination of the
Christian sources of the history of our Divine Saviour. Few are aware
of the host of documents which are not admitted to the canonical collection (the *New Testament*), vigorous, if uncritical in their legendary and
historical contributions. In the main they add nothing valid to the
Gospel stories, but in a few cases furnish collections of the words of our
Lord which were not despised by men as ancient, as erudite, and as
acute as Origen, Eusebius, and St. Jerome, together with certain similar
remains restored from Egyptian papyri by scholars who have unearthed
them in the past twenty-five years or so. Negatively, they are often
valuable, at least, for fixing the text of the Gospels and, in the case of
the papyri, for confirming some Gospel allusion (in Luke, for instance)
which some "higher critic" had declared unhistorical.

With the canonical sources we come to writings attributed to St. Paul,
to whom, from day to day I grow so indebted that I must devote to him
the major part of a later chapter. The authenticity of most of St. Paul's
Epistles is now firmly established. Of those challenged we know that
they are as old and almost as valuable as the unquestioned letters of the
great missionary to the Gentiles.

St. Paul, a Jew some ten years the junior of Jesus, was a member of
a dispersed nation, but obtained the rights of Roman citizenship. Besides
the culture of his Tarsus, he imbibed the culture of Greece and Rome,
so that his literary manner became more supple and coherent than that
of his race. Indeed, Greek lyricism, which had become sterile, was reborn
in his composition which, as Edward Norton noticed, "rises even to the
level of Plato's in the *Phaedrus*."

But Paul was too masterful a man to become a mere stylist. "We can affirm," as Father Grandmaison applauds him, "without fear of contradiction by anyone who has tried to translate a few of his pages, that no one has ever written like this man," that "never has there been one more passionate, more original, or in the literary sense of the word, more inspired." I have already recorded how deeply I was impressed with his profundity when at Harvard I had to struggle with each one of his words in the Gothic translation, and how I set myself to compare and contrast this text with the English ones of Wyclif, Tyndale, and the King James translators.

Among his companions were St. Mark, "the cousin of Barnabas," who was named in *The Acts of the Apostles*, as "a good man, full of the Holy Ghost and of faith," and St. Luke, "the beloved physician." And although Paul in his days as a persecutor knew not Christ in the flesh, at his conversion he saw his Lord in His risen radiance. Again and again he insists, with a sanity and a sincerity that cannot be impugned, that Divine Revelation has come to him *directly* from God.

I will never forget my astonishment when I discovered that, despite all the vicissitudes in the days of manuscripts of papyrus and later of parchment, the Good News survived in a far greater number of versions than the masterpieces of pagan Greece and Rome. In the latter case, with the exception of a few extremely popular authors like Homer or Virgil, the difficulty is, as B. H. Streeter remarks in the *Four Gospels,* "the paucity and late date of MSS. No portion of Tacitus, for example, survived the Dark Ages in more than one version. Again, apart from fragments, there are no MSS. of the Greek classics earlier than the ninth century, and very few older than the twelfth." The enemy may remark that this is the fault of medieval Christians. Any cursory study of the work on the pagan classics in the early monasteries and Catholic universities will give the lie to that slander. On the other hand, it seems little short of miraculous that such a multitude of versions of the Gospels, in part or whole, survived the fearful persecutions of the pagans, the repeated inundations of plunder-drunk barbarians, and the prolonged outrageous cruelty of the hordes of heretical Arians. Add to this Hort's outline (in *The New Testament in the Original Greek*) of his twenty-five years of investigation with Westcott of the discrepancies and similarities and identities of the multifarious material. An enormous amount of more recent comparison and collation has not seriously shaken the judgment of Hort when he concludes:

The proportion of words virtually accepted on all hands as raised above doubt is very great, not less, on a rough computation, than seven eighths of the whole. The remaining eighth, therefore, formed in great part by changes of order and other comparative trivialities, constitutes the whole area of criticism. . . . The amount of what can in any sense be called substantial variation is but a small part of the whole residuary variation, and can hardly form more than a thousandth part of the entire text.

The study of the Gospels as literature and the more familiar acquaintance with the *Koine*, or common language in the Greco-Roman world of Christ's day, has further increased the reliance of scholars on them. Similarly a comparison of the realism of the Gospels with the legendary stories in many of the lives of the early saints is most convincing evidence. What particularly impressed me were such passages as the following which I can only partially quote here from Bishop Felder's *Christ and the Critics:*

The evolution of the Church's faith was accomplished in company with, and by reason of, external, tangible facts, and obvious, manifold and well-known history. The time, the scene, the circumstances of the super-human life and activity of Jesus, and the persons participating in them, are characterized in minutest detail.

It was, for example, in Corozain, Bethsaida and Capharnaum that His divine power of performing miracles was proved in broad daylight and in the presence of all the people. In the synagogue at Capharnaum, still used by the Jews, He drove out the devil. . . . Under circumstances which are minutely described He also healed the man sick of the palsy and the servant of the centurion, and raised from the dead the daughter of Jairus, the ruler of the synagogue. Would it have occurred to the community of Christians to invent these and similar details, and would the Evangelists have had the audacity to record them, if they had been wholly or even partially invented? Must not the persons appealed to, as witnesses, have disclosed the falsity of these legends? And there were among them not merely believers in Christ, but also enemies of Christ — individuals, groups and entire villages.

Much more, as the author says, would the leaders of the people, constantly upbraided for their unbelief and the judicial murder committed by them, have given the lie to the statements made regarding the miracles and works of Christ by the disciples in the streets and squares of the city, if these statements had not been perfectly true. "This silence on the part of contemporary enemies is the most eloquent defence of Gospel history."

IX. THE SYNOPTIC GOSPELS

The first of the three Synoptic Gospels was a favorite in the early Church, partly, no doubt, because composed by one of the Twelve who had walked and conversed with Christ. Its authorship by St. Matthew is unchallenged in the early tradition and it was clearly intended primarily for the Jews, both believers and others. According to St. Irenaeus, to whom we owe much priceless information (for he was a pupil of St. Polycarp who in turn was a disciple of St. John the Divine), St. Matthew sat down to indite his Gospel "when Peter and Paul were evangelising Rome and founding the Church." His book is Jewish to its very marrow, a fact to which the Apostle himself drew attention. "From the very beginning," notes Father Grandmaison referring to Matthew's geneology of Christ, "we are plunged into the atmosphere of the Old Testament." None of the other contributors to the Gospels knew more than he about "the spiritual outlook, the manners, the customs, and the language of the educated rabbis of his time." In Matthew's work the Jewish rhythms, which so aided the hearers of oral recitation to carry away the content in memory, fairly swarm. On the other hand, nobody is as relentless as this saint, once a publican, in condemning the infidelity of the Jews to their Messiah. Even I, as a boy, felt so strongly the homely intimacy of Matthew that he was my first favorite.

St. Mark, on the other hand, did not move me. And it is only lately that I have learned to treasure for its own unique contribution, his mercilessly bare narrative with all its swift sincerity. St. Mark, it seems, was somewhat slighted by the ancients, though now he is much eulogized by our contemporaries. Papias of Hierapolis, writing about A.D. 125, quoted by Eusebius, shows how Mark was less orderly in his construction than Matthew, yet also how close was Mark to the Tradition which arose among those who knew and learned from Jesus in the flesh. Mark was Peter's disciple and, as the earliest writers of the Church agree, set down Peter's discourses precisely as he had heard them "without troubling to place in consecutive order the oracles of the Lord." When Peter learned of Mark's intention, Clement tells us, He did not make any comment, either to dissuade him from his course, or to encourage him in it." In his First Epistle Peter affectionately refers to him as "my son Mark."

The Gospel according to St. Luke is, in the opinion of the aesthete-apostate, Renan (who wrote this phrase perhaps with a wistful backward look toward the days before he cast aside his priestly cassock), "the most beautiful book that has ever been written." Perhaps I shared something of this feeling. For it gradually replaced Matthew as my favorite Gospel in my Congregationalistic boyhood hours in Sunday School, at just the time when I began to grow sensitive to the charms of literary styles. St. Luke, as we have seen, was a cultivated physician and the disciple of St. Paul. *The Acts of the Apostles,* which is quite clearly a continuation of Luke's *Gospel,* contains (about a tenth of it) passages written in the first person plural. These fragments, claims Father Grandmaison, are "generally admitted" to be "pages of the diary of a journey kept by a companion of St. Paul" who "was an eyewitness of the later facts recorded in the Acts" and "was also the author of the whole work," and therefore "of the Third Gospel." This is as good a place as any to insert the point that the wealth of wide-ranging quotations in Father Grandmaison's lifework are gleaned not only from Catholic but from Protestant and from non-Christian and anti-Christian sources.

Many authors have loved to quote as an example of Luke's marmoreal style, uniquely Hellenistic among the authors of *The New Testament,* the following flawless, preludial sentence: "Forasmuch as many have taken in hand to set forth in order a narration of the things that have been accomplished among us, according as they have delivered them unto us, who from the beginning were eyewitnesses and ministers of the word; it seemed good to me also, having diligently attained to all things from the beginning, to write to thee, most excellent Theophilus, in order that thou mayest know the verity of those words in which thou hast been instructed." Humble in his attitude toward his forerunners, St. Luke claims only the merit of careful investigation of his sources, of lucidity, coherence, and fullness. He is notable for his adoration of divine mercy. His opposition to caste snobbishness and racial intolerance made him the constant champion of the poor who have not, in their desire for wealth, forgotten God. Luke is the sole recorder of the parables of the Good Samaritan, of the Prodigal Son, and of the Pharisee and the Publican, together with his stories of the sinning woman and of the good thief who was crucified with Jesus. Luke also stands out in his tenderness. More than any of the composers of the Gospels, he lavishes special attention on St. Elizabeth, the mother of John the Baptist, on St. Anna, the venerable prophetess of the Temple, on the widow whose son was restored to life at Naim, on Mary Magdalene, on the women of Jerusalem who wept to see Christ swooningly staggering on His way to Calvary, on those who stood at the foot of the cross, on those who first heralded the Resurrection, and on many more — but above all on the Blessed Virgin Mary, Mother of Jesus, who, tradition assures us, gave him herself much priceless information.

I was carried a long way toward my ultimate convictions when I developed a practice of considering the three Synoptic Gospels taken together. Because writing materials were costly, cumbrous, and perishable, and because of the recitational habits of the early Christians, faithful to Jewish tradition and persistent in their use of modulated and rhythmical discourse "in which the very accent of the Master could survive," the works of Matthew, Mark, and Luke did not appear until the paucity of trained evangelists fell far short of the multitude of churches and until this need was reinforced by liturgical demands. St. Luke in his prologue does refer not merely to the other pair of contributors but to the "many" pioneers of information. He follows St. Mark closely, sometimes condensing but sometimes supplementing. He enriches especially the accounts of the Childhood of Jesus and of His Passion and Resurrection. St. Mark's gospel, mainly narrative, fairly throbs with "the rude vivacity," as Father Grandmaison describes it, of his instructor St. Peter. St. Matthew is "drier, less colored, but more careful." His accent is less vulnerable to "rash interpretations, and sometimes absolutely prevents them." Though it contains "very striking and numerous similarities of vocabulary" to those in the work of St. Mark, it has a definite independence "as regards facts." Its unity of plan, which "in no way savors of a compilation," is fortified with "a unity of sentiment," just such as you would expect from a comrade of Jesus Himself. Then, too, scholars note its strong traces of an earlier Aramaic version. To B. H. Streeter, in his *Studies in the Synoptic Problem,* it seems that "At every step we feel that Matthew is writing for those to whom Pharasaic Judaism is a very real and potent force of mixed attraction and repulsion." Father Grandmaison also notes as an evidence of its archaism "its absence of prejudice on the points which divided the early Christians." The notion that the writer may not have been Matthew himself finds no support in ancient tradition.

As I toiled through the tortuous efforts of the "higher critics" to reconsider the traditional dates of the Gospels, I was amused by their collective behavior which resembled that of the celebrated King of France who, with his ten thousand soldiers, marched up the hill and marched down again. They set out with a bold, iconoclastic fanfare and then executed a grudging retreat toward the position always maintained by the Catholic Church. With the passing years investigators have pushed the dates of the versions which we possess farther and farther back toward the days when Christ dwelt on earth. In 1835 Strauss dated them all, at the earliest, in the year 150. Harnack (1911) fixes our Greek version of the Aramaic of Matthew at about 70, Mark at about 65, Luke at about 67. Further, Harnack, the greatest "liberal" Protestant scholar, thinks the version of Mark, used about 67 by Luke, is a second edition and that the common source may be dated "about 50 or even earlier." He adds:

Sixty years ago, David Frederic Strauss thought that he had deprived the first three Gospels of almost all their value. . . . The historical and critical labors of two generations have succeeded in restoring it to them in great measure. . . . The Gospels are not "party documents. . . ." They belong, in their essentials, to the primitive Judaic period of Christianity, to that short period which we may call palæontological. It is a happy accident for which we ought to be thankful to history, that we still possess accounts dating from this period. . . . The absolute character of the Gospels is today universally recognized by critics. . . . That in them we are, for all essentials, face to face with primitive tradition, is incontestable.

Today, Father Grandmaison has shown further that a "careful study of the Gospel rhythms discloses in the sermons of Jesus, beneath the individual characteristics of each writer, a continuous quality of a unique type, which is guaranteed by the literary form itself. It is often possible with the help of these indications to prove directly the authenticity of the words of Jesus." He warns us that "It needs very strong views (or rather prejudices) to enable anyone to attribute the Beatitudes, the 'Consider the lilies of the field,' the 'Render to Caesar . . .' or the Parable of the Good Samaritan, to the improvisation of anonymous prophets." In *La Mission Historique de Jesus* Henri Monier insists that "The words of Jesus were clear and indestructible. . . . They could neither be imitated nor altered." And even J. Middleton Murry, the "freethinker," in *Jesus Man of Genius*, entertains similar views. Father Grandmaison points out that while Jewish Palestinian Society was crashing into ruin in the years 66–70, and *even earlier, as far back in fact as the year 44*, this region was "becoming more and more disorganized each day. . . .

It is Palestinian society before these great disturbances, and in a state of comparative peace, that the synoptic evangelists always depict and that with an exactitude which is quite striking."

X. THE GOSPEL OF ST. JOHN

And now we turn from the synoptists to *The Gospel of St. John,* the prime favorite of my Catholic days, as indeed it must be for any student of Christology. It was composed by the Apostle in his old age, at the entreaties of his friends whom he besought first to pray for him and to perform many acts of penance. He then plunged into his sublime opening chapter which is recited at the close of almost every Mass. I remember once, when it was being read in the St. James Cathedral in Seattle, how, as I followed it through in my Missal, the great organ thundered out a jubilant accompaniment which was magnificently worthy of its soaring mysticism.

As to the historical value of the Johannine narrative, even the infidel Renan, who had ridiculed its validity in the early editions of his *Life of Jesus,* qualified his position profoundly in his final version. Thirty years before him, the inconoclastic Strauss had made a similar partial recantation and confessed that he first exploited the unfavorable side "with exclusively polemical zeal" because it had been neglected. "But little by little the favorable side has regained its rights; yet I cannot ... sacrifice all the objections without more ample information." In our own day the modernist insurgent, Loisy, who had dubbed this Gospel "a theological theorem which scarcely keeps the appearance of history," decided, in the second edition of *Le Quatrieme Evangile* that the book possesses a fair measure of history. Though Loisy fancifully attributed this to unscrupulous editing and though Strauss suffered a later relapse, we may agree with Father Grandmaison that these vacillations "demonstrate that the question of the historical value of the Fourth Gospel remains an open question in face of even the most independent criticism, the most detached from all dogmatic pursuits." Attempts to explain it as a maze of allegories and symbols peculiar to St. John's own type of Christianity have been riven assunder by their "improbabilities of detail" and by their lack of power to provide a "coherent and clear hypothesis for this unfortunate attempt at a purely symbolical explanation,'" until such efforts have either been relinquished or have come to "present a spectacle of anarchy most consoling for the upholders of tradition."

In this connection no one who reads open-mindedly Bishop Felder's encyclopedic survey of this controversy will be able to doubt the veracity of tradition. "In reality," so he sums up the defense, "all the prejudices against the genuineness of John's Gospel proceed, from first to last, from the alleged incredibility of its contents. The doubts of the Johannine origin of this document are not based upon 'positive observation of the text and positive far-reaching knowledge of tradition . . . but the representatives of such hypotheses were united only in the negative decision that a personal disciple could not have written the book, since its contents are held to be incredible for various reasons, partly historical, partly psychological, partly philosophical and partly dogmatic.'

"The genuineness of John's Gospel can, therefore, be doubted only in so far as its credibility is doubtful." And when we turn to the question of its credibility we find a rapidly growing number of iconoclasts, those whose honesty has triumphed over their chagrin, paying full tribute to the historical reliability and indeed the very unusual vividness, homeliness, and precision of "the disciple whom Jesus loved." Indeed, I find it difficult to see how even the most enthusiastic theorymongers could have remained so stubborn in their efforts to turn the Fourth Gospel into mere allegory. For, as Bishop Felder says, "Personal occurrences in the life of Jesus are not presented in general, undefined features, as is necessarily the case with the hero of any allegory, but are carved, plastically, concretely and vividly from life, with an exact statement of place, time and other circumstances." The homeliness of St. John's narrative, I repeat, is so intimately fused with its high mysticism as to command a belief in its supernatural inspiration, the trait that came more and more to amaze me as I read and reread it. Bishop Felder emphasizes especially the Johannine account of the days of the Passion and Crucifixion of our Lord. "With almost the precision of a statistician, and with the deep emotion of the disciple most closely concerned in them, John describes them faithfully to the minutest details." Like another favorite mystic of mine, St. John of the Cross, this witness of the Death and Resurrection of our Lord seems all the more convincing as a mystic to me, because, whenever need be, he can keep his feet so firmly on the ground. And he is to me all the more convincing as an understanding historian because, as a mystic, he has penetrated into the very heart of the meaning of life.

Moreover, as a matter of fact, we have far more ancient materials for tracing the origin of the Fourth Gospel and for studying the life of its author than for the books and characters of the three synoptists. "But," as Father Grandmaison warns us, "tradition, which is clear when looked at from a height, becomes contentious and subject to endless disputes, if it is studied from one of its links." Our first fact, a convincing one, emerges in the *Epistle* of St. Ignatius of Antioch (about 107 or 110), a work which cannot well be explained except by supposing a long contact with and a real assimilation of that "Johannine doctrine and spirit which is extremely rare in the other ancient Christian writings." Soon after 110 or 120, St. Polycarp, who was a disciple of St. John, quotes from his master's first Epistle which is really a sort of introduction to the Gospel. In his first *Apology* (c. 150) and *Dialogue* (c. 160), St. Justin alludes unmistakingly to St. John's book. Such quotations and allusions then multiplied in the following years. And it is notable that they appear at "all points of the doctrinal and geographical horizon." Soon arose broadcast accounts (accepted by the Church) of St. John's activity, longevity, composition of the Fourth Gospel, the *Apocalypse,* and the *Epistles.* A fragment of the lost *Hypotyposes* by Clement of Alexandria makes the significant remark that "John . . . the last of all, seeing that the exterior features (of the Life of Christ) had been well brought out in the Gospels, urged on by his disciples and moved by the Spirit, wrote a spiritual Gospel."

St. Irenæus, Bishop of Lyons, recognized by Tertullian as "a very painstaking enquirer in matters of doctrine," much esteemed as an historical source for the study of heresies by the most rigorous of our modern critics, and the friend of St. Polycarp, writes: "Then John, the disciple of the Lord, he who had reclined on His breast, gave also [his version of the Gospel] while he dwelt at Ephesus." To me, as I began, from such sources, to realize what the Catholic Church meant by that Tradition which Luther so fatally discarded, it seemed that my new Mother had taken me in her arms and transported me back over the ages until I could hear the very voices of those martyrs of the subapostolic period. In admonishing Florinus, who had fallen away from orthodoxy, St. Irenæus testified:

So well do I remember it all that I could tell the place where the blessed Polycarp sat himself down to teach, and his manner of entering and of going out, his way of living, and the beauty of his appearance, the discourses he gave to the people, and the familiar conversation which he had with John and with the others who had seen the Lord, as he has related and recalled their words. And what he heard from them concerning the Lord, His miracles, His teaching, the details concerning those who had seen with their eyes the

Word of Life, as Polycarp related it, and all in conformity with the Scriptures (all these do I remember). All that has since then by the mercy of God developed upon [he narrated]; I listened carefully, and I engraved it, not on papyrus, but in my heart and forever. By the grace of God, I remember it exactly. . . . And Polycarp was not only instructed by the Apostles, and had converse with many of those who had seen Christ, but he was also established by the Apostles in Asia, as bishop of the Church which is at Smyrna. And we ourselves saw him in the flower of his age, for he was so long preserved, and passed out of life gloriously in extreme old age by the noble gate of martyrdom.

Then I caught my breath as I remembered that St. Irenæus, too, faced martyrdom serene and exultant in his memory of the spoken words of St. Polycarp. Yes, I thought, what madness of Luther's could have blinded him to these momentous facts? But when I remembered his even more perverse unresponsiveness to the evidence for oral apostolic tradition in his favorite, St. Paul, I wondered less at his contempt for the succeeding generations. But how I longed to introduce my old Protestant friends, friends who had lost their faith, as I had, largely because ignorant of these facts which Luther censored — how I longed to share with them all this spiritual wealth!

The Fourth Gospel itself, unlike its predecessors, contains brief references to its author as the disciple whom Jesus loved. A careful survey of the references to specific disciples in the earlier Gospels and to certain historical events (for example that James died in the year 43) makes John the most likely Apostle to be described as the beloved. Thus these autobiographical hints in the Fourth Gospel are congruous with both tradition and history.

That the literary unity of the Gospel according to John is highly noteworthy has been conceded even by critics who have tried to prove it the work of "two Johns," an author together with an editor. J. Weiss, for instance, in his *Das Urchristentum*, finds in the entire book "The same type of piety, of religious experience, and of style." Father Grandmaison adds:

We can defy criticism to find elsewhere than in John, half a page that can be confounded with what he has written. . . . It is not a question here merely of vocabulary or turns of style. The very essence, the profundity and unity of inspiration, are above deliberate imitation, beyond the possibility of unconscious similarity. . . . If we cannot write like John at will, it is chiefly because we do not think and feel as John thought and felt.

And the Fourth Gospel forges together, most marvelously, as we have seen, mystical and uniquely valuable historical strains. John, without being at all antisemitic (indeed he was steeped in rabbinical lore), evidently was inspired to exhort imperfectly instructed Christians and insincere ones, Gentiles, wanderers in blighted Hellenic religions and initiations, "and the schools of knowledge and the numerous sects of bewildered heretics who knew not how to interpret deeply and clearly their Christian sources." All this is fused most powerfully with a devotion to the Eucharist and to the other Sacraments. It is most difficult to understand how I, even in my naïve boyhood, or any other Protestant who sets any store in the writings of St. John could possibly cleave to the anemic notion that in the Holy Communion the worshiper consumes the symbols of, rather than the real Body and Blood of our Blessed Lord.

XI. INFALLIBILITY AND SUPREMACY

The question of papal infallibility, which may be briefly mentioned here, had never been a very serious difficulty to me. I always felt that if I could accept divine authority, divine revelation, then I could also accept a divine guardianship necessary to prevent the Church from falling into errors of faith or morals during the future centuries. Only so could Christ's promise be fulfilled that the gates of hell should not prevail against her and that He would send the Holy Ghost to be with her.

Infallibility, namely, implies nothing else than the inerrancy in matters of faith and morals on the part of the Vicar of Christ when, in virtue of his supreme authority, and as teacher and pastor of the faithful, he pronounces a definition *in matters of faith or morals that is intended to obligate the universal Church*. The object of papal infallibility must be either explicitly or implicitly contained in Scripture or Tradition. Only with all these conditions fulfilled do we speak of papal infallibility. Thus when pronouncing merely as a private theologian the pope would not be infallible. Much less does infallibility imply that the pope cannot sin. That would be impeccability, which has never been claimed for him.

Neither could the question of the supremacy of the Supreme Pontiff cause any real difficulty to me. There is no blinking the unchallenged leadership of Peter in the Acts of the Apostles, while the words of Christ, making him the holder of the keys, committing to him the entire flock, the lambs and the sheep, cannot be misunderstood. Nor were they misunderstood by the Apostles and by the early Christians, nor by that same Church through the ages which alone goes back directly to the Apostles and Christ who made Peter the Rock on which to build His Church against which no storms of violence or error should prevail.

The need of the primacy and infallibility of the pope, as promised by Christ and fulfilled in His Church, is evident from the bewilderment existing in all the other churches. No better evidence could be found than in the Episcopal or Anglican church today, claiming to be one, yet maintaining pastors ranging from the very verge of Catholicism to anarchic Unitarianism, holding all sorts of divergent views of the Virgin Birth, the Resurrection and the Christological portions of the Apostles' Creed, to say nothing of ethical problems like divorce and birth control.

CHAPTER IX

THE CITY OF GOD

---

*"It is not the Faith that evolves in the faithful, but the
faithful who evolve in the Faith."*

As I look back over the rememberable years of the half century that
was required to draw me to receive my first Holy Communion before
the high altar in St. Joseph's Church — and I have always been so given
to reminiscence both pleasurable and painful that my memory is a
veritable beehive of moods and scenes and books and persons — I feel
almost everywhere and at every time the inspiration of that divine purpose called Providence. The very name of the beloved town of my
nativity, childhood, youth, and early manhood, Providence, seems like
a symbol which haunts me "like a passion." It is true that my way has
wound not always upward. I have had many fainting spells, steep falls,
despondencies, and perversities. Yet on the whole, the general influence
of tradition and truth has been graciously cumulative. I must have received many visitations of the Holy Ghost in many an hour of burningly
conscious and dimly conscious loneliness and nostalgia. That is why I
often murmur today, as I go to my work and toward my home, the
Catholic ejaculation, "O Holy Spirit, sweet Guest of my soul, remain
with me and see that I ever remain with Thee."

It is, for a fact, a good deal of a riddle to me why our heavenly Father
withheld from me for so many buoyant springs, opulent summers, mellow
autumns, and bleak winters, through worries, through acute and dangerous illness, through temptations conquering and conquered, in spite
of my frequent uprushes of the will to believe, the measure of sanctifying grace needful to make me whole. But we Catholics develop a growing
tendency to find in many misty, dank twilights and many tribulations
the tremendous reasonableness of God's mercy. And I am forced to confess that I now believe that I received a long preparation as an alien to
the faith in order that I might assist other wanderers so often suspicious
of those born and bred as Catholics. "Jesus, meek and humble of heart,
make my heart like unto Thine."

I. FIRST AXIOM OF ARISTOTELIAN THOMISM

In an earlier chapter I observed that the thoroughly trained Catholic and the Catholic alone, in contrast with the philosophers of all the other schools, is catholic (universal) enough to make use, quite consistently, of all the ways of knowing of all the schools, skeptical, empirical, rationalistic (*a priori*), pragmatic (or, more broadly and precisely, experimental), authoritarian (dogmatic), and mystical.

Thus although the pure skeptic, if there ever was one, would refute himself by knowing that all knowledge is impossible, it is a most healthy habit to be more or less skeptical. David Hume, in particular, was without question skeptical. Bertrand Russell's work is but a wraithlike imitation of his, dolled up with a certain phraseology derived from up-to-the-minute mathematics and physics, but in fundamental content not one step forward. The trouble with Hume was that he was not skeptical enough. If he had grown a little more daringly skeptical he would have become a Thomist — horrible fate for a "freethinker" of the "Age of Enlightenment!" He criticized Descartes for beginning his philosophy by believing in too much when he said: "I think, therefore I am." Hume was right, from the point of view of the one-sided empiricist who thinks that knowledge is a mere matter of piling up sensations and images like separate bricks without mortar. When Hume, in his *Treatise on Human Nature,* searched for himself he found only a single isolated "perception." To him the "I" seemed to be a mere fiction, an unintegrated "bundle of perceptions." Russell plays the sedulous ape and says that the first certainty is merely that there is an "event," a "thought," and that what we call the "I" is a mere name for a "history" of thought-events "causally connected." What can *he* mean, on his own presuppositions, by "causally connected"? His master, Hume, was more consistent; he denied also the reality of causation and the workability of any substitute concept.

The scholastic philosopher is even more empirical, at appropriate points, than Hume and Russell for he ranges over a far vaster assemblage of facts, including many which they dogmatically deny, notably supernatural facts. But the Thomist is also more cunning in his analysis of the *a priori* concept. Hume and Russell, when they think that they find empirically that cluster of perceptions or string of thoughts called an "I" or even a single "thought," have assumed too much. How do *they* know that what they have found is a *mental* substance or even a *mental* event? The schoolman makes no such large assumption. He begins merely with the obvious remark, not that he finds a thought or idea or that a thought or idea is "given" (to whom? to what? and by whom? by what?) but that there *is something*. Whether that something is "mental" or "material" or both has yet to be seen. But there *is* a something which is what it is; in other words, x = x; whatever is, is. Here we have that principle of identity which Hegel (something after the manner of Heraclitus, whom Aristotle had disposed of some two thousand years before) undertook to deny by blurring identity with similarity, by ignoring Aristotle's profound division of "being" into the potential and actual, and his definition of change as the transition from potentiality to actuality, by declaring (with characteristically Hegelian and, later Marxian, sophistry) that "being" is the emptiest of concepts, and therefore equating it with nonbeing in order to deify a blind "becoming," whereas "being" is precisely the richest and most inclusive of all concepts.

From x = x, the Aristotelian-Thomist proceeds to the equally self-evident principle of contradiction which even almighty God cannot violate: that a thing cannot both be and not be at the same time and in the same respect, that is to say, x cannot be non-x, that x = not non-x, in other words that x = x. Onward we proceed to the equally self-evident principle of excluded middle: that between being (potential or actual with the transitional becoming) and not-being there is no intermediary thing: x is not non-x; there is no conceivable other meaning for not non-x except x; so once more x = x.

The scholastic philosopher goes on to note that whatever reality a being has, it must originate either of or by itself or else from some other being; in other words x is either self-explanatory or must be explained, as to its origin and peculiar nature, in terms of some other being as its "sufficient reason." Those contemporary philosophers, for instance the self-styled "emergent materialists" (with whom the bankrupt Marxist is just now hopefully and pathetically coming to terms), who try to deny the principle of sufficient reason, invariably, sooner or later, exemplify their nihilism by treating the purely negative and, at its best, static-mathematical concept of "chance" as if it explained or as if it were a dynamic cause, or by ascribing to some effect a cause far too fragmentary, as any scientist acquainted with the facts would discover at once. From this emasculated "cause" or "chance" they then point triumphantly to a "superior" result. In the end their position comes to this: that nothing, by exercising its own initiative, becomes something, that non-x, un-aided, becomes x. But whatever conclusion their armchair theories beget in practice, they recognize like every sane person that since a cause is what in any manner contributes to the production of being, it follows that every x must have a cause, either in Itself (the Infinite) or in another, to give it being. Those who today deny cause are either fol-lowers of Hume who erroneously made knowledge the sum of our sense experiences, and of the sense experiences alone, or they confuse the boundaries of *pure* mathematics and the physical sciences which *use* mathematics for *some* of their results.

The principle of causality, which no one can *consistently* reject outside or even inside of the madhouse, leads us ultimately to the one, infinite X, the Source of being for all other beings including Itself or Himself. This X, which Descartes vainly thought he could reach with his philos-ophy and which Hume and Russell knew that they could not reach with their imperfectly threshed out version of his philosophy, this X, which the Angelic Doctor proves conclusively to exist without any appeal to authority whatsoever, is God the Father Almighty, Creator of heaven and earth.

Then the bare proofs of the bare existence of this X, this "I am who am," carry with them the exposure of what we analogically call Its or His "attributes." These attributes include the certain presence of a dis-position to reveal Himself in various suitable ways to all His creatures. The proof of this and its consequences is set forth in Catholic Apologetics or Fundamental Theology of which we had a few glimpses when, in the chapter on "Difficulties," we considered the credibility of the Gospels and the explanation by St. Thomas Aquinas of the reasons for Divine Revela-tion. All this leads in turn to one of the two most precise and sublime of all sciences, Dogmatic Theology, wherein the Catholic philosopher may combine with his skeptical caution, his empiricism, and his *a priori* rationalism a *reasonably* anthoritarian way of knowing.

The Catholic now may and does often pursue — as a Lavoisier, a Pasteur, a Mendel, a Lemaître — that materialistic, experimental, or pragmatic way of knowing that seeks its goal in controlled and refined empirical verification; or he may pursue another experimental, a super-naturalistic experimental, an even more refined and precise technique for the discovery of the ultimate Truth. And this is the other of the two most precise and sublime sciences, the mystical, the genuinely Mystical Way which, as practised by a St. John of the Cross, does not spurn, but soars upward from, the most expert and austerely calculated achievements of the discursive reason.

II. COMPARATIVE RELIGION

The uniqueness and supremacy of the Catholic Church radiates with increased luster the more often her doctrines are compared with those of other religions, both Christian and non-Christian.

It was only as I approached closer and closer to the threshold of the Church of Rome that I learned the proper perspective in the study of comparative religion which, from my Harvard days onward, had been for me a favorite pastime. The disposition to look upon all religions except one's own as mere heathenry has always seemed to me incompatible with the conception of a God worthy of worship. Even before I read it in St. Paul, I always believed that "Truly God" — if there be a God whom men could love and trust — "hath never left Himself without witness." When I possessed only that "little knowledge" of the religions of the world "which is a dangerous thing," I shared with so many others today the disposition to level down all religions by overemphasizing their similarities. Deepening knowledge, however, revealed to me enormous differences between the so-called incarnations and so-called trinities and sacraments of other religions and those of Christianity. Nevertheless, once well confirmed in Catholicism, I found that I could reverence far more deeply than I did as Protestant or Agnostic the great truths of all the religions, particularly of China and India, while this very deepening reverence ran parallel with a clearer and clearer recognition of the supremacy of Christianity in its pristine purity, that is in its Catholicism, from St. Peter to Pope Pius XII. I wish that I might here dwell, with a charitable eloquence even remotely approaching Otto Karrer's, in his triumphantly Catholic *Religions of Mankind*, on the inspiring virtues of the many religions, even of some, like the Aztec, fever hued with the flush of decadence. But the limitations of space condemn me to the polemical attitude.

Like many other sentimentalists of my day I had my period of dabbling in some of those occidental versions of Buddhism which waylay those of us whose ignorance equals our wistfulness. But I was cured by the briefest of acquaintances.

As to the real thing, Buddhism, in the broadly taken uncritical sense of the term, is certainly one of the greatest of non-Christian faiths.

Born in a twilight of unhistorical legends, it has nonetheless spread widely; but it has done so at the cost of an utter loss of unity, a division into many sects and often a great abyss between the beliefs of the priest-hood and the tenets which the leaders deem fit for absorption by the laity. It is a religion called by some of its students atheistic, by some pantheistic. Here and there some of its proponents have risen at times to the noblest summits of theism. Yet it is well known that the Buddha himself, far from claiming the divinity imputed to him in later ages, in Japan for instance, was himself rather agnostic and certainly intent on teaching a religionless ethic. Later Buddhism has, here and there, bor-rowed more than once from Christianity, whether directly or indirectly, consciously or unconsciously. Fundamentally, however, it tends to gravi-tate toward a pole opposite to Christianity. Though it stresses, not sel-dom overstresses, our finiteness, it often encourages self-centeredness, in the desire to still all desire, in the quest for annihilation into a never clearly defined Nirvana. Though it rises at times to a touching com-passion, it often takes a supine attitude toward evil, so be it that each individual may ignore all evil in his desire to lose himself like a dewdrop in an aimless ocean of being. Buddhism, in Ceylon and India, in China and Japan, is one in little more than its name, and least of all among European and American dilettanti.

In *The Dharma of Gotama the Buddha and the Gospel of Jesus the Christ,* Dr. Charles Francis Aiken has shown that the fad of some of our supercilious intelligentsia for opposing to the miracles wrought by Christ in confirmation of His divine mission, the wonderful things which the Buddhist scriptures ascribe to their religious hero is utterly sophistic.

There is no parity between the miracles told of Christ and those ascribed to Buddha. The former are of a character in every way worthy of one who declared Himself to be the Savior of mankind, and being recorded by His apostles and disciples, who were constant eye-witnesses of His wonderful works, are beyond the suspicion of invention.

While there is thus solid reason to give credence to the Gospel narrative of the miracles of Christ, there is no ground for treating the alleged miracles of Buddha as other than idle myths. It was not till centuries after Buddha's death that they found a place in the sacred records and, moreover, the vast majority are so childish and stupid as to bear on their face the stamp of their fanciful origin. The extravagances of the *Lalita Vistara,* the prominent sacred narrative of the Northern school, would provoke a smile in most children of even tender years.

Professor August Karl Reischauer, in his *Studies in Japanese Buddhism*, has put his finger on the fundamental difficulty which makes oneness for this religion unachievable. "It must be remembered that while Buddhism has much to say theoretically about truth, that is, Absolute Truth as known by the Enlightened One, it regards all truth known to man and even all explanations of the Absolute Truth as not differing essentially from error."

I have given more space to Buddhism than I can afford to any one of the other non-Christian religions except Judaism, because its influence is greater among us. Apparently many of us still feel as I did when I thought that men like George Santayana were seers and I could be impressed by his Olympian remark in *The Realm of Essence*, that, as far as religions went, Buddhism probably approached nearest to the truth.

The oldest Indian book, the *Rigveda*, which scoffers at Christianity never tire of reminding us dates back somewhere about two thousand years before Christ, is recognized by all able scholars today as the work of a very aged and rather decadent civilization which, bewildered no doubt by the curse of original sin, had drifted so far in the ways of a troubled polytheism, that despite certain magnificent outbursts reminiscent of a primordial belief in One Infinite God, it stands in sorry contrast with the young virility of the Jewish *Old Testament* and only confirms our belief that the latter was inspired by God. When we reach the *Upanishads*, the most ancient commentaries on the *Rigveda*, although we find many sublime passages, the pervading note is that of a world-weary pantheism. No need to dwell further on the growing passivity and carnalism of the later stages of Brahminism or Hinduism, even after leaving out those versions that degenerated into atheism. Everyone knows something of the wretched caste system, the temple-prostitution, and the erotic art on the walls of the sacred edifices which would "bring a blush to the cheek of a sergeant-major."

It has been estimated in recent years that Confucianism has been the most considerable rival of Christianity, challenging the latter's 35 per cent of mankind with its 18½, and so contrasting favorably with Islam's 13½, Hinduism's 13, and Buddhism's 8½ per cent. But at the present moment, under the cataclysms which torture China, with the consequent waves of materialistic atheism on the one hand, and rapidly increasing Christianity on the other, Confucianism is waning perceptibly and substantially. For, in spite of its many admirable qualities which I have often heard the amateurs in comparative religion cite with characteristic inaccuracy in order to edge the malice of their smart gibes at Christianity, Confucianism bears many marks of senility, especially in its great emphasis on ancestor worship, a practice recognized by contemporary anthropologists as often a sign of decadence in the cycles of religious history. And like the Buddha, Confucius, though he or his disciples penned more than one soaring passage, was primarily the champion of what seemed to him to be a practical system of ethics which, as such, was largely victorious over the much more profound Taoism of the mystics of China.

Of Mohammedanism's manner of growth, carnal, bloodthirsty, and so ignoble in contrast to the prevailing Christian mode of propagation, we have already taken note. The Christian crusades, be it remembered, were wars of defense. As to Islam's oneness, we must remember first that it is itself a mere schismatic offshoot, like the many forgotten early heresies and the moribund creeds of modern Protestantism, from the pure Christian Tradition. Though Islamism is widespread (within certain sharply delimited areas from Egypt to Java); though it numbers, along with its fanatics, many who have gone much farther than the rank and file of Christians in the ways of holiness; and although it presents a formidable front to Catholic missionaries (some of whom are more learned in Mohammedan theology than the Mohammedan scholars themselves), it has, as we saw, a very vaguely historical background. This renders it peculiarly vulnerable, precisely like Protestantism, to the acute outbursts of heresy which agitate it and rend it from time to time, and which promote disintegrative tendencies, eventuating (as in the case of Protestantism) in pantheism, deism, agnosticism, and atheism. Thus, for instance, as Christopher Dawson shows in his essay on "Islamic Mysticism" in *Enquiries into Religion and Culture,* a chasm arose between Arabian mysticism, with its powerful drift toward fatalism and pantheism, and some of the Persian ecstatics who at times have come very close, and at times explicitly close, to Christianity.

Mohammedanism, too, like eastern schismatic Christianity and the Church of England, Episcopalianism, has always yielded much more to the disintegrating and corrupting influence of Caesar than has the pure Catholic Christianity of the West — even admitting the far too frequent falterings away from God of some of its members. Tirelessly does holy Mother Church beseech her Founder to inspire the Mohammedans, so holy at their best, with a reverence for Him who will withdraw all their misplaced allegiance to various Caesars and give it to His Father to whom they have so long been faithful. "Oh pardon them," prays the Church to their Divine Redeemer, "whatever in scorn of Thy Most Holy Name and of Christianity, they have done to injure Thy chosen people. With one ray of Thy light disperse the darkness in which they are involved, and in the baptism of regeneration open to them the treasures of Thy heart."

Judaism, dear to me through its embodiment in many of my finest friends; Judaism, that unique and magnificent knight-errant of monotheism, in the days of its ancient glory, always triumphing sooner or later over the wiles and violences of the decadent polytheisms which surrounded it; Judaism, faithful under many heartbreaking subjections, scattered, persecuted, and exiled, esteemed from Abraham to Moses, from Moses to David, and from David to the later prophets of Jesus, remains in its most orthodox sect uniquely impressive even to this day.

But the orthodox members are dwindling. The Judaic creeds which have accepted various degrees of "liberalism" have made a fatal surrender of the faith of their fathers. And the Ethical Culture Movement is largely a cleavage based on a nonreligious moralism that closely resembles the fatuous humanisms to which many later-day gentiles resort. Besides these variations the Jews are many-sundered by different national cultures as in Spain, Portugal, northern Europe, and southern Russia. For all of these the Roman Catholic Church, whose popes have often protected them from the persecutions and coercions of her more headstrong and unnaturally bigoted members, has never ceased to offer, like her Founder on the cross, a healing flow of prayers. "Look down," she cries, "look down with eyes of pity, O Lord, on the children of that race, which for so long was Thy chosen people; and may the blood which of old was called down upon them, be poured out on them, a cleansing stream of redemption and life." And from time to time God answers Her tireless prayers in a most healing and heartening way, as I learned when I discovered the profoundly beautiful life and meditations of the Jewish convert, Francis Libermann (1804-1852), a pioneer of the African Missions and a founder of the now most distinguished and productive Congregation of the Holy Spirit.

In 1937 David Goldstein, a courageous Jew who some years ago turned from Socialism to lead a most vivid Catholic apostolic life, drew a comprehensive picture of the religious bankruptcy of Judaism, which was reproduced in *The Catholic Digest*. Of the 15,630,000 Jews in the world, 4,228,029, or 27 per cent, reside within our American borders.

Among these, Mr. Goldstein tells us, regular synagogue membership is very small in the United States. On the basis of the 1916 *Report of Religious Bodies*, the synagogue membership would amount to 17 per cent, but an exact tabulation, he believes, would reduce this to not more than 7 per cent, of whom only one third are synagogue-attending Jews. The hostile feeling of the Reformed Jews against the Orthodox is extreme. Wage-earning Jews have to a large extent exchanged their religion for Socialism, while "Jews educated in our nonreligious institutions of learning are imbued with the notion that pantheism and rationalism alone can stand the test of right reason and science. . . . Much opposition to Jews is due to their being greatly talented and often using those talents in a nonreligious if not in an antireligious way."

With their remarkable natural gifts, it is precisely what the Catholic Church has to offer them "intellectually, esthetically, mystically, and sacramentally," that would enable them to attain to glorious achievements impossible to them "so long as they stand against the Law, as Moses, the patriarchs and prophets intended it to be understood and its fulfillment to be realized."

How, then, can they be approached with things Catholic? Mr. Goldstein has the following suggestions to offer:

First, they must be sympathetically induced to study the books of the Old Testament in the light of Catholic teachings. *Secondly*, they must be shown that the acceptance of the prophecies and their fulfillment as understood by the Catholic Church is not a denial of the faith of their fathers. *Thirdly*, there must be brought to the mind of Jews the historically established fact that the abolition of their priesthood of Aaron, which functioned by divine sanction, the destruction of their Temple and the consequent failure to reinstitute their old sacrifice, which the Orthodox Jews of today pray for, are all a part of the divine plan outlined in the Old Testament. They must be brought to the realization that the persecutions that they have had to face and are still facing, are exhortations, so to speak, of their God of Abraham.

"Meet Jews with the realization of our indebtedness to them. They gave us Moses, Abraham, David, Isaias, Jeremiah, Job, Daniel, the Mother and sons of the Machabees, John the Baptist, and other patriarchs, prophets, and spiritual heroes whom our Church loves to honor. They gave us the *Old Testament* and all the writers of the *New Testament* [except St. Luke]. From the Jews came Jesus the Christ (Messiah) in whose veins flowed the blood of Israel's kings; they gave us the holiest of all holy women, Mary the Virgin Mother of Jesus; Joseph the foster father of our Lord; the twelve Apostles, eleven of whom suffered and died for Christ; from them came the first 8000 members of our Church."

III. THE EARLY SECTS

I have already dwelt upon the time when I first felt a gentle touch of the disciplinary hand of the Church — the only church which has a pure and unequivocal oneness, unity — and how, instead of repressing, it really emancipated. Often, as I brooded happily over this episode, I have come to realize more and more that the admonitions of the spiritual descendants of Jesus and Peter and Paul are, when intelligently interpreted, invariably positive not negative. All heresies throughout the ages have been narrow in one way or another, and in the blindness of their very narrowness they hàve always suffered a paranoidal delusion that the Roman Catholic Church is narrow.

Gnosticism was anathema because it degraded matter and narrowed the conception of Jesus to that of a mere intermediary of God with matter. Thus, like Christian Science today, its attitude toward the Incarnation and toward the Atonement on the Cross was sacrilegious. How ignorant and perverse are those who accuse Catholicism of being cabined, cribbed, confined! The denunciations of the Church, the reverse of proving her to be narrow, are proof of Her Catholicity.

Her martyrs died defiant under the tortures of the Arians because these heretics said that Jesus, the "Word" of St. John, was not the equal of the Father, the true God. She opposed Nestorianism because it sundered Christ into two persons, God the Son and the man Jesus, and drained the conception of the Redemption and Resurrection of all their glory by insisting that it was only the man who died on the cross for our sins. She rebuked the Monophysite for the opposite extreme of denying the humanity of Christ and thus making nugatory His earthly life, of maintaining that there is but one nature in Christ and not the Divine and the Human natures united in one person.

The Donatists held the bigoted and blasphemous view that sinners could not belong to the Church of Him who walked with publicans and sinners. They themselves sinned egregiously, terrorizing with their roving brigandage the true followers of Christ. But they were conquered by that great sinner whom the Church received repentant, St. Augustine. It was when the tireless prayers of his mother, St. Monica, had been answered by our universal Mother Mary and her Divine Son. And so, too, down fell the Pelagians who held that death was the result merely of a law of human nature, not of the loss of sanctifying grace, when St. Augustine thundered, *Roma locuta est. . . . Causa finita est.*

Pope St. Telesphorus, the martyr, excommunicated the hypercritical Bishop Marcion when he denied the resurrection of the body, refused baptism to the married, and asserted that the true God was opposed to the God of the *Old Testament,* thus nullifying the assurance of Jesus that He came "not to destroy but to fulfil." Monothelites martyred Pope St. Martin I because of their narrow view of the will of Jesus, but were silenced when the Council of Constantinople made perfectly explicit the always implicit dogma that our Saviour has "two natural wills, without division, change, partition, or confusion; not contrary to one another but the human will following and subject to the divine."

Pope Adrian I, the friend of Charlemagne, condemned the Iconoclasts who, like the Mohammedans and like the Protestants later, destroyed sacred images, and who have impoverished to this day the Schismatic churches of the East. The inspired wisdom of Pope Adrian I becomes irrefutable to the historian when he remembers that the fury of the Byzantine Iconoclasts, who smashed the images of Jesus and Mary and the saints, accorded ill with their servile respect in leaving untouched the images of the Emperor; when he remembers that the surrender of the Eastern Schismatic churches to temporal power has weakened them everywhere and brought destruction in Russia; when he remembers how greatly iconoclasm and political fanaticism despiritualized Mohammedanism; and when he remembers how often the image-breaking Protestants, from Luther and Cranmer on, cringed before petty princes and carnal kings.

St. Dominic preached against the sterile and vicious dualism of the Albigenses who made the universe a drawn battle between good and evil, held flesh to be intrinsically vile, and therefore prohibited marriage and encouraged suicide. The Church looked askance upon Wyclif, the disappointed office seeker and hero of the later reformers, not because he justly attacked abuses among the clergy, but because he denied the unity of the Church and sought to make the Scriptures sufficient in themselves, thus anticipating that fatal lack of oneness which makes the Anglican church today to be in fact not a church at all but a chaotic confederation of congregations. The sanity of the Church of Rome was tragically justified when the Hussites, the Bohemian followers of Wyclif, exploded into a cluster of internecine sects, some abolishing the Sacrament of Extreme Unction, some denying the reality of Purgatory with its assurance of God's mercy, others at war with the confessional, and some so fanatically inclined that they blended communism with sexual promiscuity and degraded marriage, as did the Soviets until the dire results brought back a measure of sanity.

The early heresies, though now dead, are discouragingly prophetic of those which were to follow. The most formidable was that of Arianism — far more formidable than any heresy which dated from Martin Luther and Henry VIII on to Mary Baker Eddy.

Arianism arose from the misguided Greek effort to harmonize the truth that there is but one God with the truth that God is three Persons in one Substance, the Father, the Son who is true God and true Man (one Person, uncreated, eternally begotten without beginning, with two Natures), and the Holy Spirit who is forever proceeding from both the Father and the Son. We should not seek to understand our Incarnate Lord by comparing Him with a human son of a human father. Rather we should think of the human father-son relationship as the palest, most tenuous, and most remote reflection of the one absolutely and endlessly existent begetting of Son from Father — the Father's Word, which in the beginning was with God, which is God, which before Abraham was, *is*. Without this revealed mystery (and let us not forget that, as pointed out earlier, the fact of Revelation can be established by reason) the uniquely Christian conception of that sanctifying grace which so penetrates us that it makes us godlike would be impossible. God made us His adopted children by an act of condescension possible only to God, the assumption of our finite nature into which He poured His own Infinite Essence, and so shared with us our most harrowing pains, sorrows, and ignominies as to lift us up to be partakers of His own divine nature. In contrast with this colossal mystery the so-called incarnations of Egyptian, Greek, and Hinduistic mythology (which are the cynical pastimes of various dabblers in Comparative Religion today) stand out utterly insignificant.

The Arians sought to make of Christ, the Word, a mere first creature of God, instead of acknowledging Him to be, as the Nicene Creed (325) triumphantly declared in reply to them, "consubstantial with the Father." The difference was expressed by the two words: *homoiousion* (like in substance) and *homoousion* (of the same substance). It was easy for me, in my unenlightened days, to sneer with Gibbon at the theological dispute over the insertion of the little letter "i," but it was that insertion, as interpreted by the Arians, which gave a wrong significance to the Person of Christ.

What the Church stood for in the Arian crisis, even at the risk of being utterly wiped out, was the *Via Media* which she always opposes to the unnumerable anti-Catholic extremes. "Let us preserve the Jewish conception of the unity of nature," wrote St. Gregory of Nyssa, "and of the Greek conception only the distinction of persons." We are here confronted with the Mystery of the Most Blessed Trinity, for the first time most clearly revealed by none other than our Divine Lord, Jesus Christ (though the Jews saw it faintly even in the Mosaic books and more frequently in the sapiential and prophetic writings).

It was in my meditations on the Trinity that I came to see more plainly than from any other religious experience, how largely due was my agnosticism and atheism (like that of all agnostics and atheists I have known or of whom I have read) to an unrevised childhood conception of God, which I had made no effort to deepen and refine alongside my maturing scientific conceptions. It is from a curious one-sided development like this that such hysterical image-thinking arose as we find, for instance, at the beginning of *A Free Man's Worship*, by Bertrand Russell. The utter failure of my old masters and myself to rise above anthropomorphic travesties of God, which we then naïvely impute to the genuinely scientific theologians, can be speedily amended by anyone who has the curiosity to read sustainedly in the works of St. Augustine, St. Thomas Aquinas, and St. John of the Cross.

The glorious reality of the Trinity is the only possible answer to the age-old tormenting problem of the One and the Many which has paralyzed all non-Christian philosophers, from the dim audacious dawns of the forest sages of ancient India to the high dazzling noon of Plato, and so on to the murky *Götterdämmerung* of our post-Cartesian philosophy. Beautifully in his work on *The Holy Trinity*, Father J. P. Arendzen writes: "In this world man is at his greatest when he bends his head and murmurs: 'Glory be to the Father and to the Son and to the Holy Ghost, as it was in the beginning, is now and ever shall be, world without end.' Creature though he be, he enters into the life of God."

The Arian was too worldly to do this. Therefore he forfeited what the Catholic gains by losing himself: "The divine Three come and make their abode in his soul in the unity of God." And so Father Arendzen continues:

Ever since God revealed the Trinity, the sea of divine glory is to us no indifferentiated dead whiteness, well-nigh blinding our eyes and dazing our mind, showing us nothing but eternal unchangeable infinite sameness, as if it were activity without principle, aim or achievement within itself, ceaseless energy without production, without the joy of completion. For us God has ceased to be the Great Unknown, of which we know only this that He made this world, the free sport of divine artistry, betraying yet hiding by infinite remoteness the Artist who made it. We still, like Moses, put off the sandals of our feet when in the desert of dry philosophy we approach the burning bush and hear God Himself saying: "I am who am." In adoring gratitude we thank Him still for His gracious speech to Israel of old, but we are glad that in the fulness of time He told us more, and told us I am Father and I am Son and I am Holy Ghost.

Error crept in, the author concludes, when the priority of order in the Godhead was changed into a priority of time, then into a priority of inequality and of dependence, and finally when it was construed as one of nature rather than of person, "as if the divine nature could exist in a greater or less degree."

Arianism was a mere aristocratic fad of a powerful minority, an unpopular and unscrupulous smart set. Manifestly in the demand of the masses for St. Ambrose as their bishop, the childlike mind of the people in their saner moods was at one with the childlike mind of the wise and holy philosopher in its exultant allegiance to unsullied Trinitarianism. Just as the people found no more difficulty than a learned Duns Scotus or a spotless St. John Berchmans in the Dogma of the Immaculate Conception, so in this matter of the Trinity they could realize intuitively that: "It is the Godhead itself which the person of the Father eternally gives to the Son, and the Son together with the Father gives to the Holy Ghost, and in the Godhead all is infinite, eternal, sovereign and independent."

The simple folk, moreover, like the *true* scholar who is both erudite *and wise,* would never confound the perfect and infinite Trinity of Catholicism with the loosely polytheistic trios of Egypt, Babylon, and Greece, nor with the decaying blur of polytheism and pantheism of the myth-making decadent Brahmins, or with the shallow, ponderous, and verbose spellbinding of the Hegelian dialectic. It is only an awe-inspiring and tender Triune Deity which can, without intrinsic contradiction, overarch eternity and at the same moment come, as our Saviour promised, to dwell whole and entire in every one of us who prays pureheartedly for such a grace.

Yet the struggle with Arianism was intense. It brought out such great lights of the Church as the indomitable Athanasius and the heroic and beloved St. Ambrose. It lingered on still with the Goths and Vandals and other barbarian hordes and did not expire until the year 650 — as long a life as has been vouchsafed to the flickering-out Protestantism of today.

IV. THE EASTERN SCHISM

Let us turn now to the three great rebellions of Christians against Christians — the Eastern Schism, the Great Schism of the West, and the Reformation. I was never more astounded than when, coming late to a knowledge of scientific history (which after all was rarely written until the turn of this century), I discovered that here stands out most conspicuously the impregnability, the oneness of the Church of Peter, against which his Master promised him that the gates of hell should never prevail. It is here that so many have been grossly deceived, though in most cases not intentionally, by teachers and writers; and many are still being so deceived.

All of these schisms, I have learned, were motivated more by politics and avarice than by religion. As to the first, the Schism of the East, Father Philip Hughes in the first volume of *A History of the Church* has shown with great vividness and comprehensiveness how, when the pagan persecution died down and the Roman emperors became Christians, a new peril lowered on the horizon. The temporal rulers lusted more and more after ecclesiastical power to buttress their political prestige. They contended against every pope at Rome and, with the aid of weak local prelates, usurped more and more of the functions of the Holy See. It is true that the natural Persian, Greek, Roman, and even Hebrew misunderstanding of the sublime doctrine of the Trinity, despite persistent revelations of it throughout the long eras of the Old Testament and clear teaching regarding it in the New Testament, accounts in part for the origin of the heresies. But their survival was, as has been said, the result not so much of theological controversy as of political cupidity. Only gradually, over the span of centuries, did the severance of what we call today the Eastern Orthodox Church become complete. First there were minor schisms, then a grave though brief break from 867 to 868, then increasing enmity, and finally the crash in 1054 which (although the council of Lyons was something of a palliative from 1274 to 1282, and the council of Florence fared better from 1439 to 1472) has endured to the present, when now the genius and saintliness of Pope Pius XI, most brilliantly seconded by Pope Pius XII, has accomplished a good deal toward the reunion. The ambition of the See of Constantinople, allied with the political intrigues of the Eastern emperors of the Roman empire, had effected a breach which was broadened, after the capture of Constantinople, by Turkish intrigue. Into this vortex were drawn the Islam-encircled patriarchates of Alexandria, Antioch, and Jerusalem, until at last even the Russian and Slav churches succumbed to the tragic estrangement. Although it was Constantinople alone among these churches which, in 1472, spurned the council of Florence and broke clean away, the lapse of centuries has hardened the hearts of 145 million Eastern peoples against Rome, despite the fact that the dissident Eastern churches still retain a true priesthood and valid sacraments.

Repeatedly, the Eastern Orthodox churches have paid the penalty for rendering unto Caesar the things which belong to God. For their ambition-engendered apostasy, these schismatics have crumbled under almost every vicissitude, while the spiritual guardians of the Eternal City have endured a long series of bludgeonings with heads "bloody but unbowed" except in undiscouraged prayer.

Today the members of the Eastern dissident churches are hopelessly divided as belonging to four independent churches governed by their respective patriarchs. In addition, there is a confederation of autocephalous churches united in their common practice only — and even this in different languages — of the Byzantine rite: the churches of Cyprus, Russia, Georgia, Sinai, Greece, Bulgaria; the churches of the Serbs, Croats, and Slovenes; the churches of Roumania, the Ukraine, Poland, Esthonia, Finland, Czechoslovakia, Albania, and North America. Each of these is governed merely by synods of bishops under the primacy of a patriarch or other primate. The patriarch of the once proudly rebellious Constantinople has merely an honorary prestige. In general these relatively recent synods have reduced the power of the patriarchs only to see it fall a prey to politicians.

The Holy Directing Synod of Russia, the prototype of these institutions, was founded by a man of the world, Peter the Great, in 1721, to direct the growingly corrupt priestcraft, until, in 1917, it was dashed into atoms by other worldly men, the atheistic Bolsheviki. It is significant also, in this connection, to survey the frequent political earthquakes in the Balkans which have, and may yet again and again, set all Europe aflame. Eastern Orthodoxy, too, in Asia Minor, Turkey, Greece, Albania, and even to a certain extent in Russia under the Czars, in Roumania and various other countries, has repeatedly fallen under the heel of Mohammedanism, which it has never anywhere thrown off with the imperious finality of Rome-inspired Spain. While, in theory, morality and religion have been regarded as wedded in these Eastern churches they have, as a fact, become more and more incompatible.

Nothing can be more significant than to contrast the rather sentimental and often confused quasi mysticism of their greatly gifted philosopher, Berdyaev (who writes so well on social problems), with the sinewy dialectic of another contemporary, but a Catholic, Maritain. The only strength of Eastern Orthodoxy lies in the touching if superstitious devoutness of the rank and file. Perhaps the recent reception of some of their distinguished bishops among the clergy of Rome is a further symptom of ruin — but, in this case, of a ruin which will lead to a radiant, Phoenixlike rise from the ashes of the dissident Eastern churches, to a resurrection in the bosom of Rome. More striking has been the return to us of a number of their entire churches. Many of our most haunting prayers plead most tenderly for them and extol the genius of certain ancient Fathers whom we shared and still share with them. "Preserve us," concludes one of these prayers, perhaps the most beautiful of them all, "from every false step which could widen the breach between us. Grant that the spirit of peace and charity, which is the mark of thy presence with the Faithful, may hasten the day in which our prayers may be united with theirs, so that every people and every tongue may acknowledge and glorify our Lord Jesus Christ, Thy Son. Amen."

V. THE GREAT WESTERN SCHISM

Today I stand amazed when I contemplate the failure of my old teachers of history, both in their words and in their books, to view the so-called Great Western Schism in proper perspective. Even the agnostics could not seem to emancipate themselves from their Protestant upbringing. Then came the "economic determinists" who inclined toward a point of view equally warped in another direction. It is clear that here, as in the case of the Eastern Schism, politicians played a major part. But the situation was radically different in the West. For the Church of Rome was not torn in its very warp and woof by such worldly tension to the point of *actual* schism. I myself first learned the proper approach when I discovered a definition by St. Thomas Aquinas: "Schismatics properly so called are those who *willingly* and *intentionally* separate themselves from the unity of the Church." On this basis I could agree with Father Bertrand L. Conway (in *The Question Box*), and practically all genuinely scientific authorities, Catholic and Non-Catholic, that the number of unequivocal schismatics throughout the long period of bewilderment was astonishingly small.

It is true that even saints took sides. Thus St. Vincent Ferrer supported sincerely the so-called Clementine popes. Nevertheless he worked diligently toward unity, and played a significant part in its final achievement. St. Catherine of Siena, who has been called "the greatest woman in Christendom," and who never flinched from chiding a pope, was a powerful adherent to the true Pontiff, Urban VI. All Catholics, no matter what their special opinions were, though some sought to rest ultimate powers with some of the Councils, took the position, quite antipodal to that of the splitting Eastern churches, that there could be only one head, one pope. Whereas the Eastern Orthodox began and has steadily continued to deteriorate under worldly pressure, the peoples of the Western Church, the One Church, under an avalanche of conspiracies caused by avaricious men, such as has afflicted Europe today, remained steadfastly loyal to Peter and to his Divine Master. Even Gregocius, a mordant foe of the papacy, confesses that its indestructability was verified strikingly by the so-called Schism of the West. The whole event was but one of the many confirmations of the promise of Jesus that "the gates of hell shall not prevail against it."

The "Great Western Schism" had a background considerably more complicated than that of the real schism in the East. First we recall the fact that, in contrast with the cultured East, the West remained decidedly barbarous, even after the all but miraculous infiltration of Christianity from Rome which reached a climax with the Holy Roman Empire in the days of Charlemagne. It was hardly to be expected, with the menace of the Moslems from without and the numberless discordances within, that the superb but premature internationalism of those days could survive except as a vision for all who are not besotted with imperialistic capitalism, with communism, with Nazism, and with Fascism.

On the squalors and the glories, the fanaticism and the piety, the greed, the compromises, and the devotions of the crusades we cannot dwell here. Suffice it to say that many wanderers came back from the Orient with diseases of the flesh and with Saracen heresies with which they infected the stay-at-homes. A considerable number of the stay-at-homes were already much concerned with the fleshpots of Egypt. To comprehend the conditions then existing one needs but to follow, with Father Thomas M. Schwertner, O.P., the adventures of his hero, St. Albert the Great, and to realize how much of the time of that profound theologian and pioneer scientist was consumed in continual journeys throughout western and central Europe to revive fading faiths, to reconcile professors and friars, princes and merchants, merchants and princes and churchmen. This will enable us to appreciate the fact that, even in the thirteenth century, the Golden Age of Catholicism, there was a hellbroth brewing that was a ready poison for even the honest souls who were later perturbed by the spectacle of rival claimants of the See of Peter.

Gradually I came more and more clearly to understand how back of all the welter of the "Great Western Schism" surged the avarice of adolescent nations, particularly the long-standing jealousy of the French who, more than any others, had sown the germs of this ferment years before when, from 1305 to 1370, they transported the papacy to Avignon, and saw to it that those who reigned during this period were their countrymen, one and all.

It was finally my non-Catholic but unwaveringly truth-seeking friend and colleague, Professor Henry S. Lucas, who taught me how to appreciate the so-called Western Schism for better and for worse. I found myself most impressed by the fact that the popes, even of those troublous days and during the "Great Schism" and during the Renaissance and Reformation — not one of them, not even the all-too-worldly Alexander VI — ever uttered a word to weaken any well-informed faith in papal infallibility on strictly doctrinal matters. They all proved that they might make mistakes about the temporal problems of the world. And they all proved as well that they could not make mistakes when speaking *ex cathedra* to the world about the eternal problems — the matters of faith and morals — which our Lord consigned to the custody of St. Peter.

Turbulent Europe was boiling with dissensions secular and ecclesiastical when Gregory XI (1370–1378) was hesitating as to whether he should emancipate himself from the imprisonment in Avignon, where for a long time the jealous French kings had detained the pontiffs, and proceed to the Eternal City wherein St. Peter had inaugurated the apostolic rule. Hardly had be arrived at Rome when death gripped him.

Naturally there was much concern as to whether he would remain at Rome or retreat from the traditional city. Sixteen of the twenty cardinals were just then in Rome. They were of various nationalities but mainly French. Meanwhile Rome was in a mob-state. After fixing upon a compromise candidate, an Italian who took the name of Urban VI, the cardinals fled. Their fears were groundless for the populace was satisfied. And the cardinals themselves were glad to bask in his favors. It may be said at once that Urban, for all his unfortunate outspokenness, irrascibility, and ignorance of the world, was, in the face of his later rivals, the true pope. Despite the bewilderment of the people throughout Europe, occasioned by various conspiracies, despite his betrayal by his cardinals who oddly enough excused themselves on the grounds that they had been coerced by Roman mobs, despite the intrigues of kings and princes and prelates, the great Church retained in the vortex of the whirlpool its unbroken tradition of being governed by one ruler, Peter's descendant.

Nevertheless the fiery Urban estranged in various ways (not in themselves reprehensible) so many that he was presently confronted with a rival who named himself Clement VII and was plausible enough to arouse the allegiance of St. Vincent Ferrer, great Dominican confessor who, in those troublous times, traversed Spain, France, Italy, and Switzerland, credited with many miracles and with the Pentecostal gift of many tongues, a fearless preacher of penance. When holy geniuses like St. Catherine of Siena, a Dominican nun, and St. Vincent Ferrer, a Dominican friar, were sincerely at odds, no wonder that royal worldlings made the most of it and the whole issue was contaminated by the rising spirit of nationalism. It was this that had wrecked, for the time being, that magnificently internationalistic Holy Roman Empire with which Charlemagne and the Church had sought to solve the problems of rendering unto Caesar those things which are Caesar's and unto God those things which are God's.

The rival popes, perforce like kings in those days, went to war. The ambitious Clement, despite the fact that he had already achieved a record for bloodthirsty efficiency, was driven from the environs of Rome to Avignon. But Urban continued his reckless policy of mistreating promising allies. Ecclesiastical government was in a sorry state.

At the death of Pope Urban VI his legitimate successor was Boniface IX, of blameless life until the financial difficulties occasioned by the division of power forced him to become unnaturally mercenary. The clergy of Germany and France grew infuriated and defiant. In growingly nationalistic England the papacy had for some time been under suspicion as long as it tarried in Avignon, in the realms of the hated

France. John Wyclif, somewhat fanatically but with much justice, had scourged his fellow clergy and launched more than one thunderbolt charging the papacy with too much power. He had at first favored Urban VI as the true pope but had finally spurned him as being too politically minded, and unwittingly paved the way definitely toward the later Reformation which swept over England in later centuries. In Bohemia, which was also becoming nationalistic, the teachings of Wyclif inspired John Hus in his energetic but tragic career.

What was to be done to maintain the pristine and unique oneness of the Roman Catholic Church? The rivals refused voluntary abdication. They scouted the idea of decisions of arbitrators, quite rightly, since not even cardinal committees would or could be impartial. Could it be argued that the entire Church was an authority higher than Christ's vicar and could therefore, through a general council representing the Church Universal, prevail over any papal decision? Of course, the claimants would not, nay could not, admit this. But might not stark necessity ratify such a solution? No, the tragic but never absolute "Schism" was to bear fruit in a triumphant vindication of that papal supremacy which could survive even so terrible a test.

At the death of the false pope, Clement, in 1394, he was succeeded by Peter de Luna of Aragon, "a crafty intriguer," in the words of Professor Lucas. The new pretender took the name of Benedict XIII. The University of Paris, the crown, and the clergy, now hungering for unity, requested too late that the cardinals of Clement refrain from perpetuating his rule. Benedict XIII won his election from these cardinals who, however, had been prudent enough to exact from each candidate a promise to *resign voluntarily* if a majority so desired. The wily pretender replied: "I can abdicate as easily as take off my hat." But when he was esconced he availed himself of his virtuosity in canon law to sit tight. This cost him the allegiance of the French clergy and the university. At that point the ever rapacious king and nobles took over the clerical appointments and in so doing increased taxes to a distressing degree. The intermittently insane Charles VI sought fruitlessly to ally himself with the now continuously drunken Emperor Wenzel against Boniface IX. And the Duke of Orleans brought the French crown back to the support of the Avignon papacy, to Benedict.

At about the same time, unfortunately, Boniface IX was succeeded by Innocent VII who was too aged to advance the cause of Rome. He lived on for only two years. And his successor, Gregory XII, though blameless of life, was, like Innocent, too easily influenced by his younger kin and too timid to make much out of his nine years of rule. Both the rivals professed readiness to meet and negotiate. But Benedict was, as usual, moved mainly by a spirit of intrigue. And the more sincere Gregory was pliant in the hands of his ambitious nephews. Roman cardinals resented his failure to be firm in his vow that he would abdicate if Benedict did likewise. And Benedict, deprived of his main prop by the death of Orleans, fled to Perpignan after a brief struggle.

Now both Gregory's and Benedict's cardinals were at one at least in their disgust over the situation. They summoned the clergy to a great council at Pisa. Both Gregory, nephew ridden, and the Machiavellian Benedict sought to assemble councils of their own. But Gregory's failed from paucity of attendance. And Benedict was astounded to find that the prelates who answered his call concluded that he should abdicate. Nor was the Pisan council particularly effective. It was too sane to attempt to elevate its authority above that of the papacy. It was, to be sure, prepared to oust both the rivals. But a minority sought to purify the widespread abuses which were in time to lend whatever of justice there was to the real schisms of Luther, Calvin, Zwingli, Henry the VIII, and the others who, in the Reformation later, unconsciously prepared their followers for that myriad-tongued Protestantism of today which is fading out as an empty humanism.

The Pisan conclave wound up with the election of another false pope, Alexander V, who made a few gestures of reform and called another council which was excommunicated by the two deposed popes. One thing was manifest. No council could tower over the heir of Peter, no matter who that heir might be. There were now three claimants. But only one, as all Christendom knew, could be the right one.

Alexander was succeeded by his servile follower, John XXIII, a most worldly prelate. Despite or because of his machinations with the next council at Rome, nothing happened beyond the condemnation of the doctrines of Wyclif; there was no attempt by the small number attending to turn resolutely to the reform of some of the abuses which that tough old English rebel had rightly attacked. Soon John was in flight. Under German pressure, he fell into the hands of Sigismund and yielded supinely to that Emperor's suggestion that the next council be held at Constance, in Germany, where Sigismund could readily wield a strong hand.

In Constance, because of the objection to the predominance of John's

Italian bishops, no general group discussion was allowed. Under England's lead the prelates voted as nations, English, French, German, Italian, Spanish. Only a unanimous vote of all nations could be a traditionally valid basis for a conciliar decree. The results of this nationalistic approach to spiritual matters may well be guessed. The Hundred Years' War was raging. England and Germany hated France. John's Italian followers were widely suspected. And yet this political medley sought to claim the supreme ecclesiastical authority. But now, in order to evade the question of reform within the Church, John was eager to divert all attention to heresy hunting. And for this diversion Hus, the Czechist follower of Wyclif, was selected. He was summoned to Constance with a safe conduct from Sigismund. But he was imprisoned in spite of the Emperor. Sigismund finally abandoned a promise which, in the face of an ecclesiastical council, he never had the right to make and allowed Hus to be burned. This merely resulted in arousing the ire of Bohemia against both Germany and the papacy despite the fact that the real pope was not at the helm. Benedict no longer had support. The real pope, Gregory, worn out, resigned. John endeavored to stand firm. But gossip about his scandalous, unpriestly life, the bad record of his transactions, and the well-known worthlessness of his word were his undoing. Benedict was then deposed as a schismatic and a heretic.

Martin V now became the next rightfully elected pope, mainly because he was above and independent of all intrigues and all factions. But he was not destined to accomplish much of the reform from within that was the burning need. The bored, wearied, and hopelessly nationalistic council members now departed. They left behind them the menacing nemesis of the Hussite movement. The councils immediately following were pretty nearly as impotent as the Council of Constance. In his *Renaissance and Reformation* Professor Lucas makes it clear that the very impotency itself of the various councils of bishops (who quarreled so long before they united in their recognition of a legitimate pope) verifies one great point, the unassailable supremacy of the Papacy over all councils.

Thus the Great Western Schism, for all its failure to forestall the Reformation which severed so many completely from the Church, never for one moment shook the faith of the great Catholic populations in the oneness of the Church under the guidance of one supreme leader, the pope. It proved indeed what after these long centuries men are just beginning again to learn, that Christ's Church must remain one. It will not crash down in chaos before Anti-Christ.

VI. THE PROTESTANT REFORMATION

From the sixteenth century onward the "liberal reformers" of holy Mother Church have narrowed her sane and comprehensive and truly universal Catholicism until they have emasculated Christianity into almost nothing. All the heresies, ancient and modern, illustrate stages of that awful retrogression which Dr. W. E. Orchard sketches in these powerful sentences in *From Faith to Faith*:*

"If we would be human, we must be rational ethical; if ethical, evangelical; if evangelical, Catholic; if Catholic, Roman; that is the logic of progress, freedom, light. If one rejects the Roman claims, one must, eventually, reject Catholicism; if Catholicism is rejected, then gradually go doctrine, sacraments, Scripture, Christ, God, man; hell, then heaven; the next world, then this; faith goes, then hope, then love. This is the logic of denial, darkness, death."

In the American universities wherein, as teacher and student, I have spent nearly forty years of my life, I grow daily more and more sorrowfully impressed over the devastating effects of the Reformation. Those among my colleagues who still believe, are frequently too timid or too vague to make their influence felt on the youth who come often from indifferentist parents and, in rapidly increasing numbers, even from agnostic and atheistic homes. Many of the teachers remember their early religious (non-Catholic) training only with contempt, or, at best, with smiling indulgence. For this there may at times be reason. But alas, these same colleagues usually think that the whole case for religion is hatched down in the foundering faiths from which they escaped. What chance have the youths, now rapidly growing in number, who have begun to feel the need of a God conceived in all proper nobility? It is a matter for prayer. It is a matter for what St. Thomas Aquinas called the best life, "the mixed life," the life blended of prayerful contemplation and arduous apostolicity.

But there is one vast consolation, I find. The number of young men and women who grow suspicious of empty iconoclasm and of garrulous quasi-scientific solutions, is on the increase. The change is profoundly significant over the past twenty years. Almost every night my little study receives these God-seekers, unsentimental, often a bit cynical, as youth

---

* An account of his passage from Presbyterianism and Congregationalism to a highly ritualistic creed of his own making, and thence to the Church of Rome.

often feels it necessary to be, but fundamentally sincere, realistic, and merciless in their aversion for cant. One of my most interesting students at the present time is a young Japanese lady of great natural piety and acute dialectical ability. A Protestant missionary succeeded in destroying the Buddhist faith of her childhood but could do nothing reconstructive. She is now finding her way back to God through a long and very exacting study of the five proofs of St. Thomas Aquinas.

The "Reformation," that is to say, the *real* schisms and heresies that followed the "Great Western Schism," did not reform. By not awaiting the Church's own true Reformation, which soon she had under way, Luther and Zwingli, the British House of Commons, Calvin, and Knox innoculated Europe with the dreadfully diseased germ plasm that foully exfoliated to give us Louis XIV and Cardinal Richelieu and Gustavus Adolphus; Robespierre and Pitt and Napoleon and Bismarck; the British Parliament of today which finds it so difficult to formulate an unequivocally Christian policy; the atheistic leaders that were responsible for conquered France; the materialistic dictators Stalin, Mussolini, and Hitler; the anticlerical acquisitive politicians who long misruled Mexico; the Bolshevist and Anarchist "loyalists" of Spain, fiends in human form; the conscienceless bankers and militarists of Japan; the bandit generals of China. On the other hand, the Catholic Counter Reformation — with its St. Philip Neri, St. Charles Borromeo, St. Teresa and many more, notably the valiant Jesuit crusaders of love and martyrdom — proves that, had we remained steadfastly loyal to Christ and to Peter, whom He chose for the visible head of His Church, we could have escaped the Armageddon of the twentieth century.

The disintegrating tendency of the so-called Reformation was tragically manifested from the first. It will suffice here to sketch the drama of a Conference at Worms, all but unknown to English readers until set forth by Father Brodrick, S.J., in his monumental *St. Peter Canisius* (1935). Patience was the integrating virtue of this saint — patience broadened and exalted to a true mental sublimity, and supernaturalized by charity.

The conference in question was the last of a number of benevolent and rational Catholic attempts, during the Counter Reformation, to seek a mutually defined reconciliation with the leaders of Protestant Germany. St. Peter set out with his experience at the similar Diet at Regensburg (1556). But at Worms his greatest opponent was to be no less a person than Philip Melancthon whom I was taught to believe, in a certain course in Brown University, to have been one of the greatest heralds of freedom and enlightenment in Western European civilization, a man of whom Father Brodrick admits that though "a great puzzle . . . he had a fine brain and a character not only noble in many ways but full of charm." Unfortunately Melancthon's own words at the Conference proved quite sufficient, without the aid of Catholic critics, to reduce considerably my undergraduate image of his stature.

The Protestants arrived at Worms in a state of characteristic mutual dissension. Flacius in Saxony had warned his friends to be wary of the kiss of that Judas who was Melancthon, "with his pedagogue, the devil." And upon their backstairs intrigue Melancthon was not slow in taking revenge. On the other side, Peter Canisius found ample grounds for reproaching German Catholics for their apathy in the face of the vigilance and intensity of Protestant adversaries. His own efforts to keep the peace, urged upon both sides at the outset by Vice-Chancellor Seld, are sufficiently transparent in his speech at the sixth session. It furnishes us with both an admirable specimen of his temperate mode of reasoning and a perfect *précis* of the Catholic attitude toward the reciprocity of Holy Scripture and Tradition — Tradition, that only safeguard to protect us from such self-elected private interpreters of the Bible as Joseph Smith, Mrs. Eddy, and "Judge" Rutherford.

If, before all other agreements [said St. Peter], some principle has not been found on this matter of a judge of controversies, or however we name it, the Colloquy cannot possibly proceed with any profit. Indeed, there is real danger that it may break up prematurely, to the great prejudice of religion. . . . On one point we and the delegates of the other party are agreed, namely that we acknowledge the canonical Scriptures to be true, holy, internally consistent, and entirely divine, and of incomparable authority. Further, we hold that those Scriptures provided the best and soundest criterion for the adjustment of controversies in belief and religion. Whenever the Bible is clear and distinct in itself, we gladly submit to its testimony and ask for no other authority or evidence. But as soon as conflict arises about the meaning of an obscure passage and it is difficult to decide rival claims to the true meaning, then we appeal with perfect justice to the constant agreement of the Catholic Church, and go back to the unanimous interpretation of the Fathers. This is not in order that the Church may teach us without reference to the Scriptures, but that the Church may show us the true and orthodox sense of the Scriptures; not that our faith may rest upon human authority without any regard to the Divine Word, but that we may learn from the explanations and instructions of holy men what the Divine Word really says. Where the sense of Scripture is clear and unambiguous we do not appeal to the Church, but, in doubtful places, we prefer the common agreement of the

Church to the private exegesis of changeable men, who not seldom use diligent and pernicious endeavors to distort the sacred text.

It is not unreasonable for us to prefer the teaching of holy martyrs and learned confessors to that of individuals whose turn of mind is most open to suspicion — martyrs and pastors of the Church distinguished by the holiness of their lives and their knowledge of the Scriptures acquired by diligent comparison of the teaching of prophets and apostles from the earliest times. It is they who have bequeathed to us the symmetry of Catholic belief, with unanimous and harmonious accord.

Coming straight to the point in dispute, Canisius thus states the only safe and true principle to which the Church has always held and always must hold:

To sum up this question, there will be quarrelling in Germany about the sublimest objects of belief, a war of diametrically opposed views, so long as it is taught that each individual has a right to judge and decide for himself; so long as Scripture alone, interpreted privately, continues to be the final court of appeal. . . . When, therefore, any dispute that has arisen over the Scriptures is to be settled we ought to remember the warning of St. Clement of the apostolic age. The divine law, he said, must not be read or taught according to any man's private understanding of it, because in the Scriptures there is much that can be twisted to mean what some individual presumes to think it means. The sense of the text must be learned from those who have preserved it as it was truly delivered to them by their predecessors.

With serene learning St. Peter now defended some of the ancient Fathers of the Church from the accusation of false doctrine which Melancthon and Karg had rashly hurled against them. Whereas Karg, moreover, had asserted that the invocations of the saints and prayers for the dead had begun during the pontificate of St. Gregory the Great, the patient Jesuit unerringly traced these practices much farther into the past. To the usual Protestant billingsgate about idolatry and superstition he suggested that these matters might well be cleared up by reference to relevant authorities and that, though each side might heap up insults, it would be more advisable to rely on courtesy and sweet reasonableness. But it is not difficult to understand the fury of the reformers since Peter had strictly and quickly disposed of and exposed those internecine disputes of Protestants which Melancthon had fondly hoped to conceal. To cap the climax, an allusion to determinism was a direct score on Melancthon who had held at two different times two opposing views. "You have been listening," he raged, "to a sufficiently grandiloquent orator. If that is the way he wishes to contend with us we shall pay him out with interest."

Unfortunately for his "we," some of his associates charged his party of holy Pharisees with some serious doctrinal aberrations. Melancthon sought a mandate to exclude them from the Conference. But since their credentials were just as valid as those of their accusers the President found himself in a quandary. Melancthon then turned to his promise to "pay out" Peter Canisius "with interest." The gentle saint was branded idolatrous, malicious, and blasphemous. Flacius Illyricus has rendered us a report of some of the rhetorical effluvium of the Melancthonites as follows: "The chief author of the Jesuits, or certainly their restorer and propagator, is that Canisius about whose sanctity many excellent stories are told. Not the least of them is the one recounting what happened at Mainz in 1557 with an Abbess named Catella. Canisius was entertained by her in great style, and, when the two of them had reached the merry stage in their cups, they proceeded, as lovers with the common name of dog, to celebrate canine nuptials. That story was well known to everybody at the Colloquy of Worms." We may note that *catella* means puppy. And the relation between Canisius and the Latin word for dog was an incessant source of Protestant satire. Now, it just happens that Peter Canisius was not once in Mainz in 1557. Furthermore, there was no Abbess Catella there at all. But the patient Jesuit held his peace.

Philip Melancthon and his henchmen soon after departed the Conference in a dudgeon. And Peter, quite aware that when Protestants could not come to an agreement among themselves regarding fundamentals, it would be of little avail for Catholics to seek rapport with them, wrote gently to a friend, with an all but audible sigh:

Verily, the need here is for a great thirst to win souls for Christ, and for great patience in bearing with and comforting those who have begun to listen and are looking for the truth.

In the realm of German thought the followers of Luther split and sub-split until, in the nineteenth century, the "higher criticism" of Strauss sought the extirpation of the authority of Holy Scripture which Luther had perversely pitted against the authority of Apostolic Tradition. Schleiermacher retained Christianity only to reduce it, with a *reductio ad absurdum* of Luther's irrationalism, to mere romantic emotionalism. The egomania of Luther culminated in the egomania of Hegel, who placed his own arid pantheism at the crowning point of human thought and somehow combined this with a deification of the State, to justify Bismarck, Kaiser Wilhelm, and Hitler. Karl Marx thought that he had followed more logically the true dialectic of Hegel when he twisted its pantheistic pseudo-spirituality into a much more candid atheistic materialism which deified what he called "the Dictatorship of the Proletariat." But his also was really but another deification of the State whose demise he thought that he had forecast. Only with Marx the State was not Prussian Junkers and Bismarcks. Nor was it of proletarians, wage workers. It was — or is — a handful of fanatical intellectuals like Marx himself and Lenin, Trotsky, and Stalin.

In Switzerland and France, Calvinism took a somewhat sinisterly similar turn. No one, to be sure, would care to whitewash the self-styled Catholics who staged the massacre of St. Bartholomew's Eve. But Catherine de Medici was as pagan a politician as Machiavelli and his neo-pagan Nietzschean disciple, Mussolini. Calvin's philosophy began with an Omnipotent and Merciless God and ended with the ideal of an omnipotent and merciless State. For all his knowledge of the capriciousness, the cruelty, and the unbridled concupiscence of the typical rulers of his day, he would replace the Petrine Vicar of God at Rome, the servant of the servants of God, with the State which he assured us "comes of the providence and holy ordinance of God whom it pleased thus to manage the government of men." For the visible as well as invisible holy Mother Church, he substituted his merely invisible church which "cannot find collective utterance." For the sage aristodemocracy of Catholicism and its rich arborescent Tradition, he substituted, like Luther, the Bible alone. "The Bible," as Mr. Gregory tells us, "interpreted by the elders who govern the Calvinian Church. These elders of the Genevan theocracy were sincere inquisitors. They administered the divine legal system, entered all households, religiously arrested sinners, banished, excommunicated, imprisoned, burned. All sins were crimes; salvation vanished from the purpose of religion. It was replaced by an inscrutable God and an inexorable logic — in fact by the mind and person of John Calvin."*

There is little or no choice between the violent and often obscene anti-rationalism of Luther and the pedantically Procrustean rationalism of the author of the *Institutes* which "fashion a religion *de novo,* as if there had never been any religion before. Nothing that Calvin derived from the

* T. S. Gregory, *The Unfinished Universe,* a book which he began "as a Methodist minister," but which became "the story of my conversion" to the Catholic Church.

Christian scriptures is really necessary to his interpretation of the Christian faith. All he needs is logic and the dogma of divine omnipotence; deity and almightiness are synonymous terms." In fact "Calvinian theocracy . . . banished Christ from the Church." This prepared the way for the British "Whig 'realism' " of Bodin whose *Republic* "banished Christ from the State." Thus Mr. Gregory proceeds to sum up the drift of Bodin:

The Catholic [as Bodin sees it] is beaten in argument by the Protestant, the Christian by the Jew, the Jew by the philosopher and the Mohammedan, and both these last by the skeptic who finds all religions equally false, as the *Republic* found them equally useful. "Of all later systems," it has been said, "that of Montesquieu is perhaps nearer to Bodin's," and Montesquieu admired above all the Whig system of the English, who "knew best how to value those three great advantages, liberty, religion and trade."

With the British Whig system, so admired by Montesquieu, and its great philosophical champion, Locke, we hear much of that principle of "toleration" which, for so many years of my life, enthralled me as it enthralls so many of my "liberal" compatriots still. Now, if toleration is but a synonym for traditional Christian charity, then indeed it is a supreme virtue. It was, however, my mistake to confuse with the supernatural, God-given virtue of charity the very mundane naturalistic pose of toleration. And this was a great obstacle to my entrance into the Church of Rome. I did not see, as I see today, that toleration is often but a name for flabby and trimming compromise, a false charity which can quickly turn into an attitude most venomous, when expedient toleration proves inexpedient. As Tennyson says of the sorceress Vivien, "For in a wink the false love turns to hate."

Now the Whigs found it well, with the English Revolution, to temper the bigoted antitraditionalism of the Puritan with this specious tolerance. They then proceeded to construct a conveniently distant god, a deistic god, after the image of man. Superior men, like Newton, were then thinking in terms of the most promising science of mechanics which only lately has begun to fail in the field of physics and to give way to pure mathematics. As today the mathematical astrophysicist, Sir James Jeans, makes God the Supreme Mathematician so in the days of Newton and Locke, of Voltaire and the great leaders of the American and French Revolutions, man made God in the image of a Master Mechanician and banished Him far away. In the next century the mechanists banished God out of existence. It was all a natural recoil from the Calvinistic and Cromwellian God. Even today one meets many a man who, because in his childhood he lived under the shadow of the terrorist God of Calvin, cannot or will not comprehend the five arguments of St. Thomas Aquinas, the metaphysical proofs of the existence of a God not made in the image of man, but a Pure Spirit, Absolute Being, not only Omnipotent but Merciful. And these atheistic friends of mine are quite right in rejecting the tolerant deistic compromise of the Whigs. Deism was the last plausible stand of Protestantism. I can now see why I had to slough off my early religious training so largely before I could bend my steps directly and steadily toward Catholicism. No wonder that Lockian toleration made an exception by excluding atheism. No wonder that Whiggish Latitudinarianism excluded, among all Christian faiths, Rome only.

The issue today is clear and stark, Catholicism or Atheism. Anglicanism, Calvinism, Congregationalism, Unitarianism, Inquirism, these are the signposts along one road — to Atheism. Deism, mechanical or mathematical, is a blind trail which forks off the road to Atheism for a time but flounders back through a Slough of Despond. Many French revolutionists retraced their steps and hastened on along the straight path to Atheism. Their anticlerical Masonic descendants, only yesterday, allowed their spleen to obstruct the work of the great French marshal, Foch, who, despite their fanaticism, saved his country for other anticlericals to lose it again in 1940. These ultranationalists, these "Liberals" often snooped on the heels of those patriotic and pious poilus who found in the Holy Sacrifice of the Mass new courage to face once more the rusty barbwires, the yellow mud, and the rotting bodies of No Man's Land. And the red ruin which these anticlerical Masonic descendants unleashed in Mexico and "Loyalist" Spain under the smoke screen of "Liberalism" will take decades for the true historian to unmask to a people drugged with various brands of journalistic propaganda and stupidity. One road, I repeat, leads to Atheism, the other road leads to Rome. Meanwhile holy Mother Church, always praying like her Founder for the forgiveness of her enemies, offers up incessantly her prayers for the conversion of those deceived by the treacherous snares of freemasons, to Him who prayed for the men who persecuted and calumniated Him.

VII. ENCYCLOPEDISTS. AGE OF ENLIGHTENMENT

The work of the false reformers outside the Church and of their descendants, the deistic and atheistic French Encyclopedists of the so-called Age of the Enlightenment, reached a climax with the denouement of the French Revolution.

The tragic futility of all attempts, since our Divine Lord founded His Church, to establish a churchless State ought to be so clear from the lesson of the French Revolution that one is tempted today to question the sanity of Stalin and Hitler. But converted "liberals" of my type should never contemplate such anticlericals without a long prelude of reminiscence and self-diagnosis. I remember myself how much, in my youth, I was overawed by a young apostate who had been through some experiences not unlike those which made anticlericals in Rousseauistic and Voltairean France and Marxist Russia. His drunken father had aroused in him a cold hatred of the apparently inefficacious Catholic Church. In such a state of mind Haeckel's atheistic-panpsychistic *Riddle of the Universe* came to him as scripture. He assured me that no superior person in any age had ever been a really sincere believer in any religion. He did not trouble himself to produce the evidence. But he was apparently so perfectly relaxed and so calm that I felt that he must have attained to some real insight. Moreover, his conduct was on a very high level. He never indulged in any of the convivialities common to those of us who were, or had been, and who wanted to be believers. Yet he never reproached us. We had, or wanted, a religion. But religion, possessed or desired, did not seem to improve us one whit. I began to wonder whether it was necessary to renounce God in order to attain to any high degree of probity. Then, gradually, his character began to disintegrate. It began with ignoring petty financial obligations to his college chums. One saw that he had gradually come to look upon himself as one of the enlightened who could hardly be expected to be under any grave obligations to deluded weaklings like us. He was a superman. I lost sight of him long ago. May God grant that he has found his way back to the truth. But his history was, in those days, a rapidly consummated history of the typical freethinker. I have seen it repeated hundreds of times, over longer periods of time, since then.

In *Progress and Religion,* Christopher Dawson sums up the lesson that morality cannot endure unless rooted deep in traditional theology:

The revolutionaries did not limit themselves to political reforms, such as the establishment of a new constitution and a new legal code, they aspired to refashion society from its foundations. The new calendar of the revolutionary era symbolizes the complete break that was made with the past, and the belief that a new age had begun for humanity. [The same fantastic hope is manifest in the almost identical efforts of the Bolsheviks in Russia now.] The doctrines of Rousseau were the dogmas of the new state, and were surrounded by the ritual of an official cult in the feasts of the revolutionary calendar culminating in Robespierre's solemn [deistic] celebration of the Feast of the Supreme Being. But the victory of the new ideals ended swiftly in failure and disillusionment. The atrocities of the Reign of Terror were a grim commentary on the extravagant optimism of the eighteenth-century reformers and the belief of Rousseau in the essential goodness of human nature. [We have here the opposite extreme to the pessimistic Lutheran-Calvinist doctrine of human corruptness which made cynical worldliness so easy. The Catholic *via media* of "original sin" is obviously the only conception which fits the facts and lends itself to a common-sense and truly scientific meliorism.] The great apostle of the idea of Progress, Condorcet, was himself a victim of the Terror [as practically all the earlier Bolsheviks are "liquidated" by Stalin today], and the place of the generous idealists and reformers who had presided over the early stages of the Revolution was taken by self-seeking and corrupt politicians like Barras and Rewbell.

We have noted, at various points in this book, that genuine democracy springs, not from the pagan humanisms, old or new, but from traditional Christianity. We are consequently well prepared to appreciate this wise sentence from *The French Revolution* by Hilaire Belloc: "It is hardly too much to say that the Revolution would, in France at least, have achieved its object and created a homogeneous, centralized democracy, had not this great quarrel between the Republic and the Church arisen."

Christopher Hollis, in his essay on "The Church and the Modern Age" (a brilliant contribution to the fourth volume of the English Catholic Truth Society's *Studies in Comparative Religion*), furnishes us an illuminating prelude to the whole business. He contrasts the Middle Ages, when the only disputes of profound import were theological and were waged with theological weapons under the restraining influence of the Church (with her unchallenged deposit of faith), with the Reformation when theological disputes arose between rival churches and, for lack of a rational arbiter, the weapon of dispute became of necessity the sword. He then shows how out of the exhaustion rose the *politiques*, who preferred to have peace at any price rather than the truth, and enthroned in France the licentious Henry IV after his nominal conversion to

Catholicism. From all this it finally "came about that very many sincere Christians, both Catholic and Protestant, honestly thought it to be for the best that the State should be given as wide powers of Church patronage as possible. Louis XIV, with his Gallican claims, was a very sincere Christian." But now since the Gallican clergy had rendered unto Caesar the things that were God's and turned in a large measure away from Rome, what could be more natural than that they should share the corruption of the court of Louis XV when it arrived, neglect the poor who learned to forget them, flaunt their mistresses in public, and bow even to the rule of infidel bishops? What more natural than that the intellectuals should become "freethinkers" deistic or even atheistic?

What followed was a materialistic age to which the Church appeared primarily as, "the possessor of certain economic goods . . . a wealthy, landowning corporation." The next step in this philosophy was for the Revolution to seize the land. But it blundered sadly in imagining a necessary conflict between Catholicism and democracy. "The doctrine of the sovereignty of the people had been a commonplace of the medieval schools, and had been taught in modern Europe by Bellarmine, Suarez and many others a century before it was taught by Rousseau."

The Voltaires and the Robespierres were far too befuddled with the shallow sophisms of the movement to dream that, as Mr. Belloc puts it, "The swoon of the Faith in the eighteenth century is the negative foundation upon which the strange religious experience of the French was about to rise. . . . It is safe to say that where one adult of the educated classes concerned himself seriously with the Catholic Faith and Practice in France before the Revolution there are five today."

Besides the hostile intelligentsia there was also the king-hating Huguenot faction, shrunken in number, but then as today a wealthy class, envious of the Church as a sort of privileged State within a State rather than concerned any longer with genuinely religious differences.

The climax came with the presentation, on May 30, of a plan for the reform of the Constitution of the Church in Gaul which reminds one of the efforts of Hitler and his masters today, a proposal which, in a nutshell, meant the further loosening of the already loose bond between the Church of France and the Vatican, and the general subjection of ecclesiastical to a civil authority which was avowedly indifferent to religion. It is true that French Catholicism was already contaminated by temporal entanglements. But the politicians had no conception of the ineluctable piety of a minority, dwindling, uninstructed, but full of the grace which would in due time inspire the emergence of a Curé d'Ars. The revolutionists were human enough in their desire to pension off the last clergy of what they supposed to be a senile institution. What they did not see is well set forth by Mr. Belloc:

The Catholic Church was not dead, and was not even dying. It was exhibiting many of the symptoms which in other organisms and institutions correspond to the approach of death, but the Catholic Church is an organism and an institution quite unlike any other. It fructifies and expands immediately under the touch of a lethal weapon; it has at its very roots the conception that material prosperity is stifling to it, poverty and misfortune nutritious.

History has repeatedly justified our Lord's remarks about the obstacles between the rich man and heaven. History has repeatedly verified His predictions that His faithful would be persecuted but that He would be with them always.

So the plans of the revolutionists failed. But the ties that bound the Gallican Church with the King and the apparent readiness of Royalty to stake its failing prestige on the invading armies from without led the desperate champions of democracy quite naturally to brand the priesthood as traitorous. Thus came the terrorism of 1793 and the flare-up of an anticlericalism which remains unquenched in some quarters of France even today. Thus came the long procession of victorious martyrs. Then Napoleon crushed the terror.

But the advent of Napoleon was for the Church a new crisis not unlike that which occurred when Constantine legalized the faith. Caesar, for his beneficence, demands the right to meddle with things that belong only to God. Mr. Hollis sums up Napoleon's original position admirably. "Against thieves and usurers, and all the ragtag and bobtail of internationalist finance he was on the side of the persecuted Church and the ancient decencies. But he was on her side not because he loved virtue but because he hated untidiness." He realized that the internecine struggle between Church and Revolution would but pave the way for the return of the Reactionaries, who would win out by selling France into slavery under the international usurers. So he arranged with Pope Pius VII a Concordat never wholly to the liking of the Vatican. Even more reluctant was the Holy Father to crown him Emperor. Still his arrogance soared and he became so outrageous that the pope accepted imprisonment at his hands rather than submission. In due time the pope returned to

Rome honored by the world and Napoleon went to St. Helena there to utter, in his last disillusionment, his sincere and eloquent sentences on the supreme leadership and the Divinity of Jesus Christ.

During that duel between the Church and Caesar, the French clergy, now purified as by fire, were able to combine a grateful but purely political loyalty to Napoleon with an absolute allegiance to the Holy See. They were now impoverished but pure in heart. And nineteenth-century France saw a great increase of vocations to the religious life, when priests and nuns really had to take the vow of poverty, over those in the eighteenth century when children were bundled into priories and convents to provide for them an affluent career.

VIII. CHURCH AND STATE

For many years all the discussions of the desirable relations between Church and State left me with an overwhelming sense of my own stupidity. Today my frequent recognition of my own obtuseness pertains to quite other matters. For, as far as this particular problem is concerned, I now realize that my countrymen have little or no insight. And I shudder at the realization that their lack of historical perspective, not infrequently combined with emotional blindness, is one of the most serious of the focal infections from which the United States suffers today. It may yet flare out as the destruction of the last outpost of democracy.

The phrase "separation of Church and State" has been, like the ideal of union, subjected to a bewildering variety of interpretations. Certainly no sane Protestant would read it to mean that no churchman may express an opinion about matters temporal. And the view that the Church must wait upon the State to grant her any of her rights is the view of tyrants like Hitler and Calles. For us in the United States, separation means precisely what Catholicism desires it to mean, "a free Church in a free State." Only a misinformed zealot, like a member of the Ku Klux Klan, could doubt this sincerely. From the point of view of Catholicism, even in a State overwhelmingly, nay completely, Catholic, there should be enough separation to insure rendering to Caesar the things which are Caesar's and to God the things which are God's. Witness the most illuminating Concordat of 1940 in Portugal. In a genuinely Catholic country, union of Church and State implies cooperation for the common good, temporal and spiritual, but in no sense a confounding of the always distinct spheres of Church and State, of politics and religion.

Cardinal Targini has written compactly that "The civil society, even though every member of it be Catholic, is not subject to the Church but plainly independent in temporal things which regard its temporal end. . . . Temporal happiness falls only indirectly, or so far as the spiritual end requires, under the power of the Church." This gives us the clue to the Catholic principle of indirect action. As Father Wilfred J. Parsons, S.J., puts it, "This influence is not an influence exercised by individuals of the Church upon individuals of the State, but of ideas and principles taught by the Church to the collective members of the State. Moreover, it is not an influence which concerns itself with every temporal affair of the State, or with any temporal affair, unless that affair has a religious aspect or an ethical aspect which flows from a religious consideration." This last sentence has already been abundantly exemplified for the reader in the chapter which dealt with the papal encyclicals on labor. The only kind of influence for which Catholicism pleads is precisely that exercised by all groups, Protestant, Catholic, or communist, in a healthy society. But it is clear that the Church has, of her very nature, a definite message regarding such matters as the just distribution of wealth and the peace of nations, the extirpation of poverty and the control of imperialistic greed. This kind of influence, which has led in ages past to the emancipation of slaves and to the elevation of the status of women, is precisely the influence which entitles the Catholic Church to the epithet Mother of Civilization. It is the great apostasy of modern Europe which, in the past few centuries, has plunged us deeper and deeper into a chaos from which, as Christopher Dawson has shown us in an earlier chapter and Hilaire Belloc in this, humanity will have a long struggle to recover this side of heaven and purgatory and hell.

Nor can this grim diagnosis be assigned to disgruntled Catholics exclusively. Atheists like Bertrand Russell and George Santayana taught me for years, before I dreamed of becoming a Catholic, to recognize the disease, although, as I often felt almost despairingly, they do not penetrate deeply enough into its causes and they have nothing of consequence to offer for its cure. Even the once exuberantly melioristic H. G. Wells has come to face the facts, although his hatred of the one possible solution remains still as blind as was the pseudo-progressivism of my own first thirty-five years of life. Aldous Huxley has diagonized shrewdly from the first and not without an occasional hint of a glimpse of the cure. Suffice it for me here to conclude with a passage from a man who has molded my political philosophy of late more than any other contemporary, from Jacques Maritain's masterpiece on the problem of Church and State, *The Things That Are Not Caesar's,* a message invincibly Catholic:

We must assert as a truth superior to every vicissitude of time the supremacy of the Church over the world and all earthly powers. [Not a political but a spiritual supremacy is here implied, for the things of God must obviously take precedence of the things of Caesar.] If the universe is not to suffer a radical disorder, the Church must lead the nations to the ultimate end of human life, which is also that of States and must therefore, in virtue of the spiritual interests entrusted to her, direct governments and nations and bend before God the stiff necks of the powers of flesh. On that condition only will they be stable: "For He does not take away mortal kingdoms who gives the kingdom of Heaven: He confirms them." The Pope is living Authority. On the summit of humanity, we see in him the imprint of the face of Christ. If that authority is not obeyed by Christian nations what authority will hold? The economy of the world is breaking up. And if that authority is obeyed, it inspires the hearts of men with the spirit of love which constitutes unity.

It is impossible, he argues, to recover peace without justice, that is without submission to God. It was not for herself but for the good of nations and states that the Church "helped them to do their important work in such a way as suited the requirements of the supernatural end. The apostasy of the nations is exerting itself to relieve the Church more and more from any such anxiety." The Church, it is true, could not make the world holy and just in the past, for "the world remained the world," but she can make it habitable for men.

The Church's attitude is properly described as suprapolitical, Maritain continues. She has no choice between forms of government, but must defend her own rights and the liberties of her children. On the other hand, Catholics, as being also members of a terrestrial community, must contribute their share of work for the temporal salvation of the State and the world. And in the distress of mankind that has disappointed the high hopes of nationalism and humanitarian optimism, it is folly for men to reject the advice of the Church, with all her vast experience of history. In the temporal calamities the great problems of the spiritual order are bound again to engage the minds of men. With Berdyaev, Maritain agrees that there is question of a new Middle Ages. A ferment is at work within the Church herself.

All her aspirations at the moment seem to be strained towards a spiritual restoration of Christendom. The spirit of God is making her cry out with her whole heart in the hope of that holy task. We should be sorry for anyone who judged a movement of such divine origin according to the standards of politics, national conflicts and worldly interests. Jesus Christ is moving His chalice from one place to another throughout the world, extending the frontiers of the Church, augmenting everywhere within her labor and desire in distant preparation for the return of the Christian East to unity, or the end of the fratricidal schisms provoked by the Reformation, or imploring Heaven to make the scales fall from the eyes of the elder race, or extending the secular effort of the missions and solemnly inviting the nations of Asia to share in the plenitude of the priesthood and the government of the churches.

IX. THAT THEY MAY BE ONE

Our Divine Lord, as Father Conway reminds us, "never spoke of a plurality of Churches, but of 'My Church.'" At the close of the Last Supper, in the last division of His long sacerdotal prayer, the Saviour turns from commending to His Father the eleven faithful Apostles to beseech grace and unity for their followers.

> And not for them only do I pray
> But for them also
> Who through their word shall believe in me.

What is it [inquires the Most Reverend Alban Goodier, S.J., in his masterly meditation which I read every Holy Week, *The Passion and Death of Our Lord Jesus Christ*], that He asks of His Father for His universal Church? . . . He asks that its living unity, manifested to all eyes, should be a lasting proof "That Thou hast sent me," that:

> "The world may know that Thou hast sent me
> and hast loved them
> as Thou hast loved me."

This, then, in His mind was to be the first foundation of the Apostolate; the living unity of the Church, which nothing would avail to break, was of itself to be the chief means by which she would win the world to belief, to knowledge, and to love:

> "And not for them only do I pray
> But for them also
> Who through their word shall believe in me,
> That they all may be one

As Thou Father in me
And I in Thee,
That they also may be one in us,
And the world may believe that Thou hast sent me,
And the glory which Thou hast given me
I have given to them
That they may be one
As we also are one,
I in them
And Thou in me,
And the world may know that Thou hast sent me
And hast loved them
As Thou hast loved me."

When I first became exultantly aware of this oneness for which our Blessed Lord prayed and which mankind can attain through the agency of His Mystical Body, His one Church, I was so filled with zeal that I was frequently guilty of doing my neighbors more harm than good. I too frequently forgot, I still too frequently forget, the days when I so sincerely shared the delusions and the nostrums with which our sick souls strive to heal the sick world.

Gradually peace, but a militant peace, full of high reposeful activity has come to me with the recognition that the two cities of St. Augustine, the City of God and the City of the World and Satan, are perpetually at war within the breast of each one of us, whether or not we have heard, however dimly or clearly we have understood, our adorable Master's sacerdotal prayer. Now I grow at once more patient and more militant than ever as I realize that the struggle between churches, and the struggle between churches and states, are but the externalization of my own malady.

In the Roman Catholic Church I have learned to sift the faltering truths from the pervasive errors of false prophets like Calvin and Rousseau, Hegel and Marx, Spengler and Wells, Mussolini and Hitler, American pragmatists and naturalists and liberals. I have thus learned that the one *philosophy* of history which fits the facts and enables us to meet them undiscouraged and uninflated, whether they prove tragic or triumphant, is that *theology* of history which St. Augustine gave us as his *De Civitate Dei*:

Two loves have created these two cities, namely, self-love to the extent of despising God, the earthly; love of God to the extent of despising one's self, the heavenly city. The former glories in itself, the latter in God. For the former seeks the glory of men, while to the latter God, as the testimony of the conscience, is the greatest glory. The former lifts its head in self-glory, the latter says to its God: "Thou art my glory, the lifter up of my head" (Ps. 3:4). The former, dominated by the lust of sovereignty, boasts of its princes or of the nations which it may bring under subjection; in the latter men serve one another in charity, the rulers by their counsel, the subjects by their obedience. The former loves its own strength in the person of its masters, the latter says to its God: "I will love Thee, O Lord, my strength" (Ps. 17:2). Hence the wise men of the former, living according to the flesh, follow the good things either of the body, or of the mind, or of both; and such as might know God have not glorified him as God or given thanks: but became vain in their thoughts. And their foolish heart was darkened. "For professing themselves to be wise [that is extolling themselves proudly in their wisdom], they became fools. And they changed the glory of the incorruptible God into the likeness of the image of a corruptible man and of birds, and of four-footed beasts and of creeping things [for they were either the people's leaders or followers in all these idolatries] . . . and worshipped and served the creature rather than the Creator, who is blessed forever" (Rom. 1:21 *sqq.*). But in the heavenly city there is not wisdom of man but only the piety by which the true God is fitly worshipped, and the reward it looks for is the society of the saints . . . "that God may be all in all" (I Cor. 15:28).

CHAPTER X

PERENNIALLY APOSTOLIC

"Come to us, brethren, if you wish to be engrafted in the vine. We are afflicted in beholding you lying cut off from it. Count over the Bishops from the very See of St. Peter, and mark, in this list of the Fathers, how one succeeded the other. This is the rock against which the proud gates of hell do not prevail."

"Others were able to do it, so why should not I?"

"But Thou, O Lord, to whom belongs eternity, dost Thou know nought of all I say, or dost Thou see in time what passes in time? Why, then, should I pour out all these things before Thee? Not indeed that Thou shouldst know them, but that my heart may be lifted up to Thee, and the hearts of all those that read, so that I and all they may exclaim magnus Dominus et laudabilis valde."

As I look back over the long years that lead to my conversion and as I dwell with awed delight on the constantly increasing richness, painful and pleasurable but always happy, of my experience within the Church, I realize that my greatest illuminations have come from the spoken word. Not even St. John the Evangelist and St. Paul, St. Augustine, St. Thomas Aquinas, and St. John of the Cross in their most inspired moments have pierced me so deeply and opened vistas so vast and have in an instant turned a chaotic nebula of perplexities into so sudden a galaxy of silvery thoughts, as the words that have fallen upon my ears from the lips of the learned and the unlearned, the simple and the subtle, the grotesque and the grand. For this reason, although either the oneness or the holiness or the Catholicity of the Church, singly and alone, would be quite enough to convince me of her divine origin, it is her apostolicity which arouses in me the deepest and highest rapture. The relations between apostolicity and the other three great marks or notes seem to me like the relation between being itself and its properties which flow from it.

In *The Church and the Gospels*, Father Joseph Huby, S.J., neatly summarizes this truth, which perhaps I would not have found so easy to understand if I had not lived it:

Luther's greatest claim to glory, in the eyes of his followers, is that he brought the believer back to a primitive evangel, suppressing all intermediaries. Eventually there were to be no more bishops, no more popes. No more need is there for an ecclesiastical magistracy or a universal hierarchy. Take the gospel and read it; there you will find the whole religion of Christ.

Protestants flatter themselves that by doing these things they restore the Christian religion to its original purity, as one would purify a diamond by removing its dross.

Vain presumption! When Father McGoldrick was instructing me, I often chafed inwardly over the pains he took to show me the inadequacy of Protestantism. "What a waste of time!" said I. For years I had known that it was the Catholic Church or none. The presumption of Protestantism, as Father Huby describes it, is but a lamentable mistake, a twofold mistake, psychological and historical.

A psychological mistake: for what is more pitiful than that the loftiest and most sacred things in the world should be thus given over to the caprice and fancy of each individual? Was it truly worth while that God Himself came down upon earth to reveal to us the mysteries of His intimate life if these truths were to be subject afterwards to the endless quarrels of men, without an authority which could settle the arguments with finality and fix the authentic meaning of the words of Christ?

A historical mistake: the religion of Christ did not begin as the religion of a book; when first launched it was a living Church, which preached with a living voice a doctrine fallen not from the pen but from the lips of the Master.

Moreover, even for His Apostles, the work of setting forth in writing the glory of their Master was not the most immediate task. "Their most pressing task was to preach Christ as first-hand witnesses, to gather believers in Him, to develop and organize the infant Church." And in that Church, as Father Philip Hughes says in his *A History of the Church*, "authority comes from authority already recognized." He thus briefly describes this process:

The next stage in the development begins with the removal by death of the Apostles. Their office, status, power, was unique. No one ever put in a claim to be an apostle of the second generation. Because of the fact which constituted them apostles they were necessarily irreplaceable. To their authority succeeded the new hierarchy of *episcopoi* and *presbyteroi,* and as it took place this new hierarchy itself underwent a change. The college of *episcopoi* or *presbyteroi* who, under the Apostles, had ruled the local Church gave place to an arrangement where in each local Church there was but one *episcopos* whom a number of subordinates, now termed *presbyteroi,* assisted. By the time of St. Ignatius of Antioch (i.e., the end of the first century, within from thirty to forty years of the death of St. Paul) the new system — the so-called "monarchial episcopate" — is so universal that he takes it for granted as the basis of his exhortations.

The change, he remarks, took place with so little disturbance, with so general an agreement that it left no trace in history. "One can only infer that it had behind it what alone could secure it so smooth a passage, the consciousness of all concerned that this was part of the Founder's plan wrought out in detail by the Apostles He had commissioned."

So, too, the power conferred on the new officers within the Church is never from below, never derived from a prestige of superior holiness, but there is the mention of fasting, prayer, and the *imposition of hands,* "and always the imposition is the act of those already possessed of authority . . . the all-important fact is clearly that for the first generation of Christians no powers were valid, no teaching guaranteed, no authority was lawful save such as came through the Apostles."

I. DEVOTION TO MARY AND THE SAINTS

God Himself, when He united His Divine Nature in the Person of the Son with His human nature in the womb of the Blessed Virgin Mary, keeping these Natures unconfounded and distinct yet ineffably united in one Person, was His own first Apostle, the only Founder, among all the founders of great and long-enduring religions, who claimed Divinity for Himself. But since, as God the Son, He is not in time and could say "Before Abraham *was* I *am,*" we might expect to find personages who might be called proto-Apostles, persons divinely inspired, who would foretell His assumption of His human nature in the days to come, the time of His coming, and the details of His life, passion, and death. Now, in fact this is exactly what we do discover, a phenomenon or series of phenomena absolutely unparalleled by the remotest analogy in any other of the religions of mankind. Even the Jews, who reject their Messiah, often, especially if they belong to their Orthodox Church, give their allegiance to these unique portents, although in so doing they are usually led to make the most perverse misinterpretations of the meaning of passages in their own Holy Writ. This they do that they may re-echo the denials of the last Sanhedrin, doomed soon thereupon to be dissolved forever after, amidst the ruins of their Holy City, by the legions of the ruthless Titus.

Over the work of these patriarchs and kings and prophets, from Moses to Abraham, and on to the Psalms of David which contain such startlingly literal messianic forecasts, and thence onward in time to those sublime prophets of whom the greatest, Isaias, alludes with perfect clarity to the coming Virgin Birth of his people's and all peoples' Saviour, and so down at last to John the Baptist who first announced the imminence of Christ's public appearance, and in the midst of a multitude, identified the present Christ, I cannot linger. But no convert, emancipated from the pseudo-scientific denial of miracles and with a mind murmurous with the matchless beauties of the Catholic liturgy, could write about himself without recording his love of the one whose entire consecrated life was a silent and most eloquent act of adoration, the mother of the Humanity of the Son, the first earthly dwelling place of His Divinity, the Blessed Virgin Mary.

While still an infidel I was astounded when I heard the charges of "Mariolatry" urged against Catholicism. Even Protestants, who are not so ignorant and stupid as to suppose us to be idolators when we kneel before images of Jesus, of Mary, or the saints, and who realize as clearly as we do that our images are no more idols for us than are the photographs of our parents and children that hang upon our walls, yet protest that we elevate too highly the Mother of God. Some feel bound to aver that for them our prayers to Mary and to the saints becloud the ineffable radiance of the Blessed Trinity. But as a fact, our supplications for the intercession of these holy ones betoken our humility, and in reality glorify the Father, the Son, and the Holy Spirit for the tremendous inspiration and sublime sanctity with which They endowed Mary to prepare her to hold in her human womb, to robe with human flesh and suckle with human milk our Divine Lord at whose cross and sepulcher she was destined to kneel, whose Resurrection and Ascension she was privileged to witness, whose Apostles she was entrusted to hearten in the dreadful days before Pentecost. What could be more humanly and divinely logical than the Church's teaching and practice in regard to Mary, purely human as we, yet Mother of God?

Evidently William Wordsworth did not share the pathetic myopia of so many Protestants. Although no friend of Catholicism, as his *Ecclesiastical Sonnets* in general show, and apparently more or less heterodox in many respects even in the midst of the then ubiquitous and bickering English Protestant sects, yet he could sing meekly and majestically:

> Mother! Whose virgin bosom was uncrost
>   With the least shade of thought to sin allied;
>   Woman! Above all women glorified,
> Our tainted nature's solitary boast;
> Purer than foam on central ocean tost;
>   Brighter than eastern skies at daybreak strewn
>   With fancied roses, than the unblemished moon
> Before her wane begins on heaven's blue coast;
>
> Thy image falls to earth. Yet some, I ween,
>   Not unforgiven, the suppliant knee might bend
>   As to a visible power, in which did blend
>   All that was mixed and reconciled in thee
>   Of mother's love with maiden purity,
> Of high with low, celestial with terrene.

Let me also gratefully borrow from the *Salve Mater* of Dr. Frederick Kinsman, who suffered from a misapprehension of the cults of Mary and the saints before he sloughed off his Anglicanism:

Actual experience of Catholic customs [he writes] will lessen or remove this difficulty in at least three ways. In the first place, to be understood, the devotions paid to saints must be viewed in their context of continuous worship of God through our Lord. Their actual place, determined by the great fixed points of Catholic life and worship, is distinctly subordinate. This would be illustrated by the two examples of their commonest public use. After Mass, the great habitual act of worship of our Lord Himself, lasting half an hour or longer, about three minutes are devoted to veneration of our Lady in the *Ave Maria* and *Salve Regina,* and petition for her intercession and that of the other great saints.

Similarly, he shows, there is no parity between the great Sacramental Sacrifice and the short Rosary when publicly recited, as only a prelude to the special adoration of our Lord in the Benediction. Nor, for those who know what the high altar in the church signifies, can there be any disproportion between the "blaze of tapers about a saint's image on some festival" and "the one really important light [the great red Sanctuary light that burns perpetually from Holy Saturday to Holy Thursday every year] which indicates the Tabernacle [wherein dwells the 'Angelic Bread,' our Lord]. The saints always and everywhere are nothing but our Lord's retinue, and even in the case of the greatest, derive all their importance from Him."

II. THE IMMACULATE CONCEPTION

At a time when there was a considerable growth of disbelief in the Divinity of Jesus (in 1854), Pope Pius IX comforted his distracted flock with the bull *Ineffabilis*. This proclaims the Immaculate Conception of the Blessed Virgin Mary to be "a doctrine revealed by God" which "therefore must be believed firmly and constantly by all the faithful." It is surprising how many confuse this dogma with the Virgin Birth of Christ. Mary herself was conceived and born of St. Joachim and St. Anne in the natural way. But "in the first instant of her conception," our Lady was, "by a singular grace and privilege of Almighty God, in view of the merits of Jesus Christ the Saviour of the human race, preserved exempt from all stain of original sin."

It was the Angel Gabriel himself, as Luke records, who most clearly enunciated the Immaculate Conception in his words to Mary: "Hail, *full of grace*, the Lord is with thee, blessed art thou among women." Fullness of grace allowed of no particle of sin, original or actual, in Mary. But long before that, the announcement of the Immaculate Conception was contained in the words of the Almighty Himself to Satan, hidden under his guise of a serpent: "I will put enmities between thee and the woman, and thy seed and her seed; she shall crush thy head and thou shalt lie in wait for her heel." The enmity foretold here between the Serpent and the woman, who is Mary; between the Serpent's seed and her seed, who is Christ, is absolute and complete. However the passage is read in the original Greek, it excludes from Mary every sin. Nothing could stand in more stark opposition to these words than to say that Mary in her conception had succumbed to Satan, whose head she had come to crush *through her Divine Son.*

Mary is always with her Divine Son, and her function is to bring us to Him and to save us through Him. Her Immaculate Conception is for Him alone. As Faber, the English poet convert sang:

How close to God, how full of God,
Dear Mother, must thou be!
For still the more we think of God,
The more we think of thee.

This is thy gift — oh, give it us!
To make God better known.
Ah, Mother, make Him in our hearts
More grand *and more alone!*

It is her Immaculate Conception that makes us appreciate profoundly the purity of God, and it is her Motherhood of God that makes us trust in His Mercy obtained through her. She is the immaculate way of God to us and of us to God.

Though original sin, inherited by all the descendants of the fallen Adam and Eve, is not the positive corruption which many Protestants believe it to be, yet it is, even by Catholic elucidation, a tragic privation of sanctifying grace. For, since the earthly days of Christ, the entrance of grace into the soul of the ordinary human being may be opened only by the gateway of some sort of baptism, at least baptism of desire. Although men like John Dewey are wrong in holding that pure Christianity teaches that since Adam all human beings are born "totally depraved" yet, in the phraseology of the new catechism issued by the Confraternity of Christian Doctrine in 1938, we find the teaching (much more precise than Professor Dewey's) that our first parents have transmitted to us "a nature deprived of that justice and holiness which God wished us to have": nevertheless there is an abyss of meaning between the words "depraved" and "deprived."

As I said before, I could never understand the great outcry Protestants so often have made over the beautiful devotions to Mary. I remember, too, how strongly impressed I was with the atheistic Santayana's condemnation of this perversity of theirs in *The Sense of Beauty.* It was natural enough for me, therefore, after my conversion, to take a special delight in collecting an anthology of tributes to our Lady. This led me to a quickened appreciation of the oneness of the Roman Catholic Church. The doctrine that the human Mother of God must be, not merely a virgin, but also immune from the frailty of original sin is perfectly logical, and therefore in no way inconsistent with the ineluctable faith of the Apostles. Still, it often seems to the outsider a somewhat artificial and, under pressure of a crisis, a suspiciously recent appendix.

The pope's pronouncement maintained that the dogma of the Immaculate Conception was not only logical, but historically implicit from the first. The ecclesiastical tradition of this was unchallenged in the West until the time of the famous controversy in 1140, out of which a greater clarification followed in the popular mind. In the East there was even a clearer conception of it during this early period (about 250–1100). It was repudiated, perhaps to widen the breach with Rome, in 1895, by Lord Anthimos VIII, Patriarch of Constantinople.

It is impossible to assume [writes Pohle in his volume on *Mariology*] that the early Christians believed Mary to have been subject to original sin, since the Fathers of both the Greek and the Latin Church extol her as "all-holy," "a virginal paradise preserved from the curse of God," "a virgin without the slightest taint of sin," "a miracle of grace, holier and purer than the angels," etc., etc. . . . To compare Mary's sanctity to the immaculate purity of the glorious seraphs, nay to exalt it in unmeasured terms above that purity, is but one remove from the formal declaration of the Immaculate Conception.

Even as far back as the second century, St. Justin Martyr (beheaded in 165), wrote: "The First-born of the Father before all creatures became a man through the Virgin, that by what way the disobedience arising from the serpent had its beginning, by that way also it might have its undoing. For Eve, being a virgin and undefiled, conceiving the word that was from the serpent, brought forth disobedience and death; but the Virgin Mary, taking faith and joy, when the Angel told her the good tidings . . . answered: 'Let it be done unto me according to thy word.'" We might similarly cite St. Irenæus (140-205). And let us never forget that the men of the second century often received their traditions directly from the younger companions of the Apostles themselves.

St. Augustine, the greatest genius of all the Fathers, held that because original sin usually begets personal sin and because Mary was the solitary human being who was sinless, she must have been conceived without sin. Herein we have an excellent example of an implicit formulation of a view that was to become explicit as dogma. But nothing could well be more beautiful and explicit than the words of St. Ephrem, the Syrian (310–378) : "She was *as innocent as Eve before her fall,* a Virgin *most estranged from every stain of sin,* more holy than the Seraphim, the sealed fountain of the Holy Ghost, *the pure seed of God, ever in body and in mind intact and immaculate."*

Irish Catholics appeared to have been holding the Feast of the Immaculate Conception by 900. And when this festival reached Gaul from Italy, although it aroused objections, it grew more and more popular until, by the fourteenth century, it was deeply rooted in Rome. Meanwhile the East stood steadfast. And when in the West the controversy broke out in 1140 there was, as Monsignor Pohle points out, a misunderstanding of "the real points at issue. Instead of endlessly harping on the query: 'Was the blessed Virgin Mary sanctified before or after the infusion of her soul into her body?' the medieval theologians should have formulated the problem thus: 'Was the soul of the Blessed Virgin sanctified at the moment of its creation?' But they disregarded this intrinsic possibility, on which the dogma of the Immaculate Conception rests." If the scholastics had followed Duns Scotus in his view of a special kind of redemption, a preventative preredemption, they would probably have had no difficulty. Scotus contends that God could fill her with grace without the necessity of cleansing away any already existing sin. He was followed by most of his fellow Franciscans but opposed moderately by the Dominicans including, apparently, St. Thomas Aquinas, though some held that the "Angelic Doctor" was undecided. Among them, Seraphino Capponi della Porrecta, undertook to show that St. Thomas was a possible champion or at least no foe of the doctrine. Another Dominican, Cardinal Cajetan (1469–1534), the greatest of the commentators on St. Thomas and Luther's noble adversary, said that "among modern theologians the number of those who hold that the Blessed Virgin was preserved free from original sin is infinite." The Jesuits believed that the Angelic Doctor was really in accord with the Subtle Doctor. One of the greatest of them, St. Peter Canisius (1521–1597), a patron of catechists and teachers of children, was justified in remarking that "Very few now hold the contrary opinion. . . . If they dared to speak out, they would meet with public contradiction and give offense to the people; to such a degree has the opinion adverse to the Immaculate Conception been weakened, exploded, and as it were cast out."

In 1568, Pope Pius V made the Feast of the Immaculate Conception a holyday of obligation for the entire Church. The doctrine was immensely popular. And as the following centuries flowed on, it appeared more and more to the learned to be an affront to reason to presume that "she who was from all eternity predestined to be the living temple of the Logos, the *Sanctum Sanctorum* of the New Testament, should have been even temporarily tainted by original sin." One of Mary's most radiant crusaders was St. John Berchmans whose lifelong desire to see this dogma established had much to do with my own delight in it. A search among Catholic poets who wrote long before the days of Pope Pius IX, provided me, among many others, with the following gem from Henry Constable (1562–1613) a famous Elizabethan poet who on becoming a Catholic settled in Paris, but returning to England in 1603 was confined in the Tower. The first four lines are almost as explicit as the papal bull:

> In that (O Queen of Queens) thy birth was free
> From guilt which others do of grace bereave
> When in their mothers' womb they life receive
> God as his sole-borne daughter loved thee.
> To match thee like thy birth's nobility,
> He thee His spirit for thy spouse did leave
> Of whom thou didst His only Son conceive,
> And so wast linked to all the Trinity.
> Cease then, O queens who earthly gowns do wear,
> To glory in the pomp of worldly things;
> If men such high respects unto you bear
> Which daughters, wives, and mothers are of Kings,
> What honor should unto that queen be done
> Who had your God, for Father, Spouse and Son?

The very fact that the Immaculate Conception was, for a time, a source of dispute among Catholics themselves attests its deathlessness and gave the occasion for it to be enthroned as a dogma.

III. APOSTOLICITY OF THE CHURCH

We have seen that God Himself, when He united His Divine Filial Nature with His Human Nature in the womb of the Blessed Virgin Mary, was His own first Apostle. He appeared incarnate in the very spotlight of civilization where mere legends about Him could not possibly survive for long the scrutiny of hosts of highly sophisticated, hostile, and critical enemies. He appeared at the exact moment in which He might have been expected to appear, at the most tense and tremendous climax which has yet occurred in the millennia of the history of man. He selected a small group of followers, called Apostles, and he appointed Peter as their absolute head, an appointment which He reaffirmed on several momentous occasions in language so striking that only an uninformed or a very stubborn person can persist in doubt. He gave instructions that this hierarchical government should remain permanent down the ages. He entrusted to His followers alone the choice of successors and the power of conferring upon those successors alone the power of sacramentally per- petuating the line. He promised to be with them always. He promised to send the Holy Spirit to join them at their hour of greatest need and thereafter to insure to this holy Society, this Church, that gift of doc- trinal infallibility by virtue of which the gates of hell could never pre- vail against her. He promised to return for judgment in His fullest glory on the day when her measureless mission is fully accomplished on earth.

Knowing these things we may share the ethereal thrill that breathes through these beautiful words which W. H. Mallock wrote, after a life- time of agnosticism, as well as of humble and heroic search for truth:

I can understand the Catholic claim, but I cannot understand any other. The Church says to her children, you must believe these things because I tell you that I witnessed them myself, and you know that I am trustworthy. I do not refer you merely to written books, but to my continuous conscious- ness that is called Tradition. You can believe that Resurrection surely be- cause I was there and I saw it. I saw with my own eyes the stone rolled away; I saw the Lord of Life come out; I went with the Maries to the tomb; I heard the footsteps on the garden path; I saw, through eyes blind with tears but clear with love, Him whom my companion thought to be the gardener.

As eye-and-ear witnesses to these truths ten of the first twelve Apostles died preaching in far-scattered lands, exultant martyrs. The eleventh, St. John, was tortured and escaped death by a miracle. Men demonstrably sane do not die in prolonged torture and disgrace for what they know or even suspect to be lies which they could retract with a word and thereby gain great rewards. The same may be said of men like St. Polycarp, St. Irenæus, and others, who as young men learned these truths in detail from the aged lips of the last of the Apostles or from their immediate followers, and died joyously transmitting them to yet further generations of martyrs who have suffered in every decade, down to this very moment.

Of the many features, then, which constitute apostolicity we may choose three. The first and most salient is the fact of absolute continuity for two thousand years. "By apostolicity," says Father John Brunsmann, S.V.D., in the third volume of his *Fundamental Theology*, "we understand that particular property which keeps the Church essentially just as she was established by Jesus Christ in His Apostles."

The second of the most striking marks of apostolicity is its supernatural efficacy in regenerating diseased tissue within the Church which is the Mystical Body of Christ. Of this we have already had many instances. Yet I feel that I have done nothing, as I gaze helplessly and lovingly over the resplendent achievements from among all the hosts of St. Benedict and Pope St. Gregory I; of St. Bernard; of St. Dominic (in whose Third Order I have recently enrolled) and such followers as St. Thomas Aquinas, St. Vincent Ferrer, St. Raymond of Pennefort, and St. Antoninus (to choose only the reformers and ignore the brilliant pageant of missionaries); of St. Francis of Assisi, St. Bonaventure and their followers to the days of our own contemporary, Father Rector Agostino Gemelli, who rejected his Marxian Communism to don the rusty brown habit; of St. Thomas More whose death in the sixteenth century to save the England of Henry VIII was apparently in vain — but only apparently, as the Catholic revival of the nineteenth and twentieth centuries in Great Britain shows; of the Carmelites, St. Teresa of Avila and St. John of the Cross, and their followers down to St. Thérèse of Lisieux, "The Little Flower of Jesus," in our own time; of St. Alphonsus Liguori who organized the Redemptorists in the eighteenth century; of St. John Bosco who founded schools for wayward youth in the nineteenth century; of Blessed Mother Cabrini who in the twentieth century reclaimed Italian exiles in the United States; of the American Maryknoll missionaries to the Orient in our generation; of these and throngs of others.

Lastly we must remember that the term *apostolicity* applies to the missionary work, particularly and formally to the first successful missionary in any strange land, but also more broadly and informally to home missionaries, priests, nuns, and laymen. Thus the work of St. Vincent de Paul in the luxurious days of King Louis XIV among the poor, the faltering, and the apostates was just as missionary as that of Damien who died among the lepers of the Pacific only yesterday. The miracle-working St. Jean Baptiste Vianney, who resurrected the souls of the village of Ars, debauched by the French Revolution, and whose clairvoyance brought to his confessional penitents from far distances, might be recorded in both this and the preceding group. The work of St. John Bosco, in the middle of the nineteenth century, among the reform-school type of boys who had been made pariahs by a callous society, like the work of Father Flanagan in "Boys Town" in the United States today, was just as surely a work among a strange people as that of St. Hyacinth among the Poles, St. Anscar in Sweden and Denmark, St. Frumentius among the Abyssinians, and St. Francis Xavier in India and Japan. Here again, for lack of space, I must confine myself to a very few of the innumerable achievements of the past generations. And here, even into the past decade, the past year, the past month the available harvest is so plenteous that one is tempted to reach out desperately, in all directions, at random. But I may only allude to two movements which are most appropriate for a more or less autobiographical study in apologetics like this book, because of these two I have some firsthand knowledge — the work of the Missionary Sisters of the Sacred Heart organized by Mother Francis Xavier Cabrini who was beatified in November, 1938, and the exploits in the Orient and at home of Maryknoll Fathers and Sisters who, just about the time when the financiers and their diplomatic minions began the final destruction of Western European Civilization, in 1914, quietly began a real crusade to make the world safe for genuine democracy through their efforts to prove that Chinese and Japanese and Filipinos and citizens of the United States are all one in Jesus Christ. And, finally I may mention the lay apostolate in the United States called the Catholic Worker Movement, led by Peter Maurin, the "apostle on the bum," and the converted communist, Dorothy Day.

IV. ST. PAUL AND THE EUCHARIST

Of apostolic continuity we have already had a good sample in the discussion of the authenticity of the Scriptures in an earlier chapter. There we saw that Tradition is necessary to guarantee the Gospels and Epistles, a point the rejection of which has been the chief of the many causes of the ruin of Protestantism. Here again, I long to trace at least a thin line of this continuity from St. Peter, St. John, and St. Paul to the present moment. But I must needs confine myself to an attempt to discharge my own debt of gratitude to the theology of St. Paul and to a concluding glance at his immediate followers in the period which overlapped and followed him, the post-Apostolic generation, taking some comfort in the fact that the continuity stands revealed at many points in all the preceding chapters of this book.

For my tribute to St. Paul and my sketch of the post-Apostolic generation I can imagine no prelude more fitting than a passage from Walter Pater, that most wistful neopagan who died almost — perhaps, for all we know, entirely — within the arms of Jesus:

The Mass, indeed, would appear to have been said continuously from the Apostolic Age. Its details, as one by one they become visible in later history, have already the character of what is ancient and venerable. "We are very old, and ye are young!" they seem to protest to those who misunderstand them. Ritual, in fact, like all other elements of religion, must grow and cannot be made. . . . In a generous electicism within the bounds of her liberty, and as by some providential power within her [the Church] gathers and serviceably adopts, as in other matters, so in ritual, one thing here, another there from various sources — Gnostic, Jewish, Pagan — to adorn and beautify the greatest act of worship the world has seen. It was thus the liturgy of the Church came to be — full of consolations for the human soul, and destined surely one day, under the sanction of so many ages of human experience, to take exclusive possession of the religious consciousness.

"The mass indeed would appear" — Walter Pater would not have tempered his fine prose hymn which rises to such a triumphant conclusion with such a faltering beginning, if he had caught the full import of St. Paul's famous reference to the Eucharist which has long echoed in my ears like a jubilant carillon. Nearly all the great Apostle's references to the sacrament, by their very casualness, prove that, in those days, and only a few years after our Lord's Crucifixion, Resurrection, and Ascension, the Catholic doctrine of Communion, of the Real Presence of our Lord in the Host, was a central part of the universal Tradition of the Church, that Tradition which antedated and indeed authorized the canonical works of *The New Testament*. These passages are made more impressive by the fact that St. Paul traces the prophetic promise of this Holy Sacrifice of the Mass back to the utterance of Malachy in *The Old Testament* and by the fact that he places the primitive Christian rite in the sharpest contrast with similar pagan practices which he brands as idolatrous. To cap the climax, in the famous passage to which I am referring in particular and which I quote with my italics, he defends the Holy Sacrifice by asserting that he himself learned its meaning for all time not through tradition but by revelation direct from God.

For I received from the Lord what I delivered also to you, that the Lord Jesus, the night He was betrayed, took bread, and having given thanks broke it, and said, *"This is My body which is for you: do this in memory of Me."* In like manner also the Cup, at the end of supper, saying, "This Cup is the New covenant in My blood: *do this, as often as you drink it, in memory of Me." For as often as you eat this Bread and drink the Cup, you proclaim the death of the Lord until He comes. So that whoever eats the Bread or drinks the Cup of the Lord unworthily shall be guilty of the Body* *and the Blood of the Lord.* But let a man examine himself, and so let him eat of the Bread and drink of the Cup; for he who eats and drinks — eats and drinks judgment to himself, *if he does not discern the body"* (1 Cor. 11:23–29).*

In this case the words would seem to carry their own commentary irresistibly. Nevertheless, in the light of what St. Paul has suffered at the hands of a long line of perverters, from Protestant reformers like Luther and Zwingli to their lineal descendants, neopagan poets like Swinburne, it may be worth while to quote a few reflections on this passage from *The Theology of Saint Paul,* by Father Ferdinand Prat, S.J. I wish that my reader would take the trouble to scan these two noble volumes, savoring particularly this profound scholar's exquisite sensibility to the idioms of the original Greek. Father Prat writes:

Those who wish to see in Christian dogmas only the completion of a slow evolution and the result of long-continued struggles that end by combining together after long ages of antagonism must experience great embarrassment in reading this passage which was written less than thirty years after the institution of the Eucharist, and is also of an unassailable authenticity. Does the theological language of today describe in any more precise and explicit terms the most consoling and ineffable of our mysteries? Paul declares expressly that he received this doctrine from the Lord himself, for his words (1 Cor. 11:23) cannot be understood as referring to a revelation through an intermediary, which would not distinguish him at all from the least favored of the faithful. . . .

The Apostle first indicates to us the source of his information, Jesus Christ himself: "I have received from the Lord that which I delivered unto you." In describing the institution of the Eucharist, he lays stress upon the circumstances of time — "the same night in which he was betrayed to his enemies," "after he had supped," "at the end of the farewell meal" — in order to fix the scene more perfectly in the minds of the neophytes, or rather in order to put it in direct connection with the death of the Lord Jesus.

The formula of the consecration of the bread could not be more clear. It would be not only obscure, but unintelligible and contradictory if the Saviour had said: "This bread is my body"; for it is absolutely impossible that a thing should be and not be at the same time, and the difficulty would not be removed [as Luther who clung to his belief in the Real Presence sought to do] by including the body of Christ in ordinary bread [the Lutheran quibble of "consubstantiation" versus the traditional "transubstantiation"], for it would still be untrue that the real bread *is* the real body of Christ. But

* This and following quotations from St. Paul are taken with the permission of the publishers from *The New Testament of Our Lord and Saviour, Jesus Christ,* translated by Father F. A. Spencer, O.P. (New York: Macmillan, 1937).

Jesus speaks unequivocally [as recorded not only in Paul's *Corinthians* but in the versions of Matthew, Mark, and Luke]: "This is my body, which [is] for you." The subject of the phrase is the demonstrative pronoun "this" — that is to say, what you see before you, that which I indicate to you by a gesture, that which is designated still neither as ordinary bread nor as the body of Christ, but the meaning of which will be determined at the end of the proposition, when something shall have been affirmed concerning it. The substantive verb, which serves as a copula, expresses as always the identity pure and simple between subject and predicate. It is a consolation to see today the Protestant and rationalistic exegetes agreeing with the Catholics to recognize such an elementary truth and to reject the biassed exegesis [Zwingli's fatal aberration] which translated "to be" by "to signify," contrary both to biblical and profane usage. Should the ambiguity be in the predicate? Ought the word "body" to be taken figuratively as a symbol of the body? The hypothesis is already unacceptable for the reason that it distorts without reason the natural meaning of the terms, but still more is its absurdity perceived, on substituting for the word "body" its pretended equivalent: "This is the symbol of my body, which symbol is for you. Whoever shall eat the bread and drink the chalice unworthily is guilty of the symbol of the body and of the symbol of the blood of the Lord."

Nothing need be added to this argument. In the same convincing way the formula of the second consecration is treated by the author. In both consecrations the words of Christ, spoken by the priest in the place of Christ, are effective, so that in the second there is His blood as in the first there is His body. To this double consecration St. Paul then adds the command given the Apostles by Christ to perpetuate the Eucharist to the end of time. Even the rationalistic critics do not dispute the unquestionable fact that the primitive Church and the Apostles believed in this institution. What they hold is that Apostles misunderstood the words of Jesus. But the cumulative effect of their aberrations in trying to answer the question, "What then did Jesus mean?" can but confirm the belief of any sensible person in the obvious, the traditionally venerable. "Where," concludes Father Prat, mildly dumbfounded, "will the fancy of historians of dogma end?"

It is simply incontestable, if one will take the trouble to investigate, as I did, not as a dogmatic materialist but as an open-minded agnostic, that Jesus meant exactly what He very clearly and forcibly said. And the Apostles, all of them, heard Him. As Father Prat shows:

By reason of the divine command and the explanation furnished by the

Apostle, the Eucharist became a commemorative rite: "Do this in remembrance of me. For as often [continues St. Paul] as you shall eat this bread and drink this chalice, *you shall show the death of the Lord until he come.*" [My italics.] But the eucharistic rite is not a simple commemoration of the sacrifice of the cross; it is itself a commemorative sacrifice. St. Paul does not say: "This chalice is commemorative of the new covenant concluded on Calvary in my blood"; he says: "This chalice is itself the covenant"; in other words: "The blood contained in this cup seals the covenant." It is, therefore, the blood of a victim: and *the rite which sheds it mystically* [My italics.] will have the character of a sacrifice. This appears still more clearly from the parallel passage of St. Luke: "This chalice is the new covenant in my blood, which is shed for you." St. Luke does not say that the blood *will be* shed at the moment of the passion: he says that the blood is shed now . . . for men.

The separate acts of consecration, as spoken in the Holy Mass, do not *singly* indicate a sacrifice, but since by virtue of the one consecration we have only the body of Christ, and by virtue of the other we have only the blood of Christ, that separate consecration of the two implies the mystic death of Christ. Since Christ, once bloodily sacrificed can die no longer, we actually have with His body also the blood, and with His blood also the body. That is, Christ is completely present under each separate species. Yet the body and blood are those of a victim in virtue of the rite which mystically separates them, and so possesses the character of a sacrifice.

It is tempting to go on and on with this theme. It is from St. Paul more than from any other Christian writer, and after him from St. John of Patmos, St. Thomas Aquinas, and St. John of the Cross, that I have learned one of the most significant features of Christianity, a feature absolutely unique, a feature which alone itself establishes the divine origin of Catholicism, the conception — which the human mind could never have chanced upon unaided — of an all-powerful God so infinitely condescending in His infinite Love that, not content with dwelling for a season in the womb of a simple little Jewish girl, He still, every moment, every day, in all parts of the earth "empties Himself" by becoming the substance of what was a little disk of unleavened bread, and of which now the outward species, the appearance only remains. How often have I thanked God for the opportunity that came with the years which I spent in the study of Greek in which St. Paul wrote and for the insight which came with the months which I devoted to the struggle with the

Epistles to the Corinthians in the gnarled Gothic idiom! My passage from those bewildered days to these seems now like the inevitable passage of a river that goes singing to the sea.

V. ST. PAUL AND GOD'S PROVIDENCE

From St. Paul more than from any other of the perennial apostles of nearly two millennia do I derive most of the understanding that I may dare to hope to have of God's inscrutable Providence. The Apostle's pages reverberate and thunder with their references to God's punishment on the pagans for their indifference to Him. It all reminds one terribly of our own age of growing madness. In their indifference the pagans were punished by being allowed to blind themselves — yet never utterly so. Misusing their free will, they were permitted to become the slaves of their passions so that whenever in their aching satiety they went God-seeking again, their very religions, like those of our own vain invention in these superstitious days of anthropocentric idolatries, became leprous things. And what of the Jews who had more advantages than the Pagans yet betrayed Christ? God will not abandon them. In fact, so St. Paul assures us as revealed to him, the time will come when the remnant of the Jewish nation will be converted. And from the very first they have been slowly coming in.

Indeed as we read St. Paul we catch constantly the first dawn-thrill of a hope for mankind. What should we expect God to do with a race of creatures who from the very beginning in Eden, turned their faces away from Him? He would let them punish themselves and so learn by devious ways, one by one, to love Him again. He would let them grope in the dark with false freedoms until they learned, one by one, that the only unequivocally free act is the one embodied in the cry — not of resignation, but of passionate love — "Thy will be done." He would allow them to blind themselves — yet never utterly so. For in fitful ways He would reveal Himself everywhere at all times to Polynesian mariner and Scythian warrior, to Mongolian herder and Aztec craftsman. But more than this, with His immeasurable Providence He would be training slowly, over the millennia, a special people, the Jews, to receive a special messenger in the small derided land called Palestine — Palestine, for ages a center of religious ferment from which the heralds of the long-prophesied Messias would pass forth in obedience to His mandate to teach all nations: eastward to dream-drenched India, westward to Spain at the portal of the awful Atlantic, much-harried Palestine, "The Battle Ground" (as Hilaire Belloc calls it in his great book of that name), the bridge between the rational West and the mystical East. But why one place and one people? Because during all the ages — or, rather from eternity — God was planning to become Man. By suffering unimaginable pain, humiliation, and injustice, and finally death itself, He would show His fellows how they themselves might become divine by participation in His nature. But since even God cannot violate the law of contradiction, it was necessary for Him, when He willed to imprison His Infinity in a finite being, to choose a local habitation and a particular people. Therefore, He chose the geographically perfect place, the strategically perfect moment in history, when the men of the proud Roman Empire were reeling back into chaos. And for His human blood, He selected a volatile Semitic fluid, the life stream of a tribal temperament which had long been trained by self-immolation and by selfish disloyalties, by triumphs and humiliations in a terrific rhythm to produce a few at least who would look steadfastly beyond all the worldly idolatries into eternity.

Idolatry is a mistaking of the means for the end of man's existence. Thus communism and all the other so-called humanisms are idolatrous because they regard a human social organization which functions perfectly from a primarily economic standpoint as the ultimate goal of man's aspiration. And even God's Chosen People, that is to say the wealthiest and the most influential of them, drifted into one of the subtlest of idolatries, the idolatry of Law and the pedantic, priggish, equivocating works which it imposes. Here, I found, is the clue to St. Paul's attitude toward faith and works, so tragically misunderstood by Martin Luther.

To Luther there seemed to be a conflict between the insistence on both faith and works in the *Epistle* of St. James, and St. Paul's apparently unfriendly attitude toward works in contrast with *the faith*. Consequently, Luther, despite the fact that, in his headstrong zeal to break with the Church, he had rejected Tradition (which antedated the Bible) and had declared the Bible to be the sole authority, was now constrained to denounce the lofty exhortations of St. James as "an epistle of straw." But the "works" of which St. Paul spoke warningly at times were, for the most part, the works of the Law, ritualistic observances and ethical precepts often of an artificial and pedantic nature, too often made a substitute for deeds more spiritual, more sincere, more selfless. In other words, the works which St. Paul dealt with so severely were sometimes those activities of the more decadent Pharisees, which our Lord condemned even while insisting that He came "to fulfill" the Law, and, more generally, the *human part* of man's actions in contrast with the operation of faith and grace which accompanies the morally or spiritually fruitful deeds. While St. James used the word *faith* in the homely sense of a simple assent to truth, for St. Paul the very word became a trumpet. For him it implied in addition to simple assent the vivid activity inspired by charity, the love of our neighbors as ourselves because of our love of God. There was no discrepancy whatever — other than terminological — between the Bishop of Jerusalem and the Apostle of the Gentiles who had come to a perfect understanding at the Council of Jerusalem.

St. Paul's "justification by faith" means an infusion of God's justice in a man which will come fully only when he can say, as the great Apostle said to the Galatians, "I live — yet no longer I, but Christ lives in me" (2:20). In saints like Paul and John of the Cross this does not mean at all, as purblind critics have averred, a sort of pantheistic annihilation. I have already pointed out that we are freest when we say lovingly to God "Thy will be done." The worldling knows in his heart that this is so. Yet he clings to his little wizened self. He is enslaved by each of his passing whims. He is torn by conflicting desires until he becomes less and less like a person, more and more like an explosion. In an earlier chapter I touched upon the arguments for the freedom of the will. And as a climax I emphasized what I take to be the supreme and positive proof. It must be lived to be understood. When he who tries to live in pure conformity with God's will — he who prays so incessantly "Grant, O Lord, that I may know and do Thy will" that this aspiration flows into his very actions like blood — even if he goes but a short distance along the way with St. Paul, will begin to feel within himself a growing exultant sense of freedom that spurns his last groveling doubt. He will now rediscover the lilies of the field clothed in splendors of which he never dreamed. The contemplation of his beloved will turn his prose into poetry. He will grow tender toward his enemies and admire their great qualities, as St. Robert Bellarmine never failed to do even in the midst of the most strenuous and breathless controversy. And all this will be, as I have learned from St. Paul more grippingly than from any other human being, because such an emancipated man will see in everything animate and inanimate the ever present Conserver.

Let such a man take up again the naturalistic explanation of his behavior. Let him seek cunningly all the hereditary and environmental explanations. They will indeed still account for many of his deeds. But for those of his actions which he knows to be most unequivocally his own, just because they aspire to conform with God's will — for such actions all pseudo-scientific explanations will only make him smile. For he has experienced, according to the degree of perfection to which he has attained, something of what St. Paul means when he rhapsodizes over "justification by faith." What I have thus found true I have also found true in my experiences with censors authorized by the one Church which God founded Himself. Every time they have taken issue with a phrase or a sentence of mine they have opened up some exhilarating and emancipating vista to which I had hitherto been blind. Such freedom, then, I have never found except in these two instances, submission to God and submission to His only Church.

VI. ST. PAUL AND THE HIGHER CRITICS

In St. Paul's epical vision, man, freed by baptism from the tyranny of the Mosaic Law, finds his freedom, like everything worth while, a gloriously perilous thing. Now the age-old struggle between the flesh and the spirit assumes a new phase, a phase more honorable for a man when he has put aside childish things, for a man when he has thrown off the maternal apron strings, for a man when he becomes a man. I know of nothing in the way of Protestant stupidity that has startled me into a greater indignation than my discovery of what the struggle between flesh and spirit really means in the supremely sane and soaring meditations of St. Paul. After Luther and Calvin and the Puritans blasphemed him with a praise that perverted his meaning, at last comes that idol of my youth, Swinburne, to anathematize him for expounding a morbid dualism which would have horrified him as much as it horrified the Victorian poet of paganism.

Just as the heresy of the "reformers" began by ignoring "works," because of its obsessive attitude toward faith, and turns today to a flabby toleration of any kind of "faith" because of its idolatry of "works," so these reformers began by praising St. Paul for a loathsome attitude toward the flesh which they erroneously read into him, while their "liberal" descendants, perversely accepting their leaders' travesty of the august apostle and often seconded by the "liberal" Jews of today when they attempt to pay homage to Jesus as a mere pious man, solemnly asseverate that St. Paul completely misunderstood Jesus Christ. Misunderstood Christ! — that very Jesus Christ who snatched him from his fanatical phariseeism and trained him by direct revelations to answer all the clashing excesses and deficiencies of the Gentiles by leading them always and unswervingly along a *via media*.

St. Paul, even among the morbidly dualistic Gentiles, Asiatic and Greek, never for one instant divagated from the magnificent tradition of his Jewish ancestors that God created all things except Himself, and that therefore all things, including the flesh, are good. For Paul, in consequence, the flesh is not sinful except through its misuse by souls forgetful of God.

From St. Paul more than from any other saint I have envisaged the unity of mankind down the ages. Adam and Eve caused in all men a disorder which can only be cured to the degree to which we surrender to perfect health in that Church which is the Mystical Body of Christ. Now, this general disorder which our first parents caused, works most of the havoc with our sensuous appetites and often even clouds our reason. But nobody makes it more clear than St. Paul that our reason (as conscience) never forgets the divine law and that law, itself a mere relation, implies a Lawmaker who, in this instance, is God. And to such an awakened reason the flesh, which never was sinful in itself (not even Adam's was so) — this same flesh, because created by God, is always plastic.

Moreover, to aid our embarrassed but unconquered rational souls, our heavenly Father, as St. Paul never tires of reminding us, sends His Holy Spirit with a treasure trove of gifts, gifts of which the mystic, Isaias, had written long before. They are: the lightninglike Counsel by which we can choose divine things, such as works of mercy, by our desire to do always the Will of God, in place of world-stained objects; loving Fear, which loves the all-loving God with such piercing wistfulness that it has a childlike dread of offending Him however slightly; Fortitude that, leaning on the strength of God, dares all for Him and can rejoice at the sight of rope and rack; Piety, which with filial abandon turns to God and loves even the sinner for His sake, nourishing devotion at its heart; Knowledge, that supernatural knowledge which sees in all things their Creator and Conserver and mourns most tenderly whenever these creatures forget their Source; undaunted Understanding which, increasing as our purity of heart increases, discovers richer and richer meaning in such Mysteries as those of the Trinity, the Incarnation, the Redemption, yes, even of Evil itself; and finally Wisdom, the loving knowledge that savors God, that fuses with Charity, that makes us the peacemakers, the most honored children of God. And thus ends the struggle of flesh and soul in the victory of a closer union made certain by the visit of the Holy Spirit if we only ask Him to come and coming to abide with us. This in place of the effigy of Paul besmirched by unhappy psychopaths from Luther to Swinburne! For this is the actual St. Paul, whom, with the aid of the commentaries of St. Augustine and St. Thomas Aquinas, I have discovered today on the heights of life. This is what the Apostle of the Gentiles means when he tells us that where sin abounded grace did yet more abound.

This man, aflame with charity, was the very man who took the road to Damascus aflame with a lust for the blood of the first followers of the Prince of Peace. His conversion, among the numerous miracles which have for nineteen hundred years occurred in close succession to confirm the message of Christ, has been acclaimed one of the greatest of all, second only to the Resurrection itself. Consequently the "higher critics" of the Bible have sought almost frantically to discredit it. It is obvious that the three versions of it (in the *Acts of the Apostles*) agree in all the essentials. Consequently the "freethinkers" have run pedantically amuck in their zeal to ferret out damning discrepancies.

It will probably be always at least mildly suprising to Catholics born in the faith to survey the desperate lengths to which these unnatural "naturalists" will go to explain away the obviously supernatural. To those of us who have been outside the Church it is a familiar state of mind which we have all shared. And I was one of these hapless wanderers who can testify to the acumen with which a native Catholic, Willis Dwight Nutting, has diagnosed us in *How Firm a Foundation*, which shows how the irrational "outlawing of the supernatural" has grown out of the Cartesian drift toward philosophical nihilism. To begin with, Descartes, although he did not himself deny the reality of substance, so warped the meaning and the metaphysical status of it that he paved the way for those sophistries of Russell, Whitehead, and others which we touched upon in an earlier chapter. Today, as Mr. Nutting observes, the philosophers have lost the ability "to accept existing things as fundamentally real." Explicitly or implicitly they echo the Protagorean sophism of Anatole France: "We are walled in by our senses." If they were consistent — as occasionally one of them almost is — they would see that the very arguments that they adduce against the sensibly imperceptible supernatural applies also with fatal perfection to the electrons and protons in which, with their science-idolatry, they so devoutly believe because of reasoned deduction and not because of the testimony of the senses. In other words, the same arguments which underlie their dogma that "miracles do not happen" would force them to insist that the various entities which explain the formulations of physics cannot exist. Nevertheless, armed with this superstition, the pseudo-historians, when they encounter in *The New Testament* a supernatural event of which there are severally slightly divergent accounts, conclude first that all the accounts are to be discredited. Next, in the words of Mr. Nutting, they "reconstruct what really happened. There is not much agreement as to this, except that they are all sure that what happened was something quite natural and nothing miraculous." Thus the slightly divergent accounts of our Lord's Resurrection are " 'reconstructed' into one story or another of mistake or deception, of which there is no record in any of the documents!"

I will never forget my first sensations when I first read the analysis of such difficulties in the sane and realistic pages of the Catholic exegetes. It was like passing from a stuffy department store, heavy with the odor of cheap perfume and full of apparitions of violently rouged clerks and customers, into the fresh clean air filled with the odor of living roses in some open flower stall. Of such work Father Prat's discussion of the narratives of St. Paul's conversion is a fair example.

It is conceded by everyone that the three narratives agree in all important points — viz., the occasion, the place, the time of the event, the dazzling light with which the caravan was enveloped, the dialogue between Saul, prostrate on the earth, and the mysterious voice, his temporary blindness, his baptism, his recovery, and the absolute change in his point of view, which suddenly made a persecutor an apostle. In a search for contradictions the most insignificant of details are scrutinized with the closest strictness, trifles which one would blush to notice in the case of a secular historian, circumstances external to the fact itself and relating only to the impressions experienced by the companions of the principal actor, impressions necessarily subjective and perhaps diverse.

Four differences are noted by these hypercritics, and these differences are not irreconcilable. Father Prat lists them as follows:

1. According to one account, the companions of Saul hear the voice (Acts 9:7); according to another they do not hear it (Acts 22:9). The expression used in the two cases is not the same. Ἀκούοντες τῆς φωνῆς (genitive), in Acts 9:7 means: They perceive the sound of the voice (without understanding it); τὴν φωνὴν (accusative) οὐκ ἤκουσαν λαλοῦντος μοί, in Acts

22:9, means that they "did not comprehend the voice of the one who spoke to me" (although perceiving the sound).

2. Here they see *no one*, Acts 9:7; there they see *a light*, Acts 22:9. Where is the contradiction? Is a light, a person?

3. In one case they remain standing (Acts 9:7); in the other they fall to the ground (Acts 22:9). εἰστήκεσαν ἐνεοί does not mean necessarily that *they were* standing, struck with stupefaction. It can be translated: They were, or they remained, out of themselves, as in Latin *steterunt* signifies in similar cases. One can convince oneself of this by consulting any Greek lexicon.

4. Finally, it is objected that the words of Jesus are different in different narratives. Literally, yes; but in meaning, no. The principal divergence consists in the fact that the author, according to a usage permitted at that time, unites in one single discourse (Acts 26:15-18) words uttered by Jesus Christ on two distinct occasions (Acts 22:8 and 21): perhaps also words uttered by Ananias (Acts 22:14-15) in the name of Christ.

Either the discourses are taken as a forgery, and in that case it would have been simple for a skilled writer like St. Luke to have harmonized them; or he carefully inserted all the documentary accounts as giving the full testimony, and then we must praise his historical accuracy. So again, as Father Prat further points out, if we deny the miraculous apparition to Paul, then we render inexplicable the moral miracle of his conversion. But St. Paul's own words are too clear to allow of any doubt: "He has *seen* the Lord (I Cor. 9:1); Christ has *appeared* to him finally after all the others (I Cor. 15:8); God has *revealed* his Son to him at the moment when he least thought of such a thing (Gal. 1:15-16). There is no halting in his conversion, no gradual progress towards faith."

Paul — then Saul — is halted suddenly, irresistibly. Of the Christians he knew nothing and of their doctrine less, except that they were execrated by the Synagogue. He had acted in good faith and on that ground expected mercy. As Father Prat says, all the laboriously constructed hypotheses of the critics are untenable. "In order to do away with one miracle they invent a psychological miracle still more marvelous." It was all simply the mighty grace of the Omnipotent God.

VII. ST. PAUL'S SOLICITUDE FOR ALL

Thus, by the grace of God, with which heroically he corresponded, this amazing Saul was hammered and hewn by Almighty God into a Paul of glorious paradoxes: so poor of spirit and magnanimous, so detached and charitable, so humble yet so adamantine in self-respect, so defiant and so obedient, a warrior armored in flames and a peacemaker so attentive to the faintest unuttered whisper of his Saviour, so homely in his tenderness for the blindest and most stupid and stumbling of his fellow men, and yet so piercing in his understanding of Sacred Mysteries.

Almost stolid in his refusal — except for one occasion when a prisoner at Rome — of material aid, he plied his trade of tentmaker wherever he went. He "withstood" St. Peter "to his face" when he knew that the Prince of the Apostles was wrong in his temporary shunning of Gentile table-comrades. And that brave and simple pope admitted his fault. Yet well did Paul repay his leader's humility by an equal humility in his vigilant solicitude lest he encroach upon St. Peter's jurisdiction in Rome. His scourgings and imprisonment he would generally take in silence, joyful in the opportunity to imitate the Lord. But if need be he would beard a Roman official in his hall or boast of his sufferings to those whose schismatic impulses tempted them to rationalize their own falterings by belittling his apostolic standing. No one — always excepting our Divine Lord Himself — has ever taught me so much about the examination of my conscience to detect the protean disguises of pride, the false humility which is pride, the hardly won humility which we vitiate by becoming proud of it, the self-respect which we inhibit when we ought to assert it because we are afraid that we will appear proud in the eyes of our critics and are therefore pusillanimously proud in our timid desire not to appear to be proud.

More than any other member of the Communion of the Saints, Paul has instructed and fortified me by doctrine and example in that lesson of lessons for anyone who would work as a Christian apostle, the tragic and triumphant truth that as soon as the faith makes progress in a society it will be partially destroyed from within and without, and that the moment the destruction begins the soldier of Christ must leap among the glowing and smouldering ruins to the task of rebuilding. That puissant ideal, from the days of the Apostle of the Gentiles to our own days of the Passionist and Maryknoll Fathers in tortured China, has in its continuous realization in practice accounted more than anything else, on the visible human side, for the fulfillment of our Lord's promise.

The Church in splendid and sinful Corinth, perhaps his greatest triumph, is troubled, now by the moral laxity of some of its members, again by dissensions among them. "It is actually reported that there is impurity among you," St. Paul thunders, "and such impurity as exists not even among the heathen — for one of you has his father's wife! And you are arrogant, and have not rather grieved, so that he who has done this deed might be removed from among you!" (1 Cor. 5:1, 2.) Yet he is quick to exhort them to forgive the incestuous man, once he repents. And he fairly pants to efface himself when he learns that contentious cliques are pitting his name against those of other missionaries:

Now I beg of you, brethren, by the Name of our Lord Jesus Christ, that you all speak the same thing, and that there may be no dissensions among you; but that you may be perfectly united in the same mind and in the same judgment. . . . What I mean is this: that you each declare, "I am a follower of Paul"; — "and I of Apollos"; — "and I of Kephas"; — "and I of Christ." Is Christ divided? Was Paul crucified for you? or were you baptized into the name of Paul? (I Cor. 1:10, 12–13.)

For all his tender concern for the Gentiles, St. Paul feels bound in his *Epistle to the Romans* to launch a terrible indictment of their idolatry which might well be hurled against the Fascist, Nazist, Communistic, and pseudo-democratic Liberal-Humanistic idolatries of our day. As with the Marxists and Pragmatic sophists of our time, God allowed the minds of *ungrateful* men to grow more and more confused and to take insensate delight in the turns of their unrealistic dialectic. Respectful of their free will, He leaves them to flounder in the meshes of their own creation. But for all their unnatural vices, the by-product of their perverted logic, these pagans arouse in the Apostle a triumphant tenderness. He will not give them up, nor would he have others judge them. He has none of the hideous sophistries of Calvin regarding their destiny.

But particularly charming is his letter to Philemon regarding the runaway slave Onesimus, of which Father Prat remarks: "This little masterpiece of tact, urbanity, nobility, and exquisite grace was the first Christian declaration of the rights of man." That statement, of course, Father Prat would not have us take too literally. We must, for instance, recall the implications in Mary's sublime *Magnificat,* and above all the teaching of Christ. We need but mention our Saviour's discourse to His Apostles on the eve of His Passion:

> And I come to thee,
>   Holy Father,
> Keep them in thy name
> Whom thou hast given to me
> That they may be one
> As we also are. (John 17:11.)

Starting from these words and meditating upon St. Paul's working out of their implications in his plea that Philemon show clemency to the runaway slave, who now seals his conversion to the faith by surrendering at St. Paul's suggestion, I began to see more clearly than ever before through the specious falsity of two slanders against Christianity widely prevalent today. The first is that Christianity has failed; it springs from the attribution of the sins of its betrayers to Christianity itself. Christianity has never failed, as anyone knows who follows its pure tradition from our Lord and St. Paul to St. Benedict; from St. Benedict to St. Thomas Aquinas; from St. Thomas to St. Robert Bellarmine, and from St. Robert to the papal encyclicals of our day. Christianity has never failed — when it has been lived not merely by words, but by deeds.

VIII. ST. PAUL AND CHRISTIAN DEMOCRACY

The second fallacy would seem to the reader of *The Epistle to Philemon,* on superficial first thought, to have some basis in fact. It claims that Christianity is a drug with which reactionaries strive to stupefy their unhappy victims. But we shall soon see that the truth lies in a diametrically opposite direction. It is, in fact, one of those half-truths which are much more dangerous than downright and wanton falsehood. There have been, especially since the days of the so-called Reformation, certain individuals, like Thomas Cromwell and Lord Burghley, who, while professing one creed or another, have more or less consciously sought to make religion the anodyne for those whom they exploited. At best, they have been Christians only in name. Many of them, to do them justice, have never even professed the faith. It is a fallacy popular among the so-called communists and their dupes, calling themselves "liberals," and arises from a tendency to read the history of the past four hundred years into the past two thousand or more.

The growth of capitalistic society in western civilization (if we define it as that kind of society in which the means of production are owned or controlled to a large degree by a few irresponsible individuals, the kind of society which threatens to reach its *reductio ad absurdum* in the National Socialism of Germany, and in the State Capitalism of those bourgeois Russian intellectuals who believe or pretend to believe that they have established a dictatorship of the proletariat) began with the looting of the monasteries and the guilds. It next went on to procedures like the enclosures of the commons, which completed the impoverishment of the peasant, and reached a climax in the herding of a miserable proletariat into mines and factories. The growth of this society has been accompanied by efforts, sometimes unconscious, sometimes conscious, to strangle Christianity and Democracy. Oswald Spengler may be right as far as our culture is concerned. Western civilization may be plunging downward to its death. Its only hope lies in a Christian renaissance, in a flamingly sincere echoing and re-echoing of St. Paul's exultant cry in his *Epistle to the Galatians:* "there can be neither Jew nor Greek, there can be neither slave nor freeman, there can be no male and female; for you all are one in Christ Jesus" (3:28, 29).

True democracy is a corollary of this ancient pure and perennial Christian tradition. The Greeks gave us little more than the word. For their society was rooted in the slavery which the first Christians at once undertook to dissolve, not by a violent revolution, which in any case could only have meant failure, but by a much subtler, more rational and effective method, perfectly summarized in *The Last Years of St. Paul* by the Abbé Constant Fouard:

Very different is the Church's mission on earth: into the hearts of men she drops those words of Jesus: "Ye are all brethren," and leaves it there to fructify, knowing that it will quietly and gently transform their customs and laws, healing the social body of the cancer which consumes it, not by steel or by fire, but by the infusion of a new life-blood. Certainly Paul could have found no more decisive argument against slavery than this brotherhood of man; rather, to make it more emphatic, he reminds them that all believers, by their incorporation with the Christ, are not merely sons, equally heirs to all rights, all graces emanating from the same Heavenly Father, rather their union with Him is so close that it approaches some sort of identity.

It is true that St. Paul sent the thieving, runaway, but newly converted and repentant slave, Onesimus, back to his master, Philemon. But he took ample precaution that the slave would be magnanimously, nay, lovingly received. "For perhaps," writes the Apostle in a sentence fragrant with the truest charity (that is, the love of one's fellows because of one's love of God), "for perhaps he [Onesimus] was parted from thee for a while for this reason, that thou mightest possess him forever, no longer as a slave, but far more than a slave — a dear brother. Such he is especially to me, but how much more to thee, both in earthly relations and in the Lord!" (15-16.)

Mindful of his Divine Lord's love of the fisherman and the shepherd and the poor widow, the publican and the sinner, the mighty Apostle taught incessantly, from Asia to Greece, from Greece to Rome, and from Rome to Spain, that there is neither Jew nor Greek, freeman nor slave, but that we are all one in Christ Jesus. Under this quiet but powerful influence slaves became landowning serfs and then gained more and more freedom.

The slave marketing that was revived in modern times by men who preached Christianity with their lips and blasphemed it with their deeds, the British buccaneers and Spanish conquistadors, was constantly denounced by successive popes and was heroically resisted by missionary priests who sturdily maintained that Negroes and Indians were not beasts but God's grace-adopted children. Today men like Stalin and Hitler, who would enslave the whole world, realize that their dream is impossible unless they can annihilate the Roman Catholic Church.

In the seventeenth century, when the Protestant, James I of England, proclaimed the divine rights of kings he was opposed, in the name of the pure and democratic tradition of Christianity, by the Jesuit Cardinal Robert Bellarmine, canonized in recent years and named a Doctor of the Church. A century later Thomas Jefferson, as certain of his books and marginalia preserved in the Congressional Library make amply clear, was well acquainted with the writings of St. Robert.

The most trenchant as well as constructive critics of all the anti-democratic tendencies of our day: of imperialistic plutocratic capitalism; of Fascism, Nazism, and the so-called communism of Karl Marx and his disciples, are, as we saw in earlier chapters, the great popes, Leo XIII and Pius XI, in their intrepid encyclicals. And their lips, it will be noted, are lyrical with the generous admonitions and exhortations of St. Paul. In a brilliant account of the development of Catholic dogma in his *Fire on the Earth*, Father Furfey has shown that the Church was for eighteen centuries concerned primarily with making explicit what was always implicit in Divine Revelation concerning the Trinity, the Hypostatic Union, the Redemption, the interplay of free will and grace, the basis of religion in reason as well as revelation, the basis of Christianity in Tradition as well as in the Bible. But from these pressing problems, the Church turned in our time, with Leo XIII, the Pope of the workingmen, and with his successors, to search the Scriptures and Tradition for the explication of dogmas relevant to our age of unparalleled avarice, economic exploitations, and imperialistic wars, a task to which the Church will now bring the best learning of the contemporary social scientists, fused with her infallible interpretation of the Deposit of Faith.

We owe immeasurably to St. Paul the lilt in our hope for the survival of some more or less realized Christian democracy on earth till the end of time. It may well turn out that it will once more be driven into the catacombs by the Neros and Diocletians of our day. But it will survive, as it has survived already for two thousand years, through many crises equally dreadful if not more so. It may be that black missionaries from Africa, brown ones from India, and yellow ones from China and Japan will come to bring back the crucifix to a Europe and an America which have reeled back into the beast — or below the beast. And if these orientals come to us they will come with their blood leaping to the rhythm of St. Paul's imperishable cry, "There is no longer either Jew or Greek, bond or free; all, all are one in Christ Jesus," and with the sting of his terse apothegm, the very attar of democratic idealism, "The Christ is all in all."

IX. ST. PAUL AND THE MYSTICAL BODY

"The unity of mankind," says Father Leen in *The True Vine and Its Branches*, "was very dear to the heart of Christ. His avowed intention of consecrating His life to effecting it brought Him into violent conflict with the fanatical exclusiveness of His people. His mind dwells insistently on it on the night of the Last Supper. It is a sustained note running through all the changes of thought that mark His last injunction to His disciples."

In St. Paul's magnificent exposition of the Mystical Body of Christ the same note is continuously prolonged and enshrined, even more elaborately than in the words of our Lord Himself and in those of St. John, in whose writings is recorded the Saviour's figure of Himself as the Vine, of us as the branches through whom the sap of His grace flows. So rapturous indeed is the crescendo of our Lord's principal theme in the tremendous fusion of metaphorical and literal truth in the vision of the Mystical Body of Christ that this alone would convince me that Paul was a direct recipient of Divine Revelation, who has reached to and balanced himself on such heights. As I brood happily over this ineffably consoling idea I discern flowing convergingly into it every strand of distinctly Christian thought from the highest dreams of a democracy as yet unrealized on earth to the one ultimate and unanswerable solution of the problem of evil.

"For the body is not a single member, but many." So exults St. Paul in one of his most intimate outpourings to his troublesome and beloved Corinthians. "If the foot should say, 'Because I am not a hand I do not belong to the body' — would it therefore not belong to the body? And if the ear should say, 'Because I am not an eye, I do not belong to the body' — would it therefore not belong to the body? If the whole body were an eye, where would be the hearing?" (1 Cor. 12:14–16.) And here Paul flashes before us the whole meaning of the mystery of the vast varieties and half real, half only apparent inequalities of God's created children. "If all [were] hearing, where would be the smelling? But as it is, God has placed the organs, each of them in the body just as it has pleased Him" (*ibid.*, 17, 18). For is not God reflecting His Infinity in the multifarious but vastly integrated varieties of His creatures? "But if they were all a single member, where would the body be?" (*Ibid.*, 19.)

The whole answer to the world-old philosophical problem of the one and the many is in these sentences close furled as in the tight rich bud of a sumptuous rose. And now Paul's thought rushes on in ecstatic breathlessness. "As it is, however, they are many members, yet a single body. And the eye cannot say to the hand, 'I have no need of thee!' nor again, the head to the feet, 'I have no need of you!' " (*Ibid.*, 20, 21.) Then follows a succinct, perfect, pregnant explanation of the paradox of biological and psychological inequality and spiritual equality in Christ Jesus. "Nay, much rather are those members of the body necessary which seem to be more feeble; and what we consider the less honorable parts of the body we clothe with the greater dignity; and our unseemly parts are dressed with the greater elegance" (*ibid.*, 22, 23). There is audacity, sound audacity, here. Paul means that the homeliest, lowliest parts of the Mystical Body of Christ are clean, pure, and beautiful; "our handsomer parts have no need of it. But God has combined the body in due proportion by giving greater dignity to the less regarded part; so that there might be no dissension in the body, but that on the contrary the members might have a mutual care for one another" (*ibid.*, 24, 25). It is all the most sublime manifestation of the Holy Spirit's Gift of Wisdom, of the Virtue of Charity, the Beatitude of the Peacemakers. And here follows the precious clue to the problem of evil, words which heal like some rare balsam. "And if one member suffers, all the members suffer with it; or if one member is honored, all the members have pleasure with it. Now you are the body of Christ, and individually members of it. And God has placed in the Church some to be, first, apostles, secondly, prophets, thirdly, teachers, then follow miraculous powers; then, gifts of healing, assisting governing, various kinds of languages" (*ibid.*, 26–28).

Even more healing, enlightening, and elevating, if possible, is the nuclear passage in what has been called *The Epistle to the Ephesians*, but applicable to every infant *ecclesia* of the *orbis terrarum* where he scattered so widely his seminal teachings: "So then, you are no longer foreigners and sojourners, but you are fellow-citizens with the saints, and are of the family of God, built upon the foundation of the apostles and prophets, the corner foundation-stone being Christ Jesus Himself. In Him the whole building, accurately fitted together, rises into a holy temple in the Lord; in Him you also are being built together into a spiritual dwelling-place of God" (Eph. 2:19–22).

Into the very vortex of this symphonious whirlpool of thought, which centers in that theme of oneness which our Lord had glorified in His sacerdotal speech, Paul sweeps his tender and magnanimous conception of the reciprocal love-surrender of woman to man and man to woman in marriage within the Mystical Body, that Sacrament of Marriage which in itself would be sufficient, when we contemplate by contrast the loftiest merely human *epithalamia*, to prove the Divine Origin and Eternal Verity of the Church:

Let the wives be submissive to their husbands as to the Lord; for the husband is head of the wife, even as Christ is head of the Church, Himself being the Saviour of His body. Just as the Church is subject to Christ, then, so should wives be to their own husbands in everything.

Husbands, love your wives, even as Christ loved the Church and gave Himself up for her, that He might sanctify her, purifying her in the laver of water with the Word; that He might present the Church to Himself glorious, not having spot or wrinkle or any such thing, but that she might be holy and immaculate. Even thus should husbands love their own wives as their own bodies. He who loves his own wife loves himself. For nobody ever hated his own flesh; on the contrary, he nourishes and cherishes it, just as Christ does the Church; for we are members of His body [we are of His flesh and His bones]. For this reason a man shall leave his father and mother, and shall cleave to his wife, and the two shall become one flesh. The mystery is great — I mean great, in its relation to Christ and the Church" (Eph. 5:22–32).

Full panoplied with this Pauline theology, the Church has swept aside with her sword of truth the perversions of all the sects through all the ages. In her catholicity she repeats the Apostle's assurance that God "wisheth all men to be saved and to come to knowledge," for "there is one God, one mediator also between God and men, Himself man, Christ Jesus who gave Himself for all men." In her oneness she remembers with humble audacity that Christ and herself are wedded into one Personality "for you are one with Christ." In her holiness she remembers that although Paul warned her to "put away" from the faithful the incestuous adulterer of Corinth yet was she still to treat him and all other sinners as "brethren," that is as members of her society. Indeed, her holiness is proved supreme by the very sins of her members, because she alone among institutions can heal them without being herself infected by the plague, for she alone of earthly things possesses all the means of sanctification as entrusted to her by her Bridegroom. And by the Apostle's persistent preference of the spoken word above all writing she is reminded of that perennial apostolicity, an unbroken stream of inspiration from the days of our Lord, from Peter, John, and Paul to Pope Pius XII, so that today when she speaks with the lips of her Head, she still speaks by the Paraclete, the Holy Spirit, whom at our Saviour's Ascension He promised to send to dwell perpetually within her.

She remembers that in the subapostolic era, Clement of Rome wrote to the Corinthians that:

The Apostles were instituted for us as preachers of the Gospel by the Lord Jesus Christ. Jesus the Christ was sent from God. . . . Having, therefore, received their commands . . . they [the Apostles] went forth in the assurance of the Holy Spirit, preaching the good news that the Kingdom had come. They preached from district to district, and from city to city, and appointed their first converts, testing them by the Spirit to be bishops and deacons of the future believers. . . . They afterwards added the counsel that if they should fall asleep, other approved men should succeed to their ministry.

Among many such sayings of those whom holy Mother Church knows her young men once listened to in the speech of Christ's aging twelve we must content ourselves with one more testimony, that of Papias of Hierapolis, who declared that "What I culled from books did not profit me as much as what I learned from the living and persistent voice."

Then, treading on the heels of the first subapostolic generation come the first of that long line of Church Fathers who instructed each other down the avenues of the centuries to the days of the Church Doctors.

Among these Church Fathers the first one, St. Irenæus, speaks thus of the various Gnostic sects whose occultisms and crazy symbols sound so contemporary to us who, in these days of skepticism and superstition, are afflicted by scores of mushroom fantastic and fanatical "new-thoughts" and "unities," Rutherfordisms and pseudo-Hinduisms.

> When, however, they are confuted from the Scriptures, they turn round and accuse these same Scriptures as if they were not correct . . . and that the truth cannot be extracted from them by those who are ignorant of tradition. . . . But when we refer them to that tradition which originates from the Apostles, which is preserved by means of the successions of presbyters in the churches, they object to tradition, saying that they themselves are wiser not merely than the presbyters, but even than the Apostles.

But these Gnostics, from the first century in Asia and Greece and Rome to the twentieth in Los Angeles and Salt Lake City and New York, were answered once and for all in trumpet tones by St. Paul's *Epistle* to the fadistic Colossians. The Mystical Body will be protected always by the Head who though He came late to earth, was first born before the ages:

> He is the Image of the invisible God, the First-born of all creation. For in Him were created all things in the heavens and on the earth, things visible and invisible, whether Thrones or Dominations or Principalities or Powers — all were created through Him and for Him. And He Himself exists before all things, and in Him all things hold together.
>
> He is also the Head of the Body, the Church; and He is the Beginning, the First-born from the dead, that in all things He may hold the pre-eminence. For it was the pleasure of the Father that all the fulness should dwell in Him; and that through Him He should reconcile to Himself all things, whether things that are on the earth or things that are in the heavens, making peace by the blood of His cross (1:15–20).

X. THE GLORIOUS PROCESSION OF POPES

But since I have become myself a member of the Mystical Body, the most impressive witness of Catholicity to me is the apostolic pageant of the popes. I have already, in an earlier chapter, remarked that the conception of papal infallibility was never a real difficulty. The fact that out of two hundred and sixty popes, most of whom have wielded tremendous power, many of whom have endured dreadful persecutions, and all of whom have faced crises unexampled, some four or five have proved

peccable in matters temporal, was a surprise to me only in the sense
that I marveled that under such circumstances there had not been more
that sinned and that their sins had not been greater. And even the errant
few, I saw, as anyone who takes a little trouble can see, had never made
a single doctrinal mistake. He who history has acclaimed the worst,
Alexander VI, was loved by the common people in tortured renaissance
Rome while he ruled with an iron hand those avaricious potentates who
doubtless were responsible for many slanders since cleared up. He settled
an acute difficulty over New World possessions between Spain and Portugal. But for our purposes it is most important to know that with all his
sins, he was loyal to traditional rules, wise in issuing constitutions, and
guiltless of passing a single decree at variance with Catholic faith and
morals.

Of the first thirty popes, twenty-eight won the crown of martyrdom,
some of them within a year or two of tenure, nearly all of them within
twelve years of rule. No sooner had they emerged from the catacombs,
wherein they had even planned the redemption of slaves by purchasing
their freedom, than they were beset with the heresies so fertile in the East.
Westward and northward they turned their eyes only to encounter the
hordes of barbarians, as when Pope St. Leo I, armed only with the
Crucifix, went out to meet the Huns under Attila and turned back this
"Scourge of God," and when later he confronted the Vandals of Genseric
to save for us today the treasures of that classical Roman civilization of
which, according to our traducers, our Church has taken no heed. There
were more martyrs yet to come, St. John the first, for instance, who
reigned but three years and died in prison, in 526, under Arian persecution, and St. Silverius who died (538) in an exile inspired by the heretical
Monophysites but enforced by the emperor. For, as we have seen, the
Christianized or semi-Christianized emperors, largely because of their
Caesaristic attempts to tamper with the things that are God's, were in
some respects foes more insidious than the pagan rulers. Pope St. Martin
I, because he boldly condemned the Monothelites for their attenuated
conception of Christ, was dragged a prisoner to Constantinople and
thence exiled to die, with unconquerable soul, in 655. In 1799 Pope
Pius VI died in Valence (where he had been held captive by the army
of the French Revolution) praying, like his Master, for his persecutors.
By these later popes the number of martyrs has been increased to no
less than forty.

How could I take seriously the charge that all popes have been luxurious sybarites when I knew that in a dreadful pestilence Pope Pelagius II converted his house into a hospital and died a victim of his self-sacrifice, that St. Stephen VI scattered all his own goods among the poor and fed the needy and the orphans at his own table, that John IV lavished the treasures of the Church for the redemption of captive Christians, that Theodore II died renowned for his devotion to the poor, that Martin IV fathered those starving in an appalling famine which visited even the pontifical states, that St. Celestine V resigned his office to become a hermit, that Gregory XIV, who ordered the abolition of Indian slavery in the Philippines, led a life of asceticism, prayer, and charity, that Innocent XII was a self-immolating father of the orphans and the indigent, that Benedict XIII wept at his election and held faithfully on his throne to his Dominican vow of poverty. All these are not exceptional. They are typical.

I had been brought up to think of popes as persecutors. I was to learn that Leo VII, even in the Dark Ages, condemned the enforced baptism of the Jews in Germany; that when, in the fourteenth century, the black pestilence devastated Europe, Clement VI protected the Jews against the sanguinary superstitions of the people; that in the seventeenth century Clement IX compelled the Portuguese to close their tribunal of the Inquisition; that in the eighteenth century Innocent XIII declared against those zealots who would have forbidden Chinese converts from continuing to honor Confucius and their ancestors; that in the nineteenth century Gregory XVI flinched not from reproaching his visitor, Czar Nicholas I, for his cruel persecutions of the Poles; that during the Great War in our century Benedict XV (venerated at last, after much bigoted misunderstanding, as "the Pope of Peace") was charitable to all, tireless in his solicitude for the war prisoners and the wounded on both sides, and boundless in his almsgiving to those nations which were prostrated by famine; that Pope Pius XI launched a thunderbolt at the Fascists when they railed at the Jews. All these are not exceptional. They are typical.

I had been taught that popes generally bowed the knee to temporal potentates. What of the early martyrs to whom I have just paid tribute? What of those popes who hesitated not to let the Eastern Schism take its slow but tragic course in their defiance of the political aggressions of the Christianized or semi-Christian Emperors in Greece? St. Nicholas I, in the Dark Ages, though direly besieged, championed to his death the Holy Sacrament of Matrimony against King Lothar II who had put aside Theutberga to wed Waldrada. In the tenth century Pope John XI endured imprisonment because he stood inflexible against the unlawful marriage of King Hugo. In the eleventh century St. Gregory VII compelled King Henry IV to return to his wife, and the Benedictine, the Blessed Victor III, forced the Mohammedan ruler of Tunis (even before the first Crusade) to liberate his Christian slaves. In the next century Celestine III defied the incestuous King Alphonse of Leon and Philip II of France, both of whom sought to profane the Sacrament of Matrimony. In the fourteenth century the aged Boniface, under the persecution and monstrous insults of the covetous Philip the Fair of France, stood adamant for the rights of the Church.

Coming to more recent times, in the sixteenth century Clement VII excommunicated the adulterous Henry VIII at the cost of losing England to the faith and of centuries of persecution; Pope Pius IV fearlessly forbade, under excommunication, the establishment of slavery among the Indians of the West Indies; Pope St. Pius V (in an age of luxury) remained a humble and ascetic Dominican and was dauntless and tireless in his purification of the Church from internal abuses, and Sixtus V made the pontifical states what they have since (with but a few brief relapses) remained, the best governed country on earth. Innocent XI, at the rising of the baneful nationalism toward the end of the seventeenth century, upheld the rights of the Church against King Louis XIV of France. In the eighteenth century Clement XII dauntlessly aroused a whirlwind by excommunicating that Freemasonry which allied itself with corrupt governments in their enmity to Catholicism. In the nineteenth century Pius VII, even when imprisoned at Fontainebleau, upheld the autonomy of the Church against his captor, Napoleon Bonaparte.

The revolution of 1848 drove Pius IX into exile, and the King of Piedmont robbed the Holy See of its pontifical states and Rome. In the face of this the fearless Pontiff made explicit the dogma of the Infallibility of the Pope — which had always been implicit in the one, true Christian faith — and condemned himself to imprisonment in the Vatican. Only yesterday Pope Pius XI launched his thunderbolts, contemptuous of compromise, equally against predatory capitalists of the so-called democracies, against the Fascist Mussolini, the Nazist Hitler, and the Communist Stalin. And today the world-traveled Pius XII stands with unbended knee issuing clarion calls for peace and scanning like an eagle the far-flung horizons of the missions. All these are not exceptional. They are typical.

The popes, inspired by the supernatural virtue of Charity (the love of their neighbors because of their love of God) poured into their souls by the Holy Ghost, have been the greatest mediators in history. I have already mentioned the work of Leo the Great with Huns and Vandals. Twice did St. Gregory I, that versatile and mighty genius who styled himself "the servant of the servants of God," secure peace, first between the Romans and the savage Lombards, and then between the latter and the Oriental Emperors. From these Lombards Rome was once more saved, over a century later, by St. Gregory II. In the eleventh century the German Pope, St. Leo IX, made peace between the King of Hungary and the German Emperor. In the same era that Blessed Victor III who had forced the Moslems of Tunis to relinquish their Christian slaves reconciled the same aggressive Emperor with Baldwin of Flanders and then with Godfrey of Lorraine. Toward the end of the twelfth century Gregory VIII succeeded in quelling a bitter war between Bathory of Poland and that murderous Ivan the Terrible whose bursts of fury were accounted incurable. In the same period the great purifier, Innocent, restored harmony between Portugal and Aragon, Bulgaria and Serbia, Philip of Suabia and Otho of Brunswick who strove for the rule of the empire. In the thirteenth century Honorius III mediated between France and England, Innocent IV between Emperor Rudolph and Charles of Anjou, and the benignant Boniface VIII (who in old age suffered with such august bravery under Philip the Fair) brought the incessant wars between England and France once more, for a time, to a close. The great scholar in canonical law, the French Pope John XXII, in the fourteenth century healed the animosity of Edward II of England and Robert of Scotland. In the same century Benedict XII established peace between Portugal and Spain, arbitrated successfully between the archfoes Edward III and Philip de Valois, and Gregory XI conciliated the Portuguese and Castilians. In the fifteenth century Martin V signalized the conclusion of the Great Western Schism by settling the recrudescent differences of France and England and by bringing a general peace to Europe. His successor, Nicholas V, one of the founders of the modern science (*pace* the slanderers of the Church), founder of the incomparable Library of the Vatican, about which he gathered the greatest scientists, artists, and savants of the day, repeatedly pacified Germany, Italy, and Hungary. In this same fifteenth century, furthermore, Innocent VIII ministered to Muscovy and Austria, and aided England, long torn asunder and decimated by the dreadful and futile War of the Roses, and Alexander VI, as we have seen, drew his famous papal line of demarcation between the New World holdings of Spain and Portugal. In the sixteenth century Gregory XIII (who perfected the calendar which all of us use today) once more intervened in behalf of both Muscovy and Poland.

All these are merely instances. The main point is that these apostolic achievements continue to our own moment. The "Pope of the Working-men," Leo XIII, was chosen arbitrator between Germany and Spain when they quarreled over the Caroline Islands. In the midst of his mul-tifarious activities he found time to placate Haiti and San Domingo. Despite the venemous machinations of the typical American bigots who are always trying to burke the progress of the true brotherhood of men in the Fatherhood of God, he brought to pass the settlement of the Friar question in the Philippines for the United States. And certain luminous suggestions of his *Rerum Novarum* gave origin to some of the more inspired clauses on labor in the platform of the League of Nations. We have already noted elsewhere how successfully the "Pope of Peace," Benedict XV, assisted Germany, Austria, Hungary, Turkey and England, France, Belgium, Russia, Serbia, Montenegro in the interchange of dis-abled prisoners and interned noncombatants. Before he ascended the throne, Pope Pius XI had distinguished himself as a conciliatory diplo-mat abroad. He was selected to harmonize any discords which might arise between Peru and Spain. We owe to him the deepening realization of the sanctity of marriage, the quickening of apostolic activities on the part of Catholic laymen and the spread of missions. Not the least of his aims were the economic justice for which he wrote so profoundly in *Quadragesimo Anno* and the peace of nations during this international *Götterdämmerung*. Catholicism means universality. Truly the Roman Catholic Church tends to dome the whole world. It is hard to see how any sane man could do less than pray for the acceleration of this process in an age in which we might well expect that the Anti-Christ, who will lead the human followers of Satan in the last deathlock with the Mys-tical Body of Christ, may already be born and lisping his first hellish numbers. Hilaire Belloc has written lately (in *America*, August, 1940) that it is not surprising to find men loving or hating the Church, but truly astonishing to find so many misunderstanding her. He adds, in his grim way, that after this war there will still be those who hate as well as those who love — but there will be none who do not understand.

XI. THE CHURCH'S CONSECRATED SOULS

My reader will not doubt that during my half century of life from childhood to these advancing years, both before and after I became a Catholic, I have met a very large number of nuns and priests, not a few frequently over a period of years, and a fair number on very intimate terms. I have met a few of the highest rank. I have met a number humbly at work in the most obscure positions, surrounded with squalor. I know at least one priest and one nun whose names after death may well be advanced for canonization. I have known at the other extreme a few who have seemed to be fighting a grim battle on the verge of most dreadful defeat. I have seen priests and nuns who are at times jealous and petty and vain. I have met some who, barring their vocational training, are culturally unresourceful. I have met at least two, who, to my own conclusion, have been, on the strictest analysis, unquestionably the recipients of miraculous intervention. I have met missionaries from the farthest corners of the world. I have talked with some almost ready to abandon their vocation. I have met a few, a very few, who were slothful. I have talked with a few who were rather dull. But I have never known a single one who did not, sometimes in moments most unexpected, reveal some flash of that grace which priests receive with the Sacrament of Holy Orders and nuns when they make their final vows; some almost startling, because so subtly infused and unostentatious, vein of poverty of spirit, of cleanness of heart, of most subtle and lofty prudence, of fortitude, patient or militant; some most edifying trait which I seek in vain to match in the lives of even my finest lay friends. Every one of these apostles has, at some time or other, even if but for an instant, given me, often quite unconsciously, some certain sign that he or she is a direct descendant of Christ's Twelve, or of those invincibly faithful women who hastened forth at the dawn of the first Easter to bring spices for the cold, stiff body of the beloved Teacher whose clear promise of His resurrection had, for the time being, been obliterated by grief.

While this evidently is not the place for it, I have suffered from almost intolerable longings to pour out my gratitude in eulogies of the apostolic coherence and incredible versatility of various groups, congregations, and orders within the Church, from the monks of the desert to the Utopia-building Benedictines; from the Benedictines to those twin glories of the high Middle Ages, the democratic Dominicans and the truly communistic Franciscans; from these, again, to the sternly exalting Redemptorists rallied together by St. Alphonsus Liguori in the eighteenth century, on to the Society of the Sacred Heart founded by the intrepid St. Madeleine Sophie, already storming the doors of the Vatican with such other candidates for canonization as Mother Duchesne (recently beatified), a guardian angel of black and red and white folk in Louisiana, and Mother Stuart of England, the agnostic and dashing huntress who became so delightfully humorous and holy. So I would continue on and on, down to our moment, by singing the praises of the twentieth-century born Maryknoll Fathers and Missionary Sisters of the Sacred Heart founded by the recently beatified Mother Frances Xavier Cabrini, a patron of my family, since we have adopted five of her orphans who seem to breathe her sanctity.

One intellectual adventure, however, positively demands a jubilant recall. Viewed in the light of my experiences more than twenty years later with Father McGoldrick, it would take a rather determined disbeliever to feel certain that it was merely fortuitous.

XII. LOYOLA, SOUL OF CHIVALRY

I have already recounted how Ellen Virgin, in my youth, aroused me from that dogmatic superstition with which the popular Protestant calumniation of the Jesuits had corrupted me by lending me *The Life of St. Ignatius Loyola* by Francis Thompson. At that time I shared the vulgar delusion that the Jesuits were proponents of the principle that the end justifies the means, ignorant of the fact that a substantial money prize still awaits the truth seeker who can find in their writings and teachings a single hint of such a doctrine. But the Jesuits are well used to a persecution which has seldom relaxed since the days, some four hundred years ago, when their radiantly quixotic founder sang in the prisons of the Inquisition his *magnificat* as he realized that he was experiencing in his own way and degree, the slanders and ignominies that had been heaped upon his Lord.

For a youthful chanter of the poetry of Francis Thompson, for one inflamed from childhood with romances of chivalry, it was a providential moment to read how Inigo, inditing poems to his "queen of hearts," dauntless in the tournament, persuaded a handful of madcap Basque companions, when the walls of Pampeluna fell, to retire to the citadel there to die like Roland in Roncesvalles, the Vale of Thorns, for the greater glory of the ideal of knighthood. For Inigo, though a good sort of everyday Catholic, had not yet become Ignatius, whose one thought would be to die for the greater glory of God. To a brother-in-arms he confessed his sins, he fired his troops with his defiance, and turned his face toward death. But God, out of an infinity of possible choices, had designed that this man should be one of the greatest of those who were to baffle the followers of Luther, Zwingli, and Calvin; to set aglow with an athletic repentance the faithless within the Church, and to send fire-brand missionaries to the religiously uncharted regions of the ancient Orient and the mysterious New World of the Americas. A stone dislodged by a canon shot caromed off his left leg and shattered his right.

It ought to be quite clear that Inigo was not suffering from any of those extraordinary complexes which neurotic psychologists try to discover in the buoyantly healthy saints. Far also from being a disillusioned worldling, his mind was still aflame with the prospects of a brilliant career in court and with

> . . . Emblazoned shields,
> Impresses quaint, caparisons and steeds,
> Bases and tinsel trappings, gorgeous knights
> At joust and tournament.

To avoid hopeless deformity he consented to have his bones rebroken and reset. When he recovered from the perilous fever which this painful operation caused, he found that a bone protruded below the knee of his right leg. How was he to wear the gorgeous boots befitting his state? Open the wound and saw off the grotesque portion of bone. Such was the demand of Inigo. Alas, the leg was then still too short. So he had it stretched with an iron rack.

When the fearful pain was somewhat abated he called for some romances of chivalry. But there was nothing available save a *Life of Our Savior* by Rudolph of Saxony and a copy of *Flos Sanctorum*. From these lives of saints and their master he learned

> . . . The better fortitude
> Of patience and heroic martyrdom

which he was to celebrate in the epic of deeds that crowded the rest of his active life.

At this point the psychoanalyst might intervene to assert that Inigo became a saint because he was no longer able to be a soldier. But history furnishes us with more than one example of illustrious crippled generals. Moreover, though Ignatius was to limp for the rest of his life, he many times shambled joyously over tortuous miles of pilgrim march that would have prostrated many a sturdy soldier with two perfectly good legs. Nor may the psychoanalyst honestly hint that he was sated or embittered with the military ideal. On the contrary, so full of it was he that, in the words of Father Louis Ponnelle in his life of St. Philip Neri, he set himself with unquenchable gusto his lifelong task "to organize his Company on the model of an army in the field of which discipline was to be the mainspring, and which must free itself from all *impedimenta*."

It was Ignatius more than any other personage except our Saviour Himself who taught my pagan mind what a dashing and full-blooded virtue is obedience. Notable as was his humble and exultant submission to ecclesiastical discipline, even when it was undiscerning, yet more self-effacing still was his humble and reluctant acceptance of the leadership of his infant Order when it was forced upon him by his first chosen soldiers of Jesus. Far from having lost interest in military virtues and strategy, he carried these tactics into missionary work and lent it such a unique discipline and potency that today his lightning-swift squadrons are ever the first to wheel into a breach that has been made, no matter where, in the remote frontiers of the Catholic Church.

We shall do well to insert here a brief consideration from *In the Likeness of Christ*, by Father Edward Leen, C.S.Sp., which goes to the heart of the nature of true obedience. "Now prompt and unqualified obedience cannot exist unless faith is strong and deep. Jesus loves a faith that is strong, deep, vivid, and penetrating; for without such a faith He cannot be appreciated rightly and loved with ardour. Transformation into Him demands a faith of this kind." Among all the generals and diplomats of the world Ignatius stands *sui generis* with his harmony of exactingness and kindness, of the capacity to command inextricably interfused with that capacity to obey which led him to shorten his last hours on earth and to forego the solace of a papal blessing in response to the demands of his own secretary. And this sublime dutifulness brought him the reward, this side of the Beatific Vision, of inspiring what, outside of the Liturgy, is perhaps the greatest prayer ever uttered on earth:

Suscipe, Domine, universam meam libertatem. Accipe memoriam, intellectum atque voluntatem omnem. Quidquid habeo, vel possideo, mihi largitus es; id tibi totum restituo, ac tuae prorsus voluntati trado guber-

*nandum. Amorem tui solum, cum gratia tua, mihi dones, et dives sum
satis, nec aliud quidquam ultra posco.* "Take away, O Lord, my liberty
utterly. Accept all my memory, intellect and will. Whatever I have or
own Thou hast given me of Thy largess; all this I restore to Thee and
deliver it entirely under Thy governance. Only grant me Thy love together with Thy grace and nothing further whatsoever do I ask."

XIII. THE CHURCH'S HOLINESS

I suppose all of us who become sufficiently well acquainted with
Church History find ourselves at times tempted to place the apostles of
regeneration even above the apostles of the frontiers. St. Paul (as we
have seen in my inadequate presentation of him) was pre-eminently both
the frontiersman in remote realms and the tireless regenerator of his
wide-scattered infant *ecclesiae*. With him, as with St. John the Evangelist,
as indeed with the Divine Founder Himself, the spreading of the Good
News and the consolation and purifying of the converted were parallel
processes. But, I repeat, to the student of history of holy Mother Church
there is something so awe inspiring in the way in which her apostles of
regeneration preserve her from the pathogenic growths within her, there
is something so lightninglike startling in the sudden discovery that the
very corruption of members unworthy of her is thus indirectly a proof
of her infallibility, of the perpetual presence of the Holy Ghost vouchsafed to her, that one is tempted — with all reverence to God who alone
knows — to enthrone these regenerators hard by the Right Hand where
dwells the glorified and ascended Humanity of our Saviour. Nobody
who attains to even the faintest understanding of St. John of the Cross,
for instance, will deny the force of this temptation to play at being
Dante.

The Church's supernal holiness, as I have pointed out at the beginning
of this chapter, flows out of her apostolicity as all essential properties
flow from being itself, ultimately from the Necessary and Infinite Being,
from Him who is.

"We shall be like God," says St. Augustine, "in proportion as we par-
take of His Justice and Holiness: the more just and perfect we are, the
more we shall resemble our Heavenly Father." From the days of my
boyhood, when the first beam of the holiness of the Mystical Body of
Christ caught my vision like a stunning shaft of light through a dim yet
opulent stained-glass window, my whole life has been stirred at intervals

more and more frequent, with her pageantry of devoted peoples (the Irish and Poles for instance) and of persons of unparalleled variety from among whom I have been forced to content myself with a selection almost random because of the bewildering pressure of the throngs of saints upon my joyful allegiance.

There have always been, in various institutions, good men who nevertheless could not be called holy. On the other hand, all holy men are good — except, perhaps, in the eyes of the most fanatical kind of atheist. Even some atheists have been good. But I think it is safe to say that a bitter atheist is never good, and that no atheist can be permanently good. At least we may agree that unreasoning zeal itself is evil. And to the degree that a man is fanatical, be he atheist, agnostic, or theist, he is to that degree below moral rectitude. I have already argued that no morality can endure that is not rooted in religion. But I am bound to admit that one who is a theist is not thereby good. No doubt some men have been fanatical and holy — but certainly not both at the same moment. For with the growth of holiness there must always be a lessening of fanaticism since such frenzy is a species of violence. Holiness, which means union with God, is harmony, peace. A holy personage is such to the extent to which he dedicates himself to the service of God, to the extent to which he trustingly depends upon his heavenly Father's protection, to the extent in which he seeks to be perfect as our heavenly Father is perfect. It is obvious that a man who is not a Catholic or even a Christian of any kind may be holy just so long as he is a sufficiently ardent theist. But as Abbot Columba Marmion says, in his profound and beautiful *Christ the Life of the Soul*: "All the holiness God has destined for our souls, has been placed in the Humanity of Christ, and it is from this source that we must draw." And long years have clearly taught me that the holiness of Catholics at their best is immeasurably more profound and rich than the best of any other kind. As Father Francis McGarrigle, S.J., made clear to me, "The holiness of the Church is the holiness intended by God and given through Christ. Non-Catholic holiness is not God's dispensation for man and is fragmentary."

As I went on, admiring many religions more and more, but by the very same process of thought glorying ever more and more in the uniqueness and supremacy of the Church of Rome, it gradually dawned upon me that the uniqueness of Catholic holiness began with one of the seven sayings of our Divine Saviour during His three hours of agony on the cross: "Father, forgive them for they know not what they do." We are well acquainted with all sorts of non-Christian devotional fortitudes. There was once, for instance, a Moslem standard-bearer whose right hand was lopped off. When an enemy struck away his left hand also, he seized the adored gonfalon between his bleeding stumps. But it is not recorded that he groaned out one syllable of forgiveness for his foes. Among the Christians, the Catholics down to the present moment have enormously outnumbered all others in echoing this sentence.

The first Christian martyr, after our Blessed Lord Himself, was St. Stephen. We learn in *The Acts of the Apostles* how he boldly accused the Pharisees of murdering their own Messiah. "Which of the prophets have not your fathers persecuted? And they have slain them who foretold of the coming of the Just One; of whom you have been now the betrayers and the murderers." This he said before the council, with its false witnesses. "And all that sat in the council, looking on him, saw his face as if it had been the face of an angel." Just as the meek Jesus could, in proper season, blast the faithless and unholy with terrible eloquence, so did Stephen condemn them. And just as the gentle Jesus pleaded forgiveness for his slayers, so did Stephen, even while showers of stones crashed into his body, no doubt even while his very cheekbones were crushed, pray for his foes' absolution: "And falling on his knees, he cried with a loud voice, saying: 'Lord, lay not this sin to their charge.' And when he had said this, he fell asleep in the Lord."

Interminable examples of this spirit could be given, from St. Andrew, the Apostle who preached to his tormentors from the cross, to the Jesuit Father Pro martyred in Mexico, who when his very captor was moved to implore his pardon answered: "Not only do I forgive you, but I thank you."

Pagan stoicism is at times exalted in our day, but it can bear no comparison with Christian holiness. Its humanitarianism was barren of results. In contrast we have within the Church those regenerating apostolic activities practised by a Peter Claver, a Vincent de Paul, a Philip Neri, and a galaxy of apostles of charity.

I remember [writes Father Bertram Conway, the Paulist, in *The Question Box*] meeting in Boston a Unitarian minister from Burlington, Vermont, who told me he was about to resign his ministry, because his efforts to gather in the unchurched poor of his city had met with a decided protest on the part of his wealthy parishioners. The true Church frowns on such narrowness. She always sees Christ in the poor. . . . Sinners are rarely excommunicated from her fold, and only for some flagrant sin, just as traitors and convicted criminals are debarred by the State from citizenship. [Even the excommunicated may be readmitted on making drastic reparation.] The adulterer, the drunkard, or the corrupt politician is not in "good standing" for he is not permitted to receive Communion, until he manifests a heartfelt sorrow for his sins in the Sacrament of Penance.

I have learned to realize that it is precisely because the one true Church is uniquely and supremely holy that she can purify and nurture with uncompromising sternness, harmonized with infinite tenderness, sinners so numerous and so atrocious. It is because she alone has remained absolutely faithful in continuous tradition to her adorable Founder. So she stands amidst the wreckages of the kingdoms and empires of two thousand years, in irrefragable unity amidst dead and dying heresies, palely living heresies, rival faiths and faithlessnesses sundered into uncharitable fragments; she stands, stately and compassionate, imperturbable and motherly, mightier than ever before, radiant in the light of what is for her a perpetual dawn.

XIV. THE CHURCH'S UNIVERSALITY

From this perennial apostolicity flows also the ever widening Catholicity of the Church of Jesus and Peter, Paul and John. As Saint Augustine says:

Repudiating therefore all those who seek neither philosophy in sacred things, nor holiness in philosophy . . . we must hold fast to the Christian religion and to communion with that Church which is Catholic, and is called Catholic, not only by its own members but also by its enemies. For whether they will or not, even heretics and schismatics when talking, not among themselves but with outsiders, call the Catholic Church nothing else but the Catholic Church. For otherwise, they would not be understood unless they distinguished the Church by that name which she bears throughout the whole world.

For most of my boyhood associates, in my own more intimate environment, the word "Catholic" meant bigoted and ignorant. Even under the care of my piously errant mother (for all her love of Rome) I did not learn until I was a well-grown man that "catholic" really means universal. There was, alas! — and is — plenty of evidence to confirm the bigot in his one-sided views. Among many examples I will mention one that had a lasting deterrent influence upon me often when my heart was warmed by the glamour of Catholicism. I used frequently to pass a store wherein I saw pictures and statues of our Lord with a sentimentally woeful face and a gory, half-dissected heart — a sickening travesty of that beautiful devotion quickened by St. Margaret Mary to counteract the callous paganism of modernity. There were also saccharine pictures of the Blessed Virgin, little calculated to reassure a youthful outsider who was so often told that prayers to the Mother of God were idolatrous, polytheistic. To make matters worse I found — as I still find — such things inside the churches themselves. Of course, I was but a snobbish esthete. I did not know that these crude things themselves were a proof of the catholicity of a Church which can speak the language of the connoisseur and the vulgarian, the poet, the peasant, and the street Arab without losing her dignity. Today, though I still wish, with many other Catholics, that our level of taste could be raised, I can myself pray before one of these gingerbread statues with something of the fervor of the too vocal old woman who may be kneeling at my side and deepening my own reverence and shaming my shabby sophistication with a pureheartedness which I beseech God daily that I may some time remotely approximate. Meanwhile holy Mother Church, with that tireless regenerative energy which is one of the innumerable testimonies to the truth of Christ's promise that the "gates of hell shall never prevail" against her, is sponsoring a virile and versatile movement in the liturgical arts which is bound to erase the last vestiges of this human weakness and recall the glories of the thirteenth century in traditional art organically united with appropriate contemporaneous styles.

From the day when I first learned the word *catholic* to this, I have been exploring a treasure house of its unfathomable implications. We have seen how holy Mother Church is unique in her vast embrace of the poor and the rich, the ignorant and the wise. She whispers to all men at all the seven ages of life. "Thy training and teaching," rejoices St. Augustine, "are childlike to children, forcible for youths, gentle for the aged, taking into account not only the age of the body but also that of the mind."

The Catholic Church is universal in its unequaled span of space. On the frozen borders of Labrador the patriarchally bearded bishop of our day calls the Esquimaux about him as his Blessed Lord called the children to His knee. In the land of the dragon the acolyte swings his thurible to waft heavenward the incense of the Lord to mingle on its way with the pagan incense of the yet unconverted ones of China. In

Japan, in the Fiji Islands, in Africa, and in other mission realms the work goes on more and more under native priests. Earthquakes and lightning and the bombs of soldiers destroy a mission church today. Almost before the ruins are cool, priests and parishioners are busy rebuilding it. In the southwestern United States young Mexican seminarians are in training to quicken the faith which corrupt Masonic-liberal and quasi-communistic politicians have sought more and more mercilessly, during the past seventy-five years, to destroy. In Rome a college is filled with young priests who are preparing to make a benignant invasion of Russia the moment the talons of the League of the Godless show signs of relaxing. In darkest Africa the image of the Blessed Mother replaces the fetish. Aloft on a soaring slope of the South American Andes we find a statue of the Prince of Peace upreared as a token of everlasting amity by the once warring peoples of Chile and the Argentine Republic. The gongs which lull the ears of the drowsy Buddha of India are drowned by the exultant peal of Catholic chimes. Before Sitting Bull and his braves, sinister in their war paint, only a comparatively few years ago an unarmed priest sat serene on horseback and suddenly startled the wild plainsmen to a momentary clatter of weapons, not by flourishing a bellicose standard but by unfurling a banner on which was depicted the God-man with outstreched arms and Sacred Heart aglow. During the earth's diurnal axial roll, there is, at every moment, some point where the sun's early rays fall like an aureole around some holy priest as he genuflects before the high altar and rises to elevate the Sacred Host which has just become the Body of our Divine Lord.

And as the Catholic Church is universal in space so is it universal in time. Jesus said: "Before Abraham was, I *am*." The Messiah was promised long before the Pharaohs made the first empires of history; and from Moses we learn that He was promised to the first man and the first woman at the very time that they were banished from Eden. The pages of the *Old Testament* gleam star-strewn with prophecies of His coming so accurate that it is passing strange that the Pharisees, even in the troubled days of Tiberius, when they saw Him, knew Him not and refused to welcome Him. He came, He told them, "not to destroy but to fulfill." And His promise outlives, for two thousand years, the pride of pagan and apostate, from those who burned incense before the insensate Nero to those who devil worship beside the embalmed corpse of the merciless Lenin.

XV. THE CHURCH AND OUTSIDERS

And to me, who was so long estranged from orthodoxy by what I believed to be the logically necessary uncharitable attitude of the Church of Rome toward outsiders, the most invincibly appealing implication of catholicity is to be found in a survey of the attitude of Roman Catholic theologians toward all types of unbelievers in the pure Christian Tradition. Otto Karrer, in his *Religions of Mankind*, has made this survey in an unimprovable manner.

Justin [one of the earliest Church Fathers] was led by his impressions of the various religions of his environment to the conclusion "that all who live in accordance with the Logos," that is the witness of their conscience implanted by God, "are Christians even if they have the name of atheists." It is significant that in this connection he mentions not only Socrates but Heraclitus. And Lactantius [one of the earliest Christian poets] could declare "that in spite of their idolatrous follies the great mass of pagans are pardonable . . . since they fulfil man's highest duty (the worship of God), if not in actual fact, at least in their intention. . . ."

Throughout the entire body of doctrinal pronouncements there run two distinct and seemingly conflicting series of utterances. The one proclaims the exclusive possession by the visible Church of truth and saving power. The other tells us of an invisible Church spread over the earth with power to save its members inasmuch as all who are in good faith and not responsible for their errors may belong spiritually to the Church, and so reach heaven. Neither of these two series taken by itself and to the exclusion of the other represents the full Catholic doctrine. That doctrine is mutilated when only one of the two is taught. Since they do not contradict each other — indeed they are often propounded together in the same context — they must complete each other.

Clement XI in 1713 condemned as temerarious and heretical Quesnel's proposition that "no grace is bestowed outside the (visible) Church." Similarly, in 1690, Alexander VIII had condemned the proposition of certain Gallican moral theologians that "pagans, Jews, heretics and other such receive no influence whatever from Jesus Christ, so that we must conclude that their will is naked and unarmed — being wholly devoid of sufficient grace." As early as the year 96 Clement of Rome, writing to the Corinthians, pointed out that "in every age of the world and in every generation the Lord has made purification and conversion possible to all who sincerely turn to Him." And in the same spirit the Church in her solemn condemnation of Hus at the Council of Constance affirmed the traditional teaching of St. Augustine that there are "secret Christians and elect" outside the Church and "secret pagans and reprobates" within her fold.

St. Augustine's words on this subject should never be forgotten. And I quote them the more gladly because he is widely regarded as the typical rigorist. "The term heretic" (misbeliever in a narrower or wider acceptation) should "be applied only to those who put forward false opinions from self-interest, in particular from the desire for fame or pre-eminence, or from some such motive follow these false teachers. But the man who believes them because he is deceived by a show of piety and truth, or who defends a false doctrine, be it never so perverse, not from guilty passion or pride, but because he has learned it from his parents, and with a prudent zeal seeks the truth, prepared to accept it if he finds it — such a man is by no means to be deemed separated." Such men are "well disposed and spiritual" men, "partakers of the eternal inheritance," unlike those who born and brought up in the bosom of the Church squander their partimony by an evil life. "If you ask whether a particular man is good, the answer depends not on what he believes or hopes, but on what he loves. For he who has charity has no doubt also the right faith and hope. But if a man has not charity, his faith is nought, even if what he believes is the truth."

XVI. FINALE

In my own unbelieving days I rejected the faith on rational grounds — according to my lights. Today, even after all these years of strenuous reasoning; after following the many convergent strands of proof: historical, philosophical, biological, psychological, sociological, theological, syllogistic, statistical, experimental, objective, subjective; after coming to the incandescent nucleus of the enormous web of bright rays of truth — yes even today, as when a sudden cloud obscures the sun, this hard-won faith may for an instant be veiled, but not lost. I utter an ejaculation and it shines out again. Or, more in the spirit of my earlier days of inquiry, I do not speak to God directly but I say to myself: "Well, now, just what are your *rational* grounds for disbelief?" — and I find *none*. Once I doubted rationally. Now, not infrequently in a state of perfect bodily euphoria, the semblance of a doubt may come, but wholly irrationally. At first this experience pained me acutely. Now it makes me smile. I know that it is in part merely the inertia, the after-gloom of my long years of stubbornly timid resistance to both logic and actual grace, and I find it in part a test, a purification, after each recurrence of which my faith blazes out more quietly and vividly than ever before.

Today I often wonder whether, if I had read St. John of the Cross in my youth, I would have escaped largely, indeed almost wholly, my long term of purgatorial agnosticism. I then thought that my obstacles were intellectual, rational — I now wonder whether they really were. St. John might have shown me that God was withdrawing His gifts, His toys from me in order that I might, as a grown man, seek Him Himself. I can see now that, stupid as I was, my agnosticism did clear away all sorts of naïve, childish, and sordid anthropomorphism, all sorts of silly hopes that He would grant me temporal blessings to the point of surfeit.

Then came a great eruption of "humanism." As a child I had lain awake nights in bed listening in drowsy half pleasure, half pain, to the hypnotic hum of a distant factory, wondering about the "pale, death-pale" faces of the toilers and sorrowing — ah! a bit too luxuriously — over them. Some years later I sang their wrongs in a prettily indignant Patmoresque lyric. Then, in my thirties I went mildly berserk and ranted in company with other radicals like Scott Nearing and Max Eastman, the heroes of those days. From the stages of crowded theaters we spoke in wartime, while the police lined the back of the hall and we speculated — not without a thrill of pleasant expectancy — what next? I did truly and deeply sorrow over the horrors of those days, the futile battlefields, the gaunt grim factories. I was unripely ripe for martyrdom. But I said at last to myself: "How much do these eloquent comrades of mine desire the welfare of society — and just how much do they seek their own greater glory?" And then something still deeper inside of me whispered: "And how about *you yourself,* young man?" At this point I hung my head. I knew that the dream of the proletarian revolution was futile. I foresaw, albeit dimly, the shameful egoism of the Stalins who would follow the fanatical but truly ascetical Lenins whom I had been canonizing. I did not, however, arrive apparently anywhere nearer to God. I remained a radical, a revolutionary, *in taste.* I am still a radical, far more revolutionary than ever before, *in act.* For I have become a Roman Catholic.

As I ponder these things my thoughts turn continually to our holy and mighty leader in the Vatican and I feel like one who, having brought his own paltry troubles into a spacious theater, departs in due time, after contemplating the majestic sorrows and spiritual victories of the tragic hero, departs now scornful of his own little woes by contrast with such profound and lofty sufferings. It is for me a never-failing *katharsis* to realize how, in the Vatican, today, Pope Pius XII has been passing through a veritable "Dark Night of the Soul" for the sins of this spiritually bankrupt world which has resulted from the "Renaissance" and the "Reformation." "The present age, Venerable Brethren," he writes in his second Encyclical, "by adding new errors to the doctrinal aberrations of the past, has pushed these to extremes which lead inevitably to a drift toward chaos," with its "denial and rejection of a universal norm of morality as well for individual and social life as for international relations. . . . God is hated. . . . The voice of conscience which teaches even the illiterate and the uncivilized what is good and what is bad is stilled."

But with something of a supernatural serenity, with something that suggests a knowledge of "the Spiritual Betrothal" of the great Catholic Mystics, the voice of our Holy Father adds an invincible antiphon, the eternal message, the one answer: "Whoever lives by the spirit of Christ, refuses to let himself be beaten down by the difficulties which oppose him, but on the contrary feels himself compelled to work with all his strength and with the fullest confidence in God. He does not draw back before the straits and the necessities of the moment but faces their severity ready to give aid with that love which flies no sacrifice, is stronger than death, and will not be quenched by the rushing waters of tribulation."

*　　*　　*

Here words fail me to record the utter happiness in pleasure and pain, the immense peace which the most powerful of men cannot give, which suffuses me since my surrender to "the glorious liberty of the children of God." How better can I express my thoughts than by the deep intuitions of the poet of "The Hound of Heaven" which now, at last, I really understand! Heard in my heart is that same Voice which spoke to him, richly, musically, mightily:

> Now of that long pursuit
> Comes on at hand the bruit;
> That Voice is round me like a bursting sea:
> "And is thy earth so marred,
> Shattered in shard on shard?
> Lo, all things fly thee, for thou fliest Me!
> Strange, piteous, futile thing!
> Wherefore should any set thee love apart?
> Seeing none but I makes much of naught" (He said),
> "And human love needs human meriting:
> How hast thou merited —
> Of all man's clay the dingiest clot?
> Alack, thou knowest not

How little worthy of any love thou art!
Whom wilt thou find to love ignoble thee,
　Save Me, save only Me?
All which I took from thee I did but take,
　Not for thy harms,
But just that thou might'st seek it in My arms.
　All which thy child's mistake
Fancies as lost, I have stored for thee at home:
　Rise, clasp My hand, and come!"
　Halts by me that footfall:
　Is my gloom after all,
Shade of His hand, outstretched caressingly?
　"Ah! fondest, blindest, weakest,
　I am He whom thou seekest!
Thou dravest love from thee, who dravest me."

On the Feast of the Presentation of the Blessed Virgin Mary,
November 21, 1940

INDEX